D0152328

Vincenzo Bellini

ROUTLEDGE MUSIC BIBLIOGRAPHIES

Series Editor: Jennifer C. Post

COMPOSERS

Isaac Albéniz (1998)
Walter A. Clark

C. P. E. Bach (2002)
Doris Bosworth Powers

Samuel Barber (2001)
Wayne C. Wentzel

Béla Bartók, 2nd Edition (1997)
Elliott Antokoletz

Vincenzo Bellini, 2nd Edition (2009)
Stephen A. Willier

Alban Berg, 2nd Edition (2009)
Bryan R. Simms

Leonard Bernstein (2001)
Paul F. Laird

Johannes Brahms (2003)
Heather Platt

William Byrd, 2nd Edition (2005)
Richard Turbet

Elliott Carter (2000)
John L. Link

Carlos Chávez (1998)
Robert Parker

Frédéric Chopin (1999)
William Smialek

Aaron Copland (2001)
Marta Robertson and Robin Armstrong

Frederick Delius, 2nd Edition (2009)
Mary Christison Huismann

Gaetano Donizetti, 2nd Edition (2009)
James P. Cassaro

Edward Elgar (1993)
Christopher Kent

Gabriel Fauré (1999)
Edward R. Phillips

Christoph Willibald Gluck, 2nd Edition (2003)
Patricia Howard

Charles François Gounod (2009)
Timothy S. Flynn

G.F. Handel, 2nd Edition (2004)
Mary Ann Parker

Paul Hindemith, 2nd Edition (2009)
Stephen Luttman

Charles Ives, 2nd Edition (2009)
Gayle Sherwood Magee

Scott Joplin (1998)
Nancy R. Ping-Robbins

Zoltán Kodály (1998)
Mícheál Houlahan and Philip Tacka

Franz Liszt, 3rd Edition (2009)
Michael Saffle

Guillaume de Machaut (1995)
Lawrence Earp

Gustav and Alma Mahler (2008)
Susan M. Filler

Felix Mendelssohn Bartholdy (2001)
John Michael Cooper

Olivier Messiaen (2008)
Vincent P. Benitez

Giovanni Pierluigi da Palestrina (2001)
Clara Marvin

Giacomo Puccini (1999)
Linda B. Fairtile

Maurice Ravel (2004)
Stephen Zank

Gioachino Rossini, 2nd Edition (2009)
Denise P. Gallo

Camille Saint-Saëns (2003)
Timothy S. Flynn

Alessandro and Domenico Scarlatti (1993)
Carole F. Vidali

Heinrich Schenker (2003)
Benjamin Ayotte

Alexander Scriabin (2004)
Ellon D. Carpenter

Jean Sibelius (1998)
Glenda D. Goss

Giuseppe Verdi (1998)
Gregory Harwood

Tomás Luis de Victoria (1998)
Eugene Casjen Cramer

Richard Wagner (2002)
Michael Saffle

Adrian Willaert (2004)
David Michael Kidger

GENRES

American Music Librarianship (2005)
Carol June Bradley

Central European Folk Music (1996)
Philip V. Bohlman

Chamber Music, 3rd Edition (2009)
John H. Baron

Church and Worship Music (2005)
Avery T. Sharp and James Michael Floyd

The Concerto (2006)
Stephen D. Lindeman

Ethnomusicology (2003)
Jennifer C. Post

Jazz Scholarship and Pedagogy, 3rd Edition (2005)
Eddie S. Meadows

The Musical (2004)
William A. Everett

North American Indian Music (1997)
Richard Keeling

Opera, 2nd Edition (2001)
Guy Marco

Piano Pedagogy (2009)
Gilles Comeau

The Recorder, 2nd Edition (2003)
Richard Griscom and David Lasocki

Serial Music and Serialism (2001)
John D. Vander Weg

String Quartets (2005)
Mara E. Parker

The Violin (2006)
Mark Katz

Women in Music (2005)
Karin Pendle

VINCENZO BELLINI

A RESEARCH AND INFORMATION GUIDE

SECOND EDITION

STEPHEN A. WILLIER
Temple University

ROUTLEDGE MUSIC BIBLIOGRAPHIES

NEW YORK AND LONDON

First edition published 2002
by Routledge

This edition published 2009
by Routledge
270 Madison Ave, New York NY 10016

Simultaneously published in the UK
by Routledge
2 Park Square, Milton Park, Abingdon, Oxon, OX14 4RN

Routledge is an imprint of the Taylor & Francis Group, an informa business

Transferred to Digital Printing 2009

Typeset in Times New Roman by
Swales & Willis Ltd, Exeter, Devon

Library of Congress Cataloging in Publication Data
Willier, Stephen Ace, 1952–
Vincenzo Bellini: a research and information guide/Stephen A. Willier. — 2nd ed.
p.cm. — (Routledge music bibliographies)
Includes bibliographical references and index.
1. Bellini, Vincenzo, 1801–1835 — Bibliography. I. Title.
ML134.B4415W55 2009
016.7821092—dc22 2008053331

ISBN10: 0–415–99524–8 (hbk)
ISBN10: 0–203–88887–1 (ebk)

ISBN13: 978–0–415–99524–5 (hbk)
ISBN13: 978–0–203–88887–2 (ebk)

Chi non ama Vincenzo Bellini non ama la musica.

Arrigo Boito

Contents

Preface to the Second Edition and Acknowledgements

Since the first edition of this volume was completed, a number of important events have taken place in the world of Bellini scholarship, principally the publication of the proceedings of the two conferences held in November of 2001, in Paris (item 404) and in Catania (item 406). Not only were many significant Bellini studies added to the literature, but it also became clear that Bellini is now considered a composer worth studying on a serious level. Although several landmark Bellini studies had been made (e.g., by Cambi, Pastura, Lippmann, Maguire), this situation began in earnest in 1985 with several scholarly gatherings; the momentum Bellini scholarship had gained became fully evident in the 2001 celebrations of Bellini's life and creativity. These scholarly reports are not dry, abstract discussions, but represent a kind of resuscitation or rebirth of a composer whose life and music had in many instances been relegated to the sidelines. Currently (displaying not only what is being done but also what was lacking), the initial volumes in the first Bellini critical edition have begun to appear (see items 489 and 508); a critical edition of the correspondence is planned (see item 318); serious studies of Bellini's libretti and working methods have appeared; and a number of accomplished Bellini and *primo ottocento* scholars have emerged, their work, along with that of the existing experts, taking Bellini studies to a completely new level. To be especially noted is the work of Marco Beghelli, Alessandro Roccatagliata, Luca Zoppelli, among others. In short, Bellini is now accorded the kind of attention Giuseppe Verdi began to receive in the 1970s and that had been traditionally reserved mainly for Austro-Germanic composers. Thus, this research guide has been greatly enriched since it was first published a few short years ago. I intended the first guide to be a record of Bellini scholarship, and one thing the entries and their annotations made clear was that there had been many falsehoods, misconceptions, myths, legends, and mistakes in the published materials, starting with Bellini's great friend and champion, Francesco Florimo, whose mythmaking was, from various motives, deliberate. Many authors even seemed unaware of Bellini's correct birth and death dates, a situation symptomatic of other misinformation or gaps in knowledge. Obviously a critical edition of the correspondence surrounding Bellini, bearing in mind that Florimo both destroyed and rewrote some of it, is a necessary basis for reexamination of many established conceptions about the composer. A critical edition of Bellini's operas should prove a revelation about the composer's style and working methods, about which there have been many almost mythic reports, starting with the "Letter to Agostino Gallo" (see item 145). One of the more pressing needs is an integrated life-and-works study with meaningful analyses of the music. Orrey's volume (see item 270) was promising but too short by design. Weinstock's volume (item 279) was somewhat of a gallimaufry, ultimately not very readable, and the latest entry, by Galatopoulos (see item 265) certainly does not provide much illumination of the music. A number of sources have provided worthwhile insights into how Bellini's music might or should be examined, notably encyclopedia articles by Mary Ann Smart (see item 118) and Fabrizio della Seta (see item 106), but no integrated study has appeared, a prime example of which is R. Larry Todd's magisterial volume on Mendelssohn.

Some 180 new entries, among the most illuminating and scholarly in the entire literature, have been added to this edition. There have been very few deletions. If this choice represents inclusion rather than exclusion, the annotations are meant to explain the relative worth of each volume in the sense that suspect or controversial sources have been so identified. This volume is a guide to research but it is also a history of Bellini scholarship. The entries in total add up to a picture of Bellini and in fact an account of changing music historical concepts of primo ottocento opera of the last two centuries. In one sense, this volume is not only a guide to research but also a study in reception history that says as much about the musical establishment as it does about Bellini and his contemporaries. Only by examining all types of sources can a scholar reach worthwhile, independent conclusions.

For this edition I would like to thank Dean Robert Stroker of the Boyer College of Music, Temple University, for his generous support and also the staff of the Bibliothèque de l'Opéra, Paris, where I have spent some of the most absorbing days of my life.

Preface to the First Edition and Acknowledgements

The year 2001, during which this volume was essentially completed, was the bicentennial of Vincenzo Bellini's birth. The first half of the year was dominated in the operatic and musicological world by celebrations of Giuseppe Verdi, who had died a century earlier. By November 2001, however, Bellini was receiving his due. Special issues of journals devoted to "the swan of Catania" had appeared (e.g., *The Opera Quarterly* summer issue) and Bellini conferences were held in both Catania, his birthplace, and in Paris, where he died far from home at the age of thirty-three. In Catania an institute was founded, along the lines of the Verdi Institute in Parma and the Rossini Institute in Pesaro, that will publish a journal devoted to the composer (*Quaderno belliniano*) and a Commissione Epistolario e Documentazione "Vincenzo Bellini" plans to publish a much-needed critical edition of Bellini's letters. Furthermore, a critical edition of the composer's works, beginning with six volumes (five operas and one volume of instrumental music) is to be published by Casa Ricordi, Milan.

As with Verdi, Bellini's reputation has experienced a number of vicissitudes since his death, and even during his lifetime. There was a controversy brewing already in the 1830s between his partisans and those of Rossini, because Rossini was the model for Italian opera. Bellini was sometimes deemed "filosofico" by Italians (such as Gioachino Rossini) and even somewhat Germanic (by Robert Schumann no less), because of his great attention to text-setting and because he reflected upon his art and set down his method of composition in a number of letters, principally the "Letter to Agostino Gallo" (see item 145), although the authenticity of that document is in doubt.

Bellini enjoyed a period of great popularity around the middle of the nineteenth century, but his Italian reputation was at a low ebb between 1890 and 1920. This was only with the critics, however, never with the public. The centennial of his birth in 1901 produced many tributes but little scholarship of note apart from *Omaggio a Bellini* until the appearance in 1915 of Ildebrando Pizzetti's landmark essay, followed two decades later by the study by Andrea della Corte and Guido Pannain. Pizzetti's assessment of Bellini's art, only the first of a number of subsequent publications on Bellini by the Italian composer, dispelled some of the criticisms about Bellini's harmony, counterpoint, and orchestration. Pizzetti saw Bellini as a pure melodist, an elegiac vocal composer, a viewpoint that became even more accepted when Verdi was being rediscovered in the 1920s and 1930s and Bellini's music was compared with his. There was a notable revival of interest in Bellini's music in the 1930s, reflected in Alfredo Casella's 1935 article in the periodical *Quadrivio* and Igor Stravinsky's discussion of his work in his second lecture on musical poetics at Harvard during the academic year 1939–1940.

The transferral of Bellini's remains from Paris to Catania in 1876 and the Bellini centennial in 1935 also produced many laudatory writings but little scholarship. Italians and especially Sicilians adored their genius and spoke of him in the most heartfelt but empty poetic language. In the next two decades, however, important landmarks in Bellini research by Italians appeared: Luisa Cambi's *Epistolario* in 1943, including all known extant and authentic letters, and Francesco Pastura's authoritative *Bellini secondo la storia* in 1959, based on letters and other documentary evidence. Both are indispensable volumes that no subsequent Bellini scholar can proceed without. Cambi also produced a *Vita* and Pastura a collection of letters.

Attention to and performance of Bellini's music has ebbed and flowed in part due to the ability of singers to interpret his highly personal style in a meaningful way. His special vocal lines were created for legendary singers whom we can never hear: Giuditta Pasta, Giulia Grisi, Giovanni Battista Rubini, Maria Malibran, Antonio Tamburini, Luigi Lablache, and others. We do have, however, many accounts of their performing styles and, most importantly, the music itself, which is one of the many compelling reasons a Bellini critical edition is needed; because there are many textual corruptions in the printed scores.

A number of the great soprano and mezzo-soprano interpreters of Bellini's difficult music from the 1950s, 1960s, and 1970s—the period we can now look back on as a golden era of bel canto singing in the twentieth century—are now deceased or retired. These include illustrious names such as Maria Callas, Joan Sutherland, Montserrat Caballé, Marilyn Horne, Leyla Gencer, Elena Souliotis, Renata Scotto, Beverly Sills, and Fiorenza Cossotto. Fortunately, they and others (more recently Edita Gruberova and Mariella Devia) have left a valuable legacy of both studio and live recordings. From earlier in the century we have splendid interpretations of individual arias and scenes by artists such as Rosa Ponselle and Claudio Muzio, not to mention Gina Cigna's complete *Norma*.

In an era of mass musical production and planned obsolescence, Bellini's was a unique voice. He achieved great success with only his third opera, whereas it took Donizetti upwards of thirty. Unlike most of his contemporaries and other composers in all musical styles—Johannes Brahms being a notable exception—Bellini never held a post at a court, church, conservatory, or opera house, but made a living from commissions. He worked slowly, knew his worth, and demanded—and got—higher fees than his predecessors and contemporaries. To a degree his works were less formulaic than much of the work produced by his contemporaries Gioachino Rossini and Gaetano Donizetti, ingenious though they both were.

Bellini wrote ten operas, an average of only one each year from 1825 to 1835, compared to dozens by Donizetti. Part of this may be attributed to Bellini's short life, yet an even greater contributing factor is his deliberate working method in which declamation of the text took precedence over melodic formulas. He often reserved the fioriture and high notes—all the trappings of vocal virtuosity—expressly to display outbursts of heightened emotions and drama, rendering these effects even more potent when they were used sparingly. Instead, he wrote melodies to be declaimed (notably in *Il pirata* and *La straniera*) or, as in the case of *Norma*, extensive sections of melodic recitative.

Bellini was trained in Naples by aged musicians such as Nicola Zingarelli, throwbacks to the simpler melodic style of Domenico Cimarosa and Giovanni Paisiello and deliberately anti-Rossinian. Bellini's music requires a sympathetic interpreter to make it come alive and we have had few of these: the great Normas of the twentieth century may still be counted on one hand.

If Rossini was the "savior" of Italian opera's international status with his great comic and serious hits of 1813 and 1816, Bellini was instrumental in maintaining this reputation in the late 1820s and early 1830s at a time when Rossini had retired from composing operas. His career represents a journey northward to the great opera capitals of the day: from Sicily to Naples, to Milan, to Venice, and finally to London and Paris. His early death prevented him from writing more than one work (*I puritani*) for the Théâtre-Italien in Paris. Had he lived longer, he would certainly have continued to write Italian operas for that theater and also would have achieved his goal—as did Rossini, Donizetti, and Verdi later—of writing a French opera for the Opéra. He apparently was considering several libretti by Scribe, including *Gustave III* (later set by Auber and in an Italian transformation by Verdi) and *Un duel sous Richelieu* (which gave Donizetti the subject for his opera *Maria di Rohan*). The prospects are tantalizing.

Raised with a basically Germanic outlook—which focuses on harmonic and contrapuntal complexity, the power of the orchestra, and Wagnerian principles of opera creation—opera critics in Europe and America have often criticized the works of nineteenth-century Italian opera composers, particularly those of Bellini, for deficiencies in these areas. In Bellini's case, in terms of musicodramatic effectiveness, many of these criticisms are manifestly unfounded. Bellini was a supreme melodist with faultless text setting. When this is understood and emphasized in analysis, his harmonic usage (which is sometimes rather bold), limited use of counterpoint, and orchestrational choices can be seen to work together to serve his musicodramatic ends: the expression of human emotions by the singing voice in which timbre also plays a central role. An analysis of Bellini's melodic construction has been undertaken principally by Friedrich Lippmann, to a lesser degree by Carl Dahlhaus, and, in the second edition of *New Grove*, by Mary Ann Smart.

Historically, whenever Bellini as a melodist is recognized—as by Pizzetti, for example—others have jumped in with the unfair criticism that he was "only" a melodist, a "supreme failing" of nineteenth-century Italian opera. It becomes a circular argument. Bellini's melody types are very individual; Verdi spoke of these "lunghe, lunghe melodie," and his predecessor's prodigious melodic talent was not the only factor that impressed the later composer. One cannot, for example, imagine the power of the opening storm in Verdi's *Otello* without the example provided by *Il pirata*, premiered exactly sixty years earlier. Wagner himself, although no champion of Italian opera when it served his ends, was inordinately fond of Bellini's *Norma*, incorporating ideas and structural devices from it into the conclusions of *Tristan und Isolde* and *Die Götterdämmerung*, and even going so far as to compose an added aria for the bass, Oroveso. Wagner's concept of "unendliche Melodie" in general and the rising sequential pattern of the "Liebestod" (vis-à-vis the finale of *Norma*) specifically illustrate Wagner's admiration of and indebtedness to Bellini, which he also made clear in several prose writings.

Cambi and Pastura have already been noted for their landmark scholarly work on Bellini. The German scholar Friedrich Lippmann has written indispensable works on Bellini's melodic types, aria structures, and other facets of his art. The most recent Bellini anniversary, the sesquicentennial of his death in 1985, brought a new flurry of Bellini scholarship, mainly by Italians, evidence of which are the activities of Salvatore Enrico Failla in Catania. Exhibitions were held, catalogues published, and musical and literary sources surveyed and documented. With the work of Lippmann, Rosario Maria Adamo, Failla, and Fabrizio Della Seta, Bellini scholarship is now on square footing. Leslie Orrey, writing in 1972, felt that trends had shifted toward acceptance of scholarly attention to this repertoire; at that point, however, there was still much to be done, especially through an examination of autograph sources. Writing a few years before Orrey, Andrew Porter in 1967 gave a measured outlook on Bellini's reputation:

> This is not an essay about the eloquence and beauty of Bellini's melody; nor a defense of his apt, skillful orchestration; nor a tribute to Felice Romani's masterly libretto. These things can be taken for granted now. If anything, Bellini is overpraised today, for his weaker operas are not sufficiently distinguished from the strong; and with the uneven pieces, pleasure in the general rediscovery of a style once despised can obscure perception of the specifically Bellinian achievements. (item 659)

A systematic, annotated bibliography of Bellini research is the clearest way of showing what directions Bellini research, performance, and criticism have taken and, more importantly, what lacunae need to be filled. There is a basic problem with documentation in that Bellini's letters were rearranged, suppressed, and part even forged by his great lifelong friend and executor, Francesco Florimo. The extent of this tampering, although known and previously mentioned in a number of sources (most eminently by Pastura), has only begun to be recognized and discussed more generally, in such works as John Rosselli's *The Life of Bellini* from 1996. Great caution and critical judgement is needed to untangle and verify authentic material. Rosselli has also done important archival work concerning Bellini's finances.

It must be said, however, that there is no decent treatment of Bellini's musical style in English; Orrey did not have the space (and one wishes he had for he displays some of provocative insights) and Weinstock makes too many musical errors and provides no synthesis of style or artistic growth. For one thing, he discusses the operas in alphabetical rather than chronological order. Mary Ann Smart's article in the second edition of *New Grove* is an excellent start, providing many valuable insights and connections. Although not in English, the article in the latest *Musik in Geschichte und Gegenwart* by Fabrizio Della Seta is a stimulating synthesis of Bellini's life and career. Thus we have two excellent, current treatments of the composer, although neither is by definition a full-length study. Della Seta, for example, presents Bellini's art in certain ways often overlooked by many writers. He notes that the connection within scenes in Bellini's operas becomes clear when one tries to remove certain parts or rearrange them; as opposed to manipulating component parts in Rossini's *Semiramide*, for example, one finds it nearly impossible. Bellini was also the first to give each opera a specific "tinta" and differentiate one work from another in this way, a concept we usually attribute to Verdi. For this idea, Della Seta points to an article in *L'Eco* of 20 February 1829, given in Cambi, *Epistolario*, p. 199.

One problem facing writers on Bellini has been lack of insight concerning the mechanics of the nineteenth-century Italian libretto. On this subject, Alessandro Roccatagliati has written valuable studies of the craft of Felice Romani and explored the connections of the libretto with the composers, the singers, and the theatrical productions involved in the creation of an opera. Much more needs to be done concerning performance practice—including issues of cadenzas, appoggiatura, and ornamentation—because Bellini's music does not sing or interpret itself. Some of these insights may be gleaned from recordings of great interpreters, notably Maria Callas, especially in terms of phrasing, but once again the need for a critical text is essential. Andrew Porter, who well could have done a masterly job with this topic, suggests that a monograph could profitably be written tracing the interconnections among key works of Bellini and his declared nemesis, Gaetano Donizetti. One such obvious connection is between *Anna Bolena* and *Beatrice di Tenda*, which to a great degree employ the same plot.

Concerning Bellini's life and character, there are a number of myths or misapprehensions that have been passed down too readily through generations of writers. While Bellini, like Franz Schubert, seems almost like a Hollywood model of a Romantic composer—a blond, blue-eyed Sicilian who died young in a foreign city—many have disparaged Bellini the man even while lauding his music. Many issues have proven controversial, among them his love affairs and often criticized treatment of the women who loved him, notably Maddalena Fumaroli and Giuditta Turina; his supposed effeminate nature and the connection of that to his "elegiac" musical style (we face the same situation with Frederic Chopin, a composer with whom Bellini is often linked, a musical connection that also needs to be examined in critical detail); Heine's characterization of him as "a sigh in dancing pumps"; Bellini's jealousy of and hostility toward his "rivals" such as Giovanni Pacini and Gaetano Donizetti; and his relationship with the slightly older mentor Rossini after Bellini went to Paris.

The operas of both Donizetti and Bellini are discussed often by music historians in terms of the "Code Rossini." A major problem for scholars of primo ottocento opera is that too little is known not only about Bellini's predecessors such as Cimarosa and Paisiello, but also about his lesser contemporaries such as Mayr, Pacini, and Mercadante. Until more of these connections are made, our view of Rossini, Bellini, Donizetti, and early Verdi may be off balance. This perspective, however, is inherent in our view of opera history, which is mostly based on masterworks and standard repertoire, although many would still argue that many of the works of Rossini, Bellini, Donizetti, and early Verdi actually belong to the category of "standard repertoire."

It is hoped that this guide, which consists of a critically annotated *bibliographie raisonnée* with a certain amount of cross-referencing, will provide those interested with the means to address some of these and other issues. I believe the categories encompass all the necessary facets of Bellini's life and music and the scholarship and reactions attendant upon them. The goal of this bibliography has been to be as inclusive as possible, although no claim can ever be made for completeness in a project of this kind. Thus, a number of popular, nonscholarly, even error-ridden accounts have been included in order to show the path of Bellini reception and scholarship (or sometimes lack thereof). This is not to say that such sources are meaningless and should be omitted, for they do provide a multitextured view of Bellini's reputation. At times he has been held in such low esteem that even writers such as Alfred Einstein and Guglielmo Barblan (in the original *Musik in Geschichte und Gegenwart* article) have provided incorrect birth and death dates. (Incorrect birth and death dates have proliferated throughout the Bellini literature. Even a monograph in Italian, published in Sicily no less and as recently as 2001, has him born on November 13.) Furthermore, when popular sources such as *Opera News* or *Opera* include viewpoints by authors such as Andrew Porter or William Ashbrook, there is no doubt of their value. Some of the entries have remained unannotated, but they are included for the sake of completeness and in the hope that those who are made aware of their existence may benefit from them. In many cases, titles provide a guide as to general content.

Completion of this project would have been difficult without the support of Temple University, Philadelphia, from which I have received a Study Leave, a Summer Fellowship, a Grant-in-Aid-of-Research, and monetary support through the former Dean of the Boyer College of Music at Temple, Jeffrey Cornelius, for which I am profoundly grateful. I would like to thank the staffs of the various archives and libraries in which I have conducted research: the Samuel Paley Library at Temple University, Philadelphia; the Library of the Teatro alla Scala in Milan; the British Library in London; the Van Pelt Library of the University of Pennsylvania in Philadelphia; the Bibliothèque de l'Opéra in Paris; and the Museo belliniano in Catania.

1

Bellini's Life and Career

OUTLINE OF KEY EVENTS IN HIS LIFE

1767–68 Bellini's grandfather, Vincenzo Tobia Bellini (1744–1829), moved from Torricella, a small village in the Abruzzi, to Catania; he had studied in Naples at the Conservatory di San Onofrio a Capuana; became *maestro di cappella* at Catania Cathedral; was a pedagogue and composer.

1801 Vincenzo Bellini, the eldest of eleven children, born November 3 in Catania, Sicily, to Rosario Bellini (1776–1840) and Agata Ferlito (1779–1842); Rosario was a *maestro di cappella* and composer, although not as influential on the young Vincenzo as his grandfather.

1807–08 Wrote first compositions; an anonymous manuscript written after Bellini's death by a relative or acquaintance and now found in the Museo belliniano ("L'Anonimo" hereafter) exaggerates the young Bellini's musical prowess, stating, for example, that he sang an aria at eighteen months.

1808 Began to study composition with his grandfather: his first work is a "Gallus cantavit"; wrote a great deal of sacred music for churches, e.g., Versetti for Good Friday and "Salve regina" for chorus and orchestra, and ariettas and instrumental pieces for salons, e.g., "La farfalletta."

1819 In May the Catania City Council, as a result of a *supplica* addressed to them, granted Bellini support to study in Naples; left in June to study at the Naples San Sebastiano Conservatory (Real Collegio di Musica), first with Giovanni Furno, then Carlo Conti; he was there for eight years, the least-known period of his life, even though Francesco Florimo, his lifelong closest friend, biographer, and protector of Bellini's reputation, was a schoolmate.

Instruction at the school was notably conservative, that is, anti-Rossinian. Bellini studied the theatrical works of Niccolò Jommelli, Giovanni Paisiello (*Nina, o sia La pazza per amore* was always a model), Giovanni Battista Pergolesi, Domenico Cimarosa, and other Neapolitan masters.

1820 Performed well in the annual examinations and earned a free place at the Conservatory.

1821 Undertook counterpoint studies with the aged Giacomo Tritto.

1822 Studied with the director of the Conservatory, septuagenarian Nicola Zingarelli (solfège, the Neapolitan school of opera, instrumental works of Mozart and Haydn); also studied aspects of singing with the great castrato Girolamo Crescentini.

Met Gaetano Donizetti and heard his opera, *La zingara*, then being given in Naples; Bellini admired and modeled himself after Donizetti until professional jealousy intruded.

Became infatuated with a young woman in Catania, Maddalena Fumaroli; gave her singing lessons and wrote songs for her.

1823 Composed Sinfonia in E-flat and a concerto for oboe.

1824 Due to success in annual examinations, Bellini was promoted to *primo maestrino* at the Conservatory; he was granted the privilege of visiting the Teatro San Carlo twice weekly. Either in 1824 or 1825 Bellini left the Conservatory and made an "emergency" visit to Sicily.

1825 Conservatory production given in the *teatrino* of Bellini's *Adelson e Salvini* with an all-male cast; repeated for several Sundays. Bellini reworked it subsequently for the Teatro del Fondo but this revision was not produced until 1992.

1826 Success of *Bianca e Fernando* at Teatro San Carlo, Naples, in May; the work had to be given as *Bianca e Gernando* because of the death of King Ferdinand I of Naples. *Adelson e Salvini*, seen by the most prestigious contemporary operatic impresario, Domenico Barbaja, had led to this commission. Maddalena Fumaroli's father failed to give permission for his daughter's marriage; Bellini received a *scrittura* from Domenico Barbaja for an opera at La Scala, Milan; little is known of Bellini's activities during the summer and autumn of this year, nor for the winter of 1826 to 1827.

In autumn, the site of the conservatory was moved to the rococo ex-convent of San Pietro a Majella, its present location.

1827 Departed from Naples on April 5, leaving behind the relationship with Maddalena Fumaroli; Bellini left his scores with his friend Florimo, among them four of Rossini's Neapolitan operas, Spontini's *La vestale*, some of Mozart's symphonies, and volumes of chamber music.

Bellini arrived in Milan in April, where he had a contract from Domenico Barbaja; renewed contact with Saverio Mercadante, a friend and classmate from Naples, who helped him to find lodgings and introduced him to important musicians and poets, including Felice Romani; there he composed *Il pirata*, his third opera. It was a huge success, premiered on October 27 at La Scala. We know very little about his life from his arrival in Milan up to the date of the premiere.

Il pirata was his first work with Felice Romani, resident poet at La Scala, his exclusive librettist for every subsequent work except his last, *I puritani*; it was also the first of his operas to gain international stature, the ultimate criterion for which was a Parisian performance. Bellini remained mostly in Milan from 1827 to 1833, where he was invited into the most elegant homes and salons, such as those of Count Barbò, the Duchess Litta, and the Countess Belgioioso, whom he was later to encounter in Paris; he stayed with Francesco and Marianna Pollini, older musicians who practically adopted him.

1828 Early in the year *Il pirata* was given in Vienna, the first time a Bellini opera was heard outside of Italy; in April the second version of *Bianca e Fernando* was given successfully at the Teatro Carlo Felice in Genoa using some new verses by Romani; Bellini composed two new arias for the Bianca, Adelaide Tosi. There he began a passionate love affair with Giuditta Turina (née Cantù), the wife of a wealthy silk merchant Ferdinando Turina, which lasted until 1833, when he left Italy forever.

Bellini's works began to be published by the firm of Ricordi in Milan.

1829 Very successful premiere of *La straniera* at La Scala in February, leading to controversy about its novel, unadorned, un-Rossinian style. Bellini was now called a "filosofico"; rejected setting *Cesare in Egitto* for Parma; spent March and April composing *Zaira*, which in May was a failure at the new Teatro Ducale in Parma. In August Bellini met Rossini in Milan, who was returning to Bologna after the premiere of *Guillaume Tell* in Paris.

For long periods at a time from 1829 to 1833, Bellini stayed at the country estates of the Cantù and Turina families, thus saving money and gaining more artistic freedom. Bellini also gave Giuditta his money to invest.

Ricordi published Bellini's *Sei ariette* and the Silver Medal of the Royal Order of Francesco Primo was conferred on the composer by the King of Naples, Francis I.

1830 At the beginning of the year Bellini went to Venice for a production of *Il pirata*; in May he suffered a violent attack of amoebic dysentery, the disease that eventually was to kill him; he spent the summer recuperating at Lake Como. Due to the illness of Giovanni Pacini, Bellini was asked to provide a new opera for the Teatro La Fenice, Venice; success of *I Capuleti e i Montecchi* using Romani's revision of his own libretto for Niccola Vaccai's *Giulietta e Romeo* (1825). *I Capuleti* was one of the last operas of any significance to call for a contralto hero, the part having been created for Giuditta Grisi.

Revival of *La straniera* in August at Bergamo, Donizetti's hometown, directed by Bellini; worked on the never-finished *Ernani* in the summer and autumn at Giuditta Turina's estate at Moltrasio near Lake Como where he had been recovering from his illness in the spring. *Ernani* was abandoned possibly because of fears of censorship or that it could not compete with Donizetti's successful *Anna Bolena*; several numbers from the work were used in subsequent operas. At Lake Como he met Giuditta Pasta, a singing-actress with a flawed voice but who was possessed of a striking histrionic ability, for whom he created the title roles in his next three operas. We know little about Bellini from the latter part of this year, except that he and Romani decided on *La sonnambula* as their next operatic subject.

1831 In March *La sonnambula* was premiered with great success at the Teatro Carcano, Milan, starring Giuditta Pasta. Bellini spent the summer with Giuditta Turina at Moltrasio on the western shore of Lake Como, specifically to write the role of Norma for Pasta; he seemed interested in marrying Pasta's daughter, Clelia. Other than this, we know little about Bellini's daily life between the premiere of *La sonnambula* in March and the premiere of *Norma* on December 26. At the opening of the 1831/32 Carnival season at La Scala, *Norma* had a relatively unsuccessful premiere, purportedly described by Bellini as "fiasco, fiasco, solenne fiasco," although the authenticity of this letter has been called into question; it is probably spurious. After the premiere, subsequent performances went smoothly.

1832 On January 5 Bellini left for a triumphal return to Naples and Sicily; accompanying him was Giuditta Turina. *Il fu ed il sarà*, to a libretto by Jacopo Ferretti, was heard privately in Rome on January 18 during a brief visit there by Bellini. No score exists; it was most probably a pasticcio of selections from Bellini's previous operas. He was honored in Naples with a performance of *I Capuleti e i Montecchi* at the San Carlo with King Ferdinando II in attendance.

Bellini continued to Sicily with Francesco Florimo and without Giuditta Turina. In Palermo in April, he posed for two likenesses, an oil painting by Giuseppe Patania and one in marble by Giuseppe Pollet. Returning to northern Italy in May, he directed rehearsals of *Norma* in Bergamo and Venice. In early September he returned to Milan and in November he and Romani determined that their next opera would be *Cristina di Svezia*, based on Alexandre Dumas's *Christine, ou*

Stockholme, Fontainebleau et Rome, but it was dropped in favor of *Beatrice di Tenda*, one of the first Italian operas based on events from Italian history. Pasta and Bellini had seen a ballet version of *Beatrice* at La Scala that autumn and decided it would be a worthy vehicle for the prima donna.

1833 In March his new opera for La Fenice, *Beatrice di Tenda*, was not accorded a positive reception. The libretto was late; the impresario Alessandro Lanari sent the police after Romani; recriminations and a break occurred between Bellini and his librettist. In the journalistic polemic that ensued in the *Gazzetta privilegiata di Venezia*, Romani placed the blame for the delayed premiere on Bellini and claimed that his artistic vitality had been undermined by "the three Giudittas": Grisi, Pasta, and Turina.

Never to see Italy again, Bellini left Venice on March 28 for London with Giuseppe and Giuditta Pasta; he arrived in the English capital at the end of April and stayed until mid-August; on the way he stopped in Paris to meet with the director of the Opéra, Louis-Désiré Véron, from whom he hoped to receive a commission.

At the King's Theatre, London—where he had been invited by the manager, Pierre-François Laporte, to conduct and supervise performances of his works—*Il pirata, Norma*, and *I Capuleti e i Montecchi* were somewhat successful with Pasta, Méric-Lalande, and Donzelli as leading singers; Malibran caused a sensation when she sang the title role in *La sonnambula* in English at Drury Lane Theatre. Other famous singers such as Laure Cinti-Damoreau, Rubini, and Tamburini also appeared in his works in London. Bellini took part in the social life of the city. (See *Musical Times* of September 1901 for information on Bellini in London.)

In May compromising letters Bellini had written to Giuditta Turina fell into her husband's hands. In September Bellini wrote to her saying that he no longer had ardent feelings for her.

Bellini returned to Paris in August, where *Il pirata* and *I Capuleti e i Montecchi* were given successfuly in the autumn at the Théâtre-Italien; established himself in the Bains Chinoix, Boulevard des Italiens, near the Théâtre-Italien, close to Rossini, with whom he renewed his acquaintance. Unsuccessful negotiations with the Opéra took place; Bellini devoted quite a bit of time to Parisian social life, becoming close to Rossini and becoming acquainted with Chopin, Carafa, Paër, and others; met Heinrich Heine and also undoubtedly such luminaries as Victor Hugo, Alfred de Musset, George Sand, and Franz Liszt at the salon of Princess Belgioioso; also met Ferdinand Hiller and heard Beethoven symphonies, including the "Pastoral," played at the Conservatoire.

1834 Received a definite commission from the Théâtre-Italien and began work on *I puritani* to a libretto by Count Carlo Pepoli, an Italian expatriate. Around the same time he received a commission from San Carlo, Naples, to write a new opera; he declined but remained in contact with the San Carlo's directors; finally it was decided he would write a new version of *I puritani*, for Maria Malibran, Duprez, and Porto.

Success of *La sonnambula* at Théâtre-Italien. Composed *Quattro sonetti* to words by Pepoli, a "Sapphic Ode," and some other songs, none of which is extant. Rossini urged him to work on his orchestration. Bellini and Romani resumed correspondence, but due to Bellini's death the following year, they never had the chance to work together again. Bellini experiences brief recurrence of gastric problems.

1835 Triumph of *I puritani* in January in Paris, with famous quartet of Grisi, Rubini, Tamburini, and Lablache (the only version of this opera to be published); wrote a second version of the opera for the San Carlo, Naples, to be sung by Maria Malibran and Gilbert Duprez, but the score did not reach Naples in time and it was not performed until 1985 in London. Bellini appointed a Chevalier of the Légion d'Honneur; engaged in many negotiations with the Opéra and the Opéra-Comique, all of which came to nothing. He became terminally ill at the end of August with the amoebic dysentery he had first experienced in 1830; on September 23 he died alone at the country house of S. Levy in Puteaux, a suburb of Paris; Dr. Montallegri was the attending physician; on September 25 Dr. Delmas performed the autopsy, confirming the diagnosis of dysentery, complicated by an abscessed liver.

A Requiem Mass was given at the Church of the Invalides on October 2 with Paër, Cherubini, Carafa, and Rossini as pallbearers; François-Antoine Habeneck was principally in charge of the music. One item sung was a four-part "Lacrymosa" using the tenor melody from Act III of *I puritani* as the theme, performed *a cappella* by Rubini, Nicholas Ivanoff, Tamburini, and Lablache. Even though it rained continuously, the funeral was attended by the most noted musicians and artists in Paris. Bellini was buried at Père-Lachaise Cemetery. Rossini took care of sending Bellini's possessions to his family in Catania.

1876 After years of negotiations between French and Sicilian officials, Bellini's remains were removed from Père-Lachaise Cemetery in Paris to Catania Cathedral. The ceremonies were held in Paris on September 15 and the remains reached Catania on September 23, 1876, exactly forty-one years after Bellini died. Francesco Florimo was still alive for the occasion. Commemorative festivities were held in Catania and throughout Italy.

COMPLETED OPERAS; CASTS OF PREMIERES

Adelson e Salvini, opera semiseria in three acts, libretto by Andrea Leone Tottola, after P. Delamarre; premiered at the San Sebastiano Conservatory, Naples, between February 10 and 15, 1825; second version in two acts, done either in 1826 or 1828–29 as *dramma semiserio*, unperformed until September 1992 in Catania at the Teatro Massimo Bellini.

Principal singers included an all-male cast from the Conservatory for the nineteenth-century production: Antonio Manza (Lord Adelson), Giacinto Maras (Nelly), and Leonardo Perugini (Salvini). In Catania in 1992 the cast included Fabio Previati (Adelson), Bradley Williams (Salvini), Alicia Nafé (Nelly), Aurio Tomicich (Bonifacio), and Roberto Coviello (Struley).

Bianca e Fernando, melodramma in two acts, libretto by Domenico Gilardoni, after *Bianca e Fernando alla tomba di Carlo IV* by Carlo Roti; premiered as *Bianca e Gernando* at the Teatro San Carlo, Naples, May 30, 1826; second version, libretto revised by Felice Romani, premiered as *Bianca e Fernando* at the Teatro Carlo Felice, Genoa, April 7, 1828. Bellini replaced the short introduction with a full-scale overture, added four new numbers and made changes to all but two of the other numbers.

The 1826 opera was written for Adelaide Tosi, Giovanni David, and Luigi Lablache, but when the premiere was postponed the cast consisted of Henriette Méric-Lalande (Bianca), Giovanni Battista Rubini (Gernando), and Luigi Lablache (Filippo). In 1828 principal singers included Adelaide Tosi (Bianca), Giovanni David (Fernando), and Antonio Tamburini (Filippo).

Il pirata, melodramma in two acts, libretto by Felice Romani, after Charles R. Maturin and Charles Nodier/L. J. S. Taylor, *Bertram, ou Le pirate*; premiered at La Scala, Milan, October 27, 1827.

Principal singers included Giovanni Battista Rubini (Gualtiero), Henriette Méric-Lalande (Imogene), and Antonio Tamburini (Ernesto).

La straniera, melodramma in two acts, libretto by Felice Romani after *L'Etrangère* by V.-C. Prévôt d'Arlincourt and from *La straniera*, a dramatized version of the novel by the Baron Giovan Carlo Cosenza (1827); premiered at La Scala, Milan, February 14, 1829.

Principal singers included Henriette Méric-Lalande (Alaide), Stanislao Marcionni (Il Signore di Montolino), Caroline Unger (Isoletta), Domenica Reina (Arturo), and Antonio Tamburini (Baron Valdeburgo).

Zaira, tragedia lirica in two acts, libretto by Felice Romani after Voltaire; premiered at the Teatro Ducale, Parma, May 16, 1829.

Principal singers included Henriette Méric-Lalande (Zaira), Teresa Cecconi (Nerestano), Carlo Trezzini (Corasmino), Luigi Lablache (Orosmane), and Mario Rinaudo (Lusignano).

I Capuleti e i Montecchi, *tragedia lirica* in two acts, libretto by Felice Romani after L. Scevola's *Giulietta e Romeo*; premiered at Teatro la Fenice, Venice, March 11, 1830.

Principal singers included Giuditta Grisi (Romeo), Rosalbina Carradori-Allan (Giulietta), Lorenzo Bonfigli (Tebaldo), Gaetano Antoldi (Capiello), and Rainieri Pocchini (Lorenzo).

La sonnambula, *melodramma* in two acts, libretto by Felice Romani after Eugène Scribe and J.-P. Aumer's ballet scenario set to music by F. Hérold; premiered at Teatro Carcano, Milan, March 6, 1831.

Principal singers included Giuditta Pasta (Amina), Giovanni Battista Rubini (Elvino), Elisa Taccani (Lisa), and Luciano Mariani (Il Conte Rodolfo).

Norma, *tragedia lirica* in two acts, libretto by Felice Romani after Alexandre Soumet's *Norma; ou, L'Infanticide* and his own libretto for Pacini's opera *La sacerdota d'Irminsul* (1820); premiered at La Scala, Milan, December 26, 1831.

Principal singers included Giuditta Pasta (Norma), Giulia Grisi (Adalgisa), Domenico Donzelli (Pollione), and Vincenzo Negrini (Oroveso).

Beatrice di Tenda, *tragedia lirica* in two acts, libretto by Felice Romani after C. Tebaldi-Fores; premiered at Teatro la Fenice, Venice, March 16, 1833.

Principal singers included Giuditta Pasta (Beatrice), Anna del Serrre (Agnese), Alberico Curioni (Orombello), Orazio Cartagenova (Filippo), and Alessandro Giacchini (Anichino).

I puritani, *melodramma seria* in three acts, libretto by Count Carlo Pepoli after the dramma *Têtes rondes et Cavaliers* by Jacques-Arsène-François-Polycarpe Ancelot and Joseph-Xavier Boniface [Saintine]; premiered at Théâtre-Italien, Paris, January 24, 1835.

Premiere sung by the "Puritani" quartet, Giulia Grisi (Elvira), Giovanni Battista Rubini (Arturo), Antonio Tamburini (Riccardo), and Luigi Lablache (Giorgio).

Naples version for Malibran, Duprez, and Porto (no contemporary performances; premiere not until December 14, 1985, in London).

2

Bibliographies, Works-Lists, Catalogues

BIBLIOGRAPHIES

1. Adamo, Maria Rosaria. "Aggiornamento alla Bibliografia belliniana di Orazio Viola." In *Vincenzo Bellini: Critica-Storia-Tradizione*. Ed. Salvatore Enrico Failla, pp. 82–105. Catania: Maimone, 1991. ISBN 88–77510–56–0. ML410.B44 V5 1991.

   An addition to Orazio Viola's comprehensive bibliography, first published in 1901 and updated in 1923. See item 14. Valuable essay-discussion of important scholarly writings devoted to Bellini from approximately 1935 to 1990. Organized by chronology and subject matter. Mostly Italian sources.

2. Damerini, Adelmo. "Bellini e la critica del suo tempo." In *Vincenzo Bellini, le sue opere, la sua fama*. Ed. Ildebrando Pizzetti, pp. 215–50. Milan: Fratelli Treves, 1936. ML410.B44 P58.

   An important assessment of the contemporary critical writings on Bellini's operas, written at the time of the centennial of the composer's death. Many quotations from nineteenth-century reviews, well documented. Includes bibliographic references and citations, including newspaper articles.

3. Deiss, E. "Zur deutschsprachigen Bellini-Literatur." *Dissonance* 14 (November 1987): 423–25. ML1.D57.

   List current for 1987 of Bellini literature in German.

4. Della Seta, Fabrizio. "Literatur." In "Bellini, Vincenzo [Salvatore Carmelo Francesco]." *Die Musik in Geschichte und Gegenwart, Allgemeine Enzylopädie der Musik begrundet von Friedrich Blume*. Zweite, neuarbeitete

Ausgabe herausgegeben von Ludwig Finscher. Kassel: Bärenreiter, 1999. Personenteil, 2. Band, cols. 1023–26. ISBN 37–61811–10–1. ML400.M92 1994.

Includes an excellent bibliography with a number of recent scholarly studies (in *Festschriften* and congress reports, for example) that were not cited elsewhere in the Bellini literature as of date of this publication.

5. Law, Joe K. "Selected Bibliography of Literature on Vincenzo Bellini." *Opera Quarterly* 17/3 (Summer 2001): 464–67. ISSN 0736–0053. ML 1699.O65.

   A selective bibliography, current for the bicentenary of the composer's birth, part of *Opera Quarterly*'s Bellini Commemorative Issue.

6. Lippmann, Friedrich. "Bellini, Vincenzo" (bibliography). In *The New Grove Dictionary of Music and Musicians*. 6th ed. 20 vols. Ed. Stanley Sadie. New York: Macmillan, 1980. Vol. 2 (2001): 453–55. ISBN 15–61592–39–0. ML100.N48 2001.

   Extensive bibliography divided into a number of categories: Works-Lists, Bibliographies, Discographies, Letters, Iconography, Life and Works, Biographical and Character Studies, Critical Studies, Specific Aspects of Works, and Individual Works.

7. ——. "Vincenzo Bellini" (bibliography). In *The New Grove Masters of Italian Opera*. Ed. Philip Gossett, pp. 181–89. New York: Norton, 1983. ISBN 03–93016–85–4. ML390.N466 1983.

   Extensive bibliography, updated from *New Grove* 1980, divided into a number of categories: Works-Lists, Bibliographies, Discographies, Letters, Iconography, Life and Works, Biographical and Character Studies, Critical Studies, Specific Aspects of Works, and Individual Works.

8. —— and Mary Ann Smart. "Bellini, Vincenzo" (bibliography). In *The New Grove Dictionary of Music and Musicians*. 2d ed. 29 vols. Ed. Stanley Sadie and John Tyrrell. New York: Macmillan, 2001. Vol. 3: 209–12. ISBN 15–61592–39–0. ML100.N48 2001.

   Extensive bibliography divided into a number of categories: Works-Lists, Bibliographies, Discographies, Letters, Iconography, Life and Works, Biographical and Character Studies, Critical Studies, Specific Aspects of Works, and Individual Works.

9. Maguire, Simon. "Vincenzo Bellini" (bibliography). In *The New Grove Dictionary of Opera*. 4 vols. Ed. Stanley Sadie. New York: Macmillan, 1992. Vol. 1: 395–407. ISBN 09–35859–92–6. ML102.O6 N5 1992.

   Extensive bibliography divided into a number of categories: Works-Lists, Bibliographies, Discographies, Letters, Iconography, Life and Works,

Biographical and Character Studies, Critical Studies, Specific Aspects of Works, and Individual Works.

10. Pugliatti, Salvatore. "Problemi della critica belliniana." In *Chopin e Bellini*. Ed. Salvatore Pugliatti, pp. 93–113. Messina: La Editrice Universitaria, 1952. ML410.C54 P94.

    Explores the musicodramatic connections in Bellini's operas. Bibliography and discussion of critical writings on Bellini.

11. Riehn, Rainer. "Auswahlbibliographie." In *Musik-Konzepte 46: Vincenzo Bellini*. Ed. Heinz-Klaus Metzger and Rainer Riehn, pp. 109–16. Munich: Edition Text & Kritik, 1985. ISBN 38–83772–13–5. ML410.B44 V5 1985.

    A "selective" but extensive bibliography, current for 1985.

12. Ronga, Luigi. "Note sulla storia della critica belliniana." *A Vincenzo Bellini. Bollettino dei musicisti, Mensile del Sindacato Nazionale Fascista Musicisti* 2/3 (December 1934): 70–74. Rpt., Luigi Ronga, *Arte e gusto nella musica*. Milan/Naples, 1956, pp. 244–57. ML160.R78.

    A survey, in essay form, of critical writings on Bellini's operas. An important assessment around the time of the centennial of the composer's death.

13. Tintori, Giampiero. Bibliography from *Bellini. La musica*. Milan: Rusconi Libri, 1983, pp. 343–51. ML410.B44 T56 1983. ISBN L24000.

    A monograph on Bellini's life and works. Bibliography on pp. 343–51.

14. Viola, Orazio. "Saggio bibliografico delle più antiche edizioni dei libretti musicali da Vincenzo Bellini." Appendix to Orazio Viola, "Bibliografia belliniana." In *Omaggio a Bellini nel primo centenario dalla sua nascità*. Ed. G. Giuliano, pp. 336–84. Catania: Maimone, 1901; republished 1902. 2d ed. rev. and supplemented, Catania: 1923. ML410.B44 C.

    The 1923 edition contains 888 items but ignores Lloyd (1909); in fact it contains nothing in English. Includes many newspaper articles, many of which may be found in folders in the Museo belliniano in Catania. Preceded by an essay with fourteen reproductions of paintings and other illustrations. Indices of authors and subjects. See item 1.

15. Weinstock, Herbert. *Vincenzo Bellini: His Life and His Opera*. New York: Knopf, 1971. ISBN 03–94416–56–2. ML410.B44 W4.

    Extensive list of the most important bibliographic items at that time, pp. 547–54.

WORKS-LISTS AND CATALOGUES

There is currently no thematic catalogue for the works of Bellini.

16. *Collezione delle opere teatrali poste in musica dal celebre maestro Vincenzio* [*sic*] *Bellini*. Flautina, 1834.

17. Della Seta, Fabrizio. "Bellini, Vincenzo [Salvatore Carmelo Francesco]." In *Die Musik in Geschichte und Gegenwart, Allgemeine Enzylopädie der Musik begrundet von Friedrich Blume*. Zweite, neuarbeitete Ausgabe herausgegeben von Ludwig Finscher. Kassel: Bärenreiter, 1999. Personenteil, 2. Band, cols. 1014–16. ISBN 37–61811–10–1. ML400.M92 1994.

18. Lippmann, Friedrich. "Bellinis-Opern—Daten und Quellen." *Vincenzo Bellini und die italienische Oper seiner Zeit, Analecta musicologica* 6 (1969): 365–97. ML160.S893. ISSN 0585–6086; Italian trans., rev. in Rosa Maria Adamo and Friedrich Lippmann, *Vincenzo Bellini*. Turin: Edizione RAI Radiotelevisione Italiana, 1981, pp. 523–49. ML410.B44 A43 1981.

    See item 262.

19. ——. "Bellini, Vincenzo" (Works-List). In *The New Grove Dictionary of Music and Musicians*. 6th ed. 20 vols. Ed. Stanley Sadie. New York: Macmillan, 1980. Vol. 2: 452–53. ISBN 15–61592–39–0. ML100.N48 2001.

20. ——. "Bellini, Vincenzo" (Works-List). In *The New Grove Masters of Italian Opera*. Ed. Philip Gossett, pp. 181–89. New York: Norton, 1983. ISBN 03–93016–85–4. ML390.N466 1983.

21. Maguire, Simon. "Bellini, Vincenzo" (Works-List). In *The New Grove Dictionary of Opera*. 4 vols. Ed. Stanley Sadie. New York: Macmillan, 1992. Vol. 1: 394–95. ISBN 09–35859–92–6. ML102.O6 N5 1992.

22. —— and Mary Ann Smart. "Bellini, Vincenzo" (Works-List). In *The New Grove Dictionary of Music and Musicians*. 2d ed. 29 vols. Ed. Stanley Sadie and John Tyrrell. New York: Macmillan, 2001. Vol. 3 (2001): 208–9. ISBN 15–61592–39–0. ML100.N48 2001.

    Includes the following information for each opera: title, genre-acts, librettist, literary source, premiere, MS source, printed scores. Then a listing of Sacred, Other Vocal, and Instrumental Works.

23. Pastura, Francesco. "Elenco delle opere." In *Bellini secondo la storia*. Parma: Guanda, 1959, pp. 709–12. ML410.B44 P38.

    A list of Bellini's *oeuvre* that divides the works into Musica teatrale, Musica da chiesa, Musica da camera, and Musica strumentale. Within each category works are listed chronologically and original casts are given for the operas.

24. Riehn, Rainer. "Werkverzeichnis." In *Musik-Konzepte 46: Vincenzo Bellini*. Ed. Heinz-Klaus Metzger and Rainer Riehn, pp. 105–8. Munich: Edition Text & Kritik, 1985. ISBN 38–83772–13–5. ML410.B44 V5 1985.

3

Encounters with Bellini and Contemporary Critical Reception

This section consists of encounters with Bellini and descriptions and impressions of him by his contemporaries, particularly by his friends and fellow musicians, critics, and others in the arts. A number of them are from accounts in diaries and memoirs. Others deal with critical reception. Bellini met many artists, politicians, and aristocrats in Paris, among them Countess Belgioioso, Mme Jaubert, Victor Hugo, Alfred de Musset, George Sand, Alexandre Dumas père, Heinrich Heine, Michelet, Guizot, Thiers, Augustin Thierry, Chopin, Liszt, Paër, Carafa, Cherubini, and of course Rossini. Bellini's French was notoriously poor and thus in Paris he did not say much in society. For that reason many artists who probably had met him made no references to him in their journals, diaries, or in other places. These include Balzac, Stendhal, Mérimée, George Sand, Musset, Sainte-Beuve, Hugo, and others.

There are also numerous reviews and essays in nineteenth-century newspapers and periodicals not listed here.

25. Abbadessa, Emanuela Ersilia. "Da Parigi a Catania: Il mito di Bellini tra storia, iconografia e musica." *Vincenzo Bellini et la France* (2007): 595–631. See item 404.

    This study takes into account not only Bellini's musical achievements but also his portrayal in the belletristic world, notably in the novel *Gli anni perduti* by Vitaliano Brancati (reprinted Milan, 1976), as well as in popular literature. Abbadessa examines iconographical sources to try to identify what made Bellini material for portrayal as a typical Sicilian mythic figure, the epitome of a Sicilian "lover" and son as often depicted in Sicilian fiction. Photos and portraits.

26. Acquino, Baron Aimé d'. *Journal* (1835). His account was first published in Florimo, *Bellini: Memorie e lettere*. Florence: G. Barbèra, 1882. Rpt., Florence: G. Barbèra, 1976. See item 44. ML410.B44 F6.

    One of Bellini's friends in Paris, the Baron d'Acquino, a nephew of the composer Michele Carafa, visited the sick Bellini on 11 September 1835, and attempted to see him several times further, but was denied entrance by the gardener. In his *Journal*, d'Acquino gives an extensive account of arriving at Puteaux on the morning of 23 September, only to be told that Bellini had succumbed early that morning and that "M. and Mme Lewis" had precipitously left for Paris.

27. Amore, Antonino. *Brevi cenni critici*. Catania: N. Giannotta, 1877.

    Amore was among the nineteenth-century biographers of Bellini. See his biographical writings, items 144, 216, and 285. Here he discusses Bellini's critical reception.

28. Barbieri, Raffaello. *La principessa Belgiojoso, i suoi amici e nemeci, il suo tempo. Da memorie mondane inedite o rare e da archivii segreti di stato.* Milan: Treves, 1902.

    Belgioioso held salons in Milan and Paris where Bellini met many eminent artists. See items 31, 75, and 992.

29. Basevi, Abramo. *Studio sulle opere di Giuseppe Verdi*. Florence: Tofani, 1859. Rpt., Bologna: Antiquae Musicae Italicae Studiosi, 1978. ML410. V5 B3.

    One of the earliest Verdi studies, concluding with *Un ballo in maschera*. Bellini is discussed on pp. 17–18, mainly the use of dissonance in his melodies.

30. Bauwr, Alexandrine-Sophie Goury de Champgrand, Comtesse de. *Mes Souvenirs*. Paris, 1853.

    The Countess lived in Paris from 1773 to 1860, studied composition with Grétry and singing with Boieldieu, and was in contact with many musicians. Before she married de Bauwr she was married to St-Simon, founder of the Saint Simeons.

31. Belgioioso, Cristina, Countess. *Souvenirs dans l'exil*. In *Le National* (September 5 and October 12, 1850). Rpt., Milan: Istituto Editoriale Italiano, 1946. DG551.8.B3 A3.

    The Countess, who kept salons in Milan and Paris where Bellini met many notable persons, wrote to Madame Jaubert from Athens in 1849:

    "Bellini's melodies are often on my lips and I run my fingers over a piano that, bad as it is, helps me render my musical thought. I often recall with sadness the premature death of that great composer, not with the egotistical feeling of regret over the masterpieces he carried to the tomb, but because death was so frightening to him." Translation from Beth Archer Brombert; see item 992.

Cristina's letter to Madame Jaubert relays information about the meeting at her country house, La Jonchère, between Heine and Bellini that provided the impetus for Heine's famous posthumous essay on Bellini. This account is often drawn from Jaubert's *Memoirs* but her information came from Belgioioso. Heine ribbed Bellini about the death of young geniuses, saying maybe he had nothing to worry about, if he were not a genius. Bellini was notoriously superstitious and considered Heine to have the "evil eye" because he wore glasses and had reddish tints in his blond hair, attributes of the devil. Bellini died not much later. See item 51.

32. Bellaigue, Camille. *Etudes musicales et nouvelles silhouettes de musiciens*, 1st series. Paris: Delagrave, 1898. ML60.B42.

    Bellini is discussed in Chapter VII under "Nouvelles Silhouettes de Musiciens," pp. 382–87. Bellaigue, a noted critic and friend of Verdi, was transported by Bellinian melody, inspiring him to reread the five-hundred-page work of Antonino Amore. See item 144. Bellaigue speaks of the melancholy, sentimental, but not always profound nature of Bellini's arias and the decadence of this music and its creation for singers. According to Bellaigue, the first ten measures of "Casta diva" are the most beautiful evocation of the moon in music. "*Piangere . . . far piangere*, this word comes up on every page of Bellini's correspondence." States that Bellini was twenty-one when he died.

33. ——. "Hommage à Bellini." In *Echos de France et d'Italie*. Paris: Delagrave, 1911, pp. 267–88. (Also *Revue des deux mondes* LXXXVIII (15 October 1918), pp. 923–34.) AP20.R3 1918 title: "Hommage à Bellini d'après un livre recent."

    Another assessment of Bellini by the noted French critic. See previous item.

34. Berlioz, Hector. "Bellini: Notes nécrologiques." In *Les Musiciens et la musique*. Paris, 1903, pp. 167–69. Rpt., Farnborough: Gregg, 1969. ML60.B6469 1969.

    Originally appeared in *Journal des Débats* on July 16, 1836: ". . . the simplicity of Cimarosa, as well as so much of the penetrating charm of Mozart, as well as the pathetic elevated by Gluck . . . but always a marked difference between his style and that of Rossini." Berlioz prefers *La straniera* among Bellini's works. Of Bellini: "[only] slightly versed in the science of harmony, a bit of a stranger to orchestration . . . a musician of the second rank . . . [but] his deep sensibility is just and true, as well as . . . the naive simplicity with which his best ideas are presented." Berlioz believed in technological progress in music and faulted Bellini for not displaying this in his operas.

35. ——. *Cauchemars et passions.* In *Musique et musiciens.* Comp. and ed. Gerald Condé. Paris: J.C. Lattès, 1981. ML60.B4689.

An anthology of articles by Berlioz written from 1829 to 1863 that were not included in his own collections. Many are about his contemporaries, Bellini, Cherubini, Chopin, Gounod, and Le Sueur. Also discusses major works by Mozart, Gluck, Rameau, and Grétry. Bibliography and Index.

36. Blaze de Bury, Henri-Ange, Baron. *Musiciens contemporains.* Paris: Michel Lévy Frères, 1856. ML385.B64.

These essays were written years before this publication date, appearing originally in the *Revue des deux mondes*. Compares Bellini with Mercadante. Author notes the two spectators during a performance of *Norma* who exclaim: "Rossini fait l'amour, Bellini aime!" Blaze contends that "love is the basis of Bellini's music; each measure, every note breathes love, an ardent, passionate, sublime love." Other contemporary composers discussed include Rossini, Donizetti, Cherubini, and Mercadante.

37. Castil-Blaze (François-Henri-Joseph Blaze). *L'Opéra-Italien de 1548 à 1856 (Théâtres Lyriques de Paris)*. Paris: Castil-Blaze, 1856. ML1727.8. P22 T52.

Father of Henri-Ange Blaze de Bury and the first music critic of a Paris paper, the *Journal des Débats*. His discussion of Bellini's music is tied to a treatment of the great interpreters of that music. On pp. 440–54 he deals with the singers Malibran, Lablache, Tamburini, and Rubini.

38. Chorley, Henry. *Thirty Years' Musical Recollections*. Ed. with an introduction by Ernest Newman. New York: Knopf, 1926. Originally published in 2 vols. London: Hurst and Blackett, 1862. ML423.C55 C5 1926. Rpt. in 2 vols. New York: Da Capo Press, 1984. ML1731.C58 1984.

Chorley gives Bellini's dates as 1802 to 1836. In assessing Bellini's operas, Chorley states that he was "ostensibly educated at Naples," and judges that "the acquirements with which he began to write must have been of the slenderest possible quality and quantity, a little exceeding those of any amateur who can combine a few chords, orginate simple tunes, and show some feeling for the grouping of voices and instruments." He continues in this vein but concedes that Bellini's melodies do come alive in a great singer's throat—and Chorley heard most of the original interpreters, such as Rubini, Pasta, and Giulia Grisi.

Mainly a chronicle of performances Chorley saw from 1830 to 1859 as a critic for the London *Atheneum*. In 1836, for example, he writes about (among other works) Bellini's *La straniera*, *Beatrice di Tenda*, *Norma*, and

I puritani, and the singers Giulia Grisi, Rubini, Tamburini, Lablache, and others. Speaks rapturously of *I puritani* in London with Grisi, Rubini, and Lablache. Chorley was considered an excellent judge of singers and one who described them fairly, both their strengths and their faults.

39. Conestabile, Giovanni Carlo. *Vita di Paganini*. Perugia: Tipografia di V. Bartelli, 1851. ML418.P2 C7. Rev. expanded 2d ed. by Federico Mompellio. Milan: Società Editrice Dante Alighieri, 1936. ML418.P2 C7 1936.

    A chapter, "Bellini e la critica musicale," pp. 304ff., was inserted into his life of Paganini. Plates, portraits, and facsimiles, including music.

40. Cox, John E. *Musical Recollections of the Last Half-Century*. 2 vols. London: Tinsley Brothers, 1872. ML423.C87.

    On *I puritani*: "But for the manner in which this opera was sung, it must have proved a fiasco from the very first, as it had inevitably been whenever it has in later times been resuscitated. Except by four such interpreters as Grisi, Rubini, Tamburini, and Lablache, nothing can ever be made of it, and as it is not to be expected that there may be such a concentration of talent as this again met with, it will never be considered by those best competent to judge to have been a loss that it is now almost wholly upon the shelf." Cox provides much information about nineteenth-century singers, among them Rubini, who created three roles for Bellini. See item 767.

41. Damerini, Adelmo. "Bellini e la critica del suo tempo." In *Vincenzo Bellini, l'uomo, le sue opere, la sua fama*. Ed. Ildebrando Pizzetti, pp. 215–50. Milan: Fratelli Treves, 1936. ML410.B44 P5.

    Contemporary critical reception of Bellini's works. See item 2.

42. De La Fage, Juste Adrien. "Vincenzo Bellini." *Revue ou Gazette musicale de Paris* 19–20 (1838).

    A long essay on Bellini, later translated into Italian by the author and appearing, with various additions and changes, in *Rivista musicale di Firenze* nos. 19ff., 1840–41. Very negative assessments of Bellini's orchestration, even his melody, which the author claims is static and has nowhere to go—"only in *Norma* are the arias sufficiently developed." Bellini provided influential ideas for the rest of the century, however. De La Fage also wrote about Bellini in *Miscellanées musicales*. Paris: Comptoir des Imprimeurs unis, 1844. ML60.L18. Rpt. Bologna: Forni, 1969. ML60.L18 1969.

43. De Rosa, A., Marchese di Villarosa. *Memorie dei compositori di musica dei conservatori del Regno di Napoli*. Napoli: Dalla Stamperia Reale, 1840. ML107.N2 V4.

    Bellini is treated on pp. 237–40.

44. Author unknown. *Dello stile musicale di Bellini, articolo dell Indicatore* X (1832). Handwritten essay, signed “Di G. B—a.”, found in Paris, Bibliothèque de l’Opéra (Liv. It. 3588). Followed in same volume by a copy of *Osservazioni di G.B. all’articolo dell’ Indicatore sullo Stile Musicale del Maestro Bellini*. Milan: Giacomo Pirola, 1832, a riposte to G.B.’s article of “rare sarcasm.”

    Some of the contemporary Rossini versus Bellini debate is featured. See items 46, 67, and 83.

45. Escudier, Léon. *Littérature musicale. Mes Souvenirs*. Paris: Dentu, 1860; 2d ed., 1863. ML390.E7.

    Escudier was a noted French publisher who described Bellini as “blond as the fields of corn, sweet as the angels, young as the dawn, melancholy as the sunset,” and compared him to Mozart and Pergolesi, both of whom were eighteenth-century musicians who had died tragically young.

46. Ferrer, Cavaliere di. *Rossini et Bellini. Réponse de M. le Marquis de San Jacinto à un écrit publié à Palerme. Revue, réimprimée à Bologne et traduite en français par M. le chevalier de Ferrer*. Paris: Everat, 1836. 23 pp. Published in Italian as *Rossini e Bellini: Riposto al parallelo pubblicato sul merito di loro. Cronica e Critica sull’ entità musicale dei Maestri Italiani*. [On a second title page:] *Rossini e Bellini: Riposta ad uno scritto pubblicato a Palermo. Dissertazioni analitica e paragonata sulle opere dei due maestri. Cenno storico degli antiche compositori. Osservazioni sull’enità musicale dei Maestri Italiani dei nostri giorni*. Faenza: Montanari e Marabini, 1843. 52 pp. ML410.R8 F3.

    The author, Cavaliere di Ferrer, identifies himself as a public instructor in the city of Naples and an adjunct at the city’s university. Ferrer did a French translation that was published in Paris of San Jacinto’s original reply (see item 83) to Liborio Musumeci’s *Parallelo dei due maestri Bellini e Rossini* published in 1832 in Palermo (see item 67). Ferrer’s *Réponse* defends the Rossini style and is based on San Jacinto. Ferrer also treats other contemporary Italian composers such as Carafa, Donizetti, Mercadante, and Pacini.

47. Florimo, Francesco. *Bellini: memorie e lettere*. Florence: G. Barbèra, 1882. Rpt., Florence: G. Barbèra, 1976. ML410.B44 F6.

    The first part of Florimo’s publication (“Biografia” and “Dichiarazioni e Aneddoti”) is a reworking of the chapter on Bellini in Florimo’s *Cenno storico sulla scuola musicale di Napoli*, vol. 2. Naples, 1871. See item 131. Also includes “Translazione delle ceneri di Vincenzo Bellini,” concerning the transferral of Bellini’s remains from Paris to Catania in 1876.

48. Gautier, Théophile. *Histoire de l’art dramatique en France depuis vingtcinq ans*. 6 vols. Leipzig: Durr, 1858. PN2634.G27.

The nineteenth-century poet and critic discusses performances of Bellini's operas with extensive discourses on the famous singers interpreting them. Table of contents and index.

49. Glinka, Mikhail Ivanovich. *Memoirs*. Trans. from the Russian by Richard B. Mudge. Norman, Oklahoma: University of Oklahoma Press, 1963. ML410.G559 A15.

    The "father of Russian opera" was present at the premiere of *La sonnambula* at the Teatro Carcano in Milan. He wrote that the opera made "a tremendous impression and that Pasta and Rubini sang with the most evident enthusiasm . . . and in the second act the singers themselves wept and carried their audience along with them." In the spring of 1832 Glinka began to compose a serenade based on a theme from *La sonnambula*; it was later finished and performed.

50. Greville, Henry. *Leaves from the Diary of Henry Greville*. Ed. the Viscountess Enfield. London: Smith Elder, 1883. DA536.G82.

    Henry Greville was an exact contemporary and friend of Bellini in London. His diary provides information about Bellini in his last years. He characterized the composer as "a simple-minded, amiable fellow, with a capital understanding and a strong perception of the ridiculous, which is generally the case with Italians."

51. Heine, Heinrich. *Florentinische Nächte*: "Erste Nacht." In *Sämtliche Werke*, vol. 2. Munich, 1969. First published in *Salon*, Hamburg, 1837; English version *The Works of Heinrich Heine*. Trans. from the German by Charles Godfrey Leland. New York: Printed for the subscribers only by Crosup and Sterling, 190-. Vol. 1: *Florentine Nights*.

    Famous contemporary literary portrait of Bellini by the poet and journalist Heinrich Heine, who met Bellini in Paris. Portrays him as a dandy, "a sigh in dancing pumps and silk stockings." Bellini, according to Heine's memoir, "spoke French as badly as can be in England." Nevertheless, Heine admitted that "his character was thoroughly noble and good. His soul certainly remained pure and unsullied by anything hateful." For English translations see *Opera News* 33/8 (December 21, 1968): 16 (Marek's translation from *The World Treasury of Grand Opera*, ed. George R. Marek, 1957) and "Heinrich Heine (1797–1856) on Vincenzo Bellini (1801–1835)." *About the House* 4/7 (1974): 66. ISSN 0001–3242. ML5.A22.

52. Hiller, Ferdinand. "Vincenzo Bellini." *Deutscher Rundschau*, Berlin (April–June 1878): 308–17. Also in *Künstlerleben*, pp. 144–59. Köln: Du Mont-Schauberg, 1880. ML410.H654.

    The composer Hiller wrote: "His personality was like his melodies—it was captivating—just as charming as it was sympathetic." But "he was far from being the kind of purely instinctive artist that many like to portray him as."

Reprint in *Musik Konzepte 46: Vincenzo Bellini*. Ed. Heinz-Klaus Metzger and Rainer Riehn, pp. 95–108. See item 458. See also "Ferdinand Hiller's Impressions of Bellini and His Music," in Weinstock item 279, pp. 413ff. See items 421, 458, and 954.

53. Hogarth, George. *Memoirs of the Musical Drama*. 2 vols. London: Bentley, 1838. ML1700.H71.

    See item 54.

54. ——. *Memoirs of the Opera in Italy, France, Germany, and England. A New Edition of the Musical Drama in Two Volumes*. Vol. 2. London: Bentley, 1851. Photocopy rpt., New York: Da Capo Press, 1972. ISBN 03–06702–56–8. ML1700.H72 1972.

    Bellini is discussed on pp. 116–18. His birth date is given as 1806, thus all the subsequent dates of premieres make Bellini the incorrect age. The death date is correct but Hogarth believes Bellini died at the age of twenty-nine. Also states that the composer was mainly taught by his father, rather than grandfather. Hogarth's assessment of *Il pirata* states, "The music betrays great want of artistic skill in the construction of the concerted pieces and in the management of the orchestra; but the simplicity, beauty, and impassioned character of some of the airs and duets, were sufficient to insure the success of the work." Of Bellini's character: "He appears to have been singularly pleasing in his manners and amiable in his character, and the personal interest which he everywhere excited contributed to heighten the grief felt for his loss as an artist." In later pages Hogarth deals with many of the interpreters and creators of roles in Bellini's operas.

55. Jaubert, Mme Caroline. *Souvenirs de Madame C. Jaubert*. Paris: J. Hetzel et Cie, 1881. PQ291.J3.

    Madame Jaubert, who was intimate with most of the people Bellini met in Paris, described the composer as "blond, blanc, rose et bon enfant, avec un parler et des manières enfantines" and spoke of "le jeune maestro, alors à l'apogée de sa gloire, fêté, adulé par les plus jolies femmes de Paris, à la mode en un mot, pouvait appliquer à lui-même ce vers de 'la jeune Captive', de Chénier: *Ma bienvenue au jour me rit dans tous les yeux*." Her account of Heine's last meeting with Bellini at Countess Belgioioso's salon, when Heine ribbed Bellini unmercifully, is often cited. But this incident was in fact related to her in a letter written by the Countess (Athens, 1849), later published in the Countess's *Souvenirs dans l'exil*, from which Beth Archer Brombert quotes in her study of Cristina, Countess Belgioioso. See item 992, pp. 248–50.

56. Kümmel, Werner Friedrich. "Vincenzo Bellini nello specchio dell' *AMZ* di Lipsia 1827–1846." *Nuova Rivista Musicale Italiana* 7 (1973): 185–205. ISSN 0029–6228. ML5.N93.

Kümmel shows that Bellini's reception in Germany began early: in 1828 writers in the *Allgemeine musikalische Zeitung* (*AMZ*) considered Bellini acquainted with the German classics. Indeed, he had studied the great instrumental works of Haydn and Mozart at the Conservatory. Characteristics that labeled him as "filosofico" in Italy were considered by German critics as "Germanic." Robert Schumann labeled Bellini a "butterfly who fluttered around the German oak," but wrote of the weakness of his modulations, thus displaying the typical German fascination and disdain for Italian opera. The first performance of a Bellini opera north of the Alps was of *Il pirata* in Vienna on February 25, 1828; the *AMZ* review noted that Bellini was familiar with the German school, i.e., the Viennese Classics, thus making him the only contemporary Italian opera composer to be acceptable. Many examples, citations, quotations from *AMZ*.

57. Levenson, Gower F., ed. *Letters of Harriette Countess Granville, 1810–1845*. London: Longmans Green, 1894.

Countess Granville lived from 1785 to 1862. The Countess was the younger daughter of the fifth Duke of Devonshire and wife of the first Earl Granville.

58. Lippmann, Friedrich. "Ein neu entdecktes Autograph Richard Wagners: Rezension der Königsberger *Norma*-Aufführung von 1837." *Musicae scientiae collectanea: Festschrift Karl Gustav Fellerer zum 70. Geburtstag*. Cologne: Volk, 1973. ML55.F35 1972.

This article by Wagner, considered to have been lost since Glasenapp's time, was discovered in the possession of the Juilliard Library, where it had been since 1911, one of three autographs bound together. The article is about the performance of *Norma* in Königsberg in March 1837. Wagner describes the performance and discusses Bellini's compositions. Lippmann compares Wagner's essay with his other writings about opera from this period in which he theorized about the differences between Italian and German opera, beginning with *Die deutsche Oper* (1834) and concluding with *Bellini. Ein Wort zu seiner Zeit* (1837). See item 95.

59. ——. "Wagner und Italien." *Analecta musicologica* 11 (1972): 200–47. ISSN 0585–6086. ML160.S893.

Wagner visited Italy, a country he adored and that gave him inspiration and strength in his older years, nine times. He loved certain works of art, architecture, and literature by writers such as Dante, Tasso, and Ariosto, and was even interested in and affected by Italian politics. Lippmann presents Wagner's theories on Italian music and discusses the composer's love of the music of Bellini and how this influenced him, discussing specifically what is Italian in Wagner's texts, musical forms, and musical style (melody, harmony, rhythm). Includes numerous extensive music examples from all periods of Wagner's career but especially from the early operas. Quotations from, among others, a letter Wagner wrote to Arrigo

Boïto in 1871. Lippmann divides Wagner's writings about Italian music into three period-categories: early writings, opera reform essays between 1849 and ca. 1860, and writings after 1860.

60. Liszt, Franz. *Gesammelte Schriften von Franz Liszt*. Band 3, 1. Abteilung: *Dramaturgische Blätter*, pp. 85–98. Leipzig: Breitkopf und Härtel, 1881. ML410.L7 A1.

In 1854 Liszt had to conduct *I Capuleti e i Montecchi* in Weimar. He wrote an article about this "stale production of an old-fashioned school," that "owed its being to the amalgamation of Rossini's legacy with the newly discovered principles of the romantic school." Many times Liszt uses the word "schwach" (weak) for the work and makes a great deal of the superiority of German music, for Liszt was now Kapellmeister at Weimar. He speaks of the composer as "this fair haired, weak, womanish, poor-spirited Bellini with the seeds of consumption in him, with his elegant laissez-faire, with the melancholy grace of his whole mental and bodily outfit."

61. Littlejohn, Jean. "France Meets Bellini: The Critical Reception of François-Joseph Fétis." *Vincenzo Bellini et la France* (2007): 743–54. See item 404.

Fétis's articles in *La Revue musicale* provided the French public with one of the earliest sources on Bellini. The critic's perspective on Italian music and his admiration for Rossini formed his critical opinion of Bellini's works. Fétis relied on second-hand information about Zingarelli and the Naples Conservatory, mainly through François Kandler's "Etat actuel de la musique à Naples, troisième et dernier article: Saint-Sébastien," *Revue musicale* IV (1829), in which the author states that Zingarelli permitted none of his pupils ever to study works of the modern school ("de l'école moderne") and showed a great aversion to the music of Mozart and his "imitators." See item 79.

62. Lobe, Johann Christian. "Bellini." In *Fliegende Blätter für Musik: Wahrheit über Tonkunst und Tonkünstler*. Leipzig: Baumgärtner's Buch-handlung, 1855, pp. 262–80. ML5.FR62. Rpt. in *Musik-Konzepte 46: Vincenzo Bellini*. Ed. Heinz-Klaus Metzger and Rainer Riehn, pp. 47–63. Munich: Text und Kritik, 1985. See item 458. ISBN 38–83772–13–5. ML410.B44 V5 1985.

Lobe was a composer of five operas, a flutist, and a noted writer on music. He was the editor of the *Allgemeine musikalische Zeitung*, and then started his own series, *Fliegende Blätter*, which ran from 1853 to 1857. He wrote a number of composition treatises and believed in composing according to eighteenth-century rationalism as opposed to Romanticism.

63. Mazzini, Giuseppe. *La filosofia della musica* (1836), new edition, based on the "Opere complete." With an introduction and notes by Adriano Lualdi. Milan: Fratelli Bocca, 1943. ML3800.M25 1943.

In this essay, the great Italian patriot Giuseppe Mazzini expressed his ideas about contemporary music. He saw a conflict between the individualism of Italian musicians and the mysticism of the Germans in terms of the future of nineteenth-century music. Rossini had summarized the past, Donizetti was on somewhat the right path, but Bellini had not met the challenge. See item 87.

64. Meyerbeer, Giacomo. *Briefwechsel und Tagebücher*. Ed. Heinz Becker. Berlin: De Gruyter, 1960. ML410.M61 A4.

    Meyerbeer's correspondence and diaries. He and Bellini came to prominence in Paris in the early 1830s.

65. Morgan, Lady Sidney Owenson. *Lady Morgan's Memoirs: Autobiography, Diaries and Correspondence*. Rev. ed. in 2 vols. London: Allen, 1863. Rpt. New York: AMS Press, 1975. ISBN 04–04567–93–2. PR5059.M3Z5 1975.

    The Irish novelist Lady Morgan (1783–1859) knew Bellini in London. She heard of his death on October 11, 1835; she notes it but does not write an extended reaction. She writes extensively about Giuditta Pasta, however.

66. Mount Edgcumbe, Richard. *Musical Reminiscences of the Earl of Mount Edgcumbe, Containing an Account of the Italian Opera in England from 1773 to 1834*. New York: Da Capo, 1973. Rpt. from the 4th ed. London, 1834. ISBN 03–06700–08–5. ML1731.3.E23 1973.

    Richard, Earl of Mount Edgcumbe, attended the opera for many decades and heard some of the greatest singers spanning the final flourishing of the great castrati to the rise of the title heroine and the heroic tenor. In the Supplement (1829–34) he reports that he heard Bellini's *Pirata* and *Sonnambula*, which he deems, of the new operas in the early 1830s, "the only tolerably good ones, and he is the best of the present composers. All the rest, Mercadante, Pacini, Coccia, &c., either feebly imitate Rossini, or if they attempt originality, run into extravagances greater than those of the master of the new school, and in both instances are of course inferior." Among other Bellini interpreters, he heard and wrote about Pasta and Malibran.

67. Musumeci, conte Libeo (Liborio). *Parallelo de' due maestri Bellini e Rossini*. Palermo, 1832.

    Part of the polemic comparing Rossini and Bellini in the 1830s. Musumeci exalts Bellini over Rossini. Devotes many pages to showing how Bellini has "graciously married the richness of Rossini with the melodic regularity and simplicity of Paisiello and Cimarosa. . . ." See item 46.

68. Musumeci, Mario. *Discorso di Musumeci Mario, in occasione del ritorno in patria di Bellini nella gran Sala Comunale di Catania il 18 marzo 1832*. Catania, 1832.

Appeared on the occasion of Bellini's visit to Catania in the spring of 1832. Lauds Bellini's art, which captures the essence of Greek melopea, the purity of his line and architecture, the feeling and heroic nature of his tragedy. In this—what Weinstock (see item 279) terms "flatulent"—speech, Musumeci announced that Bellini had given the autograph score of *I Capuleti e i Montecchi* to the city of Catania (it is now in the Museo belliniano), and that a medal was to be struck in his honor. The latter did not occur, to the composer's intense displeasure. Musumeci's speech was reprinted in *Omaggio a Bellini nel primo centenario dalla sua nascita*, Catania, 1901. See item 238.

69. Naumann, Emil. *The History of Music (Illustrierte Musikgeschichte)*. 5 vols. Trans. F. Praeger. Ed. Sir F.A. Gore Ouseley. Vol. 5. London: Cassell, 1886. ML 160.N29 1886a.

Bellini is discussed on pp. 1131–33, deemed "the second in importance of Rossini's disciples." He was "endowed with the gift of spontaneous melody," and wrote no comic operas, having a "dreamy nature and inclination for melancholy sentiment." Naumann praises *Norma* and discusses its orchestration. "Bellini, whose character was similar to that of Chopin, invested the *cantilena* with a breath of romance which differed from the realism of Rossini." Beginning on p. 1137 Naumann discusses Giuditta Pasta, Rubini, and other creators and interpreters of Bellini's music.

70. ——. *Italienische Tondichter von Palestrina bis auf die Gegenwart*. Berlin: R. Oppenheim, 1883. ML390.N292

Based on a series of lectures given by Dr. Naumann. See item 69.

71. Ortigue, Joseph. *Le Balcon de l'Opéra*. Paris: Librairie D'Eugène Renduel, 1833. ML1704.O77.

The author enters into a discussion of the different goals and styles of French and German opera. He discusses Italian operas by Donizetti, Rossini, Bellini, and others. For Bellini he reviews two operas he heard at the Théâtre-Italien in Paris. First is *La sonnambula* from October 27, 1831 (pp. 169–77), about which he wrote, "Despite these faults in execution, and the scant dramatic interest of the libretto, *La Sonnambula* afforded great pleasure and the success of this opera will lead to further performances." Later, writing of *Il pirata* on 14 February 1832, he reveals that there were in fact no further performances of *La sonnambula* and that the public found the music "so pale and used and old" that, despite the talents of the singers Pasta and Rubini, the piece was received coldly. In *Il pirata* the author found many pieces to praise but felt the work did not show compositional progress. In this sense, he meant in terms of the works of Rossini, considering Bellini an imitator: "The greatest injuries that genius receives are not from its enemies but really from those who throw a dead corpse into the genius's system."

72. Pacini, Giovanni. *Le mie memorie artistiche*. Ed. F. Magnani. Florence: Le Monnier, 1875. Rpt., ed. Luciano Nicolosi and Salvatore Pinnavaia, with a critical essay by Stefano Adabbo. Lucca: Pacini Fazzi, 1981. ML410.P11.

    Giovanni Pacini, another native Catanese, who attended rehearsals of *Bianca e Fernando* and took much credit for helping to launch Bellini's career, proposed to Barbaja to commission a work from Bellini for La Scala. Bellini came to consider him and his mistress, the Countess Samoyoff, as dangerous rivals. Includes bibliographical references.

73. Pagliara, Rocco. *Intermezzi musicali*. Naples, 1889.

    Pagliari was a successor of Florimo at the library of the Naples Conservatory.

74. Pepoli, Carlo. *In morte di Bellini*. 1867.

    Bellini's librettist for *I puritani* reminiscing about the composer.

75. Petacco, Arrigo. *La principessa del nord. La misteriosa vita della dama del Risorgimento, Cristina di Belgiojoso*. Milan: Mondadory, 1993. ISBN 88–04367–25–3. DG551.8.B3 P48 1993.

    Belgioioso held salons in Milan and Paris where Bellini met many eminent artists. See items 28, 31, and 992.

76. Pistone, Danièle. "Vincenzo Bellini dans l'imaginaire musical français contemporain." *Vincenzo Bellini et la France* (2007): 821–39. See item 404.

    An examination of the consciousness of Bellini in the contemporary French mind through a survey of publications (records, scores, books, periodicals), theater programs and various statistics. Also an attempt "to draw peculiarities of this image in comparison to other composers, e.g., Chopin." Five appendices.

77. Pouget, Jean-Pierre. "Une amitié et son souvenir littéraire: Alexandre Dumas père et Vincenzo Bellini." *Vincenzo Bellini et la France* (2007): 215–27. See item 404.

    Concerns the friendship between the composer and Dumas, who left a few highly complimentary pages about Bellini in various biographical writings. Bellini wrote a letter for Dumas, to facilitate a voyage he made to Italy and Sicily, a letter that remained unpublished until the present day. Dumas claimed to have met Bellini's father and to have spoken briefly with him in Catania.

78. Ricci, Federico. "Una lettera di Federico Ricci su Bellini." In *Bellini: memorie e lettere*. Ed. Francesco Florimo, pp. 140–48. Florence: G. Barbèra, 1882. Rpt., Florence: G. Barbèra, 1976. ML410.B44 F6.

Ricci, along with his brother Carlo, was a fellow student of Bellini at the Naples Conservatory and an opera composer.

79. Ricci, Franco Carlo. "Aspetti della critica francese contemporanea a Vincenzo Bellini." *Vincenzo Bellini et la France* (2007): 719–41. See item 404.

    Stresses the importance of French criticism, which carried much authority and prestige, in Bellini's career. Berlioz openly showed contempt and Fétis was no less severe, but while he condemns Bellini's orchestration he also muses whether "all this [does] not have the stamp of genius, of an ignorant genius, it is true, all spontaneity, in whom science, alas, could not come to the aid of imagination." Also explored are opinions by de la Fague, Scudo, Blaze de Bury, Castil-Blaze, and Pougin, with many contradictory positions among them. See item 61.

80. Riehl, Wilhelm Heinrich. *Musikalische Charakterköpfe, Ein Kunstgeschichtliches Skizzenbuch*. 2 vols. Vol. 1: *Zwanzig Jahre aus der Geschichte der romantischen Oper*. Stuttgart: J. G. Cotta, 1853. Subsequent editions published throughout the century. ML60.R55 (1868–69).

    Chapter One, pp. 3–75, deals with Rossini, Bellini, and Donizetti. Bellini is discussed on pp. 51–64. Notes the originality of melody found in *Il pirata* and discusses critical opinions of whether Bellini's subsequent works added something new or whether they repeated themselves. Discusses the nature of Bellini's melodies, the connection of his operas with famous singers—created for specific interpreters, the history of Bellini's operas is the history of singers' triumphs. Riehl quotes from Schilling's *Musical Lexikon* of 1835: "Bellini befindet sich in einer Krise; geht er glücklich aus derselben hervor, so kann er der Luther der italienischen Musik werden."

81. Rovani, Giuseppe. "Bellini." In *Le tre arti considerate in alcuni illustri italiani contemporanei*. 2 vols. Milan, 1874.

    Rovani (1818–74) was an Italian writer and aesthetician whose most important philosophical writing was *Le tre arti*, which includes an entire chapter on Vincenzo Bellini. He looks at *Norma*, for example, from the viewpoint of an Italian patriot who experienced the Risorgimento and is now living in a united Italy and as a lover of primo ottocento opera who does not care for new trends such as "music drama." See Kimbell (item 646), pp. 95–99.

82. ——. "Bellini e Meyerbeer." *Italia musicale* 3, 8, 11, 26, 28, 29, 37, 38, 43, 46, 57. Milan, 1856. *Italia musicale* is available in a modern edition in 5 vols. Ed. Marcello Conati, from Center for Studies in Nineteenth-Century Music at the University of Maryland, College Park. Ann Arbor: University of Michigan Press, 1992. ML5.I89 Suppl.

A comparison of the two composers, both of whom had successes in Paris in the early 1830s.

83. San Jacinto, Marchese di (Stefano Mira e Sirignano). *Osservazioni sul merito musicale dei maestri Bellini e Rossini*. Bologna, 1834. Rpt. in *Rossiniana: antologia della critica nella prima metà dell' Ottocento*. Ed. Carlida Steffan with a preface by Bruno Cagli, pp. 197–207. Pordenone: Edizioni Studio Tesi, 1992. ISBN 88–76923–43–8. In French as *Observations sur le mérite musical des maestri Rossini et Bellini en réponse à un parallèle entre ces mêmes compositeurs publié à Palerme*.

A reply to Musumeci. See item 67. The author is identified as Stefano Mira e Sirignano, founder of the Accademia Filarmonica di Palermo. (See Carlida Steffan, "Presenza e persistenza di Rossini nella riflessione estetico-musicale del primo Ottocento" in *Il testo e la scena*, pp. 76–91.) Part of the Bellini versus Rossini polemic that occurred during the early 1830s. The author states that Rossini is "the true genius of our century." See item 2. The French version may be found in a bound volume of various pieces, *Recueil de pièces sur la musique* [C. 4417 (1–12)] in Paris, Bibliothèque de l'Opéra. See item 46 by Ferrer, who translated it into French.

84. Scammacca, Carlo Zappalà. *Bellini racconta storia*. Catania: Stabilimento Tipografia Bellini, 1876.

Copy in Museo belliniano. Informal, storytelling nature. Begins with the Maddalena Fumaroli saga. Much imaginary conversation is put into various people's mouths.

85. Scherillo, Michele. *Belliniana: nuove note*. Milan: Ricordi, 1883.

Chapter topics include a comparison between Bellini's *Capuleti e i Montecchi* and Vaccai's *Giulietta e Romeo*; Bellini and popular music; Bellini's lovers; conversations with Florimo about Bellini, Rossini, Pepoli, and Pacini and Romani's widow, Emilia Branca.

86. ——. *Vincenzo Bellini: note aneddotiche e critiche*. Ancona: A.G. Morelli, 1882. ML410.B44 S34.

Not a biography but a series of anecdotal and critical accounts. Contents include: Le lettere al Florimo, Bellini carbonaro, Felice Romani, *La sonnambula*, *Norma*, *Beatrice di Tenda*, *Nina* del Paisiello e le opere belliniane, and La riforma melodrammatica di Vincenzo Bellini. Arthur Pougin characterized it thus: "Ce charmant petit volume, un peu capricieux dans sa forme, trés arbitraire dans son plan, n'en est pas moins fort agréable et d'un attrait piquant." See item 151.

87. Schumann, Robert. *Gesammelte Schriften über Musik und Musiker*. 4 vols. Leipzig: G. Wigand, 1854. ML410.S4 A1. 3d ed. Ed. Herbert Schulze. Leipzig: Reclam, 1974. ML410.S4 A12 1974.

Schumann labeled Bellini a "butterfly who fluttered around the German oak," but wrote of the weakness of his modulations. See item 56.

88. Seay, Albert. "Classics of Music Literature: Giuseppe Mazzini's *Filosofia della musica*." *Notes* 30/1 (September 1973): 24–36. ISSN 0027–4380. ML27.U5 M695.

    See item 63.

89. Spencer, Michael. "Théophile Gautier, Music Critic." *Music & Letters* 40 (1968): 4–17. ISSN 0027–4224. ML5.M64.

    Pages 12 and 13 deal with Bellini. Specific reviews from *La Presse*, *Le Ménestrel*, *Les Beautés de l'Opéra*, and others, are cited. Gautier's reviews of his music are relatively unenthusiastic. He detested *Beatrice di Tenda*, finding it lacked the melodic inspiration found in his other works and criticized the "harmonic poverty of the opera as a whole." *Il pirata* inspired Gautier to a uniform criticism of Italian opera. *Norma* is examined in *Les Beautés de l'Opéra*. See item 644.

90. Stendhal. *Vie de Rossini*. Life of Rossini, transl. and annotated by Richard N. Coe. London: Caler & Boyars, 1970. ISBN 07–14503–41-X. ML410.R8 B513 1970b.

    The early-nineteenth century novelist was a major fan of opera. He provides not just a life of Rossini but a study and opinion of current operas, singers, and performances. An especially good chapter on Giuditta Pasta, who created several roles for Bellini but not for Rossini, although she sang a number of roles in Rossini's operas.

91. Tarallo, Alfredo. "Il culto di Bellini a Napoli dagli esordi al successo parigino." *Vincenzo Bellini et la France* (2007): 553–93. See item 404.

    The two ends of Bellini's career. Neapolitan journals of the era are consulted to trace the trajectory of Bellini's rise to success. The cult of Bellini helped to exalt the Neapolitan School, which had been undergoing a crisis. Tarallo then jumps to the end of Bellini's career, examining Parisian chronicles and post-mortem honors organized by Florimo. Appendices including facsimiles of music and letters.

92. Ullrich, Hermann. "Alfred Julius Becker als Wiener Musikkritiker. Ein Beitrag zur Geschichte der Wiener Musikkritik." *Österreichische Musikalische Zeitung* 27/11 (November 1972): 596–607.

    Becker, who with August Schmidt and Otto Nicolai helped to establish the Vienna Philharmonic in 1842, wrote for August Schmidt's *Allgemeine Wiener Musikzeitung* from 1841 to 1843 and for Ludwig A. Frankl's *Sonntagsblättern* from 1842 to 1844. He rejected the great Baroque masters, admiring Mozart and Beethoven. Becker supported Berlioz but disdained Donizetti, Bellini, and the young Verdi. He attempted to fight dilettantism.

93. Vaccai, Giulio. *Vita di Nicola Vaccai*. Written by his son Giulio. Preface by A. Biaggi. Bologna: N. Zanichelli, 1882. ML410.V113.

 Nicola Vaccai was the composer of *Giulietta e Romeo*, to Felice Romani's libretto. Romani adapted this libretto for Bellini's *I Capuleti e i Montecchi*, which was often performed using Vaccai's penultimate scene.

94. Verdi, Giuseppe. Letter to Camille Bellaigue, May 2, 1898. *I copialettere di Giuseppe Verdi*. Ed. Gaetano Cesare and Alessandro Luzio with a preface by Michele Scherillo, pp. 415–16. Milan: A cura della Commissione escutiva per la onoranza a Giuseppe Verdi nel primo centenario della nascita, 1913. Rpt., Bologna: Forni, [1968]. ML410. V4 1987.

 As Verdi wrote late in his life to Bellaigue, "Bellini's harmony and orchestration is poor, it is true . . . but he is rich in feeling, and in a melancholy which is all his own. Even in less known operas—in *Straniera* and *Pirata*—there are long, long melodies, such as none before him had written. And what truth and power there is in his declamation—the duet between Pollione and Norma, for instance! What loftiness of idea in the first phrases of the Introduction, and another, just as sublime, a few bars later, badly orchestrated, but beautiful, heavenly, beyond the reach of any other pen."

95. Wagner, Richard. "Bellini. Ein Wort zu seiner Zeit" (1837). In *Richard Wagner. Sämtliche Schriften und Dichtungen*. Ed. Hans von Wolzogen and Richard Sternfeld. Leipzig: Breitkopf und Härtel, 1911. Vol. 12 (1983), pp. 19–21. In *Richard Wagner. Dichtungen und Schriften*. 10 vols. Ed. Dieter Borchmeyer. Vol. 5. Frankfurt: Insel Verlag, 1983. ML410.W1 A1 1983. In *Richard Wagner's Prose Works*. Vol. 8. Trans. and ed. William Ashton Ellis, 1892–99. London: K. Paul, Trench, Trübner. ML410.W1 A127.

 Article on *Norma* by Wagner from the program of the performance of this opera conducted by Wagner in Riga. First appeared in *Zuschauer* 7/19 (Riga, December, 1837). Rpt. in *Bayreuther Blätter* (December, 1885). Rpt. in *Musik-Konzepte 46: Vincenzo Bellini*. Ed. Heinz-Klaus Metzger and Rainer Riehn, pp. 5–11. See item 458. Wagner writes of Bellini's limpid melody, the noble beauty of his music, and urged Germans to study Bellini more deeply: "Sing, sing, and sing, you Germans."

96. ——. "Letter sur la musique (à la suite des *Quatre poèmes d'opéra*)." *Mercure de France*, 1841. ISSN 1149–0292. AP20.M5.

97. ——. *Mein Leben: Richard Wagner. Sämtliche Schriften und Dichtungen*. 6th ed. Vols. 23–25. Ed. H. von Wolzogen and R. Sternfeld, 1914.

 Upon the occasion of hearing Wilhelmine Schröder-Devrient as Romeo in Bellini's opera in Leipzig, 1834: "I shall never forget the impression that a Bellini opera made upon me . . . Simple and noble Song made its appearance again." Andrew Porter: "For a while, *I Capuleti* became a stick that Wagner used to whack Weber's *Euryanthe* and all 'solid' German music." See item 594.

98. ——. "Pasticcio von Canto Spianato" (1834). In *Richard Wagner. Dichtungen und Schriften*. 10 vols. Ed. Dieter Borchmeyer. Vol. 5. Frankfurt: Insel Verlag, 1983. ML410.W1 A1 1983.

Wagner urges Germans to study Bellini's music and to learn to make their music sing. Of German opera: "This damned erudition."

99. Weinstock, Herbert. *Rossini: A Biography*. New York: Knopf, 1968. ML410.R8 W35. Rpt. New York: Limelight Editions, 1987. ML410.R8 W35 1987.

On pp. 168–69 Weinstock provides a translation of the part of the letter that Bellini wrote to his uncle Vincenzo Ferlito in Catania, describing his first encounter with Rossini, in Milan (letter of August 28, 1829). Rossini heard the final performance of *Il pirata* and, in Bellini's words, "said to all Milan that he found in the whole of the opera a finish and an organization worthy of a mature man rather than a young one, and that it was full of great feeling and, in his view, carried to such a point of philosophic reasoning that at some points the music lacked brilliance./That was his feeling, and I shall go on composing in the same way, on the basis of common sense, as I have tried to do it that way in my enthusiasm."

Rossini wrote to their mutual friend, Filippo Santocanale, on January 26 of the successful premiere of Bellini's last opera, which Rossini called *I Puritani in Iscozia*. From Weinstock's translation, pp. 188–89: "The singers and the composer were called out twice onto the stage, and I should tell you that these demonstrations are rare in Paris and that only merit obtains them. You will see that my prophecies have been realized and with a sincerity beyond our greatest hopes. This score shows notable progress in orchestration, but I urge Bellini daily not to let himself be seduced too much by German harmonies, but always to rely for his structure on simple melodies full of real effect."

Then, after Bellini's death he wrote to Santocanale on October 3, 1835, describing the funeral. Rossini was instrumental in settling Bellini's estate and having his effects shipped to Catania.

100. Ziino, Agostino. "Luigi Romanelli ed il mito del classicismo nell'opera italiana del primo Ottocento." *Chigiana* XXXVI (1979) [ma 1984]: 173–215. ISBN 0069–3391.

See the entry below by Ziino.

101. ——. "Minima belliniana: dalla storiografia alla storio." In *Belliniana et alia musicologica. Festschrift für Friedrich Lippmann zum 70. Geburtstag*.

Ed. D. Brandenburg and Th. Lindner, pp. 310–33. Vienna: Präsens, 2004 (*Primo Ottocento*).

Deals with the assessment of a composer, who must be Bellini, by Luigi Romanelli in 1832: "questo intraprendente Giovane Siciliano, Compositore di Musica" who had the merit of not following in the footsteps of the Rossini imitators. Contains a discussion of the eighteenth-century Neapolitan School and the connection between Metastasio and Romani. Music examples.

4

Biographical Studies

ENCYCLOPEDIA AND DICTIONARY ARTICLES

102. Anglés, Hijini and Joaquín Pena. "Bellini, Vincenzo." In *Diccionario de la música Labor*. 2 vols. Ed. Joaquín Pena. Barcelona: Labor, 1954. Vol. 1: 237–38. ML105.P4.

Gives date of birth as November 1, 1801, and death date as September 24, 1835. Speaks of Bellini's music as elegiac, discusses his influence on Chopin, Liszt, Verdi, and Wagner's admiration for him. Works-List of operas and some non-operatic compositions.

103. Barblan, Guglielmo. "Vincenzo Bellini." In *Storia dell' opera*. 3 vols. in 6. Vol. 1. "L'Opera in Italia." Turin: Unione Tipografico-Editrice Torinese, 1977. ML1700.S89.

Part 6 of Vol. 1/2 (Opera in Italy) is devoted to Bellini, pp. 213–38. Subheadings include "L'esordio," "Le opere del 1829–1830," "La maturità," and bibliography. Musical analysis; some comparisons with Chopin. Music examples, illustrations.

104. ——. "Bellini, Vincenzo." In *Die Musik in Geschichte und Gegenwart*. Ed. Friedrich Blume. Kassel-Basel: Bärenreiter, 1949. Vol. 1, cols. 1611–16. ML100.M92.

Gives dates as November 1, 1801, to September 24, 1835. Life; List of Works; Musical Style; short bibliography. Facsimile of autograph page (Act One "March of the Druids") from *Norma*.

105. D'Amico, Fedele. "Bellini, Vincenzo." In *Enciclopedia dello spettacolo*. 9 vols. Ed. Sandro D'Amico. Rome: Unione Editoriale, 1952–1962;

Aggiornamento. 1955–1965, Rome, 1966; *Indice-Repertorio*, Rome: Le Maschere, 1968. Vol. 2, cols. 204–10. PN1579.E51968.

Gives dates as November 1, 1801, to September 24, 1835. Biography, discussion of musical style, list of theatrical works, bibliography. Several pages of plates showing costumes, singers, stage sets, some in color.

106. Della Seta, Fabrizio. "Bellini, Vincenzo [Salvatore Carmelo Francesco]." In *Die Musik in Geschichte und Gegenwart, Allgemeine Enzylopädie der Musik begrundet von Friedrich Blume*. Zweite, neuarbeitete Ausgabe herausgegeben von Ludwig Finscher. Kassel: Bärenreiter, 1999. Personenteil, 2. Band, cols. 1009–26. ISBN 37–61811–10–1. ML400.M92 1994.

Valuable biography and discussion of Bellini's style and place in music history from a noted Bellini authority. Works-List.

107. Fétis, François-Joseph. "Bellini, Vincenzo." In *Biographie universelle des musiciens et Bibliographie générale de la musique*. 2d ed. 8 vols. 1873. Vol. 1: 327–28; and 2 vols. *Supplément et complément*. Ed. Arthur Pougin, Paris: Firmin Didot, 1878–80. Vol. 1: 66. Rpt. of 2d ed. Brussels: Culture et Civilisation, 1972. ML105.F42 1972.

Gives dates as November 3, 1802, to September 24, 1835. Paints him as an instinctive musician, self-made, rather than a product of a great school—even though he spent a number of years at the Naples Conservatory. Critical of the Italian school of the nineteenth century. Seven items in bibliography, all from 1835 and 1836. Errors, including "Gherardi" instead of "Gerardi" for *Biografia di Vincenzo Bellini*, 1835. See item 148.

108. Honegger, Marc. "Bellini, Vincenzo." In *Dictionnaire de la musique publié sous la direction de Marc Honegger*. 2 vols. Ed. Marc Honegger. *Les Hommes et leurs oeuvres*. Vol. 1 (A–K): 107–8. Paris: Bordas (1970); rpt. 1986. ML100.D65.

Brief summary of Bellini's life and works; bibliography included.

109. Lippmann, Friedrich. "Vincenzo, Bellini." In *Dizionario enciclopedia universale della musica e dei musicisti*. 8 vols. Diretto Alberto Basso. Turin: Unione Tipografia-Editrice Torinese, 1985. "Le Biografie." Vol. 1 (A–Bur), pp. 426–32. ISBN 88–02039–30–5. ML105.D65 1985.

Presentation of biography, discussion of style; works-list and bibliography provided by the editorial staff.

110. ——. "Bellini, Vincenzo." In *The New Grove Dictionary of Opera*. 4 vols. Ed. Stanley Sadie. New York: Macmillan, 1992. Vol. 1: 389–97. ISBN 09–35859–92–6. ML102.06 N5 1992.

Lippmann's article covers the following topics: Education and Early Career (1801–26); Operatic Success (1827–33); Final Activity: London and Paris (1833–35); Character; Sources of Style; Words and Music;

Melody and Sonority; Other Aspects of Style. Music examples and facsimile of autograph of opening of Act Two of *Norma*.

111. ——. "Bellini, Vincenzo." In *The New Grove Dictionary of Music and Musicians*. 20 vols. Ed. Stanley Sadie. New York: Macmillan, 1980. Vol. 2: 446–55. ISBN 03–33231–11–2. ML100.N48.

Education and Early Career (1801–26); Operatic Success (1827–33); Final Operas: London and Paris (1833–35); Character; Origins of Bellini's Style; Words and Music; Melody; Other Aspects of Style. Complete works-list and extensive bibliography.

112. ——. "Vincenzo Bellini." In *The New Grove Masters of Italian Opera*. Ed. Philip Gossett, pp. 153–89. New York: Norton, 1983. ISBN 03–93016–85–4. M1390.N466 1983.

Article on nineteenth-century Italian opera composers from *New Grove* (1980) updated and corrected.

113. Monterosso, Raffaello. "Bellini, Vincenzo." In *Dizionario biografico degli Italiani*. 55 vols. Dir. Alberto Basso. Rome: Istituto della Enciclopedia Italiana, 1960/2000, Vol. 7: 718–39. CT1123.D5 Biog.

Extensive life-and-career with works-list and bibliography. Quotes from a number of Bellini's letters.

114. *Nuovo dizionario Ricordi della musica e dei musicisti*. Ed. Riccardo Allorto, et al. Milan: Ricordi, 1976. "Bellini, Vincenzo," pp. 75–76. ML100.N975.

This publication is based on and uses some of the material from the 1959 edition by Claudio Sartori. Biography. States that Donizetti heard *Adelson e Salvini* but it was *Bianca e Fernando*. Brief discussion of works; chronological works-list.

115. Pizzetti, Ildebrando. "Bellini, Vincenzo." In *Enciclopedia italiana*. Ed. Giovanni Gentile and Calogero Tumminelli. Milan, Rome: Istituto Giovanni Treccani, 1930. Vol. 6: 562–66.

A general assessment of Bellini's style and place in opera history, followed by a short biography.

116. ——. "Bellini, Vincenzo." In *Enciclopedia della musica* (Ricordi). 4 vols. Milan: Ricordi, 1963. Vol. 1: 225–27. ML100.E45.

Opens with introductory essay, then life-and-works. *Zaira* is not in the works-list, although it is mentioned in the text.

117. Schmidl, Carlo. "Bellini, Vincenzo." In *Dizionario universale dei musicisti*. Milan: Ricordi, 1887. ML105.S36; *Supplemento al Dizionario universale dei musicisti*. 2 vols. Milan: Sonzogno, 1929.

118. Smart, Mary Ann. "Bellini, Vincenzo." In *The New Grove Dictionary of Music and Musicians*. 2d ed. 29 vols. Ed. Stanley Sadie and John Tyrrell. New York: Macmillan, 2001. Vol. 3: 194–212. ISBN 15–61592–39–0. ML100.N48 2001.

Some data indebted to John Rosselli's 1996 findings (see item 273), particularly in providing payment figures for various operas. Several errors involve dating: on p. 200, should read "in 1830"—not 1831 as stated here—"Bellini and Romani began work on an *Ernani*"; and p. 204, "In spring 1832"—not 1833 as stated here—"he [Bellini] paid an extended visit to Naples and Sicily, returning home for the first time in five"—not six as stated here—"years." Likewise, "The following spring he spent four months in London" indicates 1834 in Smart's text, whereas his time in London began in April 1833. These errors do not occur in the works-list, however. Good treatment of melody types and formal structures. Particularly good with stylistic periods within Bellini's career and the French nature of many elements throughout his operas, long before he arrived in Paris. Analysis is synthesized with life and career. Ends with valuable overview, Reception and Influence.

BELLINI GIOVANE: ORIGINS, YOUTH IN CATANIA, EARLY COMPOSITIONS, EDUCATION IN NAPLES

Bellini's early works include: four masses (*Kyrie* and *Gloria* only), more than a dozen shorter religious works for soloists and chorus; an organ sonata; nine songs or arias; a wedding cantata; six two-part overtures (S–F); a short Oboe Concerto in E-flat major; fragments of concertos for violin, flute, and bassoon; and other works that are lost.

119. "L'Anonimo" [thus called by Pastura and Weinstock]. See item 271 and item 279, pp. 5–11. [*Nonno del Vincenzo, manuscritto di epoca imprecisata conservato presso il Museo Civico Belliniano di Catania.*]

Anonymous and undated. Grammatical mistakes and syntactical immaturities. Twelve handwritten pages in Museo belliniano giving a biographical précis, providing details especially, whether true, of the composer's early life. Pastura believed that the author must have surely been a relative or the friend of the composer, quite possibly his musical grandfather (*Nonno*).

120. Baccini, Giuseppe. *L'autografo del primo lavoro musicale di Vincenzo Bellini nella Real Biblioteca Nazionale Centrale di Firenze*. Florence, 1935.

The autograph was acquired in 1892 from the Commendatore Desiderio Chilovi by the Biblioteca Nazionale Centrale di Firenze. This "first musical work" was an *Allegretto* of eleven measures for solo piano dedicated to Angelica Paola Giuffrida.

121. Barrica, Maurizio. *Nei luoghi di Vincenzo Bellini*. Catania: Maimone, 2000. ISBN 88–77511–48–6.

 A tour of Bellini's Catania; introduction by Caterina Andò. Contents include Bellini's birthplace, which is now a museum and library, various churches including the cathedral, the Teatro Massimo "Bellini," and the Bellini monument. Several color plates, including portraits of the composer, the Bellini museum, and the house at Puteaux where the composer died. Short bibliography; fairly extensive source citations.

122. Cambi, Luisa. "La fanciullezza e l'adolescenza." In *Vincenzo Bellini, le sue opere, la sua fama*. Ed. Ildebrando Pizzetti, pp. 13ff. Milano: Fratelli Treves, 1936. See item 242. ML410.B44 P58.

 Bellini's boyhood and adolescence in his native Catania.

123. Castorina, P. *Notizie dei musicisti di Catania del passato e volgente secolo.* Manuscritto inedito giacente presso le Biblioteche Riunite "Civica e A. Ursinon Recupero" di Catania.

 Unpublished manuscript shedding light on musical life in Catania.

124. *Catania nell'Ottocento; corso di conferenze tenuto da diverse autori*. Catania: Società di storia patria per la Sicilia orientale, 1934.

 Catania in the early nineteenth century; background for Bellini's early years.

125. Cilea, Francesco. "Prefazione." In *Vincenzo Bellini, Composizioni giovanili inedite. Riprodotte in facsimile*. Ed. Francesco Cilea. Rome: Reale Accedemia d'Italia, 1941.

 A reproduction of some unpublished juvenile compositions by Bellini.

126. De Logu, Giuseppe. "La casa di Bellini." *Emporium; rivista mensile illustrata d'arte*. March 1931. AP37.E5.

 Bellini's youth in Catania, the house in which he was born. Illustrations.

127. *Enciclopedia di Catania*, V. Consoli, ed. "Bellini, Vincenzo Tobia." Vol. I. Catania, 1987.

 A fairly recent Catanese source on Bellini's musical grandfather.

128. Failla, Salvatore Enrico. *Bellini Vincenzo in Catania*. Introduction by Giuseppe Giarrizzo; photographs by Mario Rossi Trombatore. Catania: Maimone, 1985.

 Written by the Catanese Failla, one of the current authorities on Bellini sources. An essay with copious photographs. Many quotations, citations, and music examples. Begins with a quotation from Ercole Patti's account of his visit to the Bellini birthplace. See item 240. Includes notes for a catalogue of the works Bellini composed in Catania—a table of works with information about each composition. Includes an extensive bibliography and a chronological table with reference to Bellini's period in Catania, 1801 to 1819. An appendix includes the "Biografia di Anonimo" with facsimile. Bibliography and index. Illustrations, facsimiles, music examples.

129. Ferrara, F. *Storia di Catania sino allo fine del secolo XVIII con la descrizione degli antichi monumenti ancora esistenti e dello stato presente della città.* Catania, 1989. Ristampa anastatica della prima edizione del 1829.

130. Florimo, Francesco. *Cenno storico sulla scuola musicale di Napoli*. 2 vols. Naples, 1869–71.

This is the original version of the following item.

131. ——. *La scuola musicale di Napoli e i suoi conservatori: con uno sguardo sulla storia della musica in Italia*. 4 vols. Vol. 3. Bologna: Forni, 1969. Rpt. of Naples, 1880–83. ML290.8.N2 F6 1969.

A revision of his previous two-volume study, *Cenno storico sulla scuola musicale di Napoli* (Naples, 1869–71). A great part of vol. 3 is devoted to the Real Collegio di Musica di San Sebastiano e di San Pietro a Majella, where Bellini was a student and "maestrino."

132. Gallo, Agostino. "Prime scintille del genio di Vincenzo Bellini da Catania. Canzoncina da lui posta in musica a dodici anni, ed ora per la prima volta pubblicata." In "L'Olivuzza," *Ricordi del Soggiorno della Corte Imperiale Russa in Palermo nell'inverno del 1845–46*. Palermo, 1846, pp. 42–53, 109–11.

The original publication of the undoubtedly spurious "Letter to Agostino Gallo," supposedly written around 1829 and first published in Florence in 1843, which has since appeared in nearly every book about Bellini. It describes Bellini's purported method of setting text to music. "L'Olivuzza" was a commemorative pamphlet ("numero unico") issued in Palermo in connection with the residence there of the Russian royal family. L'Olivuzza was the name of the villa where they were staying.

133. Menza, A. "Bellini a Catania." In *Omaggio a Bellini nel primo centenario dalla sua nascità*. Ed. G. Giuliano, pp. 247ff. Catania: Maimone, 1901. See item 238. ML410.B44 C3.

Bellini's first nineteen years, from his birth and early musical training until his departure for the Naples Conservatory.

134. Moschino, Ettore. *Vincenzo Bellini e la sua origine abruzzese*. L'Aquila: n.p., 1940.

The origins of the Bellini family was in the Abruzzi. Bellini's grandfather had moved to Sicily in the late 1760s.

135. Nataletti, Giorgio. "1819–27: gli anni di Napoli." *A Vincenzo Bellini. Bollettino dei Musicisti, Mensile del Sindicato Fascista Musicisti* 13/3 (December 1934): 45–49.

A 1934 Fascist publication from the time of the centenary of Bellini's death. Bellini's years as a student and "maestrino" at the Naples Conservatory are explored.

136. Pannain, Guido. *Il r[eal] conservatorio di musica San Pietro a maiella di Napoli*. Florence: Le Monnier, 1942. MT5.N42 C84.

Includes information about Bellini's years as a student and "maestrino" at the Naples Conservatory.

137. Pasqualino, Giovanni. *Vincenzo Tobia Bellini dall'Abruzzo alla Sicilia.* Foggia: Bastogi Editrice Italiana, 2005. ISBN 88–8185–748–0.

Bellini's grandfather and father (Appendix: "Rosario Bellini, Il padre dimenticato") are studied through an examination of documents from archives and libraries. Facsimiles, music examples. Bibliography, appendix noted above.

Chapter 1: "La vita di Vincenzo Tobia Bellini"; Chapter 2: "I libretti musicati dal Maestro"; Chapter 3: "Le composizioni superstiti di Vincenzo Tobia Bellini"; Chapter 4: "Un contratto fra due musicisti del 1700."

138. Pastura, Francesco. "1801–1819: A Catania." *A Vincenzo Bellini. Bollettino dei Musicisti, Mensile del Sindicato Fascista Musicisti* 13/3 (December 1934): 41ff.

From the same publication as item 135, intended to glorify Italy's past and to coincide with the upcoming Bellini centenary. Describes Bellini's early years in Catania before he left for Naples.

139. ——. "'Le tre ore di Agonia,' Una composizione giovanile di Bellini sinora sconosciuta." Extract from *Catania, Rivista del Comune*, Serie 2, nos. 2–3 (April–September 1953). Catania: Fratelli Viaggio-Campo, 1953.

Published as a separate booklet; copy in Museo belliniano. On Bellini's music as a youth; on the rediscovered manuscript of "Versetti da cantarsi il Venerdì Santo," composed when Bellini was around fourteen. At the time of writing, the manuscript of this youthful composition by Bellini was owned by Professor Titomanlio Manzella, a Catanese living in Rome. Pastura compares this with other known manuscripts from Bellini's early years in order to authenticate it. Includes facsimiles and illustrations.

140. Peters, Brooks. "Letter from Sicily." *Opera News* 66/5 (November 2001): 44–47. ISSN 0030–3607. ML1.O482.

A modern-day visit to Bellini's Catania: the Teatro Massimo Bellini, the Cathedral, Bellini's birthplace, now the Museo belliniano, the Piazza Bellini. Finds Catania "strangely exotic. With a sultry, slightly louche atmosphere, more African in feeling than any other part of Italy, it brings to mind some far-off port of call in an old Hollywood movie of the '40s." Also visits Palermo, the setting of Bellini's *Pirata*, and compares it with Catania.

141. Policastro, Guglielmo. *Vincenzo Bellini (1801–19)*. Catania: Studio Editoriale Moderno, 1935. ML410.B44 P6.

A study of Bellini before he left for Naples in 1819. Begins by dealing with Bellini's background and family: Catania at the beginning of the nineteenth century; his grandfather, mother, father, siblings. Bellini's early training and compositions, early love affairs (relying quite a bit on Hans Peter Holst, *L'amante di Bellini*. See item 150). Numerous illustrations, portraits of relatives, places; facsimiles of letters, songs, other music manuscripts. Weinstock (see item 279) deems this source "generally unreliable."

142. Raso, Carlo. *Guido musicale del centro antico di Napoli*. Naples: Colonnese, 1999. ISBN 88–87501–01–7.

A musical guide to the historical center of Naples. Eleven itineraries are included. Bellini is discussed on pp. 56–61 and others. Extensive index of places, people, and works. Illustrated with photographs and drawings.

143. Verlengia, F. "Gli antentati abruzzesi di Vincenzo Bellini." *Rivista abruzzese*, Chieti, 1952.

Bellini's ancestry may be traced back to 1660 to the mountain village of Torricella Peligna in the Abruzzi.

BIOGRAPHICAL AND CHARACTER STUDIES FROM THE NINETEENTH CENTURY

144. Amore, Antonino. *Vincenzo Bellini*. 2 vols. Catania: N. Giannotta, 1892–94. ML410.B44 A6.

An amalgamation of the two volumes previously written by Amore: *Vincenzo Bellini: Arte. Studi e ricerche* (Catania, 1892); and *Vincenzo Bellini: Vita. Studi e ricerche* (Catania: N. Giannotta, 1894. ML410.B44 A6). Begins with a discussion of the Bellini family, then proceeds through each opera in chronological order. Deals with Bellini's chroniclers and biographers from earlier in the century: Cicconetti, Pougin, Florimo, and others. Bellini's relations with other composers and librettists. Appraisal by critics and other composers: Castil-Blaze, Donizetti, Auber, Soffredini, Fétis, Wagner, and others. Comparison of Italian and German opera theories and styles. Contains letters written to Bellini, including correspondence from Ricordi, Milan.

145. Cicconetti, Filippo. *Vita di Vincenzo Bellini*. Prato: Alberghetti, 1859. ML410.B44 C2.

First substantial attempt at a life of Bellini; Gerardi was the first to appear (1835). See item 148. Reprints the "Letter to Agostino Gallo," supposedly written around 1829 and first published in Florence in 1843, which has since appeared in nearly every book about Bellini. It describes Bellini's purported method of setting text to music.

146. Di Ferrer, Cavaliere. *Rossini e Bellini—Risposta a uno scritto pubblicato a Palermo nel settembre 1832*. Faenza: n.p., 1834; Cesena: Tipografia Biasini e socii, 1843. ML410.R8 F3.

Part of the Bellini versus Rossini polemic that went on during the early 1830s. Also in French: *Rossini et Bellini, réponse de M. le marquis de San-Jacinto à un écrit publié à Palerme, revue, réimprimée à Bologne et traduite en français par M. le Chevalier de Ferrer*. Paris: Everat, 1835.

147. Florimo, Francesco. *La scuola musicale di Napoli e i suoi conservatori: con uno sguardo sulla storia della musica in Italia*. Vol. 3. Bologna: Forni, 1969. Rpt. of Naples, 1880–83. ML290.8.N2 F6 1969.

A great part of volume 3 is devoted to Real Collegio di Musica di San Sebastiano e di San Pietro a Majella, in which, covering pp. 175–224, is a biography of Vincenzo Bellini, followed by "Dichiarazioni ed aneddoti" on pp. 225–97. This latter section presents documents such as Bellini's birth and death certificates, letters, notices from composers such as Rossini and Wagner, and deals with topics such as Bellini and Malibran, Bellini and his first loves, relationship between Bellini and Pacini, between Bellini and Donizetti, and others. Concluding is a list of Bellini's compositions found in the library of the Naples Conservatory, where Florimo served as chief librarian for many years.

148. Gerardi, Filippo. *Biografia di Vincenzo Bellini*. Rome: G. Salviucci & Figlio, 1835. ML410.B44 G3.

The earliest biography of Bellini, appearing only a few weeks after his death. Twenty-four pages. Cicconetti's subsequent work (1859) was more substantial and reliable. See item 145.

149. Grassi, M. *Degli omaggi resi in versi tempi dalla città di Acireale a Vincenzo Bellini. Ricordo storico per Mar. Grassi*. 2d ed. Acireale: Tipografia Danzuso, 1877.

The name Bellini surfaces in Acireale in 1774 for the "Musica del Festino" in the Chiesa Madrice and the traditional Dialogo in the piazza; this is one Vincenzo Bellini from Naples, grandfather of the illustrious swan of Catania. The sacred drama *Il sacrificio di Gefte* was presented with great success, in the cathedral square, from July 23 to 26. Cf. Musumeci, Z. "Del culto della musica in Acireale," in *Atti e Rendiconti dell'Accademia Dafnica di Acireale*, serie II, Vol. 2. Acireale, 1905–1910.

150. Holst, Gian Pietro (Hans Peter). *L'amante di Bellini*. Trans. from the Danish by Gustavo Straffordello. Milan: Sonzogno, 1885. Rpt. 1891, 1924.

Originally printed as part of *Sicilianske Skitze* (Copenhagen, 1853). A fictionalized account, sometimes cited in other literature. See item 141.

Deals with Bellini's youthful passion in Catania for Maria Anna Politi. Holst visited Sicily in 1842 for background. No letters or other documents exist about Bellini's relationship with Maria Anna.

151. Pougin, Arthur. "Bellini et ses nouveaux biographes." *La Musique populaire* 3/53 (19 October 1882): 2–3.

A portrait of Bellini is on the cover of this issue. Pougin reviews three new works on Bellini: Florimo's *Bellini: Memorie e lettere* (see item 47), Scherillo's *Vincenzo Bellini, note aneddotiche e critiche* (see item 86), and *Felice Romani ed i più riputati maestri di musica del suo tempo* by Emilia Branca (see item 335). He finds Florimo's work very touching in its devotion, revealing biographical data unknown to anyone else, presenting many letters including ones written to Bellini by musicians such as Rossini, Auber, Lablache, and Mercadante. Pougin characterizes Scherillo's volume in this way: "Ce charmant petit volume, un peu capricieux dans sa forme, très arbitraire dans son plan, n'en est pas moins fort agréable et d'un attrait piquant." He commends Branca for the inclusion of letters from many famous men in her account, seventeen years after his death, of her husband Felice Romani.

152. ——. *Bellini, sa vie, ses oeuvres*. Paris: L. Hachette et Cie, 1868. ML410. B44 P8.

A major biography that appeared within the next decade after Cicconetti's 1859 study. One of the few sympathetic treatments outside of Italy until modern times, even though Pougin talks of Bellini's defects such as technical "ignorance," "monotony," "lack of development." He may have inherited this viewpoint from Fétis. See item 107. Rossini helped the critic Pougin with this book and thus some of the criticism may have been felt by him. Florimo shared a number of documents with Pougin; this was fourteen years before Florimo's own *Memorie e lettere* (see item 47) appeared.

228 pp.

Chapter 1: Une dynastie musicale; Chapter 2: Le Conservatoire de San-Sebastiano; Chapter 3: Premier amour de Bellini, premier douleur; Chapter 4: Felice Romani; Chapter 5: Bellini arrive à Milan; Chapter 6: Détails sur la façon de travailler de Bellini; Chapter 7: Troisième voyage à Milan; Chapter 8: La Pasta—*La sonnambula*; Chapter 9: *Norma* (Lettre de Bellini sur le fiasco de *Norma*); Chapter 10: Voyage à Naples, puis à Catane; Chapter 11: Bellini signe des traités avec les administrations des deux théâtres italiens de Londres et de Paris; Chapter 12: *I puritani di Scozia*—Désespoir de Bellini—Sa mort; Chapter 13: Funérailles de Bellini; Chapter 14: Le Génie de Bellini; Appendices: Compositions de Bellini en dehors du théâtre. Chronological list of operas; bibliography; autographs, facsimiles: *Canone libero a quattro voci*; Letter to the French baritone Baroilhet of July 1, 1835.

153. Scudo, Paul (Paolo). "Donizetti et l'école italienne depuis Rossini." In *Critique et littérature musicales*. Ed. Paul Scudo. Paris: Amyot, 1850. ML60.S53.

   An essay written in July 1848, shortly after Donizetti's death. Aside from a short biography of the composer and a discussion of some of his works, Donizetti is discussed in terms of his contemporaries Rossini, Bellini, and Verdi. Notable for assessing Bellini as "Nature fine et délicate, génie mélodique plus tendre que fort et plus ému que varié." Scudo notes that Bellini escaped the influence of Rossini, having been inspired directly by eighteenth-century masters, especially Paisiello.

Note: Nineteenth-century biographical treatments of Bellini also include the following rarities:

154. Beltramo, Pietro. "Cav. Vincenzo Bellini." In *Biografia degli italiani illustri nella scienze, lettere ed arti*. Ed. Emilio de Tipaldo. Venice, Tip. di Alvisopoli, 1835. Vol. 2: 451–61. Z2350.T59; reprinted as *Biografia di Vincenzo Bellini*. Venice, 1836.

155. Bruschetti, A. *Vincenzo Bellini a Milano*. Naples, 1878.

156. Bürkli, G. *Biographie von Vicenz [sic] Bellini*. Zurich, Gedruckt bei Orell, Füssli und compagnie, 1841. ML5.N48, no. 29.

157. Cristoadoro, Antonino. *Cenni biografici dell'illustre Cigno catanese cav. Vincenzo Bellini*. Catania: Tipografia Roma, 1866.

158. Dobelli, Ferdinando. *Biografia di Vincenzo Bellini*. Milan: Gnocchi, 1867.

159. Labat, M. *Bellini*. Bordeaux: Gounouilhou, 1865.

160. Neumann, W. *Vincenzo Bellini: Eine Biographie*. Kassel, 1854.

161. Regaldi, Giuseppe. *Cenni biografici su Vincenzo Bellini*. Naples, 1842.

162. Ricucci, Giuseppe. *Vincenzo Bellini: le sue opere ed i suoi tempi*. Naples: G. Cozzolino, 1899.

163. Scuderi, Luigi. *Biografia di Vincenzo Bellini: Le biografie degli illustri catanesi del secolo XVIII*. Bologna: A. Forni, 1840. DG975. C28 S38 1975.

164. Ventimilia, Domenico. *Biografia di Vincenzo Bellini*. Messina, 1835.

CIRCUMSTANCES SURROUNDING BELLINI'S DEATH AND BURIAL

165. Bournon, Fernand. "La Maison mortuaire de Bellini à Puteaux." *Journal des Débats politiques et littéraires* 117/264 (September 23, 1905).

   Bellini died at the house of Samuel Levys [Lewis] in the Parisian suburb of Puteaux. Explores the composer's final days there.

166. Brunel, Pierre. "La Mort de Bellini: Réactions littéraires et musicales." *Vincenzo Bellini et la France* (2007): 505–17. See item 404.

Explores the early nineteenth-century French love of funeral oration poetry in terms of literary and musical reactions to Bellini's untimely death. Alfred de Musset, one year later, ties Bellini's death to that of the young singer Maria Malibran.

167. Carp, L. "How Did He Die?—The Rumors and Myths Surrounding the Death of Vincenzo Bellini." *Opera Canada* 17/1 (1976): 13. ISSN 0030–3577. ML5.O6715.

The nature of Bellini's final illness.

168. De Gaetani, G. *Ipotesi sulla natura della malattia che condusse a morte Vincenzo Bellini*. Catania, 1931.

Clinical aspects of Bellini's illness and death.

169. De Luca, Maria Rosa. "Vincenzo Bellini e il Barone Aymé d'Aquino: Note per un possible epilogo documentario." *Vincenzo Bellini et la France* (2007): 485–504. See item 404.

Contains facsimiles of correspondence between Florimo and Aymé. Beginning with Rosselli's documentary researches concerning Bellini's last days in Puteaux (see item 180), attempts to construct the relationship between Bellini in terms of chronicles of the times and what of Bellini's relationship with Aymé (famous for being the last to see Bellini alive) became part of the Bellini romanticized biography. As he often did, Florimo twisted the facts to dramatize them.

170. Della Corte, Andrea. "Ipotesi sulla casa dove Bellini si spense." *Musica d'oggi; rassegna di vita e di coltura musicale* 18 (1936): 268ff. ML5. M721.

Bellini's final days in Puteaux; rumors surrounding his death.

171. Franken, Franz Hermann. *Die Krankheiten grosser Komponisten*. 4 vols. *Band I: Haydn, Beethoven, Bellini, Mendelssohn-Bartholdy, Chopin, Schumann*. Wilhelmshaven: Florian Noetzel, 1986–97. ISBN 37–95904–19–6. ML390. F825 1986.

A series exploring the illnesses and deaths of famous composers. Bellini is treated on pp. 111–33. After an introduction and discussion of his personality, first his health problems up until the final illness and then the mortal illness of September 1835 are discussed. The section on Bellini ends with the funeral cermonies held in Bellini's honor, the transferral of his remains to Catania in 1876, and various diagnoses of his final illness. Illustrations include Bellini's piano in the Museo belliniano, a portrait of Giuditta Turina, an oil portrait of Bellini by Carlo Arienti, ca. 1827, and Bellini's death mask by J.P. Dantan *fils*.

172. Gheusi, Jacques. "La fin tragique de Bellini." *Musica, Disques* (Chaix) 82 (January 1961): 14–18.

Bellini's final months in Paris, from the triumph of *I puritani* in January to his death in September. One of Bellini's friends, the Baron Aimé d'Acquino, visited him on September 11, found him in bed, and was shocked by his appearance. On doctor's orders, Levys cut the visit short. D'Acquino returned two days later and was told by the gardener that no one was to be admitted. He returned the next day with Mercadante—no entry was granted. Finally the composer Carafa, d'Acquino's uncle, passing for a court physician, was admitted. Quotations from d'Acquino's journal, which tells of visiting on September 23, only to be told that Bellini had died at 5 a.m. that morning. Gheusi discusses the improbability that Bellini was poisoned by Levys or the woman with whom he was living, and the possibility that Bellini may have succumbed to cholera. Notes the strange behavior of Levys and the woman, who left immediately for Paris. No source citations.

173. Giugni, Francesco. *L'immatura fine di Vincenzo Bellini alla luce di nuove circostanze. Chi fu il suo medico curante?* Lugo: Tipografia Succ. Ferretti, 1938.

Copy found in Museo belliniano. About 10 pp. Giugni gives the name of the man in whose home Bellini died, Samuel Levys, as Lewis. Provides a list of references about Bellini's last attending physician, Dr. Luigi Montallegri, native of Faenza and "medico militare."

174. ——. *La malattia e la morte di Vincenzo Bellini*. Faenza: Stabilimento Grafico Fratelli Lega, 1939. An extract from the volume *Scritti medici in onore del Professore Fabio Rivalta*, published by La Società Medico-Chirurgica di Romagna.

Copy found in Museo belliniano. 17 pp. Illustrated with facsimiles. Provides letters written by Montallegri, Bellini's last attending physician in Paris. Gives the text of the autopsy report of September 26, 1835, by Professor A. Dalmas of the Faculty of Medicine of Paris.

175. Gunati, Giovanni. "De Mortuis nisi boni? Bellini nel necrologi di Berlioz e Mazzini e in una recensione wagneriana del 1837." *Vincenzo Bellini et la France* (2007): 519–51. See item 404.

In both Berlioz's "Notes nécrologiques" of Bellini and in Mazzini's *La filosofia della musica* (1836), Bellini's style is criticized for not being sufficiently "progressive" and emancipated from that of Rossini. This view was not shared by Wagner, who considered *Norma* a model of style that could help forge a bridge between Italian and German opera.

176. Kerner, D. "Bellinis Tod in Paris." *Das Orchester* 24 (November 1976): 712–16. ISSN 0030-4468. ML5.O68.

A German study of Bellini's final illness at the Levys' house in Puteaux.

177. Mariotti, M. "E morto Vincenzo Bellini per enterocolite amebica?" *Minerva med.* Turin 40–1 (1949): 292–94.

Medical aspects of Bellini's final illness—did he die of amoebic dysentery?

178. Neri, Carmelo. *Bellini morì di veleno?: i "diabolici intrighi" del Pacini e della contessa Samoyloff.* Preface by Giuseppe Cardillo. Catania: Prova d'Autore, 2000. ML410.B44 N48 2000.

Bellini was paranoid about the composer Giovanni Pacini and his mistress Countess Samoilova (1803–1875). Did they play any part in his premature death?

179. Rosselli, John. *The Life of Bellini.* Musical Lives Series. Cambridge: Cambridge University Press, 1996. ISBN 05–21462–27–4 (hardcover); 05–21467–81–0 (paperback). ML410.B44 R77 1996.

The author has reexamined and reevaluated published sources; new archival research has provided material, presented in the Appendix, on three people with whom Bellini was associated during his last days in Paris: Auguste Aymé, S. Levy, and Mlle. Olivier. Bellini was at Puteaux, the suburb of Paris where he died, from 26 May 1834, to 1 November of that year, then from ca. 11 May 1835, to his death on 25 September.

180. ——. "Vita e morte di Bellini a Parigi." *Rivista italiana di musicologia* 19/1 (1984): 261–76. ISSN 0035–6867. ML5. R79.

Research conducted in archives and in the register office, also drawing on Bellini's letters, to determine information about Bellini's final days and the people who were with him at that time: Auguste Aymé, S. Levy, and Mlle. Olivier. Aymé was a Franco-Neapolitan friend of Bellini who wrote about the composer in his diary. Also presents reactions in Paris at the time of his death *vis-à-vis* his place in society. Rosselli also assesses Bellini's education and epistolary skills.

NECROLOGIES: ELEGIES AND HOMAGES UPON BELLINI'S DEATH

Necrologies are in some cases synonymous with early biographies. Many of the homages to Bellini upon his death are in the form of laudatory poems, both in Italian and Sicilian. Many of these items are nineteenth-century rarities and as such do not bear the names of publishers or Library of Congress call numbers; a number of these remain unannotated but they are all of a similar elegiac nature.

181. *A Vincenzo Bellini, carme di Michele Bertolani.* Palermo, 1835.

182. Berlioz, Hector. "Bellini: Notes nécrologiques." In *Les Musiciens et la musique*, pp. 167–69. Paris, 1903; rpt. Farnborough: Gregg, 1969 (see item 34).

183. Brigandi, Pietro-Gaetano. *Elogio funebre in morte del cavaliere Vincenzo Bellini, recitato da D. Pier Gaetano Brigandi—nella città di Piazza a di 28 novembre.* Messina, 1836.

184. Capelli, Emilio. *In morte di Vincenzo Bellini*. Palermo, 1836.

     A poem on the death of Bellini.

185. Crescini, Jacopo. *Ode per la spoglia di Vincenzo Bellini tumulata solennemente il 2 novembre 1835 nel cimitero Le Père Lachaise.* Paris: De Racquenois, n.d.

     Dedicated to Rossini. 14 pp. Copy in Paris, Bibliothèque de l'Opéra. Poetic eulogy in Italian with French translation at bottom of page. Frontispiece, portrait of Bellini. The month is wrong; it was on October 2 rather than November 2 that Bellini was buried in Père-Lachaise Cemetery.

186. Francesconi, Pasquale. *In morte del cavalier Vincenzo Bellini*. Naples, 1835.

187. Gemelli, Carlo. *Elogio in morte di Vincenzo Bellini pronunciato all'Accademia dei peloritani nel [9 novembre] 1835*. Messina: Stamperia Fiumrara, 1835.

     Copy found in Museo belliniano. 15 pp.

188. La Farina, Giuseppe. *Elogio del cavaliere Vincenzo Bellini*. Messina, 1835.

     Elegy upon the death of Bellini.

189. Moreau, Elise. "Un chant mélodieux se perdit dans l'espace." *Le Journal des Débats* 9 oct. 1835. (Cited in Pougin, pp. 171–73. See item 152.)

     Concerns de Musset's elegy: see Brunel, item 263.

190. Novarro. "Necrologia di Vincenzo Bellini." *Giornale di Scienze e Lettere*. Palermo, 1835.

     A necrology of the composer.

191. *Onori alla memoria di Vincenzo Bellini*. Messina: Fiumara, 1835.

     Poetry honoring the recently deceased Bellini. 76 pp. On the cover: "Per cura della gioventù messinese."

192. Romani, Felice. "Necrologia di Vincenzo Bellini." *Gazzetta ufficiale piemontese* (October 21, 1835).

     Contains a reference to the break in their friendship and working relationship and the remark, "This last was a period of which we both felt ashamed." Romani's wife, Emilia Branca, left this sentence out of her book about her husband. See item 335. A full English translation of Romani's Necrology appeared for the first time in Weinstock, 1971. See item 279.

193. Scovazzo, Luigi. *In morte di Vincenzo Bellini*. Naples: R. de Stefano, ca. 1836.

Poetry lauding the deceased composer.

194. Scuderi, Salvatore. "In morte del cavaliere Vincenzo Bellini visione del cavaliere Salvatore Scuderi." Extract from *Giornale di scienze, lettere, ed arti per la Sicilia*, 167 (November 1936).

Copy found in Museo belliniano. 3 pp. A poetic elegy, beginning: "Di acerba nuova un suon funesta avrea/Già del triste Amenan scorso la riva."

195. Stagno, Lettorio. *Elogio in morte di Vincenzo Bellini*. Messina, 1835.

Poetic elegy honoring the deceased composer.

196. Trinchera, Francesco. *Alla madre inconsolabile di Vincenzo Bellini dalla morte nel fiore dell'età e della gloria rapito alle maggiori speranze d'Italia questo carme Francesco Trinchera dedicava*. 1825 [really 1835].

Copy in Museo belliniano. Poetic elegy on the death of Bellini, "to his inconsolable mother." The author gives Bellini's death date as September 24. An extract from the middle reads as follows: "Piangete dunque voi, piangete il fato/Sicule verginelle e più grazoni,/Del Sir della patetica armonia./Ei per desio d'onor mori lontana/Dalla materna sua terra natale."

HOMAGES AND REPORTS UPON THE TRANSFER OF BELLINI'S REMAINS FROM PARIS TO CATANIA, 1876

This was also the time when officials in Catania decided to erect a statue to the memory of Bellini; it was sculpted by G. Monteverde. See items 202 and 291.

197. Ardizzoni, Gaetano. *Parole su Vincenzo Bellini dette da Gaetano Ardizzoni nel Palazzo Municipale il dì 23 settembre 1876*. Catania: Tipografia di C. Galatola, 1876.

Copy found in Museo belliniano. 28 pp. of text. A speech delivered upon the occasion of the transferral of Bellini's remains from Paris to Catania Cathedral.

198. Cardona, Luigi. *Aneddoti lettere e motti di Vincenzo Bellini raccolti e copiati da Luigi Cardona*. Ragusa: Tipografia Piccitto & Antoni, 1876.

Copy found in Museo belliniano. A collection of items relating to Bellini, published in the year of the transferral of Bellini's remains from Paris to Catania. Topics such as "Il primo amore del Bellini" (Maddalena Fumaroli) and anecdotes about the infant Bellini ("Quando Bellini aveva un anno"); other composers and their views of Bellini, for example the Catanese Giovanni Pacini's assessment of *Norma*, and Cherubini on Bellini's instrumentation; copies of letters and mottoes; the (probably spurious) "Lettera sul modo di comporre musica sulla poesia"; Bellini's final words on September 23, 1835; a list of his works; the physiognomy of Bellini. All this in 26 pp.

199. Fétis, François-Joseph. "Un dernier hommage à Bellini." *Le Ménestrel; Journal du monde musical* (October 1, 8, and 15, 1876). ML5.M2.

In Fétis's own words: "A very complete and detailed account of the exhumation ceremony of the remains of Bellini, of their transport to Italy, and their arrival in Catania."

200. Florimo, Francesco, ed. *Premio Bellini. Introduzione, programma. Cronaca dell'inaugurazione del monumento*. Napoli: Nicotra, 1887.

Florimo was the primary force behind the erection of the Bellini monument.

201. ——. *Traslazione delle ceneri di Vincenzo Bellini. Memorie ed impressioni per Francesco Florimo*. Naples: Stabilimento Tipografia Professor Vincenzo Morano, 1877.

Copy in Museo belliniano. 192 pp. The most extensive of the many descriptions and offerings upon the occasion of the removal of Bellini's remains from Paris to Catania Cathedral in 1876. Florimo describes the background of the transferral agreement between Paris and Catania and the ceremonies and festivities that lasted several days in Catania and throughout Italy and Sicily. He speaks of "mio Bellini." Documents, texts of plaques.

202. Maione, Paologiovanni. "Florimo commitente musicale per un monumento a Bellini." In *Francesco Florimo e l'Ottocento musicale: Atti del Convegno di Studi* (Morcone, April 19–21, 1990). Ed. Rosa Cafiero and Marina Marino, pp. 99–119. Reggio Calabria: Jason, 1999. ISBN 88–81570–69–6. ML423. F63 F73 1999.

Florimo's 1876 plans for a Bellini monument in Catania.

203. Pastura, Francesco. "La traslazione delli ceneri di Bellini Anno 1876." Extract from *Rivista del Comune di Catania* (October–December 1957).

Separate bound copy in Museo belliniano. 9 pp. Another treatment of the transfer of Bellini's remains from Paris to Catania Cathedral. A national celebration, not just in Catania; reports from the detailed chronicle of Federico de Roberto, "Le feste belliniane," from *Illustrazione italiana* 3/51 (October 15, 1876), 311ff. Pastura quotes Amore's words on Bellini: "Com'è splendente di gioia! Piange e ride; avvicinato e carrezzato di tutti, lascia a tutti vedere l'orologio, la spilla, i bottoni d'oro del fratello Vincenzo, e la calma di Spagna: la famosa canna di cui parla l'Heine."

204. Percolla, Vincenzo. *Elogio biografico del Cav. Vincenzo Bellini scritto in occasione del trasporto delle sue ceneri da Parigi a Catania*. Catania: Stabilimento Tipografia Bellini, 1876.

A copy, inscribed by the author, found in the Museo belliniano. 163 pp. of text. Written on the occasion of the transferral of Bellini's body from Paris to Catania. Divided into twenty-four chapters, beginning with a discussion of Bellini's genius and the reason for this elegy, proceeding to his birth, the great influence on the composer of Rossini's masterpiece *Semiramide*, through the genesis, premieres, and reception of his operas, his travels, his death, autopsy, funeral ceremonies and honors in Paris, Naples, Palermo, Messina, Catania, the proposal for a Bellini monument in Catania, his character, his future reputation, and the singularity of his operas.

205. Ruda, Camillo. *L'Apotèosi di Vincenzo Bellini. Parole di Camillo Ruda*. Catania: Tipografia G. Musumeci, 1876.

Copy in Museo belliniano. 30 pp. Biographical, chronological outline of Bellini's life with remarks.

206. Scherillo, Michele. *Belliniana: nuove note*. Milan: Ricordi, 1883.

Contains many letters and documents, for example, letters to Florimo written in 1876, at the time of the transferral of Bellini's remains from Paris to Catania, from such musical figures as Richard Wagner (who was asked to write a composition but declined from fatigue—this was the opening year for Bayreuth), Hans von Bülow, Tchaikovsky, Liszt, Ambroise Thomas.

207. Sciuto, Agatino. *Vincenzo Bellini profilo biografico*. Catania: Tipografia di C. Galatola, 1876.

Copy in Museo belliniano. 13 pp.

Note: Other sources published on this occasion include:

208. Argenti, Nicola. *Vincenzo Bellini, scene intime in cinque parti*. Rome: Riccomanni, 1876.

209. *Ricordi delle feste belliniane*. Catania, 1876.

210. Zanghi, Coco. *Memorie e lacrime de la patria sul sepolcro di Vincenzo Bellini*. Catania, 1876.

BIOGRAPHICAL AND CHARACTER STUDIES SURROUNDING AND BETWEEN THE BELLINI CENTENARIES (CA. 1901 TO CA. 1935)

211. *A Vincenzo Bellini. Bollettino dei Musicisti, Mensile del Sindicato Fascista Musicisti* 13/3 (December 1934).

A fascist publication, supported by and helping to glorify Mussolini. The first section is "Tappe di vita," following the composer's life chronologically, written by Francesco Pastura, Ottavia Tiby, and others. It is complete with illustrations and footnote citations. The second section is "Miscellanea," consisting of more illustrations, homages, and elegies, for example: "Il mio Bellini" by Fausto Torrefranca; "Note sulla storia della critica belliniana"; and Luigi Tonelli, "I libretti di Bellini."

212. Abate, Giuseppe Raffaelo. *Cenno biografico di Vincenzo Bellini per Giuseppe Raffaele Abate*. Catania: Tipografia del Puritano, 1901.

Copy in Museo belliniano. 15 pp. Speaks of "il caro e divino Vincenzo" and the folly of trying to present the biography of such a figure in just a few pages.

213. Agnoli, Galileo. "La bella musa ispiratrice." *L'Illustrazione italiana* (January 1935). N6911.I36.

Explores Bellini's relationship with Giuditta Turina.

214. Allard, Roger. "Bellini." *Revue musicale* 156 (May 1935): 18–38. ISSN 0768–1593. ML5.R613.

An affectionate but not always accurate tribute to Bellini in essay form from the perspective of a century after his death. A review of his career and musical style (although not in an analytical manner) and his importance for the music world. The importance of Italian music is stressed as being the "nurse mother" of all European music and much attention is paid to the glorification of Wagner, which has colored our viewpoint of Bellini and other opera composers. Discusses Bellini's love life and his physical appearance: "Upon the body of the blond Orpheus of Catania love and music are intertwined like two serpents with eyes of gold."

Footnote (1) gives the "exact" age of Bellini upon his death as "33 years, 11 months and 24 days," whereas it should be 10 months and 20 days. Includes a reproduction of a portrait of Bellini by Maldarelli and photographs of the inside and outside of the house where Bellini was born, now the Museo belliniano. Gives the year of the transfer of Bellini's corpse to Catania from Paris as 1870, whereas it was 1876.

215. Ammirata, Giannina. *Vita amorosa di Vincenzo Bellini*. Milan: Edizioni Aurora, 1935. ML410.B44 A47.

Divided into chapters that follow the chronology of Bellini's career and love affairs: Land of Sicily; The First Love (Maddalena Fumaroli); Life in Milan; and Giuditta Turina, etc., with Chapter IX exploring his possible love for Maria Malibran. Bellini's correspondence is drawn upon throughout the text.

216. Amore, Antonino. *Belliniana: errori e smentite*. Catania: Giannotta, 1902. ML410.B44 A.

According to Weinstock, makes an "inflated sentimental saga" of Bellini's affair with Maddalena Fumaroli (see item 279, p. 24). Includes music examples and letters.

217. Angelis, Giuseppe Tito De. *Bellini: la vita, l'uomo, l'artista*. Brescia: Editrice "Ancora," 1935. ML410.B44 A65.

One of the writers who denigrates Bellini as a person because of the way he purportedly conducted his love life. Contains "information," the source of which is unknown, about Bellini's relationship with Maddalena Fumaroli. Divided into three parts: the Life, the Man, the Artist. Many citations of Florimo and some from Cambi, *Epistolario*. See item 288.

218. Aniante, Antonio [pseud. Antonio Rapisarda]. *La vita di Bellini*. Turin: Gobetti, 1925. Rpt. Florence: Passigli, 1986. ML410.B44 R2.

Typical of the new reception accorded Bellini after the appearance of Pizzetti's essay. See item 466. A few footnotes, no bibliography. The following year Aniante republished this work as *Vita amorosa di Vincenzo Bellini. Storie galanti e romanzesche* (Milan: Edizioni Pervinca, 1926), condensed with the guidance of the publisher. Aniante wrote that by doing this he pleased those critics who found little interest in *Vita di Bellini* from a musical standpoint, and besides, there already existed the insuperable work from the pen of Ildebrando Pizzetti. Aniante's work, then, was mainly a love story. The *Vita amorosa* consists of 191 pp. containing four chapters: Maddalena Fumaroli, Giuditta Cantù, Maria Malibran, and "Il tramonto" (Sunset).

219. Battiato, Santo. "Pri lu primu centenario di la morti di Bellini." *Collana di lirichi 'n sicilianu*. Catania, 1935.

Copy in Museo belliniano. In Sicilian. Partly a paean to Mussolini: "O magnanimu DUCI Mussulini." Discusses the premieres of many of Bellini's operas, impressions upon visiting Bellini's house, his tomb, the Bellini monument, the city of Catania.

220. Cambi, Luisa. *Bellini [La vita] con sei illustrazione*. Milan: Mondadori, 1934. ML410.B44 C13.

The illustrations include the entrance to Bellini's house, Bellini as an adolescent, Giuditta Turina, Bellini at the time of *Norma*, at the time of *Puritani*, and his funeral mask. Source documentation, which is extensive, is based to a certain extent on Florimo's work but also Bellini's letters in general. Somewhat stodgy, certainly does not romanticize Bellini. A few years later (1943) Cambi published the landmark *Epistolario*. See item 288.

221. Casella, Alfredo. In *Quadrivio* June 9, 1935. See the review "Vincenzo Bellini visto da Casella." *Musica d'oggi; rassegna di vita e di coltura musicale* 17 (July 1935): 272ff. ML5.M721.

Casella was an important voice in the Bellini revival in 1930s. Speaks of Bellini's music in an emotional way, as do many Italian writers: "His music moves in a sphere of pure contemplation, rising above human feeling."

222. Condorelli, Benedetto. "Lapidi commemorative di Vincenzo Bellini." Extract from *Catania. Rivista del Comune* 6, 11 (January–February 1934). Separate publication by Catania: S.A. Editoriale Siciliano Tipografica, 1934.

Copy in Museo belliniano. Presents "lapidi" (commemorative plaques) to Bellini found in various locations. Examples include places where Bellini composed certain works. Transcriptions of the texts of the plaques are provided.

223. D'Annunzio, Gabriele. "A Vincenzo Bellini." *Le Laudi* 1, 1901. Also "Nel primo centenario della nascita di Vincenzo Bellini." Hymn in *La Tribuna*. Rome, 1901.

Paean to Bellini in poetic form, written upon the hundredth anniversary of his birth. Reprinted in the special Bellini issue of *Revue musicale* in 1935 in the original Italian with interfacing French translation. Many Classical references, beginning with an invocation of the "isola divina" of Sicily.

224. De Felice, Francesco. *Bellini*. Trapani: Casa Editrice "Radio," 1935.

Copy in Museo belliniano. This was Pastura's copy and contains corrections, probably in his hand. A short biography of 53 pages that quotes extensively from Florimo, Policastro, and Scherillo. Several plates: portrait of Bellini; Catania, the Via Crociferi (near Bellini's birthplace); manuscript of *Il pirata*; Giuditta Turina; Giuditta Pasta; Maria Malibran.

225. Della Corte, Andrea and Guido Pannain. *Vincenzo Bellini: Il carattere morale, i caratteri artistici*. Turin: G.B. Paravia, 1935.

With twenty-four illustrations ("Indice della illustrazioni" at back), including portraits of Mayr, Mercadante, Pacini, and others, places where Bellini lived, theaters, singers in costume, and stage designs. Includes Della Corte, "L'animo," pp. 3–28, which explores his personality based on the letters; Della Corte's "La formazione," his musical education, pp. 29–48; Della Corte's "Il canto e i cantanti," pp. 49–64; and Pannain, "Saggio critico," pp. 77–123, which discusses Bellini's musical training and influences, his development, provides an analysis and description of his operas and details of self-borrowings.

226. Esposito, Vicenzo. *La vita di Vincenzo Bellini, in versi dialettali, pref. di Gaetano Emmanuel Calì*. Catania: Stabilimento Tipografia F. Zingale, 1935.

Written in verse in Sicilian dialect: "A Vicenzu Billini."

227. Fasano, Vincenzo Andronico. *Bellini (nel centenario della sua morte)*. Rome: Tipografia "La Precisa," 1936.

One of the homages to Bellini on the centenary of his death. Begins by speaking of Bellini's genius. Discusses Bellini reception, citing Rossini and Wagner. Twelve-page essay with three pages of notes and texts of letters and quotations that amplify the content of his essay.

228. Grassi, Antonio. *Bellini, Wagner, Verdi* (*1801–1901*). Milan: Casa Editrice "Erta," 1935. ML1700. G77 B4.

Discusses Bellini, "Interpretazione del Genio," pp. 7–33.

229. Gray, Cecil William Turpie. "Vincenzo Bellini (1802 [*sic*]–1835)." *Music & Letters* 7 (1926): 49–62, 177–79. ISSN 0027-4224. ML5.M64. Rpt. in Gray, *Contingencies*. London: Oxford University Press, 1947. ML60. G795.

At the time of writing there was a great prejudice against the music of Bellini, probably due to the prominence of the Wagnerians. Gray quotes Wagner at length on Bellini to support the view that Wagner greatly admired him. Gray calls Bellini "the father of modern melody, and not one of those who most decry him to-day could write as they do on every page if it had not been for him." Discusses the belief as unfounded that although Bellini had great natural talent he was technically deficient, never learning his *métier*.

230. Lloyd, W.A.C. *Vincenzo Bellini, A Memoir*. London: Sisleys, 1909.

Popular, chatty, dilettantish, undocumented; English translations of some of Bellini's letters and critical evaluation of the operas from an amateur standpoint; deals more with Bellini's character than the music. Defends the Italian school of opera against intolerance: "Though he had not the science which would have enabled him to write compositions like the 'Favorita,' 'Siege of Corinth,' or the standard German overtures, yet the opera [*Norma*] is prefaced by a singularly fine sinfonia in which he has most skilfully [*sic*] combined the dignity of the classic story with the ferocity discernible in the Druidess' character and the despair occasioned by the faithless Pollioni [*sic*]." (p. 39)

231. Lombardo, Nello. "L'ispiratrice di Vincenzo Bellini, con documenti inediti." *Rivista letteraria Cremona* 9 (September 1935).

The story of Bellini and Giuditta Turina. Laudatory, beginning: "Vincenzo Bellini, maestro! Propriamente: maestro, unicamente maestro, cioè: superiore, capo." Illustrated. Quotes from letters to Florimo. Describes Bellini's epistolary style as "disordinato, sgrammatico, e fanciullesco, ma vivace e assai espressivo."

232. Mezzatesta, Girolamo Guido. *Vincenzo Bellini nella vita e nelle opere. Nel lo centenario della morte con prefazione di Armando Troni*. Palermo: Editrice I Quaderni de la Sinossi, 1935. ML410.B44 M4.

An 188-page homage to Bellini. Copy found in Museo belliniano. Makes the point that, even though born in the nineteenth century, Bellini was very much of the eighteenth century. Ends with the quotation from Roberto Bracco: "Wagner è l'immensità, Bellini è l'infinito."

233. Mila, Massimo. "Bellini cent'anni dopo." *Nuova antologia di scienze, lettere ed arti* 70 (May 1935): 100ff. AP37.N8. Republished in *Cent'anni di musica moderna*. Milan, 1944. 2d ed., Turin: EDT Musica, 1981, pp. 29–38. ML196.M6 1981.

A noted Italian Verdi scholar, Mila is writing at the time of the centenary of Bellini's death. He speaks against the revival of Bellini's music just because of the centenary, for "the true genius of Bellini, more than any other composer, requires from the critic both an intensive and extensive feeling and knowledge."

234. ——. *Cent'anni di musica moderna*. Turin: EDT Musica, 1981. ISBN 88–70630–20-X. ML196.M6 1981.

New edition of a collection of essays first published in 1944. 212 pp. The author has supplied a new preface. Essays include a discussion of the lives and musical styles of Bellini, Rossini, Wagner, Respighi, Stravinsky, and others.

235. Miozzi, Dario. "Le celebrazioni belliniane del 1935: Un modello di strategia culturale del fascismo." *Vincenzo Bellini nel secondo centenario della nascita* (2004): 633–77. See item 406.

Explores such topics as the myths of Fascism, and the "La forza del 'Genio italico'." Discusses the highly romanticized movie *Casta diva* made in this era by Carmine Gallone, an example of cinema as "l'idolatria mussoliniana." A large bibliography on Fascism and a list of Bellini performances and publications from 1935.

236. Monaldi, Guido. *Vincenzo Bellini*. Milan: Sonzogno, 1935. ML410.B44 M6.

Part of the series *Gli uomini illustri*. 126 pp.

237. Munzone, Sebastiano. *Bellini attende ancora il suo biografo?* Catania: Edizione "Unica," [1937]. ML410.B44 M8.

A provocative title: "Is Bellini still awaiting his biography?" The author had been interested in Bellini for thirty years and this publication includes some of his earlier comments and observations. Deals with various aspects, such as singers and the publication of scores.

238. *Omaggio a Bellini nel primo centenario dalla sua nascita*. Ed. G. Giuliano. Catania: Maimone, 1901. ML410.B44 C3.

Copy in Museo belliniano. 388 pp. Contributions by several authors. Chapter 1 deals with biography and works and includes facsimiles of autographs. There is a genealogical chart of the Bellini family on p. 48.

Chapter 2 treats the modern reputation of Bellini, including poems, tributes, letters. Orazio Viola's original "Bibliografia belliniana" comprises approximately the last fifty pages. See item 14.

239. Pannain, Guido. "Vincenzo Bellini, Saggio critico." *Rassegna Musicale* 8 (1935): 1–14, 100–13, 174–82, 236–377. ML5.R18. Rpt. in Pannain, *Ottocento musicale italiano: Saggi e note*. Milan: Edizioni Curci, 1952, pp. 16–48. ML290.4.P3; and in Della Corte and Pannain, *Vincenzo Bellini: Il carattere morale, i caratteri artistici*. Turin: G.B. Paravia, 1935, pp. 77–123. ML410.B44 C6. See item 225.

Discusses Bellini's musical training and influences, his development, provides an analysis and description of his operas, with details of self-borrowings.

240. Patti, Ercole. *Diario siciliano: alla ricerca della felicità*. 5th ed. Milan: Bompiana, 1975. Originally published 1901. PQ4385.A83 D5 1975.

On pp. 111–16 describes a moving visit to the house where Bellini was born, now the Museo belliniano. See Salvatore Enrico Failla, *Bellini Vincenzo in Catania* (see item 128), for an extensive quotation from Patti.

241. Pizzetti, Ildebrando. "Hommage a Bellini." *Revue musicale* 156 (1935): 39–43. ISSN 0768–1593. ML5.R613.

Homage by one of the most important figures for reviving interest in Bellini through his 1915 essay (see item 466), and an opera composer in his own right. Pizzetti's homage begins by stating that of composers of any era and any country no one would have been more suitable to set a tragedy by Sophocles or Aeschylus than Bellini. Deems Bellini a genius who captures the essence of music, which is emotion and feeling, but whose music is also much more than that. Discusses particulars of Bellini's style in terms of his contemporaries and successors.

242. ——, ed. *Vincenzo Bellini, l'uomo, le sue opere, la sua fama*. Milan: Fratelli Treves, 1936. ML410.B44 P58.

Preface by Pizzetti. This volume includes a number of illustrations, including the young Bellini, a painting by F. Maldarelli now in the Museo belliniano; portraits of several of Bellini's teachers such as Tritto, Zingarelli, Raimondi, and Pietro. Essays include the following:

- Luisa Cambi, "La fanciullezza e l'adolescenza";
- Andrea Della Corte, "Le prime opere." The first five operas, not discussed in chronological order;
- Gianandrea Gavazzeni, "Spiriti e forme della lirica belliniana";
- Carl Holl, "Bellini in Germania." History of Bellini reception in Germany, beginning with Wagner in 1837 but only going up to Felix Mottl, who presented a production of *Norma* at Karlsruhe in 1891. Holl

spends more time discussing Italian opera history in general, rather than Bellini specifically;

- Edward J. Dent, "Bellini in Inghilterra." Dent draws on various nineteenth-century British memoirs: Henry Chorley, Lord Mount Edgcumbe, George Hogarth, Lady Morgan, from which he reproduces a number of extracts;
- Jean Chantavoine, "Bellini a Parigi." Performance history of Bellini's operas at the Théâtre-Italien during the first half of the nineteenth century, reaction in Paris to Bellini's death (poems written, the fashionable sculptor Dantan goes to Puteaux to make the death mask, the funeral ceremony);
- Adelmo Damerini, "Bellini e la critica del suo tempo." See item 2.

243. Rapisarda, A. *Vita di Bellini*. Turin, 1925. See item 218.

244. Ricca, Vincenzo. *Il centenario di* Norma. *Vincenzo Bellini: Impressioni e ricordi con documenti inedite*. Catania: Giannotta, 1932. ML410.B44 R5.

Considered the nadir of Bellini "scholarship." The lawyer Ricca presents a number of "unpublished" letters of Bellini—irretrievably lost—all of which are undoubtedly spurious. Presents no acknowledgements or verification for them and their style bears nothing in common with what we know of Bellini's authentic letters. As Frank Walker notes: "The love-letter from Bellini to Giuditta [Turina] published by Ricca is a forgery, as are all the other 'unpublished documents' in his book. They were rightly excluded by Luisa Cambi from the *Epistolario*." Illustrations of the women in Bellini's life: Fumaroli, Grisi, Malibran, and others.

After writing about Bellini's family, the author presents well over a hundred pages on the following topics: "Gli amori di Vincenzo Bellini"; "Il vero primo amore di Bellini: Maria Politi"; Maddalena Fumaroli, Giuditta Grisi, Giuditta Turina, la Malibran, Giuditta Pasta, Donizzetti [*sic*], Florimo, Beethoven, Chopin, Wagner. Then the operas are discussed in the Appendix—"Il centenario di *Bianca e Gernando*," etc.

245. Sbertoli, Vincenzo Luigi. *Vincenzo Bellini nella luce dell'arte e dell'amore*. Naples: Tipografia Editrice U. Giardini, 1936.

A copy is found in the Museo belliniano, subtitled "The brief lives and the immortal works of the composer Vincenzo Bellini and the painter Raffaello Santi, both of whom through friendly fate given the gift of eternal youth." A laudatory poem in eleven cantos, written in July of 1935.

246. Tiby, Ottavio. "Vincenzo Bellini." In *Rassegna italiana politica, letteraria e artistica* 204 (May 1935); separate copy publ. Rome: Edizione della *Rassegna Italiana*, 1935. AP37.R17.

Separate copy in Museo belliniano. 7 pp. Discusses Bellini's melodic writing, making the point that it is like no other composer's and deeming it of a deeply "pathetic" nature, embodying the dramatic essence of the scene. States that both Bellini and Beethoven "liberated" melody from conventional usage.

247. Torrefranca, Fausto. "Il mio Bellini." *A Vincenzo Bellini. Bollettino dei Musicisti, Mensile del Sindicato Fascista Musicisti* 2/3 (December 1934): 65–66.

Presentation of a concept already put forth in *Vita musicale dello spirito* (see item 248), the idea of polyphonic nature of Bellini's vocal writing, the concerted scenes.

248. ——. *La vita musicale dello spirito*. Turin: Bocca, 1910, pp. 241, 376–77.

An examination of the nature of Bellini's melodies. See item 247.

249. Voss, Paul. *Vincenzo Bellini*. Florence, 1901.

One of the few general studies of Bellini in German, preceded by Neumann (1854) and followed by Oehlmann nearly three-quarters of a century later. Discusses views of Schopenhauer (*Die Welt als Wille und Vorstellung*) and Wagner in terms of Bellini, especially the opera *Norma*.

250. Zoffoli, Giuseppe. *Per Vincenzo Bellini, dalle note della Commemorazione fatta al Giardino d'Italia il 16 maggio 1935*.

Commemorative, laudatory publication on the centenary of the composer's death. 8 pp. Copy found in Museo belliniano. Begins with the words: "E questo, Vincenzo Bellini, genio autentico, nato in terra di paradiso per cantar laudi divine d'ogni cosa terrena, onde innalzarle fine al Cielo."

Note: Additional items published during this period include:

251. Arenaprimo, G. "Bellini a Messina." In *Omaggio a Bellini nel primo centenario dalla sua nascità*. Ed. G. Giuliano, pp. 245ff. Catania: Maimone, 1901. See item 238.

252. Barblan, Guglielmo. "Bellini nel passato e nel presente." *Rassegna dorica; cultura e cronaca musicale* 6 (1935): 189–94. ML5.R145.

253. Barini, G. "Noterelle belliniane." *Rivista musicale italiana* 9, fasc. 1. Turin, 1902. ISSN 0029–6228. ML5.R8.

254. De Angelis, Giuseppe Tito. *Bellini: la vita, l'uomo, l'artista*. Brescia, 1935.

255. Gritti, A. *Discorso celebrativo nel I centenario della nascita di Vincenzo Bellini*. Palermo, 1901; and *Vincenzo Bellini*. Vercelli, 1936.

256. Heitti, Aldo. *Vincenzo Bellini*. Vercelli, 1936.

257. Malherbe, Henry. "Le Centenaire de la mort de Bellini." *Le Temps* (February 13, 1935).

258. Reina, Calcedonio. *Vincenzo Bellini (1801–1835)*. Catania, 1902. Later edition as *Il cigno catanese. Bellini, la vita e le opere*. Catania: Casa Editrice "Etna," 1935. ML410.B44 R4 1935.

259. Sabatini, G. *Vincenzo Bellini*. Catanzaro, 1935.

260. Samazeuilh, Gustave. "Pour Vincenzo Bellini." *Le Temps* (May 10, 1935).

261. Vigo-Fazio, Lorenzo. *Bellini anedottico*. 2d ed. Catania: Editio dell' Autore, 1935. ML410.B44 V5 1935a.

BIOGRAPHICAL AND CHARACTER STUDIES AFTER CA. 1935

262. Adamo, Maria Rosario and Friedrich Lippmann. *Vincenzo Bellini*. Turin: Edizione RAI Radiotelevisione Italiana, 1981. ML410.B44 A43 1981.

Two notable Bellini scholars, really two separate books. Adamo's three-hundred page scholarly biography contains four chapters: Catania, Napoli, Milano, and Parigi. This work is based on and presents numerous quotations from Bellini's letters and contemporary reviews. Adamo acknowledges her debt to Pastura's authoritative study (1959, see item 271) but adds new information from a variety of sources. She sympathizes with Bellini over the Giuditta Turina affair, whereas Weinstock (see item 279) takes Turina's side. Adamo believes, along with Pastura, that the letter to Agostino Gallo was a précis of what Bellini related to him in conversation. Many plates of manuscript facsimiles, portraits, set designs. Two autograph pages of sketches by Bellini.

The second part is an enlargement of Lippmann's *Vincenzo Bellini und die italienische Opera seria seiner Zeit* (1969, see item 343), revised and published in Italian, followed by a current discography compiled by Luigi Bellingardi. Lippmann traces the Romantic libretto from its Metastasian roots, treats the aria as the basic feature of Italian opera, and extensively analyses the nature of Bellini's melodies. As Budden points out, "Lippmann has nothing to say about Bellini's ensembles and orchestration and not much about his use of harmony. He also fails to mention a stylistic trait that struck Bellini's contemporaries most forcefully—his abundant use of appoggiaturas on strong beats in order to give poignancy of expression." Drawing from Bellini's letters, Lippmann demonstrates that the letter to Gallo is completely erroneous: Bellini did not work in that way at all, his melodies were written independently of text and dramatic situation.

Also given is an appendix with the dates of the premieres and the original casts, the principal manuscript and printed sources, and a list of Bellini's self-borrowings.

Review: Julian Budden in *Music & Letters* 64/3–4 (1983): 244–46.

263. Brunel, Pierre. *Vincenzo Bellini*. Paris: Fayard, 1981. ISBN 22–13002–63–5. ML410.B44 B7.

Modern standard life-and-works study in French. Shows an appreciation for Bellini's works. Based on previous biographies and new archival work, the result of research in French libraries. Final chapter is a summary and assessment: "Bellini, Romantic Musician," pp. 353–76. Appendices include "Bellini Today," catalogue of works, bibliography, discography, indices of names and musical works, personalia.

264. Fraccaroli, Arnaldo. *Vincenzo Bellini*. Milan: A. Mondadori, 1942. ML3925.B45 F7.

Contains forty plates, including facsimiles.

265. Galatopoulos, Stelios. *Bellini: Life, Times, Music, 1801–1835*. London: Sanctuary Press, 2002. ISBN 1–86074–405–2.

The most recent attempt at an integrated life and musical study of Bellini. The author has examined the correspondence and writings by contemporary critics but his musical analysis of the operas is unsophisticated. A number of spelling errors, particularly of names. As Law stated in his review, "As a relaxed, unbuttoned narrative the book will do well enough, but the serious and scholarly study that we need is still to seek."

Reviews: Michael Kennedy in the *Sunday Telegraph* (London), 4 August 2002; Richard Law in *Opera* 53/12 (December 2002): 1531.

266. Gallotta, Bruno. *Invito all'ascolta di Bellini*. Milan: Mursia, 1997.

Small paperback. 204 pp. Begins with a parallel chronology between the important events in Bellini's life and career and political, cultural, historical, and musical events. Provides a critical analysis of each opera and puts it into a wider literary and historical context. Other sections include a discussion of the critics, an "essential" brief bibliography, a catalogue of the operas, a discography, an index of names, and an index of works.

267. Musumeci, Caterina. *Fortuna di Bellini in Italia*. Tesi di Laurea, Università degli Studi di Catania. Typescript, Catania, 1969–70.

Typescript carbon copy found in Museo belliniano, where the author did her research. Divided into five chapters: "Infancy and Musical Adolescence"; "Career in the Theaters"; "Death and Transferral of the Body"; "Reputation of the Operas for Posterity"; "The Museo belliniano, Monuments, Squares." 216 pp. but only a bit over half of each page is covered with text. Only a few footnotes; mainly secondary research although the author does quote from letters and some nineteenth-century periodicals.

268. Neri, Carmelo. *Bellini e Giuditta Turina: Storia documentata di un amor felice*. Catania: Prova d'autore, 1998. ISBN 88–86140–26–6. ML410.B44 N47 1998.

Bellini's relations with women, focusing on the married Giuditta Turina.

269. Oehlmann, Werner. *Vincenzo Bellini*. Freiburg im Breisgau: Atlantis-Verlag, 1974. ISBN 37–61104–47–2. ML410.B44 O35.

Oehlmann's monograph, one of the few treatments of Bellini in German, provides a general synthesized overview. Intends to give a view of Bellini through the eyes of his contemporaries, although lack of space prohibits him from doing this in any detail. The strength of the book is Oehlmann's discussion of the operas. Orrey states that Oehlmann "writes sympathetically and often glowingly about his operas." No music examples or works-list. A brief bibliography that omits important works such as Cambi's *Epistolario* (see item 288), Pastura's *Bellini secondo la storia* (see item 271) and the important work of Friedrich Lippmann. This has led to several errors on Oehlmann's part, some of them pointed out by Orrey. Illustrations, including facsimiles.

Review: Leslie Orrey in *Music & Letters* 56/2 (1975): 204–05.

270. Orrey, Leslie. *Bellini*. Master Musicians Series. London: Dent, 1969; New York: Farrar, Straus & Giroux, 1969. ISBN 04–60031–32–5. ML410. B44 O8.

Synthesized view of his life and career, paying special attention to the literary sources of the libretti. Restricted by limitations of space dictated by the series of which it is a part. As Rosenthal remarks, noting that the last book about Bellini in English was Lloyd's from 1909 [Rosenthal says 1908]: "We have certainly come a long way. Who, in the inter-war years, would ever have thought that Bellini would be classed as a 'Master Musician' in this country?" Rosenthal finds it unfortunate that Orrey's monograph is far too short, "so sketchy on the musical side" and "far too kind to his subject," for Bellini was "hardly a moral person." Orrey is in fact quite objective about Bellini the man.

Klein wishes that Orrey had been able to delve deeper into *Beatrice di Tenda*, which Bellini himself believed to be the equal of *Norma*, and which has been treated unjustly ever since its unsuccessful premiere. Orrey considers *La sonnambula* to be "arguably" Bellini's best opera. Greenspan finds this a sympathetic treatment but the musical discussion is marred by Orrey's failing to consult the autographs. There are even some errors in plot.

Appendices: Calendar; Catalogue of Works; Personalia; Bibliography; Index. A number of illustrations: Bellini, Pasta, Grisi, Malibran, Turina, Lablache, stage design of *La sonnambula* by Sanquirico.

Reviews: Harold Rosenthal in *Opera* 20 (July 1969): 615; John W. Klein, *Music & Letters* 50/4 (1969): 491–95; Charlotte Greenspan in *Notes* 26/3 (1970): 517–19.

271. Pastura, Francesco. *Bellini secondo la storia*. Parma: Guanda, 1959. ML410.B44 P38.

Important authoritative critical study based on documents. It has been called "magisterial." As Leslie Orrey stated: "Pastura is to Bellini what Thayer is to Beethoven or Spitta to Bach." In this work "the facts, known and conjectured, of Bellini's life are sifted thoroughly, and earlier biographies and studies examined with scrupulous care." Reproduces in full many letters as well as a catalogue of the works. Music examples. Extensive footnote citations. Illustrations interspersed. Treats each of the operas, along with periods of life and career (e.g., "Il viaggio a Londra") in a separate chapter. Deals with the errors in Emilia Branca's *Memoirs* (see item 335). Contains "Bibliografia essenziale." No index, which makes its 700 closely printed pages and twenty-one long chapters somewhat hard to navigate. See item 401, Appendices.

272. ——. *Vincenzo Bellini*. Turin: Società Editrice Internazionale, 1959.

A more popular presentation of Bellini's life and works than item 271. Presents documentation as end notes, pp. 441–47. Plates of illustrations such as Bellini's birthplace, the Bellini monument in Catania, and others, are interspersed. Chapters, with many subheadings, include: "Catania 1767–1801"; "Figlio di Don Rosario Bellini"; "Ingresso in una scuola gloriosa"; "Contrappunto, politica e ragazzate"; "Un amore fatto di musica (Maddalena Fumaroli)"; "*Adelson e Salvini*, primo saggio operistico," and others. Thirty-six chapters in all.

273. Rosselli, John. *The Life of Bellini*. Musical Lives Series. Cambridge: Cambridge University Press, 1996. ISBN 05–21462–27–4 (hardcover); 05–21467–81–0 (paperback). ML410.B44 R77 1996.

The stated aim of this monograph, part of the Musical Lives Series, is "to provide a short critical biography of Bellini, seen in his historical context." This series attempts to integrate the discussion of the music into the biographical thread; in this case, meaningful discussion of the music is minimal. The author has reexamined and reevaluated published sources; new archival research has provided material, presented in the appendix, on three people with whom Bellini was associated in Paris: Auguste Aymé, S. Levy, and Mlle Olivier.

Rosselli challenges the published evidence we have of Bellini's life and various myths about the composer, some of which have been based on Heinrich Heine's famous description of him and much of which has been perpetuated by Bellini's great friend Francesco Florimo, who suppressed, rearranged, and faked epistolary and other evidence. As David Gutman states, "The unreliability of the letters becomes something of an *idée fixe* with Rosselli so that later parts of the book can read like a tutorial on historical musicology—all somewhat ironic given that he cannot but draw personal conclusions from the same sources." There is no bibliography *per se* but a section "For Further Reading," in which the author also discusses preferred recordings to a limited extent.

Reviews: John Steane in *The Musical Times* 138 (October 1997): 36; David Gutman in *Gramophone* 75 (September 1997): 20, 22; Julian Budden in *Opera* 48 (July 1997): 822–23; Stephen A. Willier in *Opera Quarterly* 15/1 (Winter 1999): 98–101.

274. Sangiorgi, Giuseppe. *L'Università adriatica in "Camicia nera."* Bari: Città di Castello, 1942.

A Fascist publication, glorifying Bellini as an Italian. Chapter 6, pp. 111–27, is the "Celebrazione del Cigno di Catania," a celebration held at the Reale Università di Bari upon the first anniversary of Bellini's death. Reprinted from *"Nicia" Rivista Medica d'Arte e Varietà* 3 (1936). Speaks of Bellini as a purely lyrical composer, not a "tecnico" because he did not choose to be so. The role of the "Mediterranean soul" upon Bellini's art is pursued.

275. Tiby, Ottavio. *Vincenzo Bellini. I maestri della musica*. Turin: Edizione Arione, 1938. ML410.B44 T5.

A life-and-works survey. Includes facsimiles and music examples.

276. Tintori, Giampiero. *Bellini*. Part of "La musica" series. Milan: Rusconi Libri, 1983. ML410.B44 T56 1983.

A complete survey of life and works, each analysed individually and with complete plot synopses. Appendix: "L'altro Bellini" by Quirico Principe; bibliography and index.

Bellini's life is presented in four large chapters with numerous subsections: "Maturità di un esordio"; "Scenario e mondo interiore"; "Gli anni aurei"; "Ultimo atto." Works-list.

277. Tomasi, Gioacchino Lanza. *Vincenzo Bellini*. Palermo: Sellerio, 2001. ISBN 88–38917–40–X.

Life and works divided into chapters that chronologically trace places where Bellini lived and worked, his operatic output, and women with whom he was involved. Begins by stating that the composer "came into the world" on November 13, 1801. No source citations, music examples, or index, but a fairly extensive bibliography. Attempts to provide an integrated continuity of his life and works with an assessment of the latter. 178 pp.

278. Walker, Frank. "Giuditta Turina and Bellini." *Music & Letters* 40 (January 1959): 19–34. ISSN 0027–4224. ML5.M64; Eng. trans. of "Amore e amori nelle lettere di Giuditta, Bellini e Florimo." *La Scala* 112 (1959): 13–23.

Most of what was known about Bellini's love affair with Giuditta Turina at the time this article was written came from the composer's own letters. Cambi's edition (see item 288) includes thirteen letters from Bellini to Turina but these are formal and unrevealing, often ending with greetings to Turina's husband. Bellini wrote many letters to Florimo about the affair and even though Florimo destroyed much of Bellini's controversial correspondence, Walker writes, "Enough material survives, however, for the reconstruction of the history of the affair, in broad outline and partly in detail. Gaps in the story have been filled in and further details, more or less credible, added by various biographers."

Discusses the issue of whether Bellini "served merely as a pretext for a desired breach with her husband." See p. 25 of this article for Walker's conclusions about this and several other issues involving Giuditta Turina. Walker also discusses Bellini's nature, noting that his letters "reveal a much tougher personality [than writers such as Heine had drawn], ambitious, intent on his career and his fame ('la mia gloria'), suspicious of other people's motives, without generosity of mind towards possible rivals, egoistic and calculating even in his love-affairs." Raffaello Barbiera, *Immortali e dimenticati* (Milan, 1901), is cited by Walker as providing background on Giuditta's husband, Ferdinando.

279. Weinstock, Herbert. *Vincenzo Bellini: His Life and His Operas*. New York: Knopf, 1971. ISBN 03–94416–56–2. ML410.B44 W4.

The first full-length biography in English, full of detailed information presented in text, notes, and appendices. Text divided into two large parts, the life and the compositions. Weinstock found Bellini the man unattractive and wondered if he could spend the time with him it would take to write a biographical study and also deal with him fairly. The *Life* draws extensively on two landmark Italian publications: Cambi's *Epistolario*, 1943 (see item 288), and Pastura's *Bellini secondo la storia*, 1959 (see item 271). Provides copious documentation, drawing on letters (large parts of many of them given in English translation) and contemporary newspapers and journals. Extensive notes to each chapter at end of volume. Presents for the first time in English Romani's posthumous tribute to Bellini from the *Gazzetta ufficiale piemontese* of Turin, October 21, 1835 (see item 192).

Weinstock stumbles somewhat in his musical analysis of the works. They are presented in alphabetical rather than chronological order, which destroys a sense of their connections. Many facts are given but the information is not exhaustive, for example in terms of locations of musical sources and performance histories. There is a good, comprehensive listing of Bellini's non-operatic compositions. Each scene of every opera is analysed but there are many changes of tonality overlooked; Weinstock is content to state what key each scene begins in, ignoring the coloristic, dramatic painting achieved through sometimes far-flung modulations. Orrey: "in a volume that claims to be a 'critical' biography (according to the dust jacket) one expects something more than just a scene-by-scene description of the operas. There is so much that could have been said about Bellini's (and Romani's) stagecraft; about his musical architecture, about his orchestration."

Ultimately, full of facts and difficult to read. James Ringo concludes: "Weinstock's book is fussy and overcomplicated to the point of folly. The story itself becomes lost in the ungainly tangle of quoted source material. A biography both graceful and scholarly is urgently needed for a musician of Bellini's stature; unfortunately, this is not it." Winton Dean agrees and gives a list of errors and confused thinking.

Seventeen appendices, including: Bellini's Baptismal Certificate; Bellini's Death Certificate; Ferdinand Hiller's Impressions of Bellini and His Music; Sketches of Incomplete Scenes in the Museo Belliniano at Catania; *Beatrice di Tenda*: Unpublished Passages and Variants, and others. Thirty-five illustrations, including sets by Sanquirico and portraits of Bellini (but are they all really of him?). Bibliography current for date of publication. Detailed index.

Reviews: William Shank, in *Library Journal* 97/2 (January 1972): 200–01; Leslie Orrey in *Music & Letters* 53/4 (1972): 454–57; James Ringo in *Opera News* 36 (January 22, 1972): 36; Winton Dean in *Musical Times* 113 (August 1972): 772–73.

Note: Publications in this category from this period also include:

280. Pedrocchi, G. "Natura ideale di Bellini." *Rassegna musicale* 15/7–8 (1942): 229–31. ML5.R1.

5

Letters and Documents

In connection with the November 2001 anniversary of Bellini's birth, the Commissione Epistolario e Centro di Documentazione "Vincenzo Bellini" has been formed with the goal of publishing a critical edition of Bellini's letters. See item 318.

281. Abbiati, Franco. "L'incorreggibile Vincenzillo." *La Scala* (March 1950): 20–21.

 Introduces previously unpublished documents.

282. *L'Album Bellini*, ed. Francesco Florimo and Michele Scherillo. Naples: Stabilimento Tipografico Tocco, 1886; modern edition D. Miozzi, ed. Catania: Sanfilippo, 2001. See item 394. ML410.B44 F61.

283. *L'Album pianistico Bellini: Alla memoria di Vincenzo Bellini. Album per pianoforte*, ed. D. Miozzi. Catania: Maimone, 2001. See item 290.

284. Alfieri, Gabriella. "L'Album Bellini: un 'testo misto' tra lingua usuale e stile rituale." In *Francesco Florimo e l'Ottocento musicale*. Ed. R. Cafiero and M. Marino, pp. 149–215. Reggio Calibria: Jason, 1999. See item 955.

 The *Album Bellini* that Florimo compiled in Bellini's memory in 1876.

285. Amore, Antonino. *Vincenzo Bellini: Vita. Studi e ricerche*. Catania: N. Giannotta, 1894. See item 144.ML410. B44 A6.

 Includes letters written to Bellini, including correspondence from Ricordi, Milan; see Appendix.

286. Barbiera, Raffaello. *Grandi e piccole memorie*. Florence, 1910.

 Includes a letter from Bellini to Countess Virginia Martini of April 7, 1835, not in Cambi's *Epistolario*. See item 288. Printed in this volume, pp. 484–87, this letter refers to Giuditta Turina and her possible involvement with Count Neipperg. Walker (see item 324) tells us that Barbiera's writings are "based, in about equal measure, on documents and on gossip."

287. Cambi, Luisa. "Bellinio, un pacchetto di autografi." In *Scritti in onore di Luigi Ronga*. Milan: Riccardo Ricciardi, 1973, pp. 53–90. ML55.R63 1973.

A presentation of letters that came her way since Cambi published all the letters that could be found thirty years previously. See item 288. Some of those presented here had already been published elsewhere but Cambi reprinted them for corrections and to put them into context. Cambi notes that Bellini's epistolary style is extraordinary for the frequency and continuity of correspondence with Florimo, that he writes in a conversational, at times ungrammatical, style, and that his letters, more than most of his contemporaries, provide insights into his life and career.

Each of the twenty-one documents that Cambi presents is preceded by extensive background and critical commentary that, combined with the actual letters, helps to fill in certain elements of the Bellini biography.

288. ——, ed. *Vincenzo Bellini: epistolario*. Verona: Mondadori, 1943.

Landmark scholarly collection of the letters. Incomplete, acknowledged by the author: "This collection is not and cannot be complete; it represents perhaps a small part of the letters that he wrote." She includes, however, all the letters known at the time, omitting the ones that are most certainly spurious. Somewhat different from Pastura's previous collection. See item 311. Begins with various documents, e.g., "Atto di matromonio Bellini-Ferlito" and "Atto di nascita di Vincenzo Bellini." Ends with Bellini's death notice, autopsy report, letters from Mercadante to Florimo about Bellini's death. Table of contents gives the recipient and date of each letter.

All letters provided with explanatory footnotes. Includes the "Letter to Agostino Gallo," but Cambi doubts its authenticity, indicated in a footnote.

With nine illustrations supplementing the text, including Bellini as student at conservatory; Bellini around 1830; Bellini's death mask; facsimiles of letters.

289. Caroccia, Antonio. "*La corrispondenza salvata": lettere di maestri e compositori a Francesco Florimo—Edizione critica*. Tesi di laurea, Università degli Studi di Pavia—Scuola di Paleografia e Filologia musicale di Cremona, 2001–2.

An important step toward the planned critical edition of the letters.

290. ——. "Florimo e *L'Album pianistico Bellini*." *Vincenzo Bellini nel secondo centenario della nascita* (2004): 57–76. See item 406.

The *Album pianistico* was published in 1878 in monthly installments by the Associazione Musicale Industriale di Napoli. Caroccia's article has two Appendices: (1) Copia autentica dell'Istrumento di vendita di Musica interceduto fra. . . . Francesco Florimo e la Ditta Tito di Giovanni Ricordi di Milano; and (2) Lettere per l'Album Bellini from Jules Benedict, Hans von Bülow, Giovanni Bottesini, et alia. See item 283 above.

291. ——. "Lettere inedite a Francesco Florimo per il monumento a Bellini." In *Francesco Florimo e l'Ottocento musicale*. Ed. R. Cafiero and M. Marino, pp. 33–63. Reggio Calibra: Jason, 1999. See item 955.

The copious exchange of previously unpublished letters between contributors to the Bellini monument and Florimo at the Naples Conservatory, scrupulously examined and documented by Caroccia.

292. Chisari, Giosuè. "Vincenzo scrive a suo zio Guerrera." *L'Opera* 5 (1970): 28–30.

A letter from Bellini to his Uncle Filippo Guerrera (his father's sister's husband).

293. Conati, Marcello. *L'Opera* 2 (October–December 1968): 100ff.

Conati came across three little known letters of Bellini in a volume printed in Venice (Stabilimento Tipografia Viscentini), entitled *Soccorriamo i poveri bambini rachitici—Strenna 1894—Anno Sesto, a cura del Sac. Mons. Jacopo Bernardi*. One of these is a letter from Como on July 5, 1830, to Giovanni Battista Perucchini in Venice, a Bergamasque dilettante composer of Venetian canzonette.

294. Cottrau, Guglielmo. *Letters d'un Mélomane pour servir de document à l'histoire musicale de Naples de 1829 à 1847*. Naples: A. Morano, 1885. ML290.8.N257.

Cottrau was a Neapolitan-Parisian music publisher and friend of Bellini. This is an epistolary history of music in Naples for the years cited in the title.

295. Damerini, Adelmo. "Lettere di Bellini a Donzelli." *Corriere emiliano—Gazzetta di Parma*, January 9, 1932.

Donzelli was the Italian tenor who created the role of Pollione in *Norma*.

296. De Angelis, Marcello. *Le carte dell'impresario. Melodramma e costume teatrale dell'800*. Florence: Sansoni, 1982. ML1733.4.D4 1982.

Brings to light a letter by Bellini from 1830. Forty-eight pages of plates.

297. Florimo, Francesco. *Bellini: Memorie e lettere*. Florence: G. Barbèra, 1882. Rpt. Florence: G. Barbèra, 1976. ML410.B44 F6.

So much had been written about his friend Bellini since his death, and much of it only more or less true, that Florimo decided to write his memoirs and publish many of Bellini's letters. Unfortunately, as Bellini's *fidus Achates*, Florimo heavily edited Bellini's correspondence—even destroying much of it—and perpetuated certain myths about the composer.

Very few of the letters Bellini must have written to Florimo between March 14, 1829, and a letter from Paris dated February 14, 1834, exist. Florimo must have destroyed many or given away snippets of some of the letters from this five-year period, the very time when Bellini was having his affair with Giuditta Turina, a married woman. Letters to others during this period help to fill in our knowledge of Bellini's life. The first 82 pages comprise a biography; Florimo then lists manuscripts of Bellini held at the Naples Conservatory library; "Dichiarazioni ed aneddoti"; the report of the transferral of Bellini's remains from Paris to Catania in 1876, pp. 149–243; Letters, pp. 285–512; and Romani's "Necrologia," pp. 513–15. Most of the letters are addressed to Florimo, but he also includes letters by Bellini to Romani, Carlo Pepoli, Filippo Santocanale, Guglielmo Cottrau, and others.

298. Ganguzza, Niny. "Inediti belliniani: Agosto 1830—*La straniera* a Bergamo." *L'Opera* 5/16–17 (1970).

Copy in Museo belliniano. Includes a letter by Bellini from Como written on August 24, 1830, to Count Ottavio Tasca in Bergamo concerning the performance there of *La straniera*.

299. Lippmann, Friedrich. "Belliniana: nuovi documenti." *Il melodramma italiano dell'ottocento: studi e ricerche per Massimo Mila*. Ed. G. Pestelli, pp. 281–317. Turin: G. Eunaudi, 1977. ML1733.4.M4.

Discusses newly-found Bellini documents in European and North American collections: the Pierpont Morgan Library, the New York Public Library, and the Toscanini collection, all in New York; in Europe from various collections in Italy (Siena, Naples, Genoa) and in possession of H.C. Robbins Landon in Vienna. Part 1 of this article is devoted to transcriptions of various letters: first is a letter dated February 13, 1828, to Francesco Florimo, which places it between letters XIII and XIV in Cambi's *Epistolario* (see item 288); then a letter from September 1, 1831, to Giuditta Pasta, already published in Ferranti-Giulini's *Giuditta Pasta e i suoi tempi* (see item 777), but full of errors that Lippmann has taken pains to correct. Letter 3 is from Bellini to Florimo, dated September 24, 1831; letter 4, dated April 28, 1832, to his uncle Vincenzo Ferlito in Catania, written from Naples. Letter 5 is addressed to Giovanni Ricordi in Milan, from Venice, December 22, 1832; letter 6 is to Pasta, from Paris to Como, dated August 26, 1833. Letter 7, from March 11, 1835, is to Giovanni Ricordi in Milan; letter 8, from June 10, 1825, to Joseph Denza in London; letter 9, from July 24, 1835, to Pasta in Milan; and letter 10, from August 25, 1835, to Giovanni Colleoni in Bergamo.

Part 2 treats autograph manuscripts found in the Istituto Mazzaniano di Genova (the second version of *Bianca e Fernando*); the Toscanini Collection; L'Accademia Chigiana di Siena; Conservatorio Santa Cecilia, Rome (four pages in score of the "Guerra, guerra" chorus from *Norma*); and the Pierpont Morgan Library in New York (the "Sinfonia dell'opera *Ernani*," consisting of eighteen pages; *La sonnambula* sketches, vocal ensembles *a cappella* and with orchestra). In the possession of H.C. Robbins Landon, Vienna, is a manuscript of thirty-two pages, the cover of which bears the printed title: *Studio del Contrappunto [fatto da] Vincenzo Bellini/Napoli 1819. Autografo*. Lippmann notes that from p. 17 until the end the manuscript is in a new hand. All of the above manuscripts are described in detail and music examples are provided.

300. Luzio, Alessandro. "Un amico torinese di Vincenzo Bellini." *Arti della Real Accademia delle Scienze di Torino* 47 (1932): 101ff.

In mid-October 1829 Bellini went to Turin, unacknowledged by his biographers until the publication of this article, which contains seventeen letters written by Bellini between November 3, 1829, and April 29, 1835, to a Torinese friend, Alessandro Lamperi. Luzio believes that Bellini and Lamperi first met in Genoa, while Neri (see item 308) and Weinstock (see item 279) are inclined to believe they indeed met in Turin.

301. Maione, Paologiovanni. "Florimo all'amico Bellini: 'un monumento eterno di sospiri, di slanci e di melodie'." In *Francesco Florimo a Vincenzo Bellini*. Ed. D. Miozzi, pp. 65–122. Catania: Giuseppe Maimone, 2001. See item 305.

Florimo and the Bellini monument.

302. ——. "Le lettere censurate e il culto del collezionismo: Florimo Biografo-Alchimista." *Vincenzo Bellini nel secondo centenario della nascita* (2004): 39–56. See item 406.

The Appendix (pp. 49–56) is "Campionatura delle modifiche appertate da Florimo all'epistolario di Bellini."

303. Mauceri, Marco. "Ancora su *I Puritani* per Napoli: un inedito." *Nuova rivista musicale italiana* 23 (1989): 410–17. ISSN 0029-6228. ML5.N93.

Brings to light a letter not included in Cambi, *Epistolario* (see item 288) from Bellini to Prince d'Ottaviano, written on October 14, 1834, about the "scrittura" offered by the Teatro San Carlo to adapt a version of *I puritani* for that theater. Presents modern transcriptions of the entire document on pp. 415–17. The negotiations were concluded on November 20, when Bellini received a contract from Naples. Mauceri mistakenly gives the date of the Paris premiere of *I puritani* as February 24, 1835, rather than January.

304. Mazzarino, Antonio. "Ancora due lettere di Vincenzo Bellini." *Nuovi annali della facoltà di magistero dell'Università di Messina*. Vol. 2. Rome: Herder Editore, 1975. AS 221.N86.

The two letters are from Bellini on March 21, 1831, to Augusto Lamperi in Turin and from Bergamo to Giuditta Turina at Casalbuttano.

305. Miozzi, D., ed. *Francesco Florimo a Vincenzo Bellini*. Catania: Giuseppe Maimone, 2001.

Recent publication of Florimo-Bellini materials. See item 305.

306. Musto, Dora. "Vincenzo Bellini in due autografi inediti dell'Archivio di Stato di Napoli." *Rassegna degli Archivio di Stato di Napoli* 21 (1961): 351–60.

Extract copy published separately; copy in Museo belliniano. The documents concern Bellini's application to the Naples Conservatory.

307. Neri, Carmelo, ed. *Caro Bellini . . . Lettere edite e inedite a Vincenzo Bellini*, with a preface by Giuseppe Cardillo. Catania: Prova d'Autore, 2001. ISBN 88–86140–90–8.

Letters directed to Bellini on a variety of topics from such people as Domenico Donzelli, Giuditta Pasta, Auber, Adolphe Thiers, Alessandro Lanari, Giovanni Ricordi. Most of the autographs of these letters are found in the Museo belliniano, Catania. Illustrations, Indices.

308. ——, ed. with a preface by Domenico Danzuso. *Lettere di Vincenzo Bellini (1819–1835)*. Palermo: Publisicula Editrice, 1991.

In his introduction, Neri pays homage to Cambi's collection of Bellini's letters (see item 288), "deservedly famous," the edition with the greatest number of letters and presented with the greatest accuracy and richest fund of information. Cambi is no longer in print and naturally some new letters and information have come to light; these are the justifications for this book. Neri is able to add many letters that have not appeared in previous collections—although all of these letters have been published somewhere, sometimes in isolated and currently obscure sources—and insert them in their proper chronological order, thus giving a more unbroken knowledge of Bellini's life and career. Certainly more letters will appear, but it is unlikely that the numerous letters that Bellini wrote to Florimo from March 1829 to March 1834 will ever be recovered. Neri's work is fully annotated with the autograph source of each letter, where it has been published previously, and explanatory footnotes. 309 letters; several facsimiles. Three indices: by the destination of the letters; by theatrical works; by names.

309. Pastura, Francesco. *Bellini secondo la storia*. Parma: Guanda, 1959. ML410.B44 P38.

See item 271. Contains many letters not found in 1935 *Lettere* (see item 311). Printed on pp. 675ff. are several letters written after Bellini's death from Giuditta Turina to Florimo, found in the Naples Conservatory library, that profess her love for Bellini. One of these is given in Frank Walker's *Music & Letters* article, 1959. See item 324. Discusses the arguments for and against the authenticity of the "Letter to Agostino Gallo."

310. ——. "Una lettera di Bellini a Maria Malibran e la storia della prima edizione de *I puritani*." Extract from *Rivista del Comune di Catania*, 1954.

Separate bound copy in Museo belliniano. 6 pp. Pastura writes that in the library of the music conservatory in Brussels there is a letter from Bellini written from Paris on February 27, 1835, to Maria Malibran in Venice. The letter directly involves the complex textual history of *I puritani*, specifically the autograph score found in the Museo belliniano. Bellini expresses interest in getting to know Malibran better; it is not known if Malibran responded to this letter. Pastura provides not only the text but a facsimile of the letter.

311. ——, ed. *Le lettere di Bellini (1819–35)*. First complete edition. Collected, arranged and annotated by Francesco Pastura. Catania: Totalità, 1935. ML410.B44 A2.

Precedes Luisa Cambi's collection (see item 288), which to a great extent superseded it; the contents of each collection, however, is not identical. This is the first "complete" edition of Bellini's letters, in which Pastura attempted to correct some of Florimo's damage and to include previously unpublished letters. Introduction by Pastura, in which he discusses the "umanità di Bellini" and the work of Florimo, which appeared in 1882 (see item 297). Several illustrations, facsimiles. 319 pp.

312. ——. "Lettere inedite di Bellini. Il primo incontro con Rossini avvenne a Milano nel 1829." Extract from *Rivista del Comune di Catania*, 1955.

Separate bound copy in Museo belliniano. 6 pp. Pastura moves the first encounter between Bellini and Rossini from 1827 to 1829. So far, all the major biographies have erred in this. Evidence includes that Rossini was in Paris in 1827 at the time that the two were said to have met; and a letter from Bellini to his uncle Vincenzo Ferlito dated—not by Bellini because the first page is missing—August 28, 1829, provides further evidence. During the summer of 1829 there was a revival of *Il pirata* at the Teatro della Canobbiana and it was then that the two composers met, not during the original production of *Il pirata* at La Scala in Milan. See item 956.

313. ——. "Nuovi importanti documenti assicurati al Museo belliniano." *Catania. Rivista del Comune di Catania* 6 (October–December 1958): 4ff.

Separate bound copy in Museo belliniano. 8 pp. Important new documents acquired by the Museo belliniano in Catania. These include four autograph letters, hitherto unpublished; five notes by Bellini's last attending physician, Dr. Montallegri; and several other documents. Of the letters, two are to Giuditta Turina from the early 1830s when Bellini was in Venice. Pastura gives a descripton and full text for each item and provides several fascimiles.

314. Pepoli, Carlo. *Corrispondenza epistolario del Conte Carlo Pepoli*. Bologna, 1881.

Includes letters to Carlo Pepoli from Bellini.

315. Prunières, Henri. "Bellini épistolier." *Revue musicale* 156 (May 1935): 70–72. ISSN 0768–1593. ML5.R613.

Reveals that Florimo was a "romantic who could not resign himself to present to the public letters so simple, so naive, so natural, so full of errors of syntax and spelling," that he rewrote much of them and left out much that gave them their particular flavor. Thus, Florimo's transgressions have long been known, before the publications of Rosselli's *The Life of Bellini* (see item 273). During this same year (1935), Pastura's collection (see item 311) was published. Prunières gives a general character outline of Bellini without quoting from any of his letters, considering him a pure musician who did not know about much else and who let nothing or no one interfere with his work.

316. Ricca, Vincenzo. *Il centenario di Norma. Vincenzo Bellini: Impressioni e ricordi con documenti inedite*. Catania: N. Giannotta, 1932. ML410.B44 R5.

The "previously unpublished documents" are most certainly spurious. See item 244.

317. Roncaglia, Gino. "Vincenzo Bellini: il musicista, quale appare dal suo epistolario." *Rivista musicale italiana* 1 (1948): 159–77. ISSN 0029–6228. ML5.R8.

Explores what Bellini's letters reveal about him as a musician and as a person: the ability to render in sound what has been suggested to him in his imagination—"the doubts, the torments, the anguish of the creator." They also reveal him to be full of lofty aspirations and clear ideas, hardworking, and responsible. What the letters do not tell us, Bellini's melodies do.

318. Rosselli, John. "Per una edizione critica dell'epistolario belliniano." In *Vincenzo Bellini: Verso l'edizione critica*. Ed. F. Della Seta and S. Ricciardi, pp. 291–96. Florence: Olschki, 2004. See item 493.

Calls for a critical edition of Bellini's letters. Presents various features of the nineteenth-century publication of Bellini's letters, mainly from a negative viewpoint.

319. Rossini, Gioachino. *Lettere di G. Rossini, raccolte ed annotate per cura di Giuseppe Mazzatinti, F. e G. Manis*. Florence: G. Barbèra, 1902. ML410. R8 M3.

Rossini wrote to their mutual friend, Filippo Santocanale, on January 26 of the successful premiere of Bellini's last opera, which he called *I Puritani in Iscozia*. Then, after Bellini's death he wrote to Santocanale on October 3, 1835, describing the funeral. Rossini was instrumental in settling Bellini's estate and having his effects shipped to Catania.

320. Scherillo, Michele. *Belliniana: nuove note*. Milan: Ricordi, 1883.

Includes Bellini's letter to his maternal uncle Vincenzo Ferlito dated Paris, April 1, 1835, which was first published in the *Strenna del Corriere di Catania* in 1882. In this letter Bellini praises Donizetti's *Anna Bolena*.

321. Schlitzer, Franco. "Nell'intimità di Vincenzo Bellini: lettere inedite, sparse o disperse." *Il mattino d'Italia*, June 8, 1951.

A daily newspaper in Italian published in Buenos Aires; may be found at the Library of Congress catalogued as "Newspaper 54."

322. ——. *Tommaso Traetta, Leonardo Leo, Vincenzo Bellini. Notizie e documenti raccolti da Franco Schlitzer in occasione della "IX Settimana Musicale Siennese," 15–22 September 1952. Accademia Musicale Chigiana*. Siena: Casa Editrice Ticci, 1952.

Bellini is treated on pp. 63–88. Schlitzer presents three autographs. An autograph letter from November 17, 1830, helps to fill the gap in letters written by Bellini between August 22, 1830, and January 3, 1831, noted in Cambi (see item 288). This letter is addressed to Alessandro Lamperi; Schlitzer provides a transcription of the letter. Schlitzer also presents an autograph of Romani, "Come è nato *la Sonnambula*," and from *Norma*, the first page of the autograph of the libretto by Romani, on which he wrote: "Come è stata creata la Norma."

323. Tiby, Ottavio. "Una bocciatura di Vincenzo Bellini." *La Scala* 49 (December 1953): 68ff.

Introduces previously unpublished documents.

324. Walker, Frank. "Amore e amori nelle lettere di Giuditta, Bellini e Florimo." *La Scala* 112 (1959): 13–23; English trans. as "Giuditta Turina and Bellini." *Music & Letters* 40 (1959): 18–34. See item 286. ISSN 0027–4224. ML5.M64.

The enormous collection of autograph letters left by Florimo to the Naples Conservatory library is still largely unexplored. Thirty-seven volumes of different sizes, the contents of which were in the process of being catalogued under the then librarian, Signora Anna Mondolfi. (Walker was writing in 1959.) It is still possible to make surprising discoveries. Includes letters from people writing to Florimo about Bellini and Giuditta Turina both before and after Bellini's death, including many letters from Giuditta herself: "[The letters] are completely unknown. They enable us, at last, to see this love-affair from the woman's point of view." Walker presents and translates a number of hitherto unpublished letters.

325. ——. "Lettere disperse e inedite di Vincenzo Bellini." *Rivista del Comune di Catania* 8/4 (October–December 1960): 3–15.

Walker discovered these Bellini letters in the course of his Verdi research at Harvard University, in Italian locations, and in Vienna. Walker considers that almost all known correspondence of Bellini is found in Cambi (see item 288) and Pastura's *Bellini secondo la storia* (see item 271). Here he presents a group of unpublished ones. The first two letters we know of Bellini's are the one to his uncle Vincenzo Ferlito of July 31, 1819, from Naples and to his cousin Christina Guerrera, written on July 19, 1826. Walker now presents the third chronologically, the first we have from Milan, and the sole letter sent to his sister Michela, written on the occasion of her marriage to Ascanio Marziano.

Walker deals with the famous letter to his uncle upon the success of *Il pirata* (October 1827), at this point published only in incomplete form by Cicconetti (1859, see item 145) and Cambi (see item 288). A number of letters that he presents here for the first time were subsequently published in Neri, *Lettere*. See item 308.

326. Weinstock, Herbert. "A Whale of a Story." *Opera* 22/3 (March 1971): 207–08. ISSN 0030–3526. ML5.O66.

Concerns a series of misunderstandings about a reference to a whale (*balena*) made by Bellini in a letter written on August 3, 1830, to Giuditta Turina from Bergamo, where the composer was supervising the staging of *La straniera*. Florimo thought the letter contained a disparaging reference to Donizetti's *Anna Bolena*. Finally in 1934 the mistake was cleared up by Cambi, only to be subsequently muddied by Pastura.

Note: The following are also relevant publications:

327. Cicconetti, Filippo, ed. *Lettere inedite di uomini illustri*. Rome, 1886.

328. Rapisarda, Mario. *Epistolario/a cura di Alfio Tomaselli*. Catania: F. Battiato, 1922. 523 pp.

329. Salvioli, Giovanni (anagram pseudonym of Luigi Lianovosani and Livio Nino Galvani). *Vincenzo Bellini. Lettere inedite/a cura di Giovanni Salvioli*. Milan: Ricordi, 1885. 22 pp.

6

Libretto and Literary Source Studies, Historical and Cultural Studies

Very little epistolary documentation exists between Bellini and his principal librettist, Felice Romani, to show their working methods. Some manuscripts of libretti, especially that of *Norma*, however, show that Bellini took an active part in shaping the libretto, demanding and getting many revisions. Because Bellini insisted upon these changes, Romani's libretti for Bellini are among the best he wrote. The relationship between Bellini and Count Pepoli is better documented, for Bellini practically had to train Pepoli in writing text for the theater.

330. Angermüller, Rudolph. "Grundzüge des nachmetastasianischen Librettos." *Analecta musicologica* 21 (1981): 192–235. ISSN 0585–6086. ML160. S893.

   A discussion of the loosening of the three unities after Metastasio's death, as in Foppa-Zingarelli's *Giulietta e Romeo* of 1796. Discusses Paisiello's *Nina o sia La Pazza per amore*, an important work for Bellini. No discussion of Romani, but good background to early nineteenth-century practices.

331. Arruga, Franca Lorenzo. "Incontri fra poeti e musicisti nell'opera romantica italiana." In *Contributi dell'Istituto di Filologia moderna dell'Università Cattolica di Milano*. Series Storia del Teatro I. Milan: Società Editrice Vita e Pensiero, 1968, pp. 235–90.

   The language of Italian primo ottocento opera, both literary and musical, is examined; the relationship between poet and composer is explored. Good for background and specifically for treatment of Felice Romani.

332. Ashbrook, William. "Donizetti and Romani." *Italica* 64 (Winter 1987): 606–31. PC1068.U6 A5.

An authority on the operas of Donizetti explores the working relationship between Romani, who wrote all of Bellini's mature opera libretti except for *I puritani*, and Donizetti, for whom Romani wrote *Anna Bolena*, *Parisina d'Este*, *Lucrezia Borgia*, and others.

333. Balthazar, Scott L. "Aspects of Form in the Ottocento Libretto." *Cambridge Opera Journal* VII/1 (1995): 23–35. ISSN 0954–5867. ML1699.C36.

Examines the change from the eighteenth-century Metastasian libretto to the primo ottocento's more linearly-conceived ones, which furthered greater unity of action. He discusses elements of this transformation, including the tragic ending, choice of serious subjects, minimizing of moral dilemmas, and the use of large-scale structures (e.g., the *Introduzione* and first-act finales) using examples from the operas of Rossini, Donizetti, and Bellini.

334. Beffort, A. *Alexandre Soumet: sa vie et ses oeuvres*. Luxembourg, 1908.

Soumet was the author of the French play *Norma; ou, L'Infanticide*, upon which Bellini's *Norma* was based.

335. Branca [Romani], Emilia. *Felice Romani ed i più riputati maestri di musica del suo tempo*. Turin: E. Loescher, 1882. ML423.R66 B8.

A biography written seventeen years after the death of her husband Felice Romani that, among other things, deals with Romani's relationships with the composers with whom he worked. She publishes letters to Romani from such names as Rossini, Meyerbeer, Mayr, Bellini, Pacini, Mercadante, Federico Ricci, Andrea Maffei, Cavour, and numerous others. Branca categorically denies the authenticity of the "Letter to Agostino Gallo." Suppresses information that the break between Romani and Bellini was in any way Romani's fault or that he had any shame or regrets about it. Branca claims that Bellini abandoned his setting of *Hernani* due to jealousy over the success of Donizetti's *Anna Bolena*, fearing that *Hernani* could not compete.

Weinstock (see item 279, p. 37) deems it "a blindly partisan biography of [Romani], which ever since [its publication] has been supplying misinformation and tendentious opinion about Romani himself, Rossini, Donizetti, Bellini, and the other composers with whom Romani collaborated."

336. Caswell, Elizabeth Amelia. "Norma in Paris and Gaul." *Opera News* 28 (March 22, 1954): 30–31. ML1.O482. ISSN 0030–3607.

Description of Alexandre Soumet's French tragedy, *Norma*, premiered at the Royal Odéon Theater on April 16, 1831. The ending mad scene was not used by Romani and Bellini. Mentions religious customs of the Druids. Illustrations of the Druid columns at Carnac, a village in southern Brittany.

337. Cella, Franca. "Indagini sulle fonti francesi dei libretti di Vincenzo Bellini." In *Contributi dell'Istituto di filologia moderna dell'Università cattolicoa del S. Cuore*. Vol. V: 449–576. Milan: Società Editrice Vita e Pensiero, 1968.

This essay is second in a series (the first was about Donizetti and the connections of his operas with French theater) attempting to clarify the underlying French elements of Italian opera of the early-nineteenth century. Here, for example, Cella compares passages from Soumet's *Norma* and from *L'Etrangère*, literary sources with passages from Romani's respective Italian libretti.

338. Fischer-Williams, Barbara. "Prince of Sluggards (Felice Romani, librettist of *Norma*, was the pride and despair of Italy's best composers)." *Opera News* (February 17, 1973): 24–25. ISSN 0030–3607. ML1.O482.

Bellini, although he admired Romani deeply, called him "the prince of sluggards" because of his wonted tardiness in finishing libretti. Of the dozens of composers for whom Romani wrote—including Rossini, Mayr, Mercadante, Meyerbeer, Donizetti, and Verdi (only for the unsuccessful *Un giorno di regno*)—Bellini was special among them. Discusses their working relationship and the nature of Romani's work. He wrote nothing original, relying instead on translations or adaptations of other works, many of them French sources. Bellini demanded much rewriting and Romani usually acquiesced. Also explores Romani's roles as poet, journalist, and critic, and his marriage to Emilia Branca, who wrote an unreliable posthumous biography of her husband. See item 335.

339. Galatopoulos, Stelios. "The Romani–Bellini Partnership." *Opera* 23 (November 1972): 970–77. ISSN 0030–3526. ML5.O66.

History of how Bellini and Romani met, worked together to produce seven operas, and their falling-out. No source documentation. Illustrated with reproductions of stage sets: premiere production of *Il pirata*, premiere of *La straniera*, *I Capuleti* at La Fenice, 1830, *Norma* at La Scala, 1831, *Beatrice di Tenda*, Venice, 1833. Author does not identify which scene each design represents.

340. Gioviale, Ferdinando. "Idilli imperfetti. La linea drammaturgica *Sonnambula-Puritani*." *Vincenzo Bellini et la France* (2007): 185–97. See item 404.

The scenic element in Bellini's last several operas, music vis-à-vis libretto. Quotes Rosselli that *Puritani* is weaker than *Norma* or *Sonnambula.* Includes views by Schiller, Kant, Hugo, Schopenhauer, and Wagner.

341. Goldin, Daniela. "Aspetti della librettistica italiana fra 1770 e 1830." *Analecta musicologica* 21 (1982): 128–91. ISSN 0585–6086. ML160. S893.

Not much on Bellini specifically, certainly not his mature works, but good background up to that point.

342. Lippmann, Friedrich. "Der italienische Vers und der musikalische Rhythmus. Zum Vernältnis von Vers und Musik in der italienische Oper des 19. Jahrhunderts, mit einem Rückblick auf die 2. Hälfte des 18. Jahrhunderts." *Analecta musicologica* 12 (1973): 253–369; 14 (1974): 324–410; 15 (1975): 298–333. ML160.S893. ISSN 0585–6086. Italian trans., rev. as *Versificazione italiana e ritmo musicale: rapporti tra verso e musica nell'opera italiana dell'Ottocento*. Naples: Liguori Editore, 1986. ML1733.L5716 1986.

A landmark study of text-setting in Italian opera of the nineteenth century, also with a consideration of the second half of the eighteenth century. Verse forms, musical settings. Numerous music examples, many from the works of Bellini. A previous paper given on this subject was subsequently published as "Zum Verhältnis von Libretto und Musik in der italienischen Opera seria der ersten Hälfte des 19. Jahrhunderts." In *Bericht über dem musikwissenschaftlichen Kongreß Bonn 1970*. Kassel: Bärenreiter, 1973, pp. 162ff.

343. ——. "Vincenzo Bellini und die italienische Opera seria seiner Zeit. Studien über Libretto, Arienformen und Melodik." *Analecta musicologica* 6/1–12 (Cologne and Vienna, 1969): 1–104. ML410.B44 L57. Italian trans. rev. in Adamo and Lippmann, *Vincenzo Bellini*, pp. 313–576 (see item 262).

Along with Cella (see item 337) and Roccatagliati (see items 354–57), one of the most important of the few studies of the early-nineteenth-century Italian opera libretto. Lippmann begins by discussing the opera seria libretto from Metastasio to early Verdi, maintaining that those set by Bellini are paradigmatic. The libretto's connection with Italian and literary romanticism and the character and form of the aria, ca. 1790–1835, are treated. Lippmann considers the work of Rossini, Donizetti, Mayr, Mercadante, and Pacini. Bellini is seen as the principal figure in the development of opera seria after Rossini stopped composing operas. Traces in detail the evolution of the Metastasian exit aria into the scena ed aria of the primo ottocento.

344. Mariano, Emilio. "Felice Romani e il melodramma." In *Opera & Libretto* 1. Ed. G. Folena, et al., pp. 165–209. *Studi di musica veneta*. Florence: L. Olschki, 1990. ISBN 88–22238–25–7. ML1700.O655 1990.

Discusses the "reforms" of the opera libretto suggested and carried out by Romani.

345. Mauceri, Mario. "Inediti di Felice Romani. La carriera del librettista attraverso nuovi documenti degli archivi milanesi." *Nuova rivista musicale italiana* 26/3–4 (July–December 1992): 391–432. ISSN 0029–6228. ML5. N93.

Unpublished documents of Felice Romani from Milanese archives. Includes letters, sketches of parts of several libretti, many reproduced in facsimile.

346. Mioli, Piero. *Bellini: tutti i libretti*. Milan: Newton, 1997.

The complete libretti of Bellini's operas. Contains an introduction by Giovanni Carli Ballola.

347. Morini, Nestore. "La *Norma* e le meticulosità di un revisore." *L'Archiginnasto* 13: 55ff. Bologna, 1918.

Changes made to Romani's libretto for *Norma*, many of them demanded by the composer.

348. Nicastro, Aldo. "Il caso Pepoli e il libretto de *I puritani*." *Nuova rivista musicale italiana* 21/2 (1987): 214ff. ISSN 0029–6228. ML5.N93.

In Paris, Bellini was forced to work for the first time since *Il pirata* without the librettist Felice Romani. Explores the working relationship between Bellini and the librettist of his final opera, Count Carlo Pepoli. Bellini was not shy about making suggestions for improvements to Pepoli and demanding revisions.

349. O'Grady, Deirdre. *The Last Troubadours: Poetic Drama in Italian Opera 1597–1887*. London: Routledge, 1991. ISBN 04–15054–59–1. ML2110. O4 1990.

Traces the history of the Italian opera libretto from its beginnings until the late nineteenth century. Part 1 goes through the French Revolution. Part 2 "pursues a thematic and selective vision of the nineteenth century. Opera is considered as a purveyor of European culture." Topics include: "A Cry for Freedom: High Priests and Patriots," "Of Reason and Delirium" (in which Imogene's madness in Bellini's *Il pirata* is examined), "Jester, Troubadour, and Courtesan."

350. Pepoli, Carlo. *Ricordanze biografiche: corrispondanze epistolari*. Bologna: Fava e Garagnani, 1881. 55 pp.

Pepoli was the librettist for Bellini's final, and only, Parisian opera, *I puritani*. His memoirs and a collection of his letters are presented in this volume.

351. Petrobelli, Pierluigi. "Nota sulla poetica di Bellini: a proposito de *I puritani*." *Muzikoloski Zbornik* 8 (1972): 70–85. English trans. Roger Parker as "Notes on Bellini's Poetics: A propos of *I puritani*." In Pierluigi Petrobelli, *Music in the Theater: Essays on Verdi and Other Composers*. Princeton, N.J.: Princeton University Press, 1994, pp. 162–75. ISBN 06–91091–34-X. ML410.V4 P28 1994.

Genesis of the opera, working relationship with Pepoli; the two versions of the work. Study of autograph documents. An important source for the study of Bellini's final opera.

352. Portinari, Folco. "'Pari siamo!' Io ho la lingua egli ha il pugnale." In *Teoria del melodramma ottocentesco attraverso i suoi libretti*. Turin: EDT Musica, 1981. ML1733.P67 1981.

The title is a quotation from Verdi's *Rigoletto*. Presents an attempt at codifying various genres and structures of the nineteenth-century opera libretto.

353. Rinaldi, Mario. *Felice Romani: dal melodramma classico al melodramma romantico*. Rome: Edizione De Santis, 1965. ML423.RR66 R5.

Explores Romani's Classical roots and tendencies and how he became the early Romantic librettist *par excellence*. Contains sixteen plates; bibliography.

354. Roccatagliati, Alessandro. "Felice Romani, Librettist by Trade." *Cambridge Opera Journal* 8/2 (1996): 113–45. ISBN 0954–5867. ML1699.C36.

An extensive look at Romani from an author who wrote his doctoral thesis on the librettist. The author states that he will "proceed in two stages: first, to reflect on the nature and function of Romani's dramatic-poetic creations; then to provide synchronic sketches of his working relationships, dwelling on three of the most important—with theatrical institutions, with singers and with composers." Philological, critical-textual considerations; thoroughly documented.

355. ——. *Felice Romani librettista*. *Quaderni di Musica/Realtà*.Vol. 37. Lucca: Libreria musicale italiana, 1996. ISBN 88–70961–57–5. ML423. R66 R63 1996.

The publication of his doctoral thesis from the University of Bologna (1993). Bibliography; index. Roccatagliati's writings are indispensable modern studies of the primo ottocento opera libretto.

356. ——. "Libretti d'opera: testi autonomi o testo d'uso?" *Quaderni del Dipartimento di linguistica e letterature comparate* [Bergamo] 6 (1990): 7–20; English trans. William Ashbrook as "Librettos: Autonomous or Functional Texts?" In *Opera Quarterly* 11/2 (1995): 81–96. ISSN 0736–0053. ML1699.O65.

The libretto and music of the opera as separate, autonomous texts and their interconnected functions. The two texts work together to form a third text, the theatrical performance. Focuses on Bellini's *Capuleti e i Montecchi*, Romani's working methods, variants.

357. ——. "Romani, Felice." In *The New Grove Dictionary of Opera*. 4 vols. Ed. Stanley Sadie. New York: Macmillan, 1992. Vol. 4: 17–19. ISBN 09–35859–92–6. ML102.O6 N5 1992.

Chronological works-list with genre categories. Life and career. Bibliography.

358. Rolandi, Ulderico. "Bello è affrontar la morte gridando . . . Lealtà." *Bollettino bibliografico musicale* (June 6, 1928).

Textual changes to *I puritani* by the Neapolitan censor.

359. ——. *Il libretto per musica attraverso i tempi*. Rome: Edizione delli Ateneo, 1951. ML2110.R63.

An historical survey of the opera libretto. Facsimiles; "Saggio di bibliografia del libretto per musica," pp. 221–44.

360. Schlitzer, Franco. "Cimeli belliniani: *La sonnambula. Norma*." *Quaderni dell' Accademia Chigiana* 26 (1952): 61–88. ISSN 0065–0714. ML5.S5. Republished in *Tommasso Traetta, Leonardo Leo, Vincenzo Bellini: notizie e documenti raccolta da Franco Schlitzer*. Siena, 1952, pp. 61ff., and in Franco Schlitzer, *Mondo teatrale dell'Ottocento: episodi, testimonianze, musiche e lettere inedite*. Napoli: Fiorentino, 1954, pp. 15ff. ML1733.S35.

Explores the working relationship between Bellini and Romani and publishes sketches of the libretti of *La sonnambula* and *Norma*.

361. Sebastiana, Mancuso. *Il librettista di Vincenzo Bellini*. Tesi di Laurea presentata dalla candidata Mancuso Sebastiana, 1950–51.

A thesis presented to the Museo belliniano. 103 pp. of text. Carbon copy typescript. Deems Romani "definito il Metastasio dell' '800'." Chapter topics include "Notizie sulla vita e opere minori di Felice Romani"; "Relazioni tra Felice Romani e Vincenzo Bellini"; "I libretti di Felice Romani per Vincenzo Bellini"; and Bibliography.

362. Semrau, A. *Studien zur Typologie und zur Poetik der Oper in der ersten Hälfte des neunzehnten Jahrhunderts*. Dissertation, 1993. Kölner Beiträge zur Musikforschung 178. Kassel: G. Bosse, 1995. ISBN 37–64925–03–5. ML1704.S46 1993.

Classification of language, forms and topoi in the opera libretto of the first half of the nineteenth century.

363. Smith, Patrick J. *The Tenth Muse: A Historical Study of the Opera Libretto*. New York: Knopf, 1970. ML2110.S62.

Chapter 13 deals with "The Italian Melodramma." Felice Romani is discussed on pp. 198–206. Romani is regarded as the figure "who represents the early melodramma and stands as one of the long line of premier Italian librettists." He is "par excellence a transitional figure," both looking backward to Metastasio, Goldoni, and Favart's pastorals and, "albeit with some trepidation," looking forward to "the full-blown Romanticism and melodrama of Cammarano and Piave." Smith makes the point that, as with most Italian poet-librettists, Romani was an "adaptive rather than a creative mind." He worked too quickly but his libretti for Bellini were among his best because the composer demanded extensive rewriting. During this era the composer was becoming more important than the librettist, evidenced by certain situations: e.g., rather than relying totally on the often tardy Romani, both Donizetti and Bellini turned to others; also, as highly regarded as Romani was, he could not get his works published in a complete works edition. Discusses the superiority of the libretto for *Norma*, the care with which it was written. Illustrations; facsimiles.

364. Spina, Giuseppe. "Scott–Ancelot–Pepoli–Bellini: Genesi del libretto de 'I puritani'." *Nuova rivista musicale italiana* 23 (1989): 79–97. ISSN 0029–6228. ML5.N93.

Genesis and literary sources of Bellini's last opera. The fallacious connection with Walter Scott; Ancelot; the names of the characters; the historical epoch; the dramatic situations are points of discussion. Illustrated with reproductions of contemporary prints of singers, costumes, portraits of Pepoli and Bellini, photograph of contemporary printed libretto.

365. Tomlinson, Gary. "Italian Romanticism and Italian Opera: An Essay in their Affinities." *Nineteenth Century Music* 10/1 (Summer 1986): 43–61. ISSN 0148–2076. ML1.N77.

Literary romanticism, Italian political activism, and Italian opera. Begins with Madame de Staël's indictment of Italian opera. Presents Giuseppe Mazzini's writings, including *La filosofia della musica* (see item 63), and discusses the musical implications of these views. "Opera played a prominent role in Mazzini's program for political and cultural revival." He called, however, for opera reforms and outlined them, including a turning away from Rossinian style, inclusion of elements of local color, individual musical portrayal of characters in opera, use of accompanied recitative, and chopping down of much fioriture and cadenzas. Mazzini deemed both Rossini and Bellini, each in his own way, "ambivalent Romantics." Both were transition figures, Rossini only at times displaying true Romanticism, and Bellini continuing the transition. But both *Il pirata* and *La straniera* are unambivalent in their romantic traits: breaking with Rossinian style, "in the violence of their action and the strong Schillerian emotions of their protagonists," and in being adaptations of French and English sources. Tomlinson discusses the innovative musical style of these two Bellini operas, especially with regard to melody and form. He deems *La sonnambula* and *Norma* "in comparison works of consolidation, tempering the novelties of 1827–1830 with a reassertion of Rossinian forms and gestures." The author speculates that difficulties in trying to set Hugo's play *Hernani* "may have repelled Bellini from its Romantic premises, and pushed him in different dramatic directions." Discusses Felice Romani's role in this, who was no literary Romantic. Mazzini sensed in Donizetti, in Tomlinson's words, "a vivid if incomplete realization of his ideals . . . the composer of his new Italian Romanticism, a Romanticism more urgent, energetic, and politically aware than the old."

366. Zoppelli, Luca. "Il personaggio belliniana: Poetica del Drame e poetica tragica." *Vincenzo Bellini nel secondo centenario della nascita* (2004): 131–48. See item 406.

 Intends to examine the received idea that Bellini is not an "intellectual" composer. Explores various traditional genres of drama within Italian opera and how Bellini operates within this tradition. Music examples.

Note: Other relevant publications include:

367. Albicini, C. *Carlo Pepoli, saggio storico*. Bologna, 1888.

368. Baldacci, Luigi. *La musica in italiano: Libretti d'opera dell'ottocento*. Milan: Rizzoli, 1997. ML2110.B26 1997.

369. Cella, Franca. *Prospective della librettistica italiana nell'età romantica*. Milan, 1968.

370. Cescatti, O., ed. *Tutti i libretti di Bellini*. Milano: Garzanti, 1994. ML49.B36 C47 1994.

371. Della Seta, Fabrizio. "Il librettista: L'Ottocento. Il sistema produttivo e le sue competenze." Vol. 4/2 of *Storia dell'opera italiana*. Ed. Lorenzo Bianconi and Giorgio Pestelli, pp. 233–91. Turin: EDT/Musica, 1987. ISBN 88–70630–52–8. ML1733.S75 1987.

372. Dumas, J. "Felice Romani, ou le poète jugé par un musicologue." *Revue des études italiennes* 19 (1973): 35–74. ISSN 0035–2047. PQ4001. R47.

373. Ghiron, Isaia. "Vincenzo Bellini e Felice Romani: studio." *Perseveranza*. Milan, October 1880.

374. Paschetto, Celeste. *Felice Romani*. Turin: Loescher, 1907.

375. Regli, Francesco. *Elogio al Felice Romani*. Turin, 1865.

376. Romani, Felice. *Critica letteraria*. Turin, 1883.

377. Salvioli, Giovanni [anagram pseud. of Luigi Lianovosani and Livio Nino Galvani]. *Saggio bibliografico relativo ai melodrammi di Felice Romani*. Milan, 1878.

378. Sommariva, Andrea, ed. *Felice Romani, Melodrammi, poesie, documenti*. Florence: Olschki, 1996. ISBN 88–22244–08–7. ML423.R66 R5.

379. Tonelli, L. "I libretti di Bellini." *A Vincenzo Bellini. Bollettino dei musicisti, Mensile del Sindicato Fascista Musicisti* 13/3 (December 1934): 75–82.

7

Exhibition Catalogues, Iconographies, Conferences, Congress Reports, Special Publications

380. Alajmo, Roberto. "Iconografia belliniana." In *I teatri di Vincenzo Bellini*. Ed. Roberto Alajmo, premessa di Ubaldo Mirabelli, pp. 159–223. Palermo: Edizioni Novecento, 1986. ISBN 88–37300–48–4. ML410.B44 T4 1986.

Part of a profusely illustrated volume, containing stage sets for each opera. Discusses portraits of Bellini and iconographical evidence of his life and career.

381. Andò, Caterina Rita, Domenico de Meo, and Salvatore Enrico Failla, eds. *Bellini: Mostra di oggetti e documenti provenienti da collezioni pubbliche e private italiane. Catalogo*. Catania: Maimone, 1988. ISBN 88–77510–22–6. ML141.C34 B43 1988.

Part of several research projects on Bellini carried out by Salvatore Enrico Failla and colleagues. These projects were developed with and supported by the Cattedra di Storia della Musica dell'Ateneo Catanese. The initial purpose is to collect the greatest number of documents relating to Bellini and to make copies of them, especially in microfilm. This material is then to be catalogued for publication.

Opens with essays on "La musica di Vincenzo Bellini" by Friedrich Lippmann and "Bellini fra culto e documento" by Failla. The book then is divided into fifteen sections, according to musical output, each by a different author: individual operas, theater works uncompleted, secular vocal music, sacred vocal music, instrumental music, etc. Types of materials displayed include facsimiles of printed scores, manuscripts, letters, libretti; portraits; costumes; stage sets; original reviews.

382. Andò, Caterina Rita, Salvatore Enrico Failla, Giampiero Tintori, and Piero Tosi. *Bellini, Vincenzo. Mostra di stampe, figurini e costumi per i personaggi belliniani*. Festival Belliniano, Catania, September 23–October 4, 1989. Catania: Maimone, 1989. ISBN 88–77510–29–3. ML410.B44 B4 1989.

Illustrations of contemporary and modern costumes worn by singers portraying characters in Bellini's operas; a number of photographs of Maria Callas are included. Essays include: "Vestite gli eroi" by Andò; "Immagini di personaggi belliniani" by Failla; "Il costume nell'opera dell'Ottocento" by Tintori; and "*La sonnambula* del' 55" (at the Teatro alla Scala, Milan, starring Maria Callas, directed by Luchino Visconti) by Tosi. Subsequent chapters are devoted to individual operas.

383. Baccherini, Maria Adelaide Bartoli and Raffaello Monterosso, eds. *Vincenzo Bellini ". . . in questa graziosa capitale della Toscana . . . ." Mostra bibliografico-documentaria*. Cremona: Fondazione Claudio Monteverdi, 2001.

"Eccomi in questa graziosa capitale di Toscana," wrote Bellini to Ricordi on May 24, 1832, on his way to Sicily. On the evening of May 23 the composer attended a performance of his *Sonnambula* at the Teatro La Pergola in Florence. This bicentenary exhibit displayed autograph manuscripts of scores and libretti, lithographs of Bellini, Rubini, Malibran, Tamburini, Pasta, Lablache and others, letters, costumes, plays from which libretti were fashioned. Catalog contains numerous color plates and a bibliography of works cited. Introduction by R. Monterosso on Bellini and the Florentine connection.

384. *Bellini 1980. Opera Engagement Calendar*. New York: Metropolitan Opera Guild, 1979.

Datebook from the Metropolitan Opera, a Bellini iconography copiously illustrated with portraits of Bellini and productions of his operas.

385. Bellini, Vincenzo. *Catalogo della mostra belliniana nel Castello Ursino. Catania, January–September 1935*. Ed. Guido Libertini, Benedetto Condorelli, and Francesco Pastura. Catania: Editoriale Siciliana Tipografia, [1935].

An exhibit organized by the Comune of Catania upon the centenary of Bellini's death that gathered together the majority of memorabilia of Bellini. Begins with "Notizie biografiche." Illustrated with descriptions of the objects. Many autographs displayed ("La 'Rotonda' degli autografi") from the Museo belliniano, the Naples Conservatory, private collections, and other locations. Copies of catalogue found in Museo belliniano, Catania, and Paris, Bibliothèque de l'Opéra.

386. Bellini, Vincenzo. *Numero commemorativo a cura della Rivista del Comune di Catania*. Catania, 1935.

Special publication by his native Catania on the centenary of Bellini's death. Contents include:

- G. Libertini, "Richerche tra gli autografi del Museo belliniano";
- C. Pettinato, "La morte di Bellini";
- Benedetto Condorelli, "Il volto di Bellini";
- Francesco Pastura, "Rivelazioni degli autografi musicali belliniani";
- Adelmo Damerini, "I cento anni de *I puritani*";
- F. De Stefano, "Una lettera di G. Rossini riguardante *I puritani*";
- Orazio Viola, "Interpreti di *I puritani*";
- L. Gandolfo, "Le opere rievocate nella stagione catanese";
- P. Buzzi, "Bellini";
- N. Pagliaro, "Curiosità e leggende attorno a Bellini";
- Luisa Cambi, "Piccolo mondo belliniano";
- S. Fiducia, "Monumenti a Bellini in Catania";
- S. Lo Presti, "Il cuore catanese di Vincenzo Bellini";
- A. Lualdi, "Ricordo de *La sonnambula*";
- O. Profeta, "Dantan e la Parigi di Bellini";
- V. Laurenza, "Malta e Bellini";
- R. Valensise, "Epigramme."

86 pp. Illustrations; facsimiles of letters and manuscripts.

387. Bellini—numéro spécial de *La Revue musicale*. 1935. ISSN 0768–1593. ML5.R613.

French paean to Bellini for the 1935 centenary. Begins with a poem in Italian, with French translation, by Gabriele D'Annunzio: "Nel primo centenario della nascita di Vincenzo Bellini" (1901). Other contents include:

- Roger Allard, "Bellini," pp. 18–38;
- Ildebrando Pizzetti, "Hommage à Bellini," pp. 39–43;
- Guido Pannain, "La Norma," pp. 44–51;
- Domenico de Paoli, "Bellini, musicien dramatique," pp. 52–62. Deems Bellini a "composer with a dramatic power unique in his time (at least in Italy)";
- Henri de Saussine, "Sur Bellini, harmoniste," pp. 63–64 (see items 470, 471);
- Frederik Goldbeck, "Notes sur un album oublié," pp. 65–69. Concerns the *Hexaméron, grandes variations de bravoura sur la marche des Puritains, composées pour le concert de Madame, la Princess Belgiojoso au bénéfice des pauvres, par MM. Liszt, Thalberg, Pixis, H. Herz, Czerny et Chopin*. The work was published in 1841. Focuses on the variation by Chopin and how it upholds Bellinian style. Provides music examples by Chopin and Liszt. Chopin contributed a *largo* in common time in E major and Liszt composed the Introduction, the

passages connecting the variations, and the finale. He also arranged the entire work for piano and orchestra;

- Henry Prunières, "Bellini, épistolier," pp. 70–72 (see item 315);
- José Bruyr, "En parlant de Bellini," pp. 73–74;
- Arthur Hoerée, "Un film sur Bellini," pp. 75–76. A review of the film *Casta diva*, which is a romanticized version of Bellini's life using music from several of his operas. The principal character of Maddalena Fumaroli is played and sung by the young Hungarian star Martha Eggerth. This author gives the film a good rating in terms of musical performance. This film is a predecessor of the one with the same title described in item 841;
- Luigi Colicicchi, "Reprise du *Pirata* à Rome," p. 77. Review of a recent performance of *Il pirata* featuring Benjamino Gigli, Eva Pacetti, Ernesto Basiola, conducted by Tullio Serafin.

388. Cella, Franca and Lorenzo Arruga. *Museo teatrale alla Scala: Bellini a Milano (November 30–December 28, 1985)*. Turin, 1985. ML141.M5 M9.

Contents of this eighty-page exhibition catalogue include "Il volto di Bellini"; "La voce negli autografi del Museo Teatrale alla Scala"; "Gli oggetti personali"; "I luoghi"; "Gli amici"; "Le opere milanesi" ("La fonte, il libretto," "gli interpreti"); "Gli interpreti belliniani: le altre opere"; and "Le scene, i costumi." Lavishly illustrated with portraits, facsimiles, stage designs, interiors of places Bellini stayed, some in color.

389. Condorelli, Benedetto. "Un importante dono al Museo belliniano." Extract from *Rivista del Comune di Catania* 12/6 (November–December 1933).

Condorelli was the first director of the Museo belliniano, Catania. Copy found in Museo belliniano. 4 pp. The lawyer Vincenzo Pappalardo gave a collection of Bellini's medals to the Bellini Museum, which are still on display there. Condorelli lists and describes them. They are still on display in the museum.

390. ——. *Il museo belliniano. Catalogo storico iconografico. A cura del commune di Catania*. Catania: Commune di Catania, 1935.

Condorelli was the director of the Bellini Museum and Library. Illustrated with black and white plates. Bibliography. 158 pp. The Bellini Museum and Library was inaugurated on May 5, 1930, in the house in which Bellini was born. Condorelli lists the contents of each room. Room A contains all the documents relating to the transferral of Bellini's remains in 1876. Room B is where Bellini was born and contains his piano and some of the original furniture and other personal objects; also letters and iconographical items, all relating to the first three phases of Bellini's life, from Catania, Naples, and Milan. Room C, in addition to his grand-mother's spinetta, contains various documents relating to London and Paris. Room D is dedicated to Bellini's compositions: autograph scores, study scores, libretti, creators of Bellini's great roles. In the display cases there are various autographs showing variants and unused themes; also the complete autograph manuscript of *I puritani* in which he wrote variants for Malibran for San Carlo, Naples. Room E is the mortuary: various precious relics, pieces of the original coffin from Père-Lachaise, part of the sheet that enshrouded the corpse, and the masks done by the sculptor Dantan at Bellini's death bed the morning of September 24, 1835, and the one done in 1876 in Catania by the sculptor Grimaldi from the mummified corpse after forty-one years. Room F is the library, containing editions of Bellini's works and a collection of writings about the composer, plus volumes relating to other opera composers such as Rossini, Donizetti, and Wagner. Also found here are journals, contemporary newspaper clippings, models of stage sets, play bills, and other items relating to opera production of the time.

391. Consoli, Vittorio. *Bellini*. Catania: Arti Grafiche Figli di Cesare Constantino, 1967. ML410.B44 C5.

Copy in Museo belliniano. Iconography with text, all black and white. List of illustrations at end of book. Includes some stills from the film "Casta diva." See item 841.

392. De Angelis, Marcello, ed. *Le cifre del melodrama: l'archivio inedito dell'impresario Alessandro Lanari nella Biblioteca Nazionale Centrale di Firenze: 1815–1870*. Florence: Giunta Regionale Toscana-La Buova Italia, 1982. (Inventari e Cataloghi Toscani, 11.)

Alessandro Lanari (1790–1862) was an opera impresario connected with theaters in Florence (long associated with the Pergola there), Rome, Naples, Venice, and Bologna. He commissioned *Norma*, *Capuleti*, *Beatrice di Tenda*, and also operas by Donizetti and Verdi.

393. Failla, Salvatore Enrico, director. *Atti del convegno internazionale di studi belliniani*, Catania November 4–9, 1985. Catania: Maimone, 1990.

Failla writes: "A more marked interest in Bellini studies was evident following the 'Convegno Internazionale di Studi Belliniani' organized in Catania by the Department of Literature and Philosophy of the Università degli Studi di Catania from November 4 through 9, 1985. At the convention, the absolutely first modern performance of the original draft of *Adelson e Salvini* took place. The plans for the Fondazione Bellini were laid here also."

Contents include:

- F. Giovale, "'Ah, tu perdoni. Quel pianto il dice': note sul tema del sacrificio e del perdono nei libretti belliniani di Felice Romani," pp. 25–45;
- Aldo Nicastro, "Il caso Pepoli e il libretto dei *Puritani*," pp. 47–61;

- R. Meloncelli, "La lirica vocale di Vincenzo Bellini nella produzione cameristica italiana dell'ottocento," pp. 63–111;
- Maria Rosario Adamo, "Guarda che bianca luna: una 'lettera' belliniana," pp. 113–44;
- Simon Maguire, "On the Question of Analysis in Bellini," pp. 145–56;
- Giampiero Tintori, "Lettere di Bellini e su Bellini al Museo Teatrale alla Scala," pp. 157–74;
- Roman Vlad, "Modernità di Bellini," pp. 175–85;
- F.A. Agostinelli, "'I Puritani' uno e due: la versioni napoletana," pp. 187–93;
- Salvatore Enrico Failla, "La prima versione di *Adelson e Salvini*," pp. 195–212;
- Lorenzo Arruga, "Recitazione neoclassica immedesimazione e drammaturgia," pp. 213–20;
- Julian Budden, "La fortuna di Bellini in Inghilterra," pp. 225–31;
- Marcello Conati, "La 'novella' belliniana," pp. 241–60;
- D. Cranmer, "A Portugese Perspective," pp. 261–88;
- P. Rattalmo, "I melodrammi di Bellini nelle parafrasi pianistiche coeve," pp. 289–95;
- François Lesure, "Bellini et Berlioz," pp. 297–304;
- R. Pagano, "Vincenzo Tobia Bellini e le sue Toccate per clavicembalo," pp. 305–29;
- "L'attuale situazione degli studi belliniani," pp. 331–61;
- Salvatore Enrico Failla, "Immagini di personaggi belliniani."

394. Florimo, Francesco and Michele Scherillo, eds. *Album-Bellini/pubblicato il giorno dell'inaugurazione del monumento/a Vincenzo Bellini*. Naples: A. Tocco, 1886. Naples: Nicotra, 1887. See item 282. ML410.B44 F62.

68 pp. Various poems and sonnets; tributes and quotations from Giuseppe de Luca, Wagner, Tchaikovsky, Thomas, von Bülow, Auber, Rossini, Verdi, and others. Page 61 lists those who subscribed to the Bellini Monument in Naples, including "Sua Maestà il Rè d'Italia, Umberto I (1400L)." Florimo wrote an "Inno a Bellini," calling Bellini's music "limpid as spring water, transparent as crystal, and diaphanous as the roof of our sky." At the end is a transcription for voice of an F-minor Partita of Bach, arranged and with text by Arrigo Boïto, marked, "Religioso e largo."

395. *Mostra internazionale di musica in Bologna 1988. Catalogo con brevi cenni biografici e succinte descrizioni degli autografi e documenti di celebri o distinti musicisti posseduti da Emilio Succi, Accademica Filarmonica di Bologna*. Bologna: Società Tipografica già compositori, 1988.

This catalogue from an international exhibit held in 1988 of items from the Emilio Succi collection, Bologna, includes seven items pertaining to Bellini, including signed autograph letters (to Rossini and his uncle

Vincenzo Ferlito) and autograph notes by Bellini's last attending physician, Dr. Montallegri.

396. *Museo storico musicale di S. Pietro a Majella*. Naples: Real Stabilimento Tipografico Francesco Giannini e Figli, 1930.

A listing of 734 items found in the Naples Conservatory where Bellini studied. Includes portraits of musicians, busts, autographs, musical instruments, medals, and photographs. A special archive is devoted to Bellini.

397. Neri, Carmelo. *Guida illustrata del Museo Civico Belliniano di Catania*. Catania: Maimone, 1998.

Most recent guide to the Museo belliniano, sponsored by the Città di Catania. List with extensive annotations and color illustrations of 132 items found in the museum. Includes portraits of Bellini and many of the people associated with him, autograph scores and letters, pianos, objects Bellini owned, his death mask, sculptures of the composer (by Dantan, for example), and much more. Index; bibliography with a number of relevant Italian newspaper articles.

398. *Omaggio a Bellini*. Milan: Mazzotta, 1986. ISBN 88–20206–58–7. ML410.B44 D3 1986.

Table of Contents includes:

- Domenico Danzuso, "Classicità greca e aneliti romantici";
- Francesco Gallo, "Casorati, De Chirico e Prampolini in bozzetti e figurini di scenografie belliniane";
- Raffaele Monti, "Divagazioni sulla messinscena belliniana." Over 80 pages of reproductions of costumes and stage sets;
- "Elenco delle Opere in Mostra" from 1930s to the early 1960s, stage designs for Bellini's operas from various theaters such as the Teatro Comunale di Firenze, La Fenice, Teatro Massimo di Palermo, Teatro Massimo Bellini di Catania, Teatro Reale dell'Opera di Roma.

399. *Opera, L'. Teatro Massimo Bellini, Catania* 5/16–17 (Milan, 1970).

Articles about Bellini and his operas by Niny Genguzza, Don Giosuè Chisari, Domenico Tempio, Benedetto Condorelli, and Vittorio Consoli.

400. *Opera Quarterly* 17/3 (Summer 2001). Special issue commemorating the two-hundreth anniversary of the birth of Vincenzo Bellini. ISSN 0736–0053. ML169.O65.

Opening statement by E. Thomas Glasow, editor, pp. 357–60. Articles, which are annotated in their respective proper places, include:

- Robert Ignatius Letellier, "Bellini and Meyerbeer," pp. 361–79;
- Giorgio Migliavacca and Laura Scandariato, "Turin's Links with Bellini: A Northern Capital and a Successful Southerner," pp. 380–98;

- Heather Hadlock, "On the Cusp between Past and Future: The Mezzo-Soprano Romeo of Bellini's *Capuleti,*" pp. 399–422;
- E. Thomas Glasow, "Théophile Gautier on Bellini: 'Notice sur *Norma*' ", pp. 423–34;
- Eugene H. Cropsey, "American Premieres of Bellini's Lesser-Known Operas," pp. 435–50;
- Giorgio Migliavacca, "Bellinienne Extraordinaire: A Conversation with Mariella Devia," pp. 451–63;
- Joe K. Law, "Selected Bibliography of Literature on Vincenzo Bellini," pp. 464–68.

Also includes book and recording reviews of most of Bellini's *oeuvre*, and Recordings and Videos Received.

401. *Quaderni dell'Istituto musicale Vincenzo Bellini di Catania*, Vol. II, ed. Roberto Carnevale. "Vincenzo Bellini 1801–2001, con una appendice su Francesco Pastura." Libreria Musicale Italiana. Lucca: LIM Editrice, 2001. ISBN 88–70962–84–9. ML410.B44 V463x 2001.

Articles include:

- Giuseppe Giarrizo, "Di Vincenzo Bellini (1801–1835)," pp. 3–22;
- Dario Miozzi, "Divagazioni sul mito e sulla fortuna di Bellini in Italia nell'Otocento," pp. 23–40;
- Graziella Seminara, "La melodrammaturgia incompiuta di *Beatrice di Tenda*," pp. 41–62. See item 689;
- Aldo Mattina, "Drammaturgia e lirismo delle Ariette con una breve indagine su una (im)probabile catalogazione," pp. 63–74. See item 732;
- Arcidiacono, Angela, Giuseppe Cantone, Antonella Fiorino, and Letizia Spampinato, "Analisi melodica di alcune composizioni vocali da camera di Vincenzo Bellini," pp. 75–112. See item 732;
- Antonio Caroccia, "I manoscritti e le lettere autografe di Bellini conservati nella Biblioteca del Conservatorio di musica 'San Pietro a Majella' di Napoli," pp. 113–60. See item 491.

Appendix: "Su Francesco Pastura (1905–1968): per una ricognizione della biografia e dell'attività critica."

Riccardo Insolia and Antonio Marcellino, "Appunti per un profilo biografico di Francesco Pastura," pp. 163–225.

Index of Names.

402. *Sicilia Magazine* Speciale—Teatro Massimo Bellini. Supplemento al No. 6 di *Sicilia Magazine*, 1989.

Contents include: A. Dalponte, "Editoriale"; F.P. Busalacchi, "Verso il centenario"; G. C. Ballola, "Il festival Bellini"; D. Danzuso, "Storia di un teatro"; Salvatore Enrico Failla, "Una città per la musica"; Fabrizio Della

Seta, "La musica per il dramma"; Franca Cella, "Bellini e il suoi librettisti"; G. Guclerzi, "Interpreti tra storia e mito"; B. Condorelli, "La Catania di Bellini"; Giuseppe di Stefano, "La mia Catania"; A. Foletto, "*I puritani*"; C. Orselli, "Un teatro vivo."

Some English text in this volume, pp. 57–75, but not always in an idiomatic translation.

403. Tintori, Giampiero. "Iconografia belliniana al museo teatrale alla Scala." In *Vincenzo Bellini: Critica-Storia-Tradizione*. Ed. Salvatore Enrico Failla, pp. 119–27. Catania: Maimone, 1991. ISBN 88–77510–56–0. ML410.B444 V52 1991. See item 439.

Survey of Bellini portraits with reproductions of each, including the provenance: portrait by Frederick Millet, which belonged to Giuditta Pasta; Bellini at the age of twenty-six, portrait by Sigr. Flavez in Milano; Bellini in an engraving by Di Bartolo; Bellini in a nitric acid etching by Pistrucci; Bellini in an engraving by Gandini from a drawing by Demarchi, and several others.

404. *Vincenzo Bellini et la France, Histoire, création et réception de l'oeuvre/Vincenzo Bellini e la Francia, Storia, creazione e ricezione dell'opera. Acte du Colloque international*: Paris, Sorbonne, Salle des Arts, November 5–7, 2001. Ed. Maria Rosa De Luca, Salvatore Enrico Failla, and Giuseppe Montemagno. Lucca: Libreria Musicale Italiana, 2007. With Index. ISBN 97–88870–96–5087. ML410.B44 V522 2007.

Preface (Introductory Remarks) by Pierre Brunel, "Bellini, année 2001," pp. xvii–xx. Wants to explore certain "idées reçues" about Bellini, such as his musical training, his "angelic" nature, the evenness of his oeuvre, and his purported facility.

Session topics included the following (individual papers with annotations are listed in appropriate chapters in this guide):

I. "I compositori italiani a confronto con l'ambiente musicale parigino";
II. "Sulle tracce del soggiorno parigino belliniano; immagini e relazioni musicali e letterarie";
III. "Storia di un trionfo: *I puritani*";
IV. "Morte e apoteosi di Bellini";
V. "Influenze estetiche, fonti letterarie e modelli di drammaturgia";
IV. "Bellini dopo Bellini: La ricezione musicale e la critica."

405. *Vincenzo Bellini and the Italian Celebration of 1835*. Rome: ENIT, 1935.

English edition, published by the Italian State Tourist Department. Includes an introductory survey of Bellini's life and many illustrations. These include several Bellini portraits and pictures of his birthplace. List of operas in chronological order with details of premieres; short list of references. States that in 1835 Bellini "was then only a little over thirty years of age."

406. *Vincenzo Bellini nel secondo centenario della nascita. Atti del Convegno internazionale Catania, 8–11 November 2001*, ed. Graziella Seminara and Anna Tedesco. (*Historiae musicae cultures* CVI) Florence: Olschki, 2004. ISBN 88–22253–90–6. ML410.B44 V527 2004.

Edizione critica delle opere di Vincenzo Bellini in collaborazione con Casa Ricordi; Commissione Epistolario e Centro di Documentazione "Vincenzo Bellini."

Session topics include the following. Each article is listed with annotation in the proper chapter. If one compares the conference program (printed at the beginning of the first volume) and the table of contents (at the back of the second volume), one notes that two of the papers presented at the conference are not included (one because of the author's death) and that two new essays replace them.

I. "Sull'epistolario belliniano";
II. "Libretti e drammaturgia" (1);
III. "Libretti e drammaturgia" (2);
IV. "Il linguaggio musicale";
V. "Problemi filologici" (1);
VI. "Problemi filologici" (2);
VII. "La tradizione esecutiva e della messa in scena delle opere di Bellini."

Review: Roberta M. Marvin, *Music & Letters* 88/1 (2007): 158–60.

407. *Vincenzo Bellini. La vita, le opere, l'eredità*, ed. Giorgio Taborelli. Milan: Silvana Editoriale, 2001. ISBN 88–82153–83–5. ML410.B44. V525 2002.

Contents include:

- Giovanni Carlo Ballola, "Intorno all'astro maggiore—Nascita, apogeo e fine di un sistema solare," pp. 13–27;
- Angelo Foletto, "Vita di Vincenzo Bellini: Sì presto estinto fiore," pp. 28–43;
- Aldo Nicastro, "Le opere per il teatro," pp. 44–85. Theaters, singers, stage sets. Illustrated;
- Graziella Seminara, "La 'filosofica musica' di Vincenzo Bellini," pp. 86–101. Music facsimiles and illustrations;
- Luca Zoppelli, "Bellini: Immaginario romantico e antropologia tragica," pp. 102–11. Music facsimiles and illustrations;
- Piero Mioli, "Alla ricerca del sublime ossia Bellini, i grandi cantanti e i principali fenomeni vocali del suo teatro," pp. 112–27;
- Vittoria Crespi Morbio, "Bellini in scena: Una breve storia delle scenografie belliniane," pp. 128–45. Sets by Sanquirico, De Chirico, Zeffirelli;

- Sergio Sablich, “Il Bellini dei musicisti: La fortuna del compositore presso i colleghi,” pp. 146–57. Bellini and Berlioz, Chopin, Liszt, Wagner, Pizzetti;
- Carmelo Neri, “Memorie belliniane a Catania: I segni del compositore nella sua città,” pp. 158–65. A tour of Bellini’s Catania with a splendid reproduction of “Onoranze funebre del 1876 a Vincenzo Bellini” (anon., Museo belliniano);
- Livio Aragona, “La voce tua mi suona. . .Breve video-discografia selezionata,” pp. 166–73. Photos of famous singers such as Sutherland, Caballé, and Kraus.

408. Winternitz, G. F. “I cimeli belliniani della R[eal] Accademia Filarmonica di Bologna.” *Rivista Musicale Italiana* 40 (1936): 104–18. ISSN 0029-6228. ML5.R8.

Winternitz was the archivist for the Real Accademia Filarmonica di Bologna. Presents Bellini curios and relics found in that collection.

8

Aspects of Musical Style: Aesthetics, Analysis, Performance Practice, Influences, Compositional Process

409. Balthazar, Scott L. "The *Primo Ottocento* Duet and the Transformation of the Rossinian Code." *Journal of Musicology* 7/4 (Fall 1989): 471–97. ISSN 0277–9269. ML1.J693.

Refutes the scholarly discussions that stress the "tenacity with which Rossinian procedures" of formal structure held sway throughout the first half of the nineteenth century. Balthazar studies the duets of Rossini, Bellini, Donizetti, and Verdi from 1815 to 1850, finding that "musical, poetic, and dramatic design changed substantially during this period in ways that point toward the breakdown of archetypal schemas and the concurrent rise of structural continuity in the second half of the century."

410. ——. "Ritorni's *Ammaestramenti* and the Conventions of Rossinian Melodrama." *Journal of Musicological Research* 8/3–4 (1989): 281–312. ISSN 0141–1896. ML5.M6415.

The author writes: "Carlo Ritorni's *Ammaestramenti alla composizione d'ogni poema e d'ogni opera appatenente alla musica* of 1841 provides the most complete nineteenth-century overview of the general principles of Italian operatic design that has yet come to light. It not only confirms contemporary awareness of practices that we can see in the score—occasionally amplifying modern conceptions—and provides rationales for numerous stylistic developments, but also reveals a range of influences, biases, and methodological constraints that shaped Ritorni's individual perceptions of the Rossinian legacy, offering extraordinary insight into factors that shaped perceptions of Rossini in the era of Bellini and Donizetti."

411. ——. “Rossini and the Development of the Mid-Century Lyric Form.” *Journal of the American Musicological Society* 41/1 (Spring 1988): 102–25. ISSN 0003–0139. ML27.U5 A83363.

Balthazar writes, “Traditionally, scholars have contrasted the freedom and complexity of Rossini’s melodic designs with the conventionality and simplicity of the mid-century lyric form A A’ B A’ adopted by Bellini and others. However, Rossini’s melodies embraced a wide range of options. Many of them prefigure later lyric conventions exactly, while others incorporate numerous aspects of later practice.”

The author concludes that “Rossini’s role in the development of the mid-century lyric form suggests that we should regard Bellini not as the originator of that design [A A’ B A’], but rather as the composer who solidified and popularized an approach that Rossini had already tested and made successful. Rossini’s melodies embraced a wide range of options. Many of them prefigure later lyric conventions exactly, while others incorporate numerous aspects of later practice.” See Huebner item 447 for an alternative analytical method.

412. Barblan, Guglielmo. *L’opera di Donizetti nell’età romantico*. Bergamo: Banca Mutua Popolare, 1948.

Manifestations of Romanticism in the works of Donizetti and his contemporaries, especially Spontini, Rossini, and Bellini.

413. Beghelli, Marco. “Alle origine della cabaletta.” In *L’aere è fosca, il ciel s’imbruna. Arte e musica a Venezia dalla fine della Repubblica al Congresso di Vienna*. Ed. F. Passadore and F. Rossi, pp. 593–630. Venice: Fondazione Levi, 2000.

In this and the following entries by Beghelli, he examines contemporary and changing concepts of various formal units, e.g., cabaletta, romanza, cavatina, rondò.

414. ——. “Che cos’è una Gran Scena?” In *Belliniana et alia musicologica. Festschrift für Friedrich Lippmann zum 70. Geburtstag*. Ed. D. Brandenburg and Th. Lindner, pp. 1–12. Vienna: Präsens, 2004 (*Primo Ottocento*).

415. ——. “Il contributo dei trattati di canto ottocenteschi al lessico dell’opera.” In *Le parole della musica I: Studi sulla lingua della letteratura musicale in onore di Gianfranco Folena*. Ed. F. Nicolidi and P. Trovato, pp. 177–223. Florence: Olschki, 1994.

416. ——. “Il lessico melodrammatico di Bellini.” *Vincenzo Bellini nel secondo centenario della nascita* (2004): 27–37. See item 406.

417. ——. “Tre slittamenti semantici: cavatina, romanza, rondò.” In *Le parole della musica III: Studi di lessicogia musicale*. Ed. F. Nicolodi and P. Trovato, pp. 185–217. Florence: Olschki, 2000.

418. Biget, Michelle. "Le Chant des affligés ou la musique 'se rallie au peuple'." *Corps écrit* 28 (October–December 1988): 45–54. ISSN 0751–5022. AP20.C75.

The author writes about the influence of the French Revolution on the opera house, which continues throughout the nineteenth and twentieth centuries with Bellini, Verdi, Wagner, and *verismo* composers. This is true "even if the more traditional musical composition and 'grande machine' staging practices lag greatly behind the ideological content of the librettos."

419. Black, John. "Donizetti and His Contemporaries in Naples, 1822–1848: A Study in Relative Popularity." *Donizetti Society Journal* VI (1988): 11–27. ISSN 0307–1448.

Black has compiled a chronological listing of the offerings of the five theaters that presented opera in Naples from 1822 to 1848. Eight composers are examined in terms of popularity: Rossini, Bellini, Donizetti, Mercadante, Pacini, Raimondi, Luigi Ricci, and Vincenzo Fioravanti. Donizetti's works were the most frequently performed and Bellini's works were the most popular in the smaller theaters. Pacini was the least performed and Rossini is not notably represented, as he left Naples in 1822 and the performance of his works fell off sharply after that point.

420. Brauner, Charles Samuel. *Vincenzo Bellini and the Aesthetics of Opera Seria in the First Third of the Nineteenth Century*. Ph.D. diss. Yale University, 1972. 2 vols. 776 pp. Ann Arbor, MI: UMI Press, 1982.

Discusses the change in musical style in Italian opera from Classical to bel canto, led by Rossini. From the author: "The standard scene of *opera seria* in *bel canto* style from the 1820s consists of accompanied recitative followed by two or more closed melodies separated by a spoken [?] dialogue in which dramatic action usually occurs. Bellini took over the conventional forms from Rossini and, in his mature operas, created the moderately ornamented, affective melody which is characteristic of his style. The most successful dramatic realization of the era is achieved in *Norma*, in which Bellini's melodic fluency is combined with a libretto that emphasizes the thoughts, rather than the actions, of the characters."

421. Budden, Julian. "Aspetti del rapporto tra Bellini e Chopin." *Vincenzo Bellini nel secondo centenario della nascita* (2004): 605–10. See item 406.

Explores the connection of Bellini's and Chopin's music, even though this is often not mentioned in modern biographies of both composers. Unfortunately, there is a lacuna in Chopin's letters during the years 1834–35 and Bellini never mentioned Chopin to Florimo. Yet there is other, first-hand, testimony of the connection, from Ferdinand Hiller's *Künstlerleben* (see item 52). Also examines Schumann's review of Chopin's B-flat minor sonata, where Schumann connects the two composers. Music examples.

422. Cagli, Bruno. "Vincenzo Bellini." In *Guida all' opera*. Milan/London, 1981.

Analyses *La sonnambula, Norma*, and *I puritani*.

423. Caswell, Austin. "Mme. Cinti-Damoreau and the Embellishment of Italian Opera in Paris, 1820–45." *Journal of the American Musicological Society* 27 (1975): 459–92. ISSN 0003–0139. ML27.U5 A83363.

Discussion of a set of volumes acquired by the Lilly Library at Indiana University in 1971. Written by Mme Laure Cinti-Damoreau, a leading opera soprano in Paris in the second quarter of the nineteenth century, they contain cadenzas and embellished phrases from much of the French opera repertoire of the period but also include Italian repertoire from works by Rossini, Donizetti, and Bellini. Gives a biographical account of Cinti-Damoreau, born Laure-Cinthie Montalant in 1801. A number of writers assumed that she was either born or trained in Italy. Author describes the one printed volume and several notebooks of embellishments left by Cinti-Damoreau and lists their contents. Article concludes with a number of extended music examples of cadenzas and embellishments of certain phrases. Extensive examples from the Act One aria of Bellini's *La sonnambula*. Nearly all of the soprano's variations are of passages that are already florid in Bellini's original—she leaves simple *cantabile* lines unadorned, a practice that is evident in hundreds of her examples.

424. Cataldo, Glauco. *Il teatro di Bellini. Guida critica a tutte le opere*. Bologna: Edizioni Bongiovanni, 1980.

Begins with a brief biography, then presents a listening guide with music examples for each opera. One appendix is a discography compiled by Stefano Ferrari.

425. Celletti, Rodolfo. "Il vocalismo italiano da Rossini a Donizetti." *Analecta musicologica* 5 (1968): 267–94; 7 (1969): 214–47. ISSN 0585–6086. ML160.S893.

The period surveyed comprises the three decades from 1810 to 1840 in terms of the history of the Italian opera theater. Part 1, from 1968, deals with Rossini and his vocal reforms that began with *Elisabetta, regina d'Inghilterra* in 1815. Celletti discusses famous singers and vocal requirements for specific roles, providing numerous short music examples.

Part 2 concerns Bellini and Donizetti. Rossini's operas were an Italian phenomenon but by the time of Bellini and Donizetti, Italian operas reflect European Romanticism. The expressive demands of Romantic drama seemed to deny the need for Rossinian fioriture, as evidenced in the works of both Meyerbeer and Bellini in the late 1820s and 1830s. The tenor now comes into his own as a kind of Romantic ideal of youth, sentiment, and audacity, but also of loyalty and liberty. Discusses roles sung by Rubini—

in *Bianca e Fernando*, *Pirata* [a landmark role for tenor], *Sonnambula*, and *Puritani*. Also discusses the females—Pasta, Malibran—the lower males such as Lablache and Tamburini and the roles Bellini created for them. Many music examples to illustrate his points. The Bellini discussion takes up only pp. 214–23; Donizetti's vocal writing is surveyed on pp. 223–47 in the same manner as above.

426. Cocchiara, Giuseppe. "Origine e vicende d'una canzone popolare." *Annali del museo Pitrè* 2–4 (1951–53): 68ff.

This essay, plus essays by Scherillo (see item 472) and Tiby (see item 476), all on Italian popular music, were published together in *Nuove effemeridi* 3 (1990).

427. Colas, Damien. "Duetto e dialogue a confronto dal cantabile al 'Dialogo musicale' nei duetti di Bellini." *Vincenzo Bellini nel secondo centenario della nascita* (2004): 149–83. See item 406.

An examination of the slow tempi in Bellini's duets derived from French sources. Looks at the central slow tempo as a projection of lyricism rather than pure drama. Appendices comparing texts, e.g., Soumet and Romani for *Norma*.

428. Colombau, Claudia. "Vincenzo Bellini e la sua poetica creative nella ricezione del mondo musicale francese contemporaneo." *Vincenzo Bellini et la France* (2007): 45–75. See item 404.

An analysis of Bellini's aesthetic and creative poetics in light of his reception in Paris in the 1830s. Critics were still under the influence of Rossini's "sublime" style, whereas Bellini presented something more melancholy, with neo-Classic echoes and a closer connection between text and music. Critics examined include Berlioz, Blaze de Bury, Escudier, and others, who recognized the "esprit de noctambulisme" and the connection with Chopin evinced in Bellini's sentimental melodies.

429. Conati, Marcello. "La novella scuola musicale." *Studi musicali* 21/1 (1992): 191–208. ISSN 0391–7789. ML5.S9248.

A revised and updated version of Conati's article ("La 'novella' Bellini") that originally appeared in *Atti del Convegno Internazionale di Studi belliniani*. See item 393. Illustrates how Bellini radically departed from Rossinian style and the effect this had on Donizetti and ultimately Verdi. Conati cites Carlo Ritorni's *Ammaestramenti alla composizione* (see item 410), in which Bellini is championed as the founder of a "new school." In terms of Ritorni's viewpoint, Conati concludes that Bellini's operas did not neglect features of Rossini's style, but took them towards a new kind of theatrical expression.

430. Crutchfield, Will. "The Bel Canto Connection." *Opera News* 62/1 (July 1997): 30–35; 51. ISSN 0030–3607. ML1.O482.

Discusses differences and connections between singing and ornamenting the works of Handel and those of Rossini-Donizetti-Bellini. Concludes that of the "singing style in Handel and in what we habitually call bel canto . . . the similarities far outweigh the differences." With ornamentation, the "differences are in the practical details" such as bass line and harmonic rhythm. Makes the important point that "the connection is Mozart," who went to Italy to learn operatic practice and wrote for many Italian singers throughout his career.

431. ——. "Unbroken Line: Vincenzo Bellini and Richard Wagner." *Opera News* 67/8 (February 2003): 34–41. ISSN 0030–3607. ML1.O482.

A persuasive account of the profound impact Bellini's music had on Wagner. "But the connection is probably still underestimated. Beethoven and Weber have long been seen as sources of Wagner's musical imagination; in fact, Bellini was at least as much so." Excellent exposition of elements of Bellini's musical style, especially melodic, that made a mark on Wagner. Connections between *Pirata* and *Walküre*; *Capuleti* and *Tristan*; *Norma* and *Tristan* and *Götterdämmerung*; *Pirata* and *Tristan.*

432. Dalmonte, Rossana. "La canzone nel melodramma italiana del primo ottocento: ricerche di metodo strutturale." *Rivista italiana di musicologia* 11/2 (1976): 230–312. ISSN 0035–6867. ML5.R79.

Topics include the genre of the canzona, related minor forms, and themes of these genres (nature, history). A number of canzoni within operas are examined by composers such as Mercadante, Donizetti, Mayr, Ricci, Rossini, Bellini, and others. Examples by Bellini are from *La straniera*, *La sonnambula*, *Beatrice di Tenda*, and *I puritani*.

433. Della Corte, Andrea. "Vicende degli stili del canto dal tempo di Gluck al novocento." In *Canto e bel canto*. Turin: G. B. Paravia, 1933, pp. 229–79. MT823.C67.

A discussion of Bellini's vocal style based on eighteenth-century antecedents, especially the music of Gluck.

434. Della Seta, Fabrizio. "Some Difficulties in the Historiography of Italian Opera." *Cambridge Opera Journal* X/1 (March 1998): 3–13. ISBN 0954–5867. ML1699.C36.

Noted Bellini scholar discusses problems to be aware of and perhaps overcome when writing about Italian opera, particularly the *primo ottocento*. One is the heavily Austro-Germanic scholarly tradition, which has imposed its own criteria and prejudices. In addition, there are problems of creative authorship and textual authenticity. Some approaches that Della Seta suggests include the sociological, consideration of the flexibility between written text and performance, the demands of the audiences, and the role of the star performers. Some of these aspects have traditionally been neglected or even scorned by past historians.

435. Di Giacomo, Salvatore. "Fenesta ca lucive." In *Figure e paesi*. Napoli, 1909.

Connection between Bellini's music and Neapolitan song.

436. Drac, Irina. *The Operas of Vincenzo Bellini and Gaetano Donizetti in the Context of Italian Music and Theater Culture of the Romantic Period*. Ph.D. diss., Istorija muzyki: Gosuarstvennaja Konservatoija, Kyviv, 1990.

In Russian. Includes a seventeen-page bibliography. Investigates the interaction between composers and performers in Italian musical culture during the first half of the nineteenth century, compares Bellini's and Donizetti's evolution from the opera seria to the lyric and Romantic opera, and analyses Donizetti's operas *La fille du régiment*, *L'elisir d'amore*, *Don Pasquale*, and *Lucia di Lammermoor*. The classic bel canto period is viewed as an independent stage of development in Italian musical theater.

437. Einstein, Alfred. "Vincenzo Bellini." *Music & Letters* 16 (1935): 325–32. ISSN 0027–4424. ML5.M64.

This article includes the subtitle: "Died 23rd December, 1835," which is incorrect. Written on the centenary of Bellini's death. "The measure of Bellini's greatness is still a matter of dispute. . . . Musical history, even the history of Italian opera, can be imagined without Bellini, but it would be very much poorer."

Chooses three operas to discuss: *La sonnambula*, *Norma*, and *I puritani*. Einstein's Germanic viewpoint leads him to call the plot of *I puritani* "silly": "Unlike the touching situations in *Sonnambula*, the mad scenes are external, cold, brilliant." A few tiny errors along the way, e.g., the role of Norma was not created by Maria Malibran.

438. Fabbri, Paolo. "Rossini e Bellini a paragone." In *"Musica franca": Essays in Honor of Frank D'Accone*. Ed. Frank A. D'Accone, Irene Alm, Alyson McLamore, and Colleen Reardon, pp. 283–95. New York: Pendragon Press, 1996. ISBN 09–45193–92–0. ML55.D15 1996.

439. Failla, Salvatore Enrico, ed. *Vincenzo Bellini: Critica-Storia-Tradizione*. Catania: Maimone, 1991. ISBN 88–77510–56–0. ML410.B44 V52 1991.

A major critical study of Vincenzo Bellini, each article including a number of full-page illustrations, many in color, many of cities and theaters. Plus a set of color plates ("Tavole") at the end.

Contents include:

- Giuseppe Giorrizzo, "Vincenzo Bellini (1801–1835): Tra Catania e l'Europa," pp. 10–19. Political, cultural background;
- Salvatore Enrico Failla, "Da Catania, a Napoli, Milano e Parigi. La vita e la musica di Vincenzo Bellini," pp. 20–31;
- Salvatore Enrico Failla, "Gli autografi belliniani del San Pietro a Majella [Napoli]," pp. 32–47. Cf. *La biblioteca del Conservatorio di San Pietro a Majella a duecento anni dalla fondazione*. Napoli: Istituto Italiano per

gli Studi Filosofici Centro di Ricerche Musicali Francesco Florimo, 1991;

- Emanuela Ersilia Abbadessa, "Gli eterografi belliniani del San Pietro a Majella," pp. 48–61;
- Alessandra Tosca, "Le stampe belliniane del San Pietro a Majella," pp. 62–75;
- Maria Rosa De Luca, "I Bozzetti per opere belliniane del San Pietro a Majella," pp. 76–81;
- Maria Rosario Adamo, "Aggiornamento alla *Bibliografia belliniana* di Orazio Viola," pp. 82–105 (see item 1);
- Roberto Alosi, "Bellini ad Acireale," pp. 106–17;
- Giampiero Tintori, "Iconografia belliniana al Museo Teatrale alla Scala," pp. 118–27;
- "Breve storia delle esecuzioni belliniane in Inghilterra," pp. 128–47. The first Bellini work heard in London was *Il pirata* at King's Theatre, Haymarket on July 28, 1830; includes quotations from contemporary reviews;
- Marco Goracci, "La tradizione belliniana attraverso i testi 'minori'," pp. 148–61;
- Fernando Giovale, "La scena evocativa," pp. 162–79;
- Aldo Nicastro, "Bellini e l'europa," pp. 180–99;
- Yonel Buldrini, "Vincenzo Bellini sventurato eroe di un giallo francese," pp. 200–14. Bellini the unfortunate hero in a thriller (what the French call a "jaune" or "roman policier") ? The author is Roxane Azimi, her book, *Bellini ou la mort d'Orphée*. The preface introduces the world of Paris where Bellini lived from 1833–35, with illustrious characters such as Alfred de Musset, George Sand, Balzac, Heine, Chopin, and Eugène Sue. The first part of the novel, "Il Canto d'Orfeo," consists of twelve chapters. Many famous musicians appear: the singers Tamburini, Ivanoff, and Rubini, for example. Part 2 is shorter, only six chapters, and deals with Bellini's "disappearance" to Puteaux. The article is illustrated: lithograph of transferral of Bellini's remains (original located in Museo belliniano); color incision of Princess Belgioiosi, and others. Facsimile of pages of autograph manuscript of *I puritani* located in Museo belliniano;
- Tavole, pp. 215–68. Includes reproductions, each the size of a full page, of playbills, portraits of composers and singers, facsimiles of autographs and libretti (printed and manuscript), opera house façades and auditoriums, stage sets, and Lake Como;
- Appendix, pp. 269ff.

440. ——. *Vincenzo Bellini, "zampognaro" del melodramma.* Catania: Maimone, 1985.

Influence of folk and popular music on Bellini, which in Naples and Sicily are heavily intertwined.

441. Favara, Alberto. *Corpus di musiche popolari siciliane*. Ed. Ottavio Tiby. Palermo: Accademia di scienze, lettere e belle arti, 1957. ML1750.S53 F412.

Sicilian folk music, history, and criticism; a body of music that possibly influenced Bellini.

442. ——. *Scritti sulla musica popolare siciliana*. Rome, 1959.

Essays on popular Sicilian music.

443. Ferris, George T. *Great Musical Composers: German, French, and Italian*. London: W. Scott, 1887. ML390.F38.

Discusses Donizetti and Bellini on pp. 200–12: "Their scores are singularly thin, measured by the standard of advanced musical studies." Calls Bellini "in many respects the greater of the two. There is scarcely to be found in music a more signal example to show that a marked individuality may rest on a narrow base." Too many errors: states that Bellini was born in 1802 and claims that *La sonnambula* and *Norma* were for a Neapolitan public are only two examples.

444. Greenspan, Charlotte Joyce. *The Operas of Vincenzo Bellini*. Ph.D. diss., University of California, Berkeley, 1977. 383 pp.

Investigates Bellini's ten operas, written from 1825 to 1835, eight of which achieved immediate success, from various viewpoints: the compositional process, sources, singers, theaters, and audiences. Contains tables and comparisons of self-borrowings among his operas, for example the pieces in *I Capuleti* taken from *Zaira* and *Adelson e Salvini*. Much of Greenspan's documentation comes from Bellini's letters. Speaks of Bellini's important influence even though he died at a young age. An important study.

445. Grey, Thomas Spencer and Joseph Kerman. "Verdi's Groundswells: Surveying an Operatic Convention." In *Analyzing Opera: Verdi and Wagner*. Ed. Carolyn Abbate and Roger Parker, pp. 153–79. Berkeley: University of California Press, 1989. ISBN 05–20061–57–8. MT95.A59.

One of the musicodramatic conventions Verdi adopted from Bellini and Donizetti is a certain type of phrase encountered often in *concertato* finales and other ensembles. Julian Budden coined the term "groundswell" for this type of phrase. The authors trace this phrase type in various contexts in Verdi's operas up to *Otello* (1887). Thomas S. Grey states that "the modifications of both musical pattern and dramatic context reveal much about Verdi's changing relationship to the inherited generic conventions of 19th-century Italian lyric drama."

446. Grossata, Elisa. "Aprile 1833-Aprile 1834: 'Un anno di vero sonno ferreo' della produzione belliniana." *Vincenzo Bellini et la France* (2007): 157–71. See item 404.

In April 1834 Bellini began composing *I puritani* after a year "di sonno ferreo" in which he absorbed Parisian cultural life.

447. Huebner, Steven. "Lyric Form in *Ottocento* Opera." *Journal of the Royal Musical Association* CXVII/1 (1992): 122–47. ISSN 0629–0403.

Summarizes the scholarship on Italian opera forms, including those by Lippmann and Balthazar (q.v.), both based on alpha-numeric analyses of poetic phrase structure. Huebner proposes a method that includes considerations of tonality and cadential articulation, which will help to display how melodic phrases interact with each other. He further believes this is preferable also from an historical perspective. He exemplifies his ideas with an alternative method to Scott Balthazar's analysis of melodies from *Semiramide* (see item 411).

448. Kimbell, David. *Italian Opera*. National Traditions of Opera series, ed. John Warrack. Cambridge: Cambridge University Press, 1991. ISBN 05–21235–33–2. ML1733.K55 1990.

Bellini and conventions of primo ottocento opera are discussed in Part 5: Chapter 21, "Italian Romanticism"; Chapter 22, "Dramatic Themes: The Libretto"; Chapter 23, "The Life of the Theatre" (administration, theatres and audiences, repertory); Chapter 24, "The Musical Language of Italian Romantic Opera" (primacy of song, art of singing); Chapter 26, "A Franker Romanticism" (epigones of Rossini, Bellini, mature works of Donizetti). An excellent, integrated study of Italian opera in general.

449. ——. "La musica strumentale nelle opere di Vincenzo Bellini." *Vincenzo Bellini nel secondo centenario della nascita* (2004): 391–409. See item 406.

Discusses the use, function, and form of the overture v. the prelude, instrumental introductions within the operas, and the role of instrumental music in transforming the traditional Italian melodrama into musical drama. Looks specifically at the overture to *Beatrice di Tenda* in light of the Rossinian model and the research done by Gildo Salerno (see item 688). Music examples.

450. Lang, Paul Henry. "Donizetti and Bellini." *A Critic at the Opera (The Experience of Opera)*. New York: Norton, 1971. ISBN 03–93007–06–5. ML1700.L26.

An essay based on reviews and articles written when Lang was the music critic for the *New York Herald Tribune* from 1954 to 1963. The Bellini discussion covers pp. 123–29. Lang begins by stating, "Bellini's operas present great difficulties to audiences beyond the Alps, let alone beyond the seas." Yet he believes that "Bellini's particular musico-dramatic conception is valid and viable, but nothing less than superlative singing can do justice to it and bring out its qualities." Provides an outline of his career, with special attention given to *Norma* and *I puritani*, and to the singers who created Bellini's music.

451. Letellier, Robert Ignatius. "Bellini and Meyerbeer." *Opera Quarterly* 17/3 (Summer 2001): 361–79. ISSN 0736–0053. ML169.O65.

Explores the reputations and revivals of the works of these two seemingly unrelated composers—Bellini known for melody and Meyerbeer for drama—and the truth of these conceptions. Topics include "The Bellinian Melody," "The Pre-Bellinian Meyerbeer: *Il crociato in Egitto*," "1831: Year of Destiny for Bellini and Meyerbeer," "The Impact of *Norma* and the Composition of *Les Huguenots*," "Three Meyerbeerian Modes of Melodic Response: Imitation, Appropriation, Transformation in the Duets of *Les Huguenots*," "Bellini and the Drama of Mass Resolve," and "A Lifelong Admiration." Demonstrates that Meyerbeer in a number of compositions displayed "his apprehension of the long Bellinian melody." Music examples and extensive source citations.

452. Lippmann, Friedrich. "Donizetti and Bellini, Ein Beitrag zur Interpretation von Donizettis Stil." *Studi musicali* 4 (1975): 193–243. ISSN 0391–7789. ML5.S9248.

An amplified German version of Lippmann's "Donizetti e Bellini, Contributo all'interpretazione dello stile donizettiano," in *Atti del 1º Convegno internazionale di studi donizettiani (22–28 Sept. 1975)*, Bergamo: Azienda Autonoma di Turismo, 1983, pp. 179–99. The author believes it is impossible to understand the style of either composer without comparing and contrasting the two. This Lippmann does, using Bellini's and Donizetti's mature works (from 1830 to 1844), and providing numerous musical examples to illustrate his points.

453. ——. *Studien zu Libretto, Arienform und Melodik der italienischen opera seria im Beginn des 19. Jahrhunderts (unter besonderer Berücksichtigung Vincenzo Bellini*). Dissertation: University of Kiel, 1962.

Much of this information was incorporated into Lippmann's subsequent publications on the music of Bellini.

454. ——. *Versificazione italiana e ritmo musicale. I rapporti tra verso e musica nell'opera italiana dell'Ottocento.* Naples: Liguori, 1986.

A landmark study of text-setting in Italian opera of the nineteenth century, also with a consideration of the second half of the eighteenth century. Numerous music examples, many from the works of Bellini. See item 342.

455. ——. "Vincenzo Bellini und die italienische Opera seria seiner Zeit. Studien über Libretto, Arienformen und Melodik." *Analecta musicologica* 6/1–12 Cologne and Vienna (1969): 1–104. ISSN 0585–6086. ML160. S893; Italian trans. rev. in Adamo and Lippmann, *Vincenzo Bellini*, pp. 313–576 (see item 343).

Lippmann considers the work of Rossini, Donizetti, Mayr, Mercadante, and Pacini. Bellini is seen as the principal figure in the development of opera seria after Rossini stopped composing operas. His melodic style is examined in detail. Lists and evaluates the principal musical sources and discusses variants among them.

This study initiated a discussion between Philip Gossett and Friedrich Lippmann in *Journal of the American Musicological Society*, beginning with Gossett's review of Lippmann's study: 24/2 (1971). Correspondence ensued in 25/2 (1972): 280–83; and 59/1 (1973): 175–77. One of the main issues was the labeling of formal structures vis-à-vis the published scores and the manuscripts. Specifically at issue concerning the music was Lippmann's labeling certain passages "arias," in which instances Gossett disagrees with him. Another major problem facing Rossini-Bellini-Donizetti scholars is that, in Gossett's words, "we know virtually nothing about the formal procedures of Paisiello, Simone Mayr, or Rossini's lesser contemporaries, not to mention possible internal developments in their style."

Review: Alberto Basso in *Rivista italiana di musicologia* V (1970): 332–34.

456. Maguire, Simon. *Vincenzo Bellini and the Aesthetics of Early Nineteenth-Century Italian Opera*. New York: Garland, 1989. ISBN 08–24023–44–7. ML410.B44 M3 1989.

A photographic reproduction of Maguire's doctoral thesis, prefaced by a brief chapter entitled "Italian Attitudes to Music at the Close of the Bel Canto Era." Part of the series "Outstanding Dissertations in Music from British Universities." Kimbell describes this Oxford dissertation (from Worcester College, 1984) as "the most important English-language writing yet to have appeared on the composer," and believes that "he has made a major contribution to our understanding of the composer and his world." In the preface, Maguire discusses Italian attitudes to music at the close of the bel canto era. He draws mainly on Italian critical and aesthetic writing dating from the end of an era dominated by the concept of bel canto.

The last part examines the bel canto aesthetic in some detail. The whole field of Italian opera studies has suffered from the application of assumptions and criteria derived solely from German Romanticism. "In particular, we need to decide whether the values derived from later operas, in which the orchestra generates dramatic power, are useful in understanding earlier works." The work is meant to show Bellini not as a precursor of Verdi but as a valid composer in his own right, coming out of an eighteenth-century Neapolitan tradition aligned with opera's Greek roots. As Kimbell notes, "it would hardly be an exaggeration to say that the modern perception of bel canto opera is false in almost every particular. Essentially the singer was a declaimer of poetry. . . . The priorities were an effortless clarity of diction, a dignified pose and apt oratorical gestures." Maguire cites the work of one of Bellini's teachers, Girolamo Crescentini's *Raccolta di essercizi per il canto all'uso del vocalizzo* (Paris, 1811). Crescentini, who taught Isabella Colbrán, Adelaide Tosi, and Andrea Nozarri, believed that "Il canto deve essere un'imitazione del discorso" (Singing should be an imitation of intelligible speech).

Table of contents includes: "The Aesthetic Roots of Italian Opera in the Early Nineteenth Century"; "The Role of the Singer on the Stage"; "Poetry and Drama in the Libretto"; "The Constitution of the Orchestra and its Place in the Melodramma"; "The Heritage of Bel Canto." Bibliography; Index.

Reviews: David Kimbell in *Music & Letters* 74/1 (1993): 141–43; William Ashbrook in *Notes* 49/1 (1992): 112–13.

457. Mangani, Marco. "Le sinfonie d'opera di Bellini: Alcune considerazioni analitiche." *Vincenzo Bellini et la France* (2007): 287–306. See item 404.

An analysis of Bellini's overtures. Mangani maintains that Bellini tried to create a new pattern in which the formal structure progressively acquired a dramaturgical function. Music examples.

458. Metzger, Heinz-Klaus and Rainer Riehn. *Vincenzo Bellini. Musik-Konzepte* 46. Munich: Text und Kritik, 1985. ISBN 38–83772–13–5. ML410.B44 V5 1985.

In German. Includes the following: Richard Wagner, "Bellini, Ein Wort zu seiner Zeit," pp. 5–6; Richard Wagner, "Eine Rezension," pp. 7–10; Henri de Saussine, "Bellinis Harmonik," pp. 11–16; Francesco Degrada, "Prolegomena zur Lektüre der Sonnambula," pp. 17–46; Johann Christian Lobe, "Bellini," pp. 47–63; Elisabeth Eleonore Bauer, "Klingt wie Bellini," pp. 64–94; Ferdinand Hiller, "Vincenzo Bellini," pp. 95–104; Rainer Riehn, "Werkverzeichnis," pp. 105–8; Rainer Riehn, "Auswahlbibliographie," pp. 109–116; Paolo Mezzacapo de Cenzo, "Auswahldiskographie," pp. 117ff.

459. Morski, Kazimierz. "Vincenzo Bellini, Fryderyk Chopin, Franz Liszt a Parigi: Espressione e virtuosismo nel pensiero creativo-interpretativo." *Vincenzo Bellini et la France* (2007): 77–108. See item 404.

The importance of virtuosity in Paris of the 1830s and how it was expressed in different, personal ways by these three composers. Bellini composed a new kind of vocal line in which virtuosity was used to express strong emotions. Music examples.

460. Noske, Frits. "The Notorious Cabaletta." In *The Signifier and the Signified: Studies in the Operas of Mozart and Verdi*. The Hague: Martinus Nijhoff, 1977, pp. 271–93. ISBN 90–24719–95–X. ML1700.1 N67. "Clarendon Paperbacks," New York: Oxford University Press, 1990. ISBN 01–98162–01–4. ML1700.1 N67 1990.

History of the cabaletta leading to Verdi's usage and transformation of it. Definitions, formats, developments. In addition to cabalettas by Rossini, Bellini, and Donizetti, the music of Mayr, Paër, Ricci, Pacini, and others is discussed.

461. Nowik, Wojciech. "Chopin e Bellini—'Casta diva,' manoscritto di Chopin." *Quadrivium* 17 (1976): 139–55. ISSN 0392–1530. ML5.O23.

Discusses a Chopin manuscript of "Casta diva," which for many years belonged to the famous singer Pauline Viardot-García. Displays how Chopin may have been influenced by Bellini's style. Facsimiles, comparison chart.

462. Osborne, Charles. *The Bel Canto Operas of Rossini, Donizetti, and Bellini*. Portland, Oregon: Amadeus, 1994. ISBN 09–31340–71–3. ML390.O82 1994.

An introduction and guide to these operas, 114 in all. Bellini's ten operas are treated on pp. 307–54. Osborne is especially good with literary background of the operas. He provides plot synopses of some but not all of the works, performance histories, and evaluations of the individual numbers in the opera, giving details of Bellini's self-borrowings. Very restricted bibliography and selective discography by John Carter. William Ashbrook, the noted Donizetti authority, deems it "at best a superficial reference work, useful for no more than a hasty brushup before an encounter with one or another of these operas," but Alan Blyth states, "No other book that I know of deals in one volume so comprehensively with the works of Rossini, Donizetti, and Bellini."

Reviews: William Ashbrook in *Opera News* 59 (November 1994): 59; Julian Budden in *The Musical Times* 135 (September 1994): 568; Alan Blyth in *Opera* 45 (July 1994): 841–42; Thomas G. Kaufman in *Opera Quarterly* 12/2 (Winter 1995–96): 115–18; Stephen A. Willier in *Notes* (March 1996): 812–13.

463. Pagannone, Giorgio. "Sui rapporti tra forme testuali e forme musicali in Bellini. Funzionalità drammatica dell'isoritmica." *Vincenzo Bellini nel secondo centenario della nascita* (2004): 251–65. See item 406.

Based on a statement by Lippmann (see item 342) that nineteenth-century Italian melodrama has a strong propensity for using isorhythm. Pagannone discusses the various dramatic uses of this device, in the portrayal of madness, for example. Numerous music examples.

464. Pannain, Guido. *Ottocento musicale italiano: saggi e note*. Milan: Edizioni Curci, 1952, pp. 16–48. ML290.4P3.

Reprint of "Saggio critico" from *Rassegna musicale* 8 (1935); discusses Bellini's musical training and influences, his development, provides an analysis and description of his operas, details of self-borrowings.

465. Piper, Charlotte Fakier. *A Study of Six Selected Coloratura Soprano "Mad Scenes" in Nineteenth-Century Opera*. DMA diss., Louisiana State University, 1990. 130 pp.

Piper deems the coloratura mad scene "significant in its display of the performer's talent" and a convention that "requires the ultimate combination of vocal virtuosity and dramatic expression." Scenes by Bellini examined are "Ah! non credea mirarti" from *La sonnambula* and "Qui la voce" from *I puritani*. Piper concludes that "the heroines from [Donizetti's] *Anna Bolena* and *Lucia di Lammermoor* seem most believable in their madness. In these two operas, the elements of plot, libretto, and music work together to make the insanity plausible. The performer's contribution is essential."

466. Pizzetti, Ildebrando. "La musica di Vincenzo Bellini." *La Voce* 7 Series: Riviste del Novecento, 8 (1915): 1070–85, 1121–57; also in "Opuscolo" in the volume *Intermezzi critici*. Florence, 1921, pp. 7–112; and in *La musica italiana dell'ottocento*. Turin: Edizioni Palatine, 1947, pp. 149–228. ML290.4 P6.

Proclaims the genius of Bellini: "Here was one who spoke with the voice of God." The appearance of Pizzetti's essay on Bellini did much for Bellini's reputation as a master composer, changing the viewpoint of him from an elegant composer whose music was designed for display of vocal embellishment to that of a serious musician whose style was deliberately designed to achieve his musicodramatic ends. Pizzetti believes Bellini achieves these goals: "The man whose eyes does not fill with tears when Norma bids farewell to her children is a mean and paltry wretch."

A careful and revealing analysis of the operas. Marks the beginning of a serious consideration of Bellini's art by musicians and scholars. Pizzetti concedes that there is a lack of polyphony even in Bellini's greatest operas but this misses the point; the composer makes his effects in other ways, mainly through melody and rhythm, i.e., linear aspects. This subsequently led many not to take Bellini's use of harmony and tonality into consideration. Pizzetti speaks of "una sensibiltà di prodigiosa finezza e purezza."

467. ——. "Spiriti e forme dell'arte belliniana." *Musica d'oggi; rassegna di vita e di coltura musicale*. New Series 1 (June 1958): 346–50. ML5. M721.

Continues his exploration of Bellini as "lirico puro," examining several arias: "Ah! non credea mirarti" from *La sonnambula*, "Casta diva" from *Norma*, and "Qui la voce sua soave" from *I puritani*.

468. Pugliatti, Salvatore. *Chopin e Bellini*. Biblioteca Mediterranea 4. Messina: La Editrice Universitaria, 1952. ML410.C54 P94.

Concerns Bellini's connection with Chopin, presented in two separate essays. Topics in the Chopin section include the "modernity" of Chopin's music, the breakdown of functional tonality, "impressionism." In the Bellini essay, topics include critics of Bellini's music, the character of Bellini's art, and impressions of *Norma*. Pugliatti notes that the subject of Chopin and Bellini has been recently treated by Bronarski in *Chopin et l'Italie* (see item 483), which he states is mostly an objective view that overlooks nineteenth-century writings on the Bellini–Chopin connection (e.g., Schumann writing in 1841), aside from the book by Liszt published in Paris in 1852. Pugliatti includes bibliographic commentary and discussion of compositional process, with extensive reference to Henri de Saussine's discussion of Bellini's harmonic practice. See items 470, 471. Pugliatti believes that Saussine reduces everything to technical details and harmonic analysis in examining the musicodramatic effect of Bellini's music, to the exclusion of the linear element, melody. Includes Mila's "Carattere dell'arte di Vincenzo Bellini," pp. 115–30. Extensive footnotes, source citations.

Reviews: *Rassegna musicale* 24 (April–July 1954): 178–79; *Rivista musicale italiana* 106 (January–March 1954): 193–95.

469. Rosen, Charles. *The Romantic Generation*. Cambridge, MA: Harvard University Press, 1995. ISBN 06–74779–33–9. ML196.R67 1995.

The music of a few composers, writing between 1820 and 1850, is considered. Principally a treatment of piano music and the Lied, but also opera, represented by Bellini and Meyerbeer, is treated. Forty-seven-page chapter on "Opera," with pp. 608–39 devoted to Bellini. In the extensive treatment of Chopin, Rosen does not neglect the Bellini connection and has several enlightening things to say about Bellinian melody. Extensive music examples.

Reviews: Christopher Hatch in *The Opera Quarterly* 12/3 (1996): 114–17; Susan McClary in *Notes* 52/4 (1996): 1139–42.

470. Saussine, Henri de. "L'Harmonie bellinienne." *Rivista musicale italiana* 27 (1920): 477–82. ISSN 0029–6228. ML5.R8.

It is noteworthy that this look at Bellini's harmony comes from a Frenchman, whereas the Italians after Pizzetti concentrated on melody. The French critics (but not only they) from Fétis onward accused Bellini of harmonic "ignorance." Analyses five examples from *La sonnambula, Norma*, and *I puritani*. Concludes that Bellini's harmonic usage contributes as much as melody and other features to his musicodramatic goals.

471. ——. "Sur Bellini harmoniste." *La Revue musicale* 156 (1935): 63–64. ISSN 0768–1593. ML5.R613.

This is a topic about which Saussine has written more extensively elsewhere. See item 470. A short essay listing specific passages that Wagner knew from Bellini's operas, features of which found their way into

Wagner's works. For example, from the final scene of *Norma*, an upward progression in the bass is used in the "Liebestod" in *Tristan und Isolde*. The essay concludes with a paragraph about Bellini's influence on Chopin.

472. Scherillo, Michele. "Bellini e la musica popolare." *Giambattista Basile; archivio di letteratura popolare e dialettale* 3 (1885): 4ff. PQ4186.G4.

Journal devoted to Italian folklore and Italian dialects studies. According to Scherillo, a phrase from the Amina's *Andante* in the final scene of *La sonnambula* ("Ah! non credea mirarti") is found in the Neapolitan song "Fenesta ca lucive," descended in turn from the siciliana "Baronessa di Carini." Also published, along with essays by Tiby (cf. item item 476) and Cocchiara (see item 426) in *Nuove effemeridi* 3 (1990).

473. Schweikert, Uwe. "Vincenzo Bellini: 'Mit Gesang zum Storben bringen'." *Opernwelt* 42 (2001): 60–65. ISSN 0030–3690.

The title translates as Vincenzo Bellini: "To Bring to Death with Song," quoting Bellini's own words to Rubini about the effects opera should have on the listener. An essay on Bellini for the bicentenary of his birth. Repeats a number of issues about him: he was no prodigy, his style was based on the older Neapolitan style, especially that of Paisiello, and the premiere of Bellini's third opera, *Il pirata* (1827) marked the beginning of Romanticism in Italian opera. Illustrations.

474. Smart, Mary Ann. "In Praise of Convention: Formula and Experiment in Bellini's Self-Borrowings." *Journal of the American Musicological Society* 100/1 (Spring 2000): 25–68. ISSN 0003–0139. ML27.U5 A83363.

From the author's abstract: "In the 1880s, the realization that Bellini had extensively reused melodies from early or unfinished works in his most famous operas provoked a small aesthetic crisis in Italy." This has been accepted, but, "Scholars have been slow to examine Bellini's self-borrowings for clues to the evolution of his style or to his attitudes toward the relations between melody and drama.

"Most of Bellini's self-borrowings show the composer simplifying his melodies, reducing harmonic and melodic variety as if to distance himself from *bel canto* convention." Smart argues that for Bellini "self-borrowing was entangled with the looser techniques of allusion and reliance on melodic convention. For this reason, study of the self-borrowings provides a model for engaging with the musical language of early nineteenth-century Italian opera, redressing the tendency to dismiss its musical detail as 'merely' conventional and thus unworthy of analysis."

475. Tari, Antonio. *Vincenzo Bellini: Reminiscenze*. Naples, 1876. Rpt. in Antonio Tari, *Saggi di metafisica e di estetica*. Ed. Benedetto Croce, pp. 129–44. Bari: G. Laterza, 1911. BH194.T3.

Tari, a *scapigliatura*, was professor of aesthetics at the University of Naples from 1861 until his death in 1884. Cf. Kimbell, *Norma*, item 646, pp. 99–101. Croce notes that Tari wrote "pages which are of a kind very rare in our literature, and which could only have arisen from a mind cultivated in German Romantic literature, but which, for all its culture and predilections, did not lose the qualities of the southerner, clear-sighted and slightly teasing." Tari made a statement that, in his own words, "will seem very strange. And that is, that Bellini should be regarded as an embryonic Wagner. . . . So Bellinism, developed, amplified, but always given lyric form by other Italian Orpheuses of Bellinian stock, will very probably some day become the true and longed-for MUSIC OF THE FUTURE."

476. Tiby, Ottavio. "Leggenda e realtà d'una canzone popolare." In *Annali del museo Pitrè* 5/7 (1954–56): 68ff.

Also published, along with essays on Italian popular music by Scherillo (see item 472) and Cocchiara (see item 426) in *Nuove effemeridi* 3 (1990).

477. ——. *Mal di melodramma*. La Scala Museum, Milan I. Milan: Ghisoni, 1977. ML1733.4.T56

The title, "Opera Sickness," refers to a comment by Gian Francesco Malipiero about Italian musical life in the nineteenth century. This contains essays about various aspects of that musical life—the theaters, the public, the singers, the censor (particularly about *La traviata*). The monograph concludes with sketches about the vocal styles of Rossini, Bellini, Donizetti, and Verdi.

478. Wadsworth, Stephen. "Bonynge on Bel Canto." *Opera News* 40/16 (February 28, 1976): 18–22. ISSN 0030–3607. ML1.O482.

An interview with the conductor Richard Bonynge at a time when he and his wife, Joan Sutherland, were performing *I puritani* at the Metropolitan Opera, about interpreting Bellini and other early-nineteenth-century music. Bonynge talks about bel canto and Bellini style: "Handel, Bellini, and Massenet were three composers who I think understood the human voice more than any others." Bonynge also calls Bellini a composer of great originality because of his long melodic lines and the careful setting of his recitatives. Discusses ornamentation of Bellini's music: it needs very little, only in repeat of cabalettas; Bellini writes in most of the appoggiaturas in the recitatives. One writes ornaments in the style of the composer from knowing the composer's works; most published ornaments are from the wrong period, around 1890 or 1900. We do have some ornaments and cadenzas that Pasta and Rubini actually sang but it is not necessary to stick to them. Discusses how singing might have changed since Bellini's day; certainly the production of the tenor voice is quite different. In Bellini's day a mixture of head voice and falsetto was learned for the high register, whereas today we hear high Cs from the chest.

Treats Bellini's female singers—Grisi, Pasta, Malibran—and how they would not hesitate to transpose his music down a step or a third. Discusses possible cuts in *I puritani*, Pepoli's libretto, and the orchestration of Bellini's final opera.

479. Witzenmann, Wolfgang. "Grundzüge der Instrumentation in italienischen Opern von 1770 bis 1830." In *Analecta musicologica* 21 (1981): 276ff. ISSN 0585–6086. ML160.S893.

Includes some specific references to Bellini. A general study of Italian opera orchestration that provides a basis for the study of Bellini's practices.

480. Zedda, Alberto. "La strumentazione nell'opera teatrale." In *Atti del primo Convegno internazionale di studi donizettiani*. Bergamo: Azienda Autonoms di Turismo, 1983, pp. 453–542.

A survey of the instrumentation of the typical primo ottocento opera orchestra, how various formal elements (i.e., arias, scenas, ensembles, finales) are orchestrated, and the special use of individual instruments.

Note: Additional relevant materials include:

481. Bénédit, G. *Vincenzo Bellini, Etude musicale et dramatique, lue dans la séance publique de l'Académie de Marseille, 22 mai 1853, par G. Bénédit.* Publié par *la Revue Meridionale*, avec un tiré à part, et reproduite par *le Sémaphore de Marseille.*

482. Bertetti, Maria. *Contributo allo studio di alcuni problemi drammatici nel melodramma di Vincenzo Bellini*. Tesi di laurea in storia della music—Milano Università, Facolta di lettere e filosofia, 1966–67. Relatore: Prof. G. Barblan.

483. Bronarski, Ludwik. *Chopin et l'Italie*. Preface by D.-E. Inghelbrecht. Lausanne: Editions La Concorde, 1947. ML410.C54 B84.

484. Clementi, Filippo. *Il linguaggio dei suoni: Belliniani e Wagneristi*. Rome: Tipografia Roma, 1881. ML410.W12 I82.

9

Manuscript Studies, Collections, Collected Editions, Critical Evaluation of Editions of Bellini's Works, Editors, Publishing Firms

Italian libraries and archives containing Bellini manuscripts include: Naples, Library of the Conservatorio di Musica "S. Pietro a Majella"; Rome, Library of the Conservatorio di Musica "S. Cecilia"; Milan, Library of the Conservatorio di Musica "Giuseppe Verdi"; Catania, Museo belliniano; Milan, Casa Ricordi (which lost most of its correspondence with Bellini and Romani during World War II); Palermo, Biblioteca Comunale; Naples, Biblioteca Lucchesi Palli; and others. Collections in Great Britain, France, the United States, and other countries to a lesser extent also contain manuscript sources by Bellini.

See item 22, works-list by Simon Maguire and Mary Ann Smart in *New Grove Dictionary* for location of manuscripts and early printed sources.

A complete critical edition is in progress: Edizione Critica delle opere di Vincenzo Bellini. Milan: Ricordi (2008–ca. 2020), Fondazione Teatro Massimo Bellini di Catania. See items 489, 492, 493, and 508.

Many of the entries in this section have to do either with editing problems in general or with manuscripts found in specific collections. Manuscript issues and problems also appear in Studies of Individual Operas in Chapter 10. For example, see the volumes in the series *Early Romantic Opera*.

485. Abbadessa, Emanuela Ersilia. "Le carte belliniane del Civico Museo Bibliografico musicale e della Biblioteca del Conservatorio di Musica G. B. Martini di Bologna." *Note su note* 3 (1995): 12–75. ISSN 1122–0252. ML5.N793.

Bellini holdings in Bologna. See items 395 and 408.

486. ——. "Gli eterografi belliniani del San Pietro a Majella." In *Vincenzo Bellini: Critica-Storia-Tradizione*. Ed. Salvatore Enrico Failla, pp. 48–61. Catania: Maimone, 1991 (see item 439).

Looks at sources such as orchestral parts, choral parts, reductions for organ, piano, or band—sources not in the composer's hand—found at the Naples Conservatory; illustrated with portraits of Maddalena Fumaroli, the singer Henriette Méric-Lalande, and a watercolor of Bellini from the Scala Museum, Milan, by Louis Dupré.

487. Adami, Giuseppe. *Giulio Ricordi e i suoi musicisti*. Milan: Trevisini, 1933. ML427.R54 A3.

Giulio Ricordi (1840–1912). Giulio was not born until after Bellini's death but he and his firm were central to the history of publication of Bellini's works.

488. Basso, Alberto. "La collezione di autografi musicali della RAI di Torino." In *Nuova rivista musicale italiana* 3/5 (1969): 942–49. ISSN 0029–6228. ML5.N93.

These six autographs, acquired by RAI of Turin because of the interest of Giulio Razzi, include letters of Johann Sebastian Bach, Ludwig van Beethoven, Bellini, and Georges Bizet. Also included are two music autographs of Bellini. Description and diplomatic transcriptions are given of each.

489. Bellini, Vincenzo. *I Capuleti e i Montecchi, tragedia lirica in two acts* by Felice Romani, ed. Claudio Toscani. In 3 vols. Full score and commentary. Chicago: University of Chicago Press, 2008 (Distributed for Casa Ricordi). ISBN 978–88–7592–729–5.

The first volume to appear in the Critical Edition of the Works of Bellini (WVB) in Series I: Operas. The popularity of this opera led to its being used in a multitude of various reworkings for different performances. Through the years, these alterations led, for one example, to a much heavier orchestration than the composer intended. This new critical edition corrects those emendations and restores the composer's original dynamic and expressive markings. Also, material that has traditionally been cut from performance is now restored. Features both the original version and Bellini's revisions for its performance in Milan in December 1830.

490. Brauner, Patricia B. "Le edizioni critiche di opera italiana dell'Ottocento: scopi, fonti, metodi e futuro." *Fonti musicali italiana* IV (1999): 207–18. ML111.C378 1989.

491. Caroccia, Antonio. "I manoscritti e le lettere autografe di Bellini conservati nella Biblioteca del Conservatorio di musica 'San Pietro a Majella' di Napoli." In *Quaderni dell'Istituto musicale Vincenzo Bellini di Catania*, Vol. II. Ed. Roberto Carnevale, pp. 113–60. Libreria Musicale Italiana.

Lucca: LIM Editrice, 2001. See item 401. ISBN 88–70962–84–9. ML 410.B44. V463x 2001.

A comprehensive listing of the Bellini holdings in one of the most important collections of Belliniana. Includes musical manuscripts of all genres and autograph letters. Documentation for each entry is extensive, done according to the uniform cataloging model of the Istituto Centrale per il Catalogo Unico delle bibioteche italiane e per informazioni bibliografiche, ed. Massimo Gentili Tedeschi, published Rome, 1989. Introductory essay with extensive bibliographical footnotes, especially concerning Francesco Florimo.

492. Della Seta, Fabrizio. "Conversazione belliniana," conducted by Stephen Hastings. *Musica, rivista di informazione musicale e discografica* 131 (November 2001): 34–36.

An interview with a current Bellini authority, the general editor of the Bellini critical edition, which is to be published by Ricordi, Milan. Della Seta speaks of the difficulties of publishing a critical edition: it will take up to twenty-five years, the cost of the volumes will be high, and most musicians seem to be satisfied with the current, corrupt scores. Also discusses the Bellini celebrations in Catania in November 2001 (a list of events is provided on the back cover of this publication); the foundation of a Center for Bellini Studies (similar to those for Verdi in Parma and Rossini in Pesaro) and their plans to publish a critical edition of Bellini's letters; multiple versions of certain operas (e.g., *Adelson e Salvini* and the short musical setting of Gualtiero's suicide at the conclusion of *Il pirata*); and Bellini and politics in terms of *Norma* and *I puritani*.

493. Della Seta, Fabrizio and Simonetta Ricciardi, eds. "Vincenzo Bellini: Verso l'edizione critica." *Atti del Convegno internazionale*, Siena, 1–3 June, 2000. *Chigiana* XLV. Florence: Olschki, 2004. ISBN 88–22252–99–3.

Conference held to discuss plans and criteria for a Bellini Critical Edition. Contents include:

- Friedrich Lippmann. "Cosa possiamo imparare dale fonti per la conoscenzo dello stile belliniano? Filologia e interpretazione," pp. 1–14.
- Pierluigi Petrobelli. "Antiche radici e nuove funzioni della melodia belliniana," pp. 15–22. Compares Rossinian melody, in which "l'ornamentazione non è altro che una estrema manifestazione del principio della dimunizione," with that of Bellini, whose melodic forms "determinano lo svolgimento del discorso musicale."
- Charles Brauner. "Decisioni critiche per l'edizione critica di Bellini," pp. 23–47. Presents several examples, particularly from the autograph of *Norma*, with which the editors of the Bellini critical edition will be confronted. Facsimiles of music autographs.
- Marco Beghelli. "D'acciaccature, d'accenti e d'altre minuzie," pp. 49–59. Many specific examples. Autograph facsimiles from *I puritani*.

- Markus Engelhardt. “Bellini sacre,” pp. 61–75. Makes the point that Bellini wrote quite a number of sacred compositions and a complete works edition will help bring them to light and indeed will be incomplete without them. The main focus is Bellini’s four settings of “Tantum ergo.” Music examples.
- Andrea Chegai. “La musica strumentale di Bellini e le prime sinfonie d’opera: Elementi di prassi compositiva,” pp. 77–100. Analysis and comparison of some of these early sinfonie: compositional methods, formal organization.
- Marco Uvietta. “Da *Zaira* a *I Capuleti e I Montecchi*: Preliminari di un’indagine filologica sui processi di ricomposizione,” pp. 101–39. Examples of music from Bellini’s operatic failure *Zaira* being used extensively in *I Capuleti* and to a lesser degree in *Norma*. Music examples, facsimiles. Tables comparing texts.
- Claudio Toscani. “*I Capuleti e I Montecchi*: Note margine all’edizione critica,” pp. 141–61. Examines sources for the opera. Questions, principles, methods, choices for a critical edition. Cites work done on editions of Rossini, Donizetti, Verdi, and Meyerbeer. Music facsimiles.
- Philip Gossett. “Trasporre Bellini,” pp. 163–85.
- Fabbri, Paolo. “Per un’edizione critica del *Pirata*,” pp. 187–217. Many specific details for a critical edition of *Il pirata.*
- Alexander Weatherson. “ ‘Nell’orror di mie sciagure’: Pacini, la parodia e *Il pirata*,” pp. 219–34. On November 20, 1826 Pacini visited the Naples Conservatory and Zingarelli. The previous night had seen the great success of his opera *Niobe*. This was probably Pacini’s first encounter with Bellini, who came to regard the fellow Catanese with suspicion and jealousy. This article explores the textual and musical parallels between Pacini’s *I cavalieri di Valenza* and Bellini’s *Il pirata*. Further attention is given to Gualtiero’s suicide scene, abandoned after the premiere of *Pirata*, leaving the conclusion of the opera to Imogene and her *gran scena di pazzia*. Rubini sang the tenor ending at the Teatro Comunale in Bologna in the autumn of 1830, but at whose instigation, his or Bellini’s? Weatherson calls the tenor ending “questo finale alla Ravenswood *avant la lettre*.” Text of this *scena ultima*, “Tu vedrai la sventura,” is given in one of several Appendices. Music examples. Facsimiles of stage sets.
- Domenico De Meo. “Stessi versi, altra musica—Le diverse redazinoni del Coro ‘Guerra, Guerra!’,” pp. 245–70.
- A. Roccatagliata and Luca Zoppelli. “Testo, Messinscena, tradizione: Le testimonianze dei libretti,” pp. 271–96. Discusses two issues: what are the places of the libretto and the tradition of staging as part of a critical edition?
- John Rosselli. “Per un’edizione critica dell’epistolario belliniano,” pp. 291–96. Concerned with a critical edition of Bellini’s letters, especially in light of Florimo’s actions in falsifying and withholding a number of them.

- Emanuele Senici. "Per una biografia musicale di Amina," pp. 297–314. See item 620.
- Damien Colas. "Le revisioni delle parti vocali negli autografi di Bellini," pp. 315ff.

494. Fabbri, Paolo. "*Il pirata* e il suo processo compositivo." *Vincenzo Bellini nel secondo centenario della nascita* (2004): 321–90. See item 406.

Discusses three manuscript sources: autograph musical sketches including transcriptions and facsimiles; early manuscript versions of the libretto; and facsimile pages from the autograph score, mostly autograph, which shows evidences of compositional process. Many textual and musical variants are presented.

495. Failla, Salvatore Enrico. "Gli autografi belliniane del San Pietro a Majella." In *Vincenzo Bellini: Critica-Storia-Tradizione*. Ed. Salvatore Enrico Failla, pp. 32–47. Catania: Maimone, 1991. See item 439.

A discussion of the Bellini autographs in the library of the Naples Conservatory. Illustrated, facsimiles.

496. ——, Emanuela Ersilia Abbadessa, and Maria Rosa De Luca. *Minima belliniana. Tre saggi*. Bonanno: Acireale, 1996. ISBN 88–77960–86–8. ML410.B44 A33 1996.

This volume is part of the research project on Bellini supported by the Cattedra di Storia della Musica dell'Università degli Studi di Catania (Dipartimento di Scienze Storiche, Antropologiche e Geografiche) and financed by the Assessorato dei Beni Culturali della Regione Siciliana. It contains three essays dealing with Bellini materials in both Italian and foreign libraries.

The essay by Emanuela Ersilia Abbadessa analyses the sources and the history of these documents. Treating these subjects and summing up the situation are the other two essays by Maria Rosa De Luca and Salvatore Enrico Failla.

497. Lippmann, Friedrich. "Abbozzi di Vincenzo Bellini nella Biblioteca Communale di Mineo." *Nuovi annali della Facoltà di magisterio dell'Università di Messina* 2 (1984): 839–44. AS221.N86.

Bellini sketches found in the Biblioteca Communale, Mineo.

498. ——. "Belliniana II." *Vincenzo Bellini nel secondo centenario della nascita* (2004): 431–56. See item 406.

Updates his 1977 "Belliniana" but of the works he discusses, admits that only one is definitely by Bellini, the quartet "T'intendo sì, mio cor," about which he adds information missing from his previous discussion of the work in "Belliniana." Disputes his former belief (given in *New Grove Dictionary* 1980) that Sonata in F Major for four hands is by Bellini, which turned out to be a transcript of the "Polacca" from Beethoven's Serenade, Op. 8. The authenticity of a piano version of the overture to *I puritani* is deemed "incerta." Facsimiles and extensive music examples.

499. ——. "Pagine sconosciute de *I Capuleti e i Montecchi* e *Beatrice di Tenda* di Vincenzo Bellini." *Rivista italiana di musicologia* 2/1 (1967): 140–51. ISSN 0035–6867. ML5.R79.

Includes facsimiles. A study of the sources for these two operas. The most important non-autograph source for *I Capuleti e i Montecchi* is in the Archivio Ricordi in Milan. It includes, however, numerous autograph sections including the previously unknown arioso "Morir dovessi ancora" (given in facsimile), composed for the performance at La Scala, Milan. A number of newly discovered details in the sources for *Beatrice di Tenda* are presented.

500. ——. "Quellenkundliche Anmerkungen zu einigen Opern Vincenzo Bellinis." *Analecta musicologica* 4 (1967): 131–53. ISSN 0585–6086 ML160.S893.

The author described this now forty-year-old article as "a preliminary study for a critical edition of the works of Bellini." Sources of Bellini's operas and some variant problems are presented. Cf. individual operas where this article is cited.

501. Maguire, Simon. "La grafia di Bellini in alcuni autografi." *Vincenzo Bellini nel secondo centenario della nascita* (2004): 457–85. See item 406.

Bellini's hand in musical sketches acquired by Sotheby in the early 1990s and in other music manuscripts and letters, examined by forensic musicologist and Bellini scholar Maguire. Sources for *Adelson e Salvini* and other works by Bellini. Facsimiles. Appendix listing manuscripts examined.

502. ——, ed. *Adelson e Salvini* facsimile. British Library MS Add. 33361 and 33362. Cremona: Fondazione Claudio Monteverdi, 2002.

The publication of a facsimile edition of Vincenzo Bellini's *Adelson e Salvini* by Simon Maguire is part of the initiation of the critical edition of Bellini's works. The facsimile edition of these two British Library manuscripts represents a revised version in two acts of Bellini's three-act original, dating from 1824 or early 1825. Maguire has determined that the manuscript is entirely in the hands of copyists and possibly even dates from after Bellini's death in 1835. This version contains significant and extensive variations from all other known sources of the opera: included, for example, are orchestrally accompanied recitatives not found elsewhere and a different setting of the heroine's aria, "Dopo l'oscuro nembo," which, as Maguire notes, "alone would make it worthwhile bringing this score to wider attention." Contains an extensive and authoritative essay by the author.

Review: Stephen A. Willier, *Journal of the American Liszt Society* 52/3 (Fall 2002/Spring 2003): 174–80.

503. Morelli, Giovanni. "L'edizione critica delle opere di Giuseppe Verdi." *Venezia Arti* II (1998): 197–99.

Considerations for a critical edition of a nineteenth-century Italian opera composer.

504. Parker, Roger. "A Donizetti Critical Edition in the Postmodern World." In *L'opera teatrale di Gaetano Donizetti*. Ed. Francesco Bellotto, pp. 57–68. Bergamo: Comune di Bergamo, 1993.

Problems and methods for a critical edition of a *primo ottocento* opera composer, Bellini's close contemporary Donizetti.

505. Pastura, Francesco. "Rivelazioni degli autografi musicali belliniani: varianti e temi inediti." *Vincenzo Bellini: numero commemorativo a cura della Rivista del Comune di Catania*. 1925, pp. 25–34.

Presents unpublished variants found in Bellini's manuscripts.

506. Porter, Andrew. "Footnotes on *Norma*." *About the House* 2/8 (Christmas 1967): 12–14. ISSN 0001–3242 ML5.A22.

Cites six passages in *Norma* that are taken from earlier works; discusses editions: "None of the scores currently available faithfully represents Bellini's autograph; and that autograph (published in facsimile in 1935) presents problems in the form of cancellations, subsequently reinstated with the words 'si fa.' But we can distinguish between bars lightly crossed through, as if for a particular performance, and bars heavily excised in Bellini's emphatic way. On the whole the Boosey vocal score is the most accurate and the most complete. Without going into small matters, I list some larger points that markedly affect a performance." This he does on page 14. Note: The 1935 facsimile is no longer in print; the current facsimile is found in *Early Romantic Opera*, vol. 4. See item 645.

507. Riva, Federica. "I documenti belliniani in Italia: lo stato della ricerca." *Vincenzo Bellini nel secondo centenario della nascita* (2004): 487–519. See item 406.

Discusses the Italian sources for a Bellini critical edition: Centro di documentazione belliniani. Table providing list of manuscripts, printed scores and libretti of Bellini's works in the data base Musica di SBN. Another table presenting a concensus of manuscripts of Bellini's works in Musica SBN, URFM, and RISM A/II comprising some 800 items. Speaks of the need to standardize bibliographical information.

508. Roccatagliati, Alessandro. "Sul cantiere dell'edizione critica della *Sonnambula*." *Vincenzo Bellini nel secondo centenario della nascita* (2004): 411–29. See item 406.

La Sonnambula will be the second of Bellini's operas to appear in the new critical edition, to be edited by Alessandro Roccatagliata and Luca Zoppelli. Sources and editorial principles are discussed.

509. Santagata, Ettore. *Il R[egio] Museo storico musicale di S. Pietro a Majella*. Naples: F. Fiannini, 1930. ML136.N15 C6.

The conservatory where Bellini studied, which now houses a Bellini archive. This work includes 155 illustrations of various types, including portraits and autographs.

510. Scherillo, Michele. *Belliniana: nuove note*. Milan: Ricordi, 1883.

Scherillo was a student of Bellini's sketches and noted that Bellini had used music originally intended for *Ernani* in *La sonnambula*. Bellini had mentioned this in a letter to Giovanni Ricordi but the claim enraged the Catanese and Bellini acquaintance Antonino Amore. The latter studied the *Ernani* sketches only to substantiate Scherillo's claim, in addition demonstrating that parts of *Ernani* were also used in *Norma*. Scherillo and Amore engaged in a heated polemic over this issue in the 1880s.

511. Tosca, Alessandra. "Le stampe belliniane del San Pietro a Majella." In *Vincenzo Bellini: Critica-Storia-Tradizione*. Ed. Salvatore Enrico Failla, pp. 62–74. Catania: Maimone, 1991. See item 439.

A discussion of the early prints of Bellini's music located in the library of the Naples Conservatory. Illustrated, facsimiles. For *Il pirata*, for example, she lists of particular importance the first printed edition, published by Ricordi in 1827; the piano reduction edited by Del Tramater (n.1. 612–13) and two copies of the engraved score for printing (n.1. 680–789).

512. Turner, J. Rigbie. "Ninetenth-Century Autograph Music Manuscripts in the Pierpont Morgan Library: A Check List." *Nineteenth Century Music* 4/1 (1980): 49–69; updates in *Nineteenth-Century Autograph Music Manuscripts in the Pierpont Morgan Library*. New York: Pierpont Morgan Library, 1982. ML136.N5 P56 1982. ISBN 08–75980–77–5; and *Four Centuries of Opera: Manuscripts and Printed Editions in The Pierpont Morgan Library*. New York: Pierpont Morgan Library/Dover Publications, 1983. ISBN 04–86246–02–7. ML141.N4 P57 1983.

Six items for Bellini, including short excerpts and sketches from *Il pirata*, *La sonnambula*, and unidentified sketches that may be from *Norma* or *I puritani*. The 1980 and 1982 publications are alphabetical listings but the 1983 publication is chronological with many facsimile reproductions. In addition to the checklist of manuscripts (pp. 121–23), the 1983 publication includes a checklist of printed opera libretti and scores (pp. 124–27).

513. Ufficio Ricerca Fondi Musicali.

The Italian RISM center in Milan. Their catalogue has extensive information about Bellini manuscripts and early prints.

514. Vittadini, Stefano, compiler. Preface by Renato Simoni. *Catalogo del Museo Teatrale alla Scala*. Milan: E. Bestetti, 1940. ML136.M6 M9 1940.

    A number of Bellini manuscripts are housed at the Scala library-museum. Cf. also this author's *Museo teatrale alla Scala, 3 vols*. Vol. 2: *Catalogo*. Milan: Electa, 1976. PN1620.M5 M8 1976.

Note: Additional revelant sources include:

515. Amore, Antonino. "A proposito di un manoscritto di Vincenzo Bellini." *La sicilia* 7, No. 320 (November 19, 1907).

516. Caselli, Aldo. *Catalogo delle opere liriche pubblicate in Italia*. Florence: Olschki, 1969. ML128.O4 C39.

517. Roberti, Giuseppe. "Da autografi di grandi musicisti." *Rivista musicale italiana* 10/4 (1903): 625–45. ISSN 0029–6228. ML5.R8.

10

Studies of Individual Operas and Bellini's Non-Operatic Works

For several of the operas there is a "Dossier d'oeuvre" at the Paris Bibliothèque de l'Opéra containing playbills, programs, libretti, and reviews from journals and newspapers both contemporary to Bellini's time and up to the present. Similar assimilations exist in other major libraries.

See works-list by Simon Maguire and Mary Ann Smart in *The New Grove Dictionary* (item 22) for location of manuscripts and early printed sources. Additional remarks about sources will be found under each title below.

518. Della Corte, Andrea. "Le prime opere." In *Vincenzo Bellini, l'uomo, le sue opere, la sua fama*. Ed. Ildebrando Pizzetti, pp. 39–80 (see item 242). Milan: Fratelli Treves, 1936. ML410.B44 P58.

Discusses Bellini's first five operas, although not in chronological order.

STUDIES OF INDIVIDUAL OPERAS

Adelson e Salvini, dramma semiseria in three acts

Libretto by Andrea Leone Tottola; spoken dialogue with a buffo role in Neapolitan dialect.

Premiere between February 10 and 15, 1825, for Naples Conservatory: staged professionally for the first time in 1985; new version in 1826–27 as *dramma semiseria* in two acts with *recitativo secco* replacing spoken dialogue, heard for the first time in 1992 in Catania. Bellini recycled some pieces for subsequent four works. Example: The soprano's opening aria ("Dopo l'oscuro nembo") was later adapted as Giulietta's first aria in *I Capuleti e i Montecchi*.

519. Bellini, Vincenzo. *Adelson e Salvini*, prima versione, partitura, revisione e trascrizione dall'autografo di Salvatore Enrico Failla. Catania: Università degli Studi, 1988.

The original version of *Adelson e Salvini*, score with revisions, based on the autograph, done by the Bellini expert Failla.

520. ——. *Adelson e Salvini*, prima versione, spartito per canto e pianoforte, riduzione dalla partitura autografia di Salvatore Enrico Failla. Catania: Università degli Studi, 1988.

The piano-vocal score of the original version of *Adelson e Salvini*, based on the autograph.

521. De Meo, Domenico. "'O raro amico, vero esempio d'amistà.' La seconda versione di *Adelson e Salvini*," *Adelson e Salvini*, program from Teatro Massimo "Bellini," Catania, 1992, pp. 9–41.

A substantial study by a Bellini scholar connected with the world premiere of the opera in Catania in 1992. The program also contains a complete libretto, pp. 65–87.

522. Failla, Salvatore Enrico. "*Adelson e Salvini* (prima versione)." In *I teatri di Vincenzo Bellini*. Ed. Roberto Alajmo, pp. 13–28, 243–57. Palermo: Edizioni Novecento, 1986. See item 750. ISBN 88–37300–48–4. ML410. B44 T4 1986

Introductory text to the opera, followed by numerous illustrations. Failla edited the score for the first version of this opera. See item 519.

523. ——. "La prima stecura di *Adelson e Salvini*." *Vincenzo Bellini et la France* (2007): 635–55. See item 404.

A further reassessment of Bellini's first opera, especially an investigation of the relationship between Fioravanti's work of 1816 and this opera. Failla refutes the perceived minor status of Bellini's work.

524. Maguire, Simon. "*Adelson e Salvini*." In *The New Grove Dictionary of Opera*. 4 vols. Ed. Stanley Sadie. New York: Macmillan, 1992. Vol. 1: 20. ISBN 09–35859–92–6. ML102.O6 N5 1992.

Lists sources of libretto, provides plot summary, and discusses genesis, musical characteristics, and revisions.

525. Marcia, Marco. "La prima versione dell' *Adelson e Salvini* e la tradizione napoletana dell'opera buffa 'alla francese'." *Vincenzo Bellini nel secondo centenario della nascita* (2004): 77–95. See item 406.

Examines manuscripts of other pupils of the Naples Conservatory who wrote student works before and after Bellini. Argues that it was common for Naples Conservatory students to start with an opera buffa in the French manner, i.e., alternating spoken dialogue and musical numbers. Enumerates the reasons why Bellini wrote his first opera in this genre and notes the two autograph versions in which Bellini's work exists.

526. Orrey, Leslie. "The Literary Sources of Bellini's First Opera." *Music & Letters* 55 (1974): 24–29. ISSN 0027–4224. ML5.M64.

Adelson e Salvini was produced at the Real Collegio Musicale, Naples, while Bellini was still a student there in 1825. It was a two-act opera buffa using the French convention of spoken dialogue (in Neapolitan dialect) rather than sung recitative. The score was never published and at the time of this article the opera had never been performed elsewhere. Bellini later produced another version, which was published twice, by Ricordi in 1903 and by the Parisian publisher Schonenberger sometime after 1853. These two scores are not at all identical.

The librettist for the original version was Andrea Leone Tottola. Orrey discusses settings of this libretto prior to and after Bellini's. The source of the libretto was the novella "Adelson et Salvini. Anecdote anglaise" (Paris, 1772) by François-Thomas de Baculard d'Arnaud (1718–1805). Orrey traces several plays of his that were fashioned into opera librettos, set to music by composers such as Dalayrac and Donizetti (*La favorite*). Orrey provides plots of both d'Arnaud's novella and Tottola-Bellini's opera, discusses the similarities and differences, and makes clear the connection to Goethe's *Werther*, published in 1774. While Tottola could have had access to d'Arnaud's works in Italian translation, "there are so many divergencies between the 'Anecdote' and Tottola's libretto that one suspects an intermediary work, and one does indeed exist." This was the three-act drama *Adelson et Salvini* by Prospère Delamare, produced in Paris and published there in 1803. Orrey has not examined this work but has used the following source for his information about it: Derk Inklaar, *François-Thomas de Baculard d'Arnaud, ses imitateurs en Holland et dans d'autres pays*, 's-Gravenhage, 1925. Orrey concludes, providing specific examples, that there "can be little doubt that this was Tottola's source."

527. Pastura, Francesco. "Appunti belliniani. La duplice redazione dell' *Adelson e Salvini*." *Gazzetta musicale di Napoli* 2/7–8 (July/August 1956): 121–24.

The two versions of Bellini's first opera are briefly explored.

528. Tottola, Leone Andrea. *Adelson e Salvini*, libretto, revisione e trascrizione dal libretto del 1816 di Salvatore Enrico Failla. Catania: Università degli Studi, 1988.

A transcription of Tottola's libretto from 1816; part of Failla's study and edition of this opera.

Note: See also facsimile edition by S. Maguire, item 502.

***Bianca e Fernando, melodramma* in two acts**

Libretto by Domenico Gilardoni; reworked by Felice Romani for Genoa (1828).

The first version was titled *Bianca e Gernando*; premiere May 30, 1826, Teatro San Carlo, Naples; second version premiered April 7, 1828, Teatro Carlo Felice, Genoa.

529. *Atti del Convegno di studi sull'opera "Bianco e Fernando" di Vincenzo Bellini*. Genoa, 1979.

The congress report of the conference on *Bianca e Fernando* held in Genoa in 1978. Papers presented include:

- Luigi Baldacci, "Il libretto di *Bianca e Fernando*";
- Edilio Frassoni, "*Bianco e Fernando* nella critica coeva." Traces early performances and reception in both Italian and foreign theaters;
- Lippmann, Friedrich. "*Bianca e Fernando*. Genesi e struttura musicale." Explores the two versions of the opera;
- Federico Mompellio, "Vincenzo Bellini nel melodramma *Bianca e Fernando*."

530. Budden, Julian. "*Bianca e Fernando*." In *I teatri di Vincenzo Bellini*. Ed. Roberto Alajmo, pp. 29–38. Palermo: Edizioni Novecento, 1986. See item 750. ISBN 88–37300–48–4. ML410.B44 T4. 1986.

A volume about productions of Bellini's operas. Each opera is given a separate chapter. There is an extensive prose introduction to each chapter, which then consists of numerous illustrations, many of them of set designs.

531. Lamacchia, Saverio. "Recezione e ideologia 'Ancien Régime' da *Zelmira* a *Bianca e Fernando*." *Vincenzo Bellini nel secondo centenario della nascita* (2004): 267–97. See item 406.

These two works by Rossini and Bellini were heard in Naples for the first time within four years of each other (1822 and 1826). The main issue here is the effect of Rossini's work on other composers, such as Pacini, Mercadante, Donizetti, and Bellini. Also mentions the precedent of *Fidelio* as a model for *Bianca e Fernando*. Extensive music examples.

532. Lippmann, Friedrich. "L'esordio napoletano di Bellini—*Bianca e Fernando*." In *Il teatro di San Carlo 1737–1987*. Ed. Bruno Cagli and Agostino Ziino. 3 vols. Vol. 2: *L'opera, il ballo*. Ed. Agostino Ziino, pp. 171–78. Naples: Electa, 1987. ML290.8.N2 M3 1987.

Bellini's debut opera at the Teatro San Carlo, Naples, by one of the leading Bellini experts.

533. ——. "Quellenkundliche Anmerkungen zu einigen Opern Vincenzo Bellinis." *Analecta musicologica* 4 (1967): 131–53. See item 500. ISSN 0585–6086. ML160. S893.

Lippmann notes that nothing is known of the literary sources for this opera. In the Neapolitan Biblioteca Lucchesi Palla, Lippmann found a prose libretto fragment connected to Gilardoni's drama. It is titled *Bianca e Fernando alla tomba di Carlo IV Duca di Agrigento. Dramma in cinque Atti*. The author is Carlo Roti. This fragment differs from the opera libretto, which is an expansion of it, in the conclusion of the plot. Gilardoni, but especially Bellini, decided to simplify the ending, just as Bellini was to do later with the ending for *Il pirata*.

Gives the locations of various copies of the music, e.g., the original version of the Act Two finale, one source of which is a piano reduction by Francesco Florimo.

534. Maguire, Simon and Elizabeth Forbes. "*Bianca e Fernando*." In *The New Grove Dictionary of Opera*. 4 vols. Ed. Stanley Sadie. New York: Macmillan, 1992. Vol. 1: 465. ISBN 09–35859–92–6. ML102.O6 N5 1992.

Discusses the genesis and versions, provides plot synopsis, and ends with an assessment of the work, deeming it an "unusual 'rescue opera' in which the theme of romantic love is avoided." The dramatic impact may be weak, but the opera gives evidence of melodic originality.

Il pirata, melodramma in two acts

Libretto by Felice Romani; Premiere October 27, 1827, Teatro alla Scala, Milan.

535. Abert, Anna Amalie. "Räuber und Räuber Milieu in der Oper des 19. Jahrhunderts." In *Die "Couleur locale" in der Oper des 19. Jahrhunderts*. Ed. Heinz Becker (Studien zur Musikgeschichte des 19. Jahrhunderts, 42), pp. 121–30. Regensburg: Bosse, 1976. ISBN 37–64921–01–3. ML1794.C68.

Survey of robber themes in late-eighteenth- and nineteenth-century opera. One paragraph (p. 126) devoted to Romani and Bellini's *Il pirata*. Gualtiero is cited as the typical heroic, unfortunate robber character, in love with an enemy's wife.

536. Brunel, Pierre. "*Le Pirate* de Bellini: le gothique humanisé." *Lyrica* 69 (February 1981): 10–13.

Exlores the humanising elements of a "gothic" subject, the "genre frénétique," the genesis and sources of *Il pirata*. Provides a description of certain scenes and a reading list (at this time nothing in French on Bellini since Arthur Pougin, so Brunel recommends Weinstock, Orrey, and Lippmann; his own monograph on Bellini was to appear later in 1981) and discography. Illustrated with stage set of opening storm scene from the premiere by Sanquirico, and with Giovanni Battista Rubini as Gualtiero.

537. Busch, Gudrun. "Die Unwetterszene in der romantischen Oper." In *Die "Couleur locale" in der Oper des 19. Jahrhunderts*. Ed. Heinz Becker (Studien zur Musikgeschichte des 19. Jahrhunderts 42), pp. 161–212. Regensburg: Bosse, 1976. ISBN 37–64921–01–3. ML1794.C68.

A survey of storm scenes in Romantic opera. *Il pirata* has an effective storm scene that Verdi must have been contemplating as he composed the opening of *Otello*, premiered sixty years after *Il pirata*.

538. Cametti, Alberto. *La musica teatrale a Roma cento anni fa ("Il Pirata" di Bellini)*. Special pub. of *Annuario della Real Accademia di Santa Cecilia*. Rome, 1928–29.

The version of *Il pirata* heard at the Rome premiere in 1829. Cametti was an authority on opera in Rome.

539. Cornwall, Barry [B.W. Procter, pseud.]. *Life of Edmund Kean*. 2 vols. in one. London: E. Moxon, 1835. PN2598.K3 P7.

The great Shakespearean actor Edmund Kean created the leading role of Bertram in Maturin's Shakespearean play.

540. Damerini, Adelmo. "Bellini e la critica del suo tempo." In *Vincenzo Bellini, l'uomo, le sue opere, la sua fama*. Ed. Ildebrando Pizzetti, pp. 215–50. Milan: Fratelli Treves, 1936. See item 242. ML410.B44 P58.

Deals with reception and criticism of *Il pirata*.

541. Gossett, Philip, ed. *Il pirata*, 2 vols. Early Romantic Opera, ed. with introductions by Philip Gossett and Charles Rosen. New York: Garland, 1983. ISBN 08–24029–00–3. ML96.5.B47.

Reproduces Bellini's autograph score from the Naples Conservatory Library. Genesis, sources, first performance, and discussion of singers. Autograph is "one of his more tormented manuscripts." Several different foliations, reflecting different stages in its history: four main ones. "Many of Bellini's changes were introduced after the first performances in Milan, indeed after the Milanese publisher Giovanni Ricordi brought out the first edition of the piano-vocal score." The first edition reflects an earlier version of the opera rather than the autograph. All later editions are derived from that first Ricordi edition, not from the autograph. "Sorting out places where Bellini made changes *before* the first performances (i.e., compositional changes), where he made changes *after* the first performance and first edition, and where changes were made in the score without his approval will prove a difficult task, one that can only be begun here. Let me describe the manuscript enough to assist readers in finding their way through it: a full consideration of its problems must await a critical edition of the opera." Describes the situation number by number in a certain amount of detail.

542. Idman, Niilo. *Charles Robert Maturin: His Life and Works*. London: Constable, 1923. PR4987.M7 Z6.

Maturin was the Irish clergyman whose play *Bertram* ultimately provided the source for the libretto of *Il pirata*. See item 546.

543. Lippmann, Friedrich. "Quellenkundliche Anmerkungen zu einigen Opern Vincenzo Bellinis." In *Analecta musicologica* 4 (1967): 131–53. See item 500. ISSN 0585–6086. ML160.S893.

Discusses literary sources, autograph sources, and variants of *Il pirata*.

In the Biblioteca Lucchessi Palli in Naples, Lippmann discovered the literary model upon which Felice Romani directly based the libretto of Bellini's first success: *Il Pirata. Dramma in tre atti di M. Raimond, raduzione dal Francese di Camiilo Mariami Pavese* (Milan, 1831). Lippmann presents the differences between literary source and libretto. Imogene's husband (Aldini = Ernesto) dies by Gualtiero's hand already in the first act finale. Here he is less of a villain than a noble soul. Discusses the different endings. Gives the ending in the original version of the libretto, the death of Gualtiero.

Although Pastura believed that Bellini set not one note of the original ending, he was mistaken. The autograph in Naples Conservatory (Rari 4. 2. 8/9) contains music for both scenes. In the one never performed, the orchestra plays music from the slow part of the overture from the early symphony in E-flat Major; the chorus of cavaliers has a dialogue with Gualtiero, the pirates leave; then, after the last choral outburst ("Che orror!") follows sixteen bars of orchestral postlude.

544. Longyear, Rey M. "The English Horn in Classic and Early Romantic Music." In *Miscellanea Musicologica. Adelaide Studies in Musicology* 9 (1977): 128–44. ISSN 0076–9355. ML5.M34.

Includes music examples. Longyear traces the use of the English horn in the Classical period, which was occasional in northern Italy and Austria and nonexistent elsewhere. Composers included Gluck, Haydn, and Mozart, with Gluck's Viennese works rescored to omit the English horn. "The renascence of the English horn occurred during the 1790s in northern Italy . . . and after 1808 in France. . . . A second revival began in the 1820s with Donizetti, Bellini, Rossini, and Berlioz." *Il pirata* is an important work in employing the English horn in an affective manner in Imogene's "mad scene."

545. Maguire, Simon and Elizabeth Forbes. "*Pirata, Il.*" In *The New Grove Dictionary of Opera*. 4 vols. Ed. Stanley Sadie. New York: Macmillan, 1992. Vol. 3: 1917–18. ISBN 09–35859–92–6. ML102.O6 N5 1992.

Bellini's first major success, his first opera for La Scala, and his first collaboration with Romani. Presents genesis, sources, singers involved

(Rubini, Méric-Lalande, Tamburini), reception. Performance history including modifications by singers, twentieth-century revivals with Callas and Caballé; plot summary. Assessment of style and importance of work: "The tormented, impulsive hero of Italian Romantic opera is presented for the first time in Gualtiero's opening cavatina." Considers this to be not quite mature Bellini. The work contains certain features, such as the echo chorus and some complex counterpoint in the Act One finale, that Bellini never repeated. The ariosos are very important, demonstrating a turning away from Rossinian style.

546. Maturin, Rev. R.C. [*sic*]. *Bertram; or, The Castle of St. Aldobrand; A Tragedy in Five Acts*. 2d ed. London: J. Murray, 1816. PR1241.L6 vol. 320; available in a modern edition from New York: Woodstock Books, 1992. ISBN 18–54771–20–5. PR 4987.M7 B4 1992.

    Ultimate source for the libretto of Bellini's *Il pirata*. Maturin's name was Charles Robert, rather than "R.C."

547. Ortigue, Joseph. *Le Balcon de l'Opéra*. Paris: Librairie D'Eugène Renduel, 1833. ML1704.O77.

    A contemporary assessment of *Il pirata*. See item 71.

548. Pantologo, Eleuterio. *La musica italiana nel secolo XIX, ricerche filosofico-critiche di E.P.* Florence: Coen, 1828. ML2904.T69.

    Some believe Pantologo was the pseudonym of Professor Luigi Picchianti and others of Conte Torriglione, romano, resident of Florence. He presents his views on *Il pirata*, challenged by Ferdinando Giorgetti (1796–1867). Cf. Damerini, item 2, pp. 218–22.

549. Pirrotta, Nino. "Rileggendo *Il pirata* di Bellini." In *Napoli e il teatro musicale in Europa tra Sette e Ottocento—Studi in onore di Friedrich Lippmann*. Ed. B.M. Antolini and W. Witzenmann, pp. 407–16. Florence: L. Olschki, 1993, also in Nino Pirrotta. *Poesia e musica e altri saggi*. Sandicci (Florence): *La nuova Italia*, 1994, pp. 255–64. ISBN 88–22114–85–X. ML3849.P55 1994.

    Notes that *Il pirata* is seldom performed. Includes quotations from Bellini's letters. Discussion of character portrayal. Music analysis, commentary, a few music examples.

550. *Tatler*. London, 1831. Library of Congress, Microfilm 01105, reel 539.

    An early review of *Il pirata*.

551. Tintori, Giampiero. "*Il pirata*." In *I teatri di Vincenzo Bellini*. Ed. Roberto Alajmo, pp. 39–48. Palermo: Edizioni Novecento, 1986. See item 750. ISBN 88–37300–48–4. ML410.B44 T4 1986.

    A volume about productions of Bellini's operas. Each work is given a separate chapter. There is an extensive prose introduction to the chapter, which then consists of numerous illustrations, many of them of set designs.

552. Willier, Stephen A. "Madness, the Gothic, and Bellini's *Il pirata*." *Opera Quarterly* 6/4 (Summer 1989): 7–23. ISSN 0736–0053. ML1699.O65.

 Explores the "gothic" literary background of Romani's libretto, comparing the Reverend Charles Maturin's play with the opera in terms of plot and character types. An examination of Imogene's psychological state and how mental deterioration is portrayed musically. A comparison of her opening "dream sequence" with her "mad scene," which closes the opera, although an additional scene was written by Romani. Topoi of the primo ottocento "mad scene" are discussed. Music examples of Imogene's mad scene. Mad scene an important model for Donizetti, i.e., in *Lucia di Lammermoor*. Verdi and the opening storm scene. Many source citations.

Note: Additional sources on *Il pirata* include:

553. Lévy, F. "Bellini et l'école frénétique de *Bertram* (1822) à *Il pirata*." *Kongressbericht*. Villecroze, 1997.

554. Villa, G. *Il pirata*. Napoli: Tipografia Flautina, 1834.

La straniera, melodramma in two acts

Libretto by Felice Romani; Premiere February 14, 1829, Teatro alla Scala, Milan.

555. Barbò, Count Giacomo di Castelmorano. *Cenni illustrativi alla nuova opera La straniera*. Milan, 1829.

 Written by a friend of Bellini in Milan at the time of the opera's premiere. Bellini socialized in his home and there is extant correspondence from Bellini to the count.

556. Cametti, Alberto. *La musica teatrale a Roma cento anni fa ("La straniera" di Bellini). La Malibran a Roma*. Rome, 1935.

 Cametti was an expert on opera in Rome. Here he features Roman performances of *La straniera* from the 1830s.

557. Damerini, Adelmo. "Bellini e la critica del suo tempo." In *Vincenzo Bellini, l'uomo, le sue opere, la sua fama*. Ed. Ildebrando Pizzetti, pp. 215–50. Milan: Fratelli Treves, 1936. See item 242. ML410.B44 P58.

 Reception and criticism of *La straniera*. Cites Fétis in *Revue musicale* V (1829), p. 136, where he lamented the lack of an overture and praised several specific numbers. Fétis noted that many Italian critics felt that Bellini had forgotten his old master Zingarelli and had become "un filosofico."

 Various polemics surrounded *La straniera*. In *Il corriere delle dame* (March 15, 1830) appeared "Osservazioni critiche" about *La straniera*, one of them by a Signor Di Moiano, who accused Bellini of plagiarizing not only from Carafa, Peter Winter, and Rossini, but also from him; he had composed several nocturnes, allegedly used by Bellini in the hunting chorus. See item 558.

558. Di Moiano, Pietro. *Alcune osservazioni critiche intorno alla musica dell' opera La straniera del sig. Vincenzo Bellini*. Milan: Giacomo Pirola, 1830.

Appeared the year after *La straniera* was premiered. Di Moiano discusses Bellini's use of canto declamato and the appoggiatura, both of which were seen as integral to the composer's style. He speaks of his esteem for Bellini, dividing his artistry into "inspiration, science, and aesthetics." 10 pp. See item 557 above.

559. Gargiulo, Piero. " 'Seule qui pleure? . . . L'Etrangère,' *La straniera* tra musica scenica e modelli di monodrame." *Vincenzo Bellini et la France* (2007): 657–80. See item 404.

The use of Charles d'Alincourt's novel of 1825 allowed Bellini to explore a number of purely theatrical effects that help to further the bond between text and music and also allow him to continue to experiment with mimodrame already successful in *Il pirata*. Gestures of the characters and the descriptive nature of Bellini's music are integrated.

560. Gossett, Philip, ed. *La straniera*. Early Romantic Opera, 5. 2 vols. New York: Garland, 1982. ISBN 08–24029–01–1. ML96.5.B47.

Genesis, sources, original cast. Many pages of Bellini's melodic sketches for this work exist in the Museo belliniano in Catania and would make a fascinating study. Bellini desperately wanted Rubini from *Il pirata* to be the tenor lead and although he had to settle for Domenico Reina at the premiere in February of 1829, the composer revised the tenor part of Rubini the following year, a process that can be seen in a manuscript now in the Biblioteca del Conservatorio "Giuseppe Verdi" in Milan (Ms. 20), which is reproduced here in facsimile. Gossett discusses these revisions, not all of which are necessarily in Bellini's hand.

561. Gutierrez, Beniamino. "*La straniera* di Vincenzo Bellini. Il delirio per I divi e l'autore nell'ombra nella cronaca del tempo," BG, Il MDCCCXXX delle scene scaligere e della patria, *La Scala nel 1830 nel 1930* (a.c. della rivista *La Scala e il museo teatrale* e della *Libreria editrice Milanese*, n.d.).

562. Lippmann, Friedrich. "Quellenkundliche Anmerkungen zu einigen Opern Vincenzo Bellinis." *Analecta musicologica* 4 (1967): 131–53. See item 500. ISSN 0585–6086. ML160.S893.

Discusses literary sources, autograph sources, and variants.

563. ——. "*La straniera*." In *I teatri di Vincenzo Bellini*. Ed. Roberto Alajmo, pp. 49–69. Palermo: Edizioni Novecento, 1986. See item 750. ISBN 88–37300–48–4. ML410.B44 T4. 1986.

A volume about productions of Bellini's operas. Each work is given a separate chapter. There is an extensive prose introduction to the chapter, which then consists of numerous illustrations, many of them of set designs.

564. ——. "Su *La straniera* di Bellini." *Nuova rivista musicale italiana* 5/4 (July–August 1971): 565–605. ISSN 0029–6228. ML5.N93.

Explores various aspects of this work: the reception history, sources of the libretto, manuscript sources of the opera, extensive discussion of style with numerous music examples.

565. Maguire, Simon and Elizabeth Forbes. "*Straniera, La*." In *The New Grove Dictionary of Opera*. 4 vols. Ed. Stanley Sadie. New York: Macmillan, 1992. Vol. 4: 560–61. ISBN 09–35859–92–6. ML102.O6 N5. 1992.

Genesis, sources, singers involved, reception. Performance history—discussion of sopranos from the original Henriette Méric-Lalande to Renata Scotto and Olivia Stapp; omits performances by Elena Souliotis, Montserrat Caballé, and Lucia Aliberti (See Discography), all of which are or have been recently available on CD in live performance. Plot summary. Romantic genre of tenor hero, called "un disperato" in the libretto. Musical style: "the extreme point of Bellini's abnegation of Rossinian melodic decoration, with little opportunity for vocal display." There is an attendant gain in dramatic tension.

566. Review of *La straniera* in *L'Eco*, February 16, 1829, given in Luisa Cambi, *Epistolario*, p. 196 (see item 288).

In speaking of the preponderance of unadorned melodic lines in this opera, the critic wrote that Bellini had attempted "di riunire la froza della declamazione alla gentilezza del canto."

567. Schlitzer, Franco. "Giorni inediti di Vincenzo Bellini, *La straniera* a Vienna (1831)." *Il Fluidoro* 4/10–12 (1958): 7–8.

Letter from Bellini in Milan, December 1831, to Neipperg in Vienna about the performance of *La straniera* that took place at the Hoftheater in Vienna on November 24, 1831. The autograph is in the "Handschriften Sammlung" of the Oesterreichische Nationalbibliothek.

568. Smart, Mary Ann. "The Woman in Black." *Opera* 58/10 (October 2007): 1196–1200. ISSN 0030–3526.

The plot and themes of this opera are examined and tied to Bellini's possible depression and paranoia over his career. Illustrated.

569. Uvietta, Marco. "*La straniera*: lontananza e mistero nell'invenzione timbrico-spaziale." *Vincenzo Bellini nel secondo centenario della nascita* (2004): 299–320. See item 406.

Spatial effects achieved by timbre and distance in Bellini's opera, one of the themes of which is "lontananza-mistero." Music examples.

Note: Additional sources include:

570. Cambi, Luisa. "*La straniera* a Bergamo ovvero pietosa istoria di una balena a Milano." *Rivista del Comune di Catania* (September–October 1934).

Zaira, tragedia lirica in two acts

Libretto by Felice Romani: Premiere Parma, Teatro Ducale, May 16, 1829. Only eight performances given; never revived during Bellini's lifetime. Some eight numbers, in addition to shorter passages (nearly half the score), went into *I Capuleti e i Montecchi* and subsequent works.

571. Alcari, Cesare. "La *Zaira* fu veramente fischiata?" *Musica d'oggi; rassegna di vita e di coltura musica* 17 (July 1935): 262–67. ML5.M721.

Genesis and sources and circumstances of the premiere of this unsuccessful opera.

572. Capra, Marco. "Un incidente imprevisto: esiti e consequenze della *Zaira* di Vincenzo Bellini." In *Belliniana et alia musicologica. Festschrift für Friedrich Lippmann zum 70. Geburtstag*. Ed. D. Brandenburg and Th. Lindner, pp. 39–48. Vienna: Präsens, 2004 (*Primo Ottocento*).

Contemporary reviews concerning the failure of the opera.

573. Maguire, Simon and Elizabeth Forbes. "*Zaira*." In *The New Grove Dictionary of Opera*. 4 vols. Ed. Stanley Sadie. New York: Macmillan, 1992. Vol. 4: 1202–03. ISBN 09–35859–92–6. ML102.O6 N5 1992.

Discussion of genesis and sources. Reception; Bellini's only lasting failure. Plot summary; musical style, "first step away from the melodic austerity of *La straniera* towards the characteristic *morbidezza* of Bellini's mature style." Cites Pastura 1959, pp. 196–213. See item 272. Reworkings of selections from this work for *I Capuleti*, *Norma*, and *Beatrice di Tenda*.

574. Nicastro, Aldo. "*Zaira*." In *I teatri di Vincenzo Bellini*. Ed. Roberto Alajmo, pp. 71–82. Palermo: Edizioni Novecento, 1986. ISBN 88–37300–48–4. ML410.B44 T4 1986.

A volume about productions of Bellini's operas. Each work is given a separate chapter. There is an extensive prose introduction to each chapter, which then consists of numerous illustrations, many of them of set designs.

I Capuleti e i Montecchi, tragedia lirica in two acts

Libretto by Felice Romani; Premiere March 11, 1830, at the Teatro La Fenice, Venice; eight performances.

In addition to the autograph score of this opera that Bellini presented to the city of Catania (now in the Museo belliniano), an autograph of the introduction is in the Museo donizettiano, Bergamo Conservatory; in Milan, Archivio storico Ricordi, there is a manuscript copy containing certain autograph numbers, showing changes for La Scala, to open the season on December 26, 1830. Some eight numbers from *Zaira*, in addition to shorter passages, went into *I Capuleti e i Montecchi*.

575. Ashbrook, William. "*I Capuleti e i Montecchi*." *Opera* 35/4 (April 1984): 370–76. ISSN 0030–3526. ML5.O66.

Genesis, sources, and reception of the opera.

576. *L'Avant-scène Opéra*. No. 122 (July 1989); issue devoted to *I Capuleti e i Montecchi*. ML5.A865.

Copiously illustrated program book from the Paris Opéra. In addition to a plot synopsis, a complete Italian libretto with a new French translation by Michel Orcel, and musical and literary commentary by Pascale Saint-André (with music examples); this volume contains various articles, all with illustrations.

- Jean-Michel Brèque, "De la difficulté d'oublier Shakespeare": examines the numerous sources of the story prior to Shakespeare, the sources of Romani's libretto with reference to Shakespeare's play;
- Pierre Enckell, "Guelfes et Gibelins, l'alibi idéologique": presents the historical situation between the Guelphs and the Ghibelins;
- Simon Maguire, "La Genèse et les créateurs": chronicles the compositional process of Bellini's opera, with special attention to the voice types and the singers who created each character. Subheadings include: "La Crise de l'après Rossini," "Six semaines pour un opéra," "La vengeance de *Zaira*," and "Un mezzo, un soprano et deux ténors";
- Pascale Saint-André, "Les Armes romantiques d'un amour légendaire": the musical language of primo ottocento Italian opera; discusses the travesti role of Romeo and its place in opera history;
- Jacques Joly, "Felice Romani ou le classicisme romantique";
- Hélène Pierrakos, "L'Habit, le moine ou le Dieu lui-même?": further exploration of the implications of the travesti role;
- There follows a discography, in which it is seen that some recordings and performances have used a tenor for Romeo, some a mezzo-soprano;
- "L'Oeuvre à l'affiche," researched by Michel Pazdro, presents a chronicle of performances throughout Europe, the world, and special lists for Catania and La Scala, Milan;
- Bibliography by Elisabeth Giuliani;
- An interview with the director of this 1989 production, Pierre-Jean San Bartolomé, entitled "*Giulietta e Romeo*: le retour aux sources."

577. Berlioz, Hector. *Memoirs of Hector Berlioz*. Paris, 1870. Trans. and ed. David Cairns. New York: Knopf, 1969. ML410.B5 A243 1969b.

Writes about *I Capuleti e i Montecchi*, which he attended in Florence at the Teatro del Pergola. Berlioz expected to find an opera based on Shakespeare: "Bitter disappointment! The opera contained no ball at the Capulets, no Mercutio, no garrulous nurse, no grave and tranquil hermit, no balcony scene, no sublime soliloquy for Juliet, no duet in the cell between the banished Romeo and the disconsolate friar, no Shakespeare, no nothing." Of Bellini: "That little fool has apparently not been afraid that Shakespeare's shade might come and haunt him in his sleep." Berlioz did concede that Bellini "contrived at one important point to extract something memorable." This occurs when the lovers, dragged apart by their parents, rush into each other's arms and sing in unison, "We shall meet again in heaven." Berlioz loved the unison, was "carried away in spite of myself and applauded enthusiastically. Since those days, duets in unison have been worked to death."

578. ——. "*Roméo et Juliette*, opéra en 4 actes de Bellini; sa première représentation au théâtre de l'Opéra." In *A travers chants: études musicales, adorations, boutades et critique*. Paris: Lévy, 1862, pp. 317–27. ML410.B5 A54 1862; Paris: Gründ, 1971. ML410.B5 A54 1971.

Berlioz discusses the premiere of what he calls Bellini's *Roméo et Juliette* at the Théâtre de l'Opéra, Paris, and the début of Madame Vestvali. Notes that there are five operas in French and Italian on this theme but none of them captures the dramatic essence of Shakespeare. Berlioz illustrates this deficiency in the case of Romani and Bellini.

579. Brauner, Charles Samuel. "Parody and Melodic Style in Bellini's *I Capuleti e i Montecchi*." In *Music and Drama*. Ed. Richard Taruskin. Studies in Music History, Vol. 2, pp. 124–151. New York: Broude Brothers, 1988. ISBN 08–45074–02–4. ML1.S899, vol. 2.

Parody is used in the sense of borrowed material. Brauner demonstrates that in borrowing material for *I Capuleti*, Bellini paid little attention to how the original dramatic context or poetic form corresponded to the new situation; rather, the factors were type of piece (i.e., aria replacing aria) and vocal range. Bellini was always concerned, however, that his melodies carry emotional conviction. Some comparisons with Vaccai's setting of the Romeo and Juliet story to Romani's libretto. Table of borrowings and music examples.

580. Brunel, Pierre. "*I Capuleti e i Montecchi*." In *I teatri di Vincenzo Bellini*. Ed. Roberto Alajmo, pp. 83–93. Palermo: Edizioni Novecento, 1986. ISBN 88–37300–48–4. ML410.B44 T4 1986.

A volume about productions of Bellini's operas. Each work is given a separate chapter. There is an extensive prose introduction to each chapter, which then consists of numerous illustrations, many of them of set designs.

581. Collins, Michael. "Bellini and the 'Pasticcio alla Malibran': A Performance History of *I Capuleti e I Montecchi*." *Note su note* IX–X (9–10 December 2002): 109–52. ISSN 1122–0252. ML5.N793.

Maria Malibran became a famous proponent of the role of Romeo but she usually substituted the last act of Zingarelli's *Romeo e Giulietta* for Bellini's ending.

582. ——. "The Literary Background of Bellini's *I Capuleti e i Montecchi*." *Journal of the American Musicological Society* 35 (1982): 532–38. ISSN 0003–0139. ML27.U5 A83363.

Shows that Romani's libretto (originally for Nicola Vaccai's 1825 *Giulietta e Romeo*) was not based on Shakespeare but on the play of the same name by Luigi Scevola, published in Milan in 1818. Romani's libretto is virtually identical in plot to the Scevola tragedy. The libretto for Bellini is in fact a somewhat abridged and altered version of Romani's original.

Romani in his Preface hinted at a different source: Giuseppe Foppa's libretto *Giulietta e Romeo*, produced in 1796 with music by Nicola Zingarelli (later Bellini's teacher). But Romani's libretto is deliberately quite different; he did not want to duplicate it. There is another possible source for Romani: a ballet dependent on both Foppa and Scevola, *Le tombe di Verona, ossia Giulietta e Romeo*, choreographed by Antonio Cherubini, first performed ca. 1820 at the Teatro Concordia in Cremona. This may in fact have been the immediate source for Romani. Yet another possible source was *Roméo et Juliette* (1772) by Jean François Ducis, a notorious adapter of Shakespeare.

Collins provides a brief summary in order to "reveal the idiosyncrasies of Romani's version." Discusses the making of the libretto according to certain operatic conventions, such as that of opening with a chorus.

583. ——. "Vincenzo Bellini's *I Capuleti e i Montecchi*: Its Debut and Reception in Paris, 1833." *Vincenzo Bellini et la France* (2007): 173–96. See item 404.

This opera was not well received by the critics at its Parisian debut in 1833. Bellini's opera, as well as Romeo and Juliet operas by Zingarelli and Vaccai were all negatively compared to Shakespeare's play. Musically Bellini's work was considered so weak that the tomb scene was soon replaced by the ending to Vaccai's opera. The Parisian premiere featured a new overture and a substitute aria for Giulietta's *romanza* by Marco Arturo Marliana. Collins concludes that the Parisian critics were unable to fathom the avant-garde lyricism and enhanced place of recitative in Bellini's style.

584. D'Amico, Fedele. "C'è modo e modo, <I Capuleti e i Montecchi> di Bellini nella revisione di Claudio Abbado." *Nuova rivista musicale italiana* 1 (May–June 1967): 136–42. ISSN 0029–6228. ML5.N93.

Performances of *I Capuleti e i Montecchi* in 1966 with Claudio Abbado provided the occasion for an interview with Fedele D'Amico. Many stimulating comments about dramatic continuity in the operas of Bellini: the place of *I Capuleti* within Bellini's output; musicodramatic continuity within the work. Romeo is a tenor in Abbado's version.

In addition to adapting the role of Romeo for the tenor, Abbado has revised the orchestration, detailed in Leonardi Pinzauti's review in *La nazione* of April 9, 1967. Ricordi published Abbado's changes in an edition that does not state this: one would not know that this score did not reflect Bellini's original intentions but was instead rather heavily "adapted."

585. Dean, Winton. "Shakespeare and Opera." In *Shakespeare in Music*. Ed. Phyllis Hartnoll, pp. 148–50. London: Macmillan, 1964. ML80.S5 H37.

From the late-eighteenth and early-nineteenth century, opera settings of the Romeo and Juliet story presented are by Zingarelli ("The music, again replete with prayers, is imperturbably platitudinous"), Vaccai, and Bellini. Dispels the commonly accepted ideas that Vaccai's and Bellini's libretti—although both are by Romani—are identical and that Malibran substituted Vaccai's finale when performing Bellini's opera. (See item 581.) The two libretti are quite different and even have different characters. It was Vaccai's penultimate scene that often replaced Bellini's ultimate one in performance and according to Malibran's biographer Arthur Pougin, this was her choice. Dean considers Vaccai's libretto the better one; Bellini chose not to set a number of sections, including an extensive duet for Lorenzo and Juliet before she drinks the potion and a scene in which the report of her death arouses strong feelings of suffering and vengeance in Capulet. Dean considers Bellini's melodramatic finale unfortunate.

Bellini's work focuses on the love triangle of Romeo, Juliet, and Tybalt, and his music is indeed superior to Vaccai's, even though he composed this work in a hurry and recycled pieces from *Adelson e Salvini* and *Zaira*. Bellini's slow melodies are exquisite and the orchestral introductions to certain scenes that use obbligato scoring provide splendid atmosphere.

586. Gherardi, Luciano. "Una novella di Matteo Bandello 'riletta' da Felice Romani per Vincenzo Bellini." *Esercizi. Arte. Musica, Spettacolo* 4 (1981): 116–26.

The source for Romani's Romeo and Juliet opera is not Shakespeare—a fact known since Berlioz revealed this in 1831—but a story by Matteo Bandello from the 1500s. Yet many discrepancies also exist between this source and Romani's libretto, changes called for by exigencies of primo ottocento opera and by the examination of Medieval sources by Romani. For other possible sources for Romani's libretto, see item 595.

587. Gossett, Philip, ed. *I Capuleti e i Montecchi*. Early Romantic Opera. New York: Garland, 1981. ISBN 08–24029–02–X. ML96.5 B47.

A facsimile edition of Bellini's original autograph manuscript, edited with an introduction by Philip Gossett. The facsimile is from the composer's autograph manuscript in the collection of the Museo belliniano in Catania; the facsimile of the *Introduzione* in Act One is from the autograph manuscript in the Museo donizettiano, Bergamo.

Discusses genesis, self-borrowings, sources. The Ricordi piano-vocal score was not based on Bellini's autograph manuscript—cites some of the significant differences between the two. Discusses musical forms used and the combination of declamatory delivery and full melodic periods. This edition also contains a plot synopsis.

588. Guiomar, Michel. "Bellini et Berlioz: *I Capuleti e I Montecchi* et *Roméo et Juliette*." *Vincenzo Bellini et la France* (2007): 229–83. See item 404.

The author compares Bellini's and Berlioz's treatments of the Romeo and Juliet story from an aesthetic point of view, based on Gaston Bachelard's theoretic system, considering the texts as a true expression of an imaginary ego that finds a voice only in artistic creation. This study also considers attitudes towards death in these works, "regeneration fully realized in the access to the sublime and fusion with the universe" and the function of cortèges as a manifestation of death and as a link that joins sleep and death. Music examples.

589. Hadlock, Heather. "On the Cusp between Past and Future. The Mezzo-Soprano Romeo of Bellini's *I Capuleti*." *Opera Quarterly* 17/3 (Summer 2001): 399–422. ISSN 0736–0053. ML1699.O65.

Deals with the problems of casting Romeo as a female: "The convention of casting women in heroic parts [at this time] was coming under fire not only for its association with the old-fashioned Rossinian vocal style, but also because it did not work within the emerging new aesthetic of visual realism." Comments on the performance of Giuditta Pasta in the role of Romeo. Discusses competition with Vaccai's setting; substitution of his tomb scene for Bellini's in early performances. Zingarelli's *Giulietta e Romeo* is also considered. Topics include "The Tradition," "The Moderns: Romani, Vaccai, Bellini," "Two Tomb Scenes," and "Past and Future." Music examples, illustrations, extensive source citations.

590. Lippmann, Friedrich. Notes to recording of *I Capuleti e i Montecchi*: Riccardo Muti, cond., Chorus and Orchestra of the Royal Opera House, Covent Garden; Edita Gruberova (Giulietta), Agnes Baltsa (Romeo), Dano Raffanti (Tebaldo), Gwynne Howell (Capellio), John Tomlinson (Lorenzo). EMI CMS 7 64846 2, live performance, Covent Garden, London, 1984.

Genesis, sources, reception, musical style of the opera by a leading authority on Bellini's music.

591. ——. "Pagine sconosciute de *I Capuleti e i Montecchi e Beatrice di Tenda* di Vincenzo Bellini." *Rivista italiana di musicologia* 2/1 (1967): 140–51. ISSN 0035–6867. ML5.R79.

Includes facsimiles. A study of the sources for these two operas. The most important non-autograph source for *I Capuleti e i Montecchi* is in the Archivio Ricordi in Milan. Two volumes: *I Montecchi e Capuleti/ Melodramma in 2 Atti/Del sigr Maestro Vzo Bellini*. It contains, however, numerous autograph sections including the previously unknown arioso "Morir dovessi ancora" (given here in facsimile), composed for the performance at La Scala, Milan. Lippmann ends the article with an exhortation for a Bellini complete-works edition, hoping that his work will help the process.

592. Maguire, Simon, Elizabeth Forbes, and Julian Budden. "*Capuleti e i Montecchi, I.*" In *The New Grove Dictionary of Opera*. 4 vols. Ed. Stanley Sadie. New York: Macmillan, 1992. Vol. 1: 724–26. ISBN 09–358–59–92–6. ML102.O6 N5 1992.

Discusses Italian, non-Shakespearean sources of the libretto, genesis of the work, singers who created the parts. Reworking of parts of *Zaira*. Plot summary. Performance history, assessment, views by Liszt, Wagner, Berlioz. Illustration of Act Two tomb scene stage set from original Fenice production.

593. Pastura, Francesco. "Storia e vicende private dell'autografo dei *Capuleti*. L'Opera che Bellini dedicò ai catanesi." Extract from *Rivista del Comune di Catania* 3 (July–September 1956).

Published as a separate booklet. Copy in Museo belliniano. Written on the occasion of the acquisition in July of 1956, by the Museo belliniano, of the autograph score of *I Capuleti e i Montecchi*, dedicated by Bellini to the people of his beloved native city, from which he had received a "medaglia d'oro." The score had previously been in the private hands of Antonio Lanari, and Pastura gives a history of its provenance. Pastura also discusses the sources and genesis of this opera. The opportunity to study this autograph, Pastura notes, clarifies many questions and brings to light many details of the text and history of the opera.

594. Porter, Andrew. "Capulets and Montagues—Tender Lyricism and Passionate Energy: An Introduction to *I Capuleti ed i Montecchi*." *About the House* 6/10 (1983): 4–9. ISSN 0001–3242. ML5.A22.

Notes that in Bellini's autograph score, the title reads *Capuleti, e Montecchi*. Quotes from Richard Wagner's *Mein Leben* upon the occasion of hearing Wilhelmine Schröder-Devrient as Romeo in Bellini's opera in Leipzig, 1834. "I shall never forget the impression that a Bellini opera made upon me. . . . Simple and noble *Song* made its appearance again."

Porter: "For a while, *I Capuleti* became a stick that Wagner used to whack Weber's *Euryanthe* and all 'solid' German music."

Genesis, sources, reception of this work; background to Bellini's previous operas. Porter notes that, although ten of the pieces for *Capuleti* employ music from *Zaira* and Giulietta's first aria, "Oh! quante volte" is a reworking of an aria sung by Nelly (in this instance a young male student) in *Adelson e Salvini*, all pieces have undergone either subtle or considerable changes. He quotes from Charlotte Greenspan's *The Operas of Bellini*: "In a musical fabric as delicate as Bellini's a subtle change can be a significant one." Also discusses Romani's "careful and thorough remodelling of an earlier work to suit Bellini's musical and dramatic ideas," *Giulietta e Romeo* as set by Nicolai Vaccai in 1825. Bellini's old teacher, Zingarelli, had set an opera to the same subject (1796) and Romani's libretto for Vaccai was set by a composer named Torriani in 1828.

Porter compares the libretti for Vaccai and for Bellini. The former is "an opera seria giving plenty of vocal opportunity to all the members of a fairly large cast. Bellini's *I Capuleti*, however, is a tight, swift, romantic drama focused on the principals and including only what might be called the 'essential' dramatic numbers. . . ." When one undertakes this comparison, "it becomes evident how definite and how individual Bellini's ideas about music-drama were," and we know that Bellini called Romani to Venice to work with him on the opera, so undoubtedly many original ideas were Bellini's; Romani, typically, apologized for any break from convention in the preface to the published libretto.

Discusses the musical nature of the two principal roles; Giulietta represents Bellini's turn to the elegiac after having won his reputation with the *canto d'azione* of *Il pirata* and *La straniera*. Within Giulietta's music, there is even a rhythmic motto, making this the most "modern" opera Bellini wrote. Notes a number of famous performers of the principal roles from past and present. Discusses Abbado's edition in which Romeo is a tenor.

595. Roccatagliati, Alessandro. "Libretti d'opera: testi autonomi o testo d'uso?" *Quaderni del Dipartimento di linguistica e letterature comparate* [Bergamo] 6 (1990): 7–20; English trans. William Ashbrook as "Librettos: Autonomous or Functional Texts?" In *Opera Quarterly* 11/2 (1995): 81–96. See item 357. ISSN 0736–0053.

Focuses on Bellini's *I Capuleti e i Montecchi*, Romani's working methods, variants.

596. Schlitzer, Franco. *"I Capuletti e i Montecchi" di Vincenzo Bellini: l'autografo della partitura con note illustrative*. Florence: Libreria Antiquaria Leonardo Lapiccinella, 1956.

Copy in Museo belliniano; 300 copies printed. 13 pp. of text. Written just before the acquisition of the autograph score by the Museo belliniano in

Catania in 1956. See Pastura, above, item 593. The score had recently passed into the hands of the antiquarian firm of Leonardo Lapiccinella in Florence. Discusses the composition of the opera, gives a description of the autograph score ("due volumi in cartonato dell'epoca, di formato oblungo, cm. 40 × 29"). Discusses the final scene, which after the premiere was often replaced by the penultimate scene of Vaccai's *Giulietta e Romeo*. Examines the provenance of the score, providing a letter by the nineteenth-century owner, Antonio Lanari, dated Milan, July 30, 1882. Four facsimiles.

597. Schmidgall, Gary. *Shakespeare and Opera*. New York: Oxford University Press, 1990. Chapter entitled "Wherefore *Romeo*?", pp. 292–97. ISBN 01–95064–50–X. ML3858.S373 1990.

Well over two hundred operas are based on the works of Shakespeare. The author notes that the playwright "was to the operatic manner born; his expressive ways and dramaturgical means are like those of composers and librettists in many ways. . . . Similarities in expressive style, scenic structure, and staging are considered, as are the charges of unreality and melodrama, the shared demand for virtuosic display, and the comparable functions of set speeches and arias." Bellini's *I Capuleti* is studied, even though we know it was not based on Shakespeare.

598. Seminara, Graziella. " 'Costretti dall'angustia del tempo, tanto il che il Maestro, ad'un estrema brevità', Bellini, Romani e la duplice 'Parodia' de *I Capuleti e i Montecchi*." *Vincenzo Bellini nel secondo centenario della nascita* (2004): 97–130. See item 406.

Discusses Romani's explanation from the "Avvertimento" of the construction of his libretto, given that he was under time constraints (as usual). Extensive music examples.

599. Toscani, Claudio. "Bellini e Vaccaj: Peripezie di un finale." *Vincenzo Bellini nel secondo centenario della nascita* (2004): 535–68. See item 406.

Examines the respective endings of each composer's Romeo and Juliet setting and the purposes of each ending: Vaacai, for example, wanted to give the soprano a concluding aria, the traditional rondò, despite the dramatic incongruence, whereas Bellini's ending is much less indebted to tradition. Here the final "number" is based on *recitativo all'arioso* without melodic elaboration. Tables. Music examples. Vaccai's text. Reviews from the time (from *Allgemeine musikalische Zeitung*, for example).

Note: An additional source:

600. "Bellinis *Montecchi und Capuletti* in Wien." *Signale für die Musikalische Welt* 29 (June 1858): 259–60.

Ernani

Only a few musical sketches to text of Romani exist, from 1830; abandoned possibly because of fears of censorship; some of this music transferred to *La sonnambula* and subsequent operas; cf. Andrew Porter. "An Introduction to *La sonnambula*," item 594.

Sketches found in Museo belliniano in Catania.

601. Engelhardt, Markus. "Verdi und andere: *Un giorno di regno, Ernani, Attila, Il corsaro*." In *Mehrfachvertonungen*. Premio Internazionale Rotary Club di Parma "Giuseppe Verdi." Vol. 1. Parma: Istituto di Studi Verdiani, 1992. ISBN 88–85965–09–0. ML410.V4 E494 1992.

     Excellent source for several of Verdi's early operas. Engelhardt compares Verdi's works with other contemporary versions. For *Ernani*, he considers settings by Bellini, Vincenzo Gabussi, and others.

602. ——. "Versioni operistiche dell'*Hernani*." In *Ernani ieri e oggi. Atti del Convegno internazionale di studi 9–10 Dicembre 1984, nel Bollettino dell'Istituto di studi verdiani No. 10*. Parma: Istituto di Studi Verdiani, 1987, p. 104.

     The sources for a libretto that satisfies many Romantic opera requirements and the process by which it becomes a libretto. Takes into consideration the proposed *Ernani* of Bellini and Romani. This is an earlier version of the section devoted to *Ernani* in item 601.

***La sonnambula, melodramma* in two acts**

Libretto by Felice Romani: Premiere at Teatro Carcano, Milan, March 6, 1831.

603. *L'Avant-Scène Opéra*. 178 (1997). Issue devoted to *La sonnambula*. ML5. A865.

     Copiously illustrated program book from the Paris Opéra. Begins with a plot synopsis and an Italian libretto with French translation by Jean-François Boukobza. Extensive musical and literary commentary, illustrations, and music examples. Several articles follow:

     - Jean-Claude Yon, "*L'Arrivée d'un nouveau seigneur, ou La somnambule* avant Bellini": Scribe's ballet from 1827 as source for Romani's libretto;
     - Jean Cabourg, "Profil des voix": voices that created and have sung the principal roles in the opera house and on recordings: Amina (created by Pasta), Elvino, and Rodolfo;
     - Rodolfo Celletti, "Soprano dramatique d'agilité,": reprint from 1978 on the bel canto artistry of Maria Callas;
     - Roland Mancini, "Le grand Cru 1955: Callas à La Scala": another reprint on La Callas from *Spécial Maria Callas*, 1978;

- Discography by Jean Cabourg with research by Georges Voisin: discusses complete versions, then recordings of individual arias for each character;
- "L'Oeuvre à l'affiche," research by Josée Bégaud: a calendar of first performances, performance history at La Scala, Catania, in France, at Covent Garden, the Metropolitan Opera, in Buenos Aires, and internationally; Bibliography.

604. Andolfi, Otello. *La sonnambula*. Rome: A. F. Formiggini Editore, 1931.

Part of "Guide Radio-Liriche." A listening guide to the opera; plot with commentary about the music.

605. Budden, Julian, Elizabeth Forbes, and Simon Maguire. "*Sonnambula, La*." In *The New Grove Dictionary of Opera*, 4 vols. Ed. Stanley Sadie. New York: Macmillan, 1992. Vol. 4: 452–54. ISBN 09–35859–92–6. ML102. O6 N5 1992.

Genesis, literary and musical sources. The only Bellini opera written for Pasta and Rubini together. Discussion of high pitch of Rubini's part, subsequent interpreters of the role of Amina from Malibran through Callas and Scotto. Detailed plot summary. *Sonnambula* as pastoral opera, reputation in nineteenth century; parodies by Gilbert and Sullivan, reference to the opera in George Eliot's *Mill on the Floss*. First work by Bellini in which his "mature style appears finally crystallized" and from which "all Rossinian hedonism has been banished." The chorus that opens Act Two has "strangely Gluckian overtones," pointing to an older, Classical style.

606. Cagli, Bruno. "Il risveglio magnetico e il sonno della ragione." *Studi musicali* 14 (1985): 157–70. ISSN 0391–7789. ML5.S9248.

Mesmerism (*Così fan tutte*) and sleepwalking. References to Amina in Bellini's *La sonnambula*.

607. Commons, Jeremy. "Readers' Letters; Amina's Bridge Extended (Early Design for Last Act)." *Opera* 13 (July 1962): 496–97. ISSN 0030–3526. ML5.O66.

No bridge is specified in the score of the final scene of *La sonnambula* although early set designs often included one. Commons provides a photograph of an early set design that shows Amina walking on the roof of the mill, with the race and mill wheel beneath her and the remains of a wall by which she may have descended to the stage. See item 617.

608. Condorelli, Benedetto. "Note sulla prima rappresentazione della *Sonnambula*." Extract from *Rivista del Comune di Catania* 9 (January–February 1931).

Condorelli was the first director of the Museo belliniano in Catania. Published as separate booklet. Copy in Museo belliniano. 5 pp. Contains stage sets designed by Sanquirico from the premiere of *La sonnambula* and portraits of the singers involved.

609. Degrada, Francesco. "Prolegomeni a una lettera della Sonnambula." In *Il melodramma italiano dell'ottocento: Studi e ricerche per Massimo Mila*. Ed. G. Pestelli, pp. 319–50. Turin: G. Eunaudi, 1977. ML1733.4.M4; also in *Il palazzo incantato. Studi sulla tradizione del melodramma dal Barocco al Romanticismo*. 2 vols. Fiesole: Edizioni Discanto, 1979, Vol. 2: 43–77; in German in *Musik-Konzepte 46: Vincenzo Bellini*. Ed. Heinz-Klaus Metzger and Rainer Riehn, pp. 17–46 (see item 458).

   La sonnambula derives from a ballet-pantomime; discusses this non-traditional derivation of the opera libretto.

610. ——. "*La sonnambula*." In *I teatri di Vincenzo Bellini*. Ed. Roberto Alajmo, pp. 95–112. Palermo: Edizioni Novecento, 1986. ISBN 88–37300–48–4. ML410. B44 T4 1986.

   A volume about productions of Bellini's operas. Each work is given a separate chapter. There is an extensive prose introduction to each chapter, which then consists of numerous illustrations, many of them of set designs.

611. *L'Eco*. Issues of March 7 and 9, 1831; reproduced in Luisa Cambi, *Bellini Epistolario*, pp. 268–69 (see item 288).

   Critic describes opening night and in March 9 issue analyses Bellini's work.

612. Fétis, François-Joseph. Review of *La sonnambula* in *La Revue musicale* of 29 October 1831.

   The Belgian critic writes, invariably comparing Bellini to Rossini: "La phrase de Rossini est en général longue et périodique: Bellini n'avait pas le génie qui fait trouver des choses neuves de si longue haleine, mais plein d'intelligence et de tact, il comprit qu'une phrase courte et symetrique est saisie plus de rapidité par le public."

613. Forbes, Elizabeth. "Sleepers Awake (Some Antecedents of Bellini's *La sonnambula*)." *About the House* 6/5 (1982): 18–20. ISSN 0001–3242. ML5.A22.

   Notes works by Scribe-Delavigne, works set to libretti of Romani on this subject by G. Rastrelli, Carafa, Luigi Ricci, Persiani, and others, ballet by Hérold, up to the premiere of Bellini's *La sonnambula*.

614. Ortigue, Joseph. *Le Balcon de l'Opéra*. Paris: Librairie D'Eugène Renduel, 1833.

   A contemporary account of the opera. See item 71.

615. Peschel, Richard E. and Enid Rhodes Peschel. "Music is Feeling, Then, Not Sound: Portrayals of Twentieth-Century Psychiatric Definitions in

Three Nineteenth-Century Operas." In *Exploration: The Nineteenth Century*. Ed. Ann B. Dobbie, Jennifer Brantley, Katherine A. Holman, and Victoria H. Spaniol, pp. 66–99. Los Angeles: Levy, 1988.

Discussion of Verdi's *Don Carlo* and Bellini's *La sonnambula* and *I puritani* from the viewpoint of psychiatry.

616. Porter, Andrew. "An Introduction to *La sonnambula*." *Opera* (October 1960): 665–70. ISSN 0030–3526. ML5.A22.

Genesis of the opera. Bellini and Donizetti both were writing operas for the 1830–31 season at the Teatro Carcano, Milan, *Ernani* and *Anna Bolena* respectively. Why did Bellini reject *Ernani* and turn to *La sonnambula*? There is no clear answer. As Porter states: "from 1882 for four years the pages of the *Gazzetta musicale* rang with argument on this subject. Today, reading through the old controversy (reprinted in 1902 by Antonino Amore, the most vehement of the disputants), we can reach no very firm conclusions." Those who weighed in on the issue include Amore, Scherillo, and Romani's widow, Emilia Branca. Some, including Branca and Scherillo, believe that Bellini feared *Ernani* could not rival the success of Donizetti's *Anna Bolena*; Bellini himself, in a letter of January 3, 1831, stated that the problem was one of censorship. In a footnote, Porter notes, "Five numbers from *Hernani* have survived, in varying states of completion." Pasta's role was to have been that of Hernani, Elvira a lighter soprano. Porter explores sources of the libretto, performance practices of *Sonnambula* interpreters, and demands of the music on the singers.

617. ——. "Readers' Letters: Amina's Bridge." *Opera* 13 (March 1962): 210. ISSN 0030–3526. ML5.O66.

No bridge is specified in the final scene of *La sonnambula* or earlier in the Scribe ballet *La sonnambule*. Yet the bridge was standard by the time of Jenny Lind's Amina in London in 1847. See item 607.

618. ——. "*Sonnambula* Scrapbook." *About the House* 3/8 (1971): 40–46. ISSN 0001–3242. ML5.A22.

The subtitle is: "Its composition, original production, and some famous sopranos." See Porter in *Opera* 1960, item 616. In this instance, concerning the conflicting reasons why Bellini abandoned *Hernani*, Porter states: "Why not, I suggest, combine the two versions? Operatic decisions, like most decisions, are seldom prompted by one reason alone." Romani's source for the *Sonnambula* libretto was a three-act ballet scenario by Scribe; Porter contends that, even though Romani moved the setting to Switzerland and changed the names, he "changed little else. Even his dialogue is often a translation of the mimed conversation described in the ballet script." He provides an example. Porter discusses the question of "Beam or Bridge?" (see item 617), the role of Amina, some famous Aminas, and Henry Bishop's adaptation of the opera to the English stage and questions of pitch. He concludes by discussing Pastura's (see item 272) brief mention of a variant reading in "Ah, non credea mirarti," providing music examples, in the final one showing the measures in question as Jenny Lind performed them.

619. Senici, Emanuele. "Amina e il CAI. Vedute alpine ottocentesche." *Vincenzo Bellini nel secondo centenario della nascita* (2004): 569–79. See items 406 and 626.

 Explores eighteenth- and nineteenth-century writers (Ruskin, Rousseau, Byron, Shelley, Kant, Schiller) and painters (David, Alexander and John Robert Cozens, Turner) who reacted strongly to the Alps and used them as an artistic subject. Treats conceptual sources of Alpine set designs of Sanquirico, Francesco Bagnara, Carlo Ferrario, and Luigi Ricci.

620. ——. "Per una biografia musicale di Amina." *Atti del Convegno internazionale*, Siena, 1–3 June, 2000. *Chigiana* XLV: 297–314.

 Elements of the character/role. Discussion of famous singers of the role: Galli-Curci, Dal Monte, Pagliughi, Sutherland, Callas. Cadenzas sung by Lind and Tetrazzini provided. Transposition and ornamentation considered.

621. Smart, Mary Ann. "Bellini's Fall from Grace." *Opera* 53/3 (March 2002): 278–84. ISSN 0030–3526.

 An examination of plot, musical themes, and historical background of the opera. Posits reasons for Bellini abandoning Hugo's *Hernani*, possibly the success of Donizetti's *Anna Bolena*. Discusses the connection between contrasting vocal styles in Bellini's work and their relationship to dramatic/psychological content. Illustrated.

Note: Additional sources include:

622. Brofferio, A. "*La sonnambula*. Melodramma di F. Romani. Musica di Maestro Bellini." *Il Messaggiere Torinese* (1839).

623. Paduano, G. "La verità del sogno: *La sonnambula*." In *Il giro di vite: percorsi dell'opera lirica*. Florence, 1992, pp. 69–83.

624. Persiano, Filippo. *La Sonnambula di Felice Romani*. Florence, 1903.

625. Principe, Quirino. *La sonnambula di Vincenzo Bellini*. Milan: Mursio, 1991. ML410.B44 P82 1991.

626. Senici, Emanuele. "From Camargue to Switzerland: *La sonnambula*'s Alpine Landscape." In *Virgins of the Rocks: Alpine Landscape and Female Purity in Early Nineteenth-Century Italian Opera*. Dissertation, Cornell University, 1998. See item 619.

***Norma, tragedia lirica* in two acts**

Libretto by Felice Romani; Premiere December 26, 1831, Teatro alla Scala, Milan.

Norma was composed over a three-month period from September to late November of 1831, followed by nearly a month's rehearsal before its premiere on December 26. Numerous sketches by Bellini exist in the Museo belliniano, Catania, and at the Accademia Musicale Chigiana of Siena there is a folder with thirty-one sheets, most covered on both sides, of the libretto in Romani's hand, with changes and suggestions in Bellini's.

627. Adamo, Rosario Maria. "*Norma*." In *I teatri di Vincenzo Bellini*. Ed. Roberto Alajmo, pp. 113–27. Palermo: Edizioni Novecento, 1986. ISBN 88–37300–48–4. ML410.B44 T4. 1986.

A volume about productions of Bellini's operas. Each work is given a separate chapter. There is an extensive prose introduction to each chapter, which then consists of numerous illustrations, many of them of set designs.

628. Andolfi, Otello. *Norma di Vincenzo Bellini*. Rome: A. F. Formiggini Editore, 1929.

Copies in Museo belliniano and Paris, Bibliothèque de l'Opéra. 41 pp. Part of "Guide Radio-Liriche." A listening guide to the opera; plot with commentary about the music. No music examples. Bibliography.

629. *Archivs du Futur Opéra: Norma*. Brussels, Editions Labor, 1994.

Contents include:

- Paul Danblon, Preface, pp. 7–10;
- Jean Abitbol, "Les coulisses de la voix," with topics on the anatomy and physiology of the vocal apparatus, voice teachers, historical considerations, with a bibliography and "filmography," pp. 11–68;
- Claude Javeau, "Divanités," pp. 69–88;
- Sergio Segalini, "Bel canto," pp. 89–102;
- Libretto, pp. 103–36;
- Francesco Corti, "*Norma*, un opéra romantique," pp. 137–40;
- Giovanni Maresta, "Notes pour une mise en scène," pp. 141–44;
- Rinaldo Olivieri and Isabella Lonardi, "Notes scénographiques," pp. 145–48.

630. Ardoin, John. "Three Facsimiles." *Opera Quarterly* 3/4 (1985–86): 38–47. ISSN 0736–0053. ML1699.O65.

The author looks at three facsimiles: Mozart's *Die Zauberflöte*, Verdi's *Falstaff*, and Bellini's *Norma*. The *Norma* facsimile is printed by Garland in the Early Romantic Opera series. See item 645. An earlier facsimile published in Rome in 1935 by the Reale Accademia d'Italia has long been out of print. There is a brief introduction by Ottorino Respighi to the 1935 facsimile, in which he notes that there are 147 pp. for Act One; on p. 116

there is a notation "Autograph of Vincenzo Bellini and his brothers Mario Bellini and Carmelo Bellini," but with no perceptible change in handwriting. There is, however, a change in the hand in Act Two (p. 101) at the "Guerra, guerra!" chorus. Respighi notes, "non sono di mano dell'autore." Respighi also gives a provenance of this manuscript, now in the Biblioteca Musicale di Santa Cecilia in Rome. Four pages of the autograph of this chorus are in the Toscanini collection in Milan.

Ardoin discusses the "slapdash" nature of Bellini's script and quotes from the "Letter to Agostino Gallo" as if its authenticity were not in question. He notes changes made in the score such as rewriting and cuts and compares several sections to the printed score.

631. Ashbrook, William. "An Air of Competition: The Climate of *Norma*'s Early Years." *Opera News* 40/17 (March 17, 1979): 16–17, 35. ISSN 0030–3607. ML1.O482.

The early reception of *Norma* in relation to other contemporary operas, especially by Donizetti. Ashbrook deals with three early productions of *Norma*: the Milan premiere, the second production in Bergamo, and the third production at La Fenice.

632. ——. "Norma—Her Ultimate Triumph." *Opera News* 18 (March 22, 1954): 3–6, 26–28. ISSN 0030–3607. ML1.O482.

A noted scholar of primo ottocento opera examines the reasons for the tepid reception of *Norma* at its premiere. The conditions and terms under which composers worked, the singers for whom Bellini wrote, Bellini's hope that *Norma* would pave the way for him to write opera in Paris, French elements in the opera, Giovanni Pacini's enmity towards the younger Bellini and its possible connection with the *Norma* premiere "fiasco" are discussed. Turns then to reasons why *Norma* has been such a subsequent success; Ashbrook considers the music to be paramount. He follows the plot of the opera and comments on the musical settings.

633. *L'Avant-scène Opéra*. No. 29 (September–October 1960). Issue devoted to *Norma*. ML5.A865.

Copiously illustrated program book from the Paris Opéra. Most illustrations are from actual productions.

Essays include:

- Jacques Gheusi, "La création de Norma," pp. 5–7;
- Gérard Mannoni, "Une héroïne romantique," pp. 8–11;
- Catherine Clément, "Norma, Médée, Sophonisbe: de la séduction à la résistance," pp. 12–15;
- A synopsis and Italian libretto with a new French translation by Yvelaine Duault;

- Literary and musical commentary by Pierre Brunel;
- Friedrich Lippmann, "Notes sur la structure musicale," pp. 82–84;
- Rodolfo Celletti, "Le style vocal," pp. 85–88;
- Giorgio Gualerzi, "Norma et ses voix," pp. 89–93;
- Sergio Segalini, "Le rôle des rôles (Pasta–Lehmann–Ponselle–Callas)," pp. 94–97;
- Alain Mérot, "*Norma* à la scène au XIXme siècle: quelques images-clefs du romantisme," pp. 98–101;
- André Tubeuf, "Discographie," pp. 106–09;
- "L'oeuvre à l'affiche," pp. 110–27;
- Lists of performances in various opera houses such as La Scala, Covent Garden, the Metropolitan, La Fenice, and others;
- Bibliography, pp. 130–32;
- Sergio Segalini, "Le bel canto," pp. 134–39.

634. Badenes Masó, Gonzalo. *Norma de Bellini. Introducción al mundo de la ópera*. Barcelona: Daimon, 1986.

A study of *Norma* that includes a Spanish translation of the libretto.

635. Brauner, Charles S. "Textual Problems in Bellini's *Norma* and *Beatrice di Tenda*." *Journal of the American Musicological Society* 29/1 (1976): 99–118. ISSN 0003–0139. ML27.U5 A83363.

Begins with the premise, "Sorting out the textual variants in an Italian opera from the early nineteenth century is likely to be an elusive, sometimes perhaps even an impossible task. In the course of composing the work and presenting it on stage, the composer is likely to have made many changes, particularly cuts. Subsequent productions may provoke further changes, by the composer or by others. It is by no means a trivial problem to establish the chronological order of the versions and to decide when a particular version was performed; it is at least as difficult to decide which the composer preferred."

Mentions article by Raffaello Monterosso (see item 653), in which he compares the autograph score of *Norma* with the full score published by Ricordi in 1915. There are many variants between the two. Monterosso's study was "meticulous" and "painstaking" but he did not examine the original piano-vocal score published by Ricordi, "a source which proves very important in resolving the problems mentioned above."

Discusses the question of whether it is possible that the piano-vocal score could antedate the autographs, which could be the situation in Bellini's case. Examines Bellini's correspondence for clues about the process of getting a score published. Concludes, "An examination of the sources often points strongly to the conclusion that Bellini made changes not reflected in the published score." Cites many examples of this for both *Norma* and *Beatrice di Tenda*. Illustrations include pages from autograph scores. Ends with a consideration of which version a conductor should choose or an editor publish.

636. Cametti, Alberto. *Bellini a Roma. Brevi appunti storici per cura di Alberto Cametti*. Rome: Tipografia della Pace di Filippo Cuggiani, 1900. ML410. B44 C15.

Copy in Museo belliniano. 19 pp. Bellini traveled through Rome twice in 1832. The autograph manuscripts of *Norma* and *Beatrice di Tenda* are in the Santa Cecilia Academy in that city. Cametti discusses the premieres and reception of these works and provides quotations from contemporary reviews.

637. Caswell, Elizabeth Amelia. "Norma in Paris and Gaul." *Opera News* 18 (March 22, 1954): 30–31. ISSN 0030–3607. ML1.O482.

Description of Alexandre Soumet's French tragedy *Norma*, premiered at the Royal Odéon Theater on April 16, 1831. The ending mad scene was not used by Romani and Bellini. Mentions religious customs of the Druids. Illustrations of the Druid columns at Carnac, a village in southern Brittany.

638. Cecchi, P. "Temi letterari e individuazione melodrammatica in *Norma* di Vincenzo Bellini." *Recercare* 9 (1997): 121–52. ML5.R184.

Begins with a brief survey of the genesis of *Norma*, emphasizing the important role played by Giuditta Pasta. An examination of topoi found in Soumet's play and the changes Romani made to the plot, which include incorporating elements from other sources, expanding the role of Adalgisa, and changing Soumet's ending radically. Using music examples, demonstrates the effectiveness of Bellini's musical setting. Cecchi notes that the final ensemble of the opera contains aspects of both French and Italian opera styles, combines elements of aria, duet, and ensemble, and uses the technique of thematic reminiscence to express Norma's inner conflict and desire for death. Includes a summary in English.

639. Cleva, Fausto. "The Baton Points at *Norma*." *Opera News* 18 (March 22, 1954): 9–10. ISSN 0030–3607. ML1.O482.

A noted conductor answers the question, "Why isn't it more popular?" This has to do with performance demands: "The public has unfortunately been deprived of *Norma* because of the very greatness of the work." Cleva speaks of "the perfection of Bellinian melodies" and the "paralysing wealth of melodies, each more beautiful than the one before," in this work. Discusses the flawlessly set recitative, the use of chorus, the classical nature of the opera, its admirers, such as Wagner, Halévy, and Rossini.

640. De Paoli, Domenico. "En relisant *Norma*: Bellini, musicien dramatique." *La Revue musicale* 106 (1935): 52–62. ISSN 0768–1593. ML5.R613.

Calls Bellini "a composer of a unique dramatic power (at least in Italy)." Examines *Norma* for its connections to Wagner, not only in *Tristan und*

Isolde but in other works such as *Tannhäuser*. But Bellini's dramatic genius remains almost inexplicable—from where does it come? Explores various aspects and details of the score and Bellini's particular style in order to explain this.

641. Deathridge, John. "Reminiscences of *Norma*." In *Das musikalische Kunstwerk: Festschrift Carl Dahlhaus*. Ed. Hermann Danuser, Helga de la Motte-Haber, Leopold Silke, and Norbert Miller, pp. 223–27. Laaber: Laaber-Verlag, 1988. ISBN 38–90071–44–9. ML55.D185.

Views of Bellini's *Norma* by prominent figures of the past are examined by a prominent Wagner scholar. The views of, among others, Brahms, Hanslick, Verdi, and Wagner are mentioned in addition to musical transformations and "improvements" by Chopin, Bizet, Wagner, and Liszt. Deathridge concludes that "Wagner came nearest to a just approval of *Norma*; but the opera still demands a fresh critical view that avoids the usual clichés about 'melody' and Bellini's alleged technical failings."

642. Foscolo, Ugo. *Dissertazione storico intorno ai druidi e ai bardi brittani* (1812), in Ugo Foscolo, *Opere edite e postume*. Vol. 2. Florence: Le Monnier, 1850. Modern edition Florence: Le Monnier, 1985– . ISBN 88–00811–11–6. PQ 4689.A1 1985.

Early nineteenth-century intellectual concepts of Celtic people and lore, from a primo ottocento Italian perspective.

643. Friedlaender, Maryla. "*Norma* Challenged Richard Wagner." *Opera News* 18 (March 22, 1954): 32. Cited in Lacchè, item 648. ISSN 0030–3607. ML1.O482.

Wagner conducted *Norma* in Riga during the 1837 season, getting out of a sickbed to do so. He had first heard the Bellini work in Königsberg the previous year. In a signed announcement of the Riga production Wagner noted that this opera was the sole work by Bellini that combined sincerity and ardor with the most profound wealth of melody. As Wagner stated, even the most intense foes of Italian opera (which surely included Wagner himself) must admire this opera. Many extensive quotations from Wagner's writings on *Norma* and Italian opera are given here.

644. Gautier, Théophile. *Les Beautés de l'Opéra ou Chefs-d'oeuvre lyriques*. Paris: Soulie, 1845. MT95.G27; also in *Souvenirs de Théâtre, d'Art et de Critique*. Paris: G. Charpentier, 1883. PQ2258.S6 1883; Trans. within introduction by E. Thomas Glasow, "Théophile Gautier on Bellini: 'Notice sur *Norma*'." *Opera Quarterly* 17/3 (Summer 2001): 423–34. ISSN 0736–0053. ML1699.O65.

Examines *Norma* in some detail in twenty-three pages of text; extensive description of plot and settings. Gautier was very critical of Bellini's music and of Italian opera in general. Speaks of the weakness of Bellini's harmony and lapses in this admittedly superior score worthy of a mediocre composer. Bellini's talent was natural, not acquired by study. He did not compose with disciplined regularity but had to wait for inspiration. See item 48.

645. Gossett, Philip, ed. *Norma/Tragedia lirica in two acts*. 2 vols. Early Romantic Opera 4. New York: Garland, 1983. ISBN 08–24029–03–8. ML96.5.B47.

Reproduces the facsimile from Bellini's original autograph manuscript in the Biblioteca di Santa Cecilia in Rome together with sketches from the Museo belliniano of Catania, the New York Public Library, and the Toscanini estate. The autograph score shows many alterations, some of which may date from the revival in Bergamo the summer after the opera's premiere. 140 pp. of sketches, drafts, and rejections versions also survive, 128 of which are in Catania. "A full study of this massive and fascinating documentation is not possible in a limited introduction of this sort. The following notes are intended only to help readers orient themselves in front of this material." Deals with problems of various sections, such as "Sinfonia." States that this brief analysis of the situation "should strongly suggest that many other pages associated with this opera once existed and may still be found in public or private collections."

Genesis and sources. Documentation is scarce for the months when Bellini was composing *Norma*. He probably divided his time between Milan and Como; no apparent problems with Romani are known. Romani's autograph libretto and sketches are at the Accademia Chigiana of Siena. Both Pastura and Schlitzer have written about Bellini's involvement with the shaping of the libretto.

646. Kimbell, David. *Vincenzo Bellini. Norma*. Cambridge Opera Handbooks. Cambridge: Cambridge University Press, 1998. ISBN 05–21485–14–2. ML410.B44 K56. 1998.

David Kimbell's volume on Vincenzo Bellini's *Norma* is part of the series of Cambridge Opera Handbooks and as such is an authoritative guide to its subject. Kimbell states that his purpose is "to provide a biographical and cultural context for Bellini's *Norma*, to examine its artistic qualities, and to suggest something of the impression it has made on our imaginations and sensibilities in the 165 years since it was produced in Milan in December 1831."

The author eschews analysis and theory "as those terms are currently understood in academic circles," for Bellini's music, notably in terms of harmony and orchestration, has often been found lacking when judged according to Verdian and Wagnerian standards. Kimbell succeeds in putting *Norma* into its own historical context both musically and culturally. Concerning the latter, it is sometimes overlooked that this work represents the voice of risorgimento Italy.

Kimbell discusses several nineteenth-century Italian assessments of Bellini, among them those of the novelist Giuseppe Rovani and the aesthetician Antonio Tari. Chapter topics include "The Composition of the Opera," in which Kimbell provides pertinent musical-political backgound and discusses Bellini's collaboration with Felice Romani and with the original singers, and the premiere. In discussing Romani's sources in Chapter 2 (Medea, Velleda, and Alexandre Soumet's play), Kimbell expounds on "The Lure of the North," reminding us of the literary background of Ossian and the writings of Klopstock in the late-eighteenth century. Chapter 3 provides a musical overview integrated with a plot synopsis. In Chapter 4, Kimbell integrates the analysis of music and poetry.

Kimbell the forensic scholar emerges in Chapter 5, "A Glimpse of the Genesis of the Opera," in which manuscript versions of drafts and sketches of both the libretto and the score are briefly surveyed, and continues in Chapter 6 with "Some Variant Readings." Chapter 8, "Critical Fortunes since the Unification of Italy," continues the discussion of *Norma*'s reception history. Kimbell concludes by contemplating five great prima donnas who have established and furthered the performance history of the opera: Giuditta Pasta, for whom the role was created, Giulia Grisi, Lilli Lehmann, Rosa Ponselle, and Maria Callas.

Appendices include treatment of Bellini's self-borrowings, the tonal plan of the opera, and a discussion of Franz Liszt's "Réminiscences de Norma." An excellent bibliography and index are included.

Reviews: Mike Ashman in *Opera* 50/7 (July 1999): 872–73; Mary Ann Smart in *Music & Letters* 80/4 (November 1999): 631–34; Stephen A. Willier in *Opera Quarterly* 17/3 (Summer 2001): 472–75.

647. Klein, John W. "Norma Today." *Opera* 18/12 (December 1967): 968–73. ISSN 0030–3526. ML5. O66.

Bellini reception since his death, in Italy (where he was always revered) and England (where he was unappreciated and scorned until after the middle of the twentieth century). Dates the revival from Callas's 1952 *Norma* at Covent Garden. Verdi's and Wagner's appreciation of Bellini. The sublimity of *Norma* with specific examples. Numerous quotations from composers and others. Influences on Verdi, Bizet, Wagner, Mussorgsky, and Mascagni, among others.

648. Lacchè, Mara. "*Norma* ou le fascination pour l'univers mystérieux des Druides, La reviviscence des légendes gauloises dans l'imaginaire créatif en France au début du XIXe siècle." *Vincenzo Bellini et la France* (2007): 681–716. See items 404 and 643.

The relationship between *Norma* and French cultural atmosphere at the beginning of the nineteenth century, when a passion for Ossianic and Druidic legends inspired musicians, writers (e.g., Chateaubriand and

Soumet) and numerous artists. *Norma* has both Romantic and "barbarian" elements—indeed, an element of Romanticism—along with a basis in Classical tragedy inherited from the operas of Spontini and Cherubini.

649. Lalli, Richard. "The *Norma* Conquests." *Opera News* 70/8 (February 2006): 34–37. ISSN 0030–3607. ML1.O482.

Examines the role of Norma, which "occupies almost a mythic place in the opera repertoire." Difficulties of casting this arduous role. Performance and reception history of the opera, with a mention of famous interpreters of the title role such as Giuditta Pasta and Maria Callas. Bellini's musico-dramatic devices, with a special consideration of the role of Adalgisa in terms of Norma.

650. Lippmann, Friedrich. "Casta diva: la preghiera nell'opera italiana della prima metà dell'Ottocento." *Recercare* 2 (1990): 174ff. ML5.R184.

A discussion of the prayer scene in primo ottocento Italian opera and why it became so important at that time. Suggests four types of prayer scenes, according to melodic and dramatic content. Composers whose works are examined include Spontini, Donizetti, Weber, and Rossini. Bellini's *Beatrice di Tenda* is featured. Includes a summary in English.

651. ——. "Quellenkundliche Anmerkungen zu einigen Opern Vincenzo Bellinis." *Analecta musicologica* 4 (1967): 131–53. ISSN 0585–6086. ML160.S893.

Notes numerous problems among autograph and early published sources of *Norma*, especially in the Act One finale and in the second act chorus, "Guerra, guerra."

652. Maguire, Simon and Elizabeth Forbes. "*Norma*." In *The New Grove Dictionary of Opera*. 4 vols. Ed. Stanley Sadie. New York: Macmillan, 1992. Vol. 3: 617–19. ISBN 09–35859–92–6. ML102.O6 N5 1992.

Genesis, sources, Bellini's role in shaping the libretto; deviation from ending of Soumet's play. Sketches, revisions of "Casta diva" and other numbers. Problems with modern editions. Singers who created the roles, reception, performance history. Detailed plot summary. Assessment. Illustration of the cast at Her Majesty's Theatre, London 1843: Lablache, Grisi, and Conti as Pollione. Cross-references to other pertinent illustrations.

653. Monterosso, Raffaello. "Per un' edizione di *Norma*." In *Scritti in onore di Luigi Ronga*. Naples: R. Ricciardi, 1973, pp. 415–510. ML55.R63 1973.

Differences between the autograph score and the score published by Ricordi in 1915 are explored.

654. Mungen, Anno. "Bellini and the Influence of Early French Grand Opera." *Vincenzo Bellini et la France* (2007): 27–43. See item 404.

A comparison between Spontini's *La vestale* and Bellini's *Norma* "to examine when and how the first masterpiece could have—even unconsciously—influenced the second." The two operas are compared from three different perspectives: (1) the libretti with their respective descriptions of female priesthood in ancient times and in the conditions in which the protagonists find themselves; (2) a similar conception of melodic patterns (i.e., non-symmetrical motivic structure); the arias of the two heroines are examined in this light; (3) the "dramaturgy of the two operas finds a topic moment in the aesthetic of the tableau, a musical interactive constellation of elements that ensures for the chorus a new, momentous presence."

655. Paduano, G. "Norma: la crisi del modello deliberativo." In *Noi facemmo ambedue un sogno strano: il disagio amoroso sulla scena dell'opera europea*. Palermo: Sellerio, 1982, pp. 152–77. ML3858.P3 1982.

Examines the libretto of *Norma* and its ancestors in the context of a larger discussion of five operas with grand heroines.

656. Pannain, Guido. "La Norma." *Revue musicale* 156 (May 1935): 44–51. ISSN 0768–1593. ML5.R613.

Comparison of Soumet's play and Chateaubriand's character Velleda from *Les Martyrs* with Romani and Bellini's *Norma*. The libretto and how Bellini's music brings the characters and dramatic situations to life. Not theoretical analysis but commentary. Demonstrates how Romani at times followed Soumet's original French text exactly. Gives the playbill from the Scala premiere.

657. Parmentola, Carlo, ed. *Norma. Opera collana di guide musicali diretta da Alberto Basso*. Turin: Unione Tipografico-Editrice Torinese, 1974. Teatro Regio, Turin. ML50.B44 N6 1974.

Extensive guide to the opera. Begins with cast of characters and complete Italian libretto. Parmentola's essays include "Norma fra tradizione e rivoluzione"; a number-by-number analysis of the opera with music examples; and very general bibliographic notes. Appendices include "La vocalità di *Norma*" by Rodolfo Celletti; and "Un'opera per 'primedonne' " by Giorgio Gualerzi.

658. Porter, Andrew. "Heroine." *The New Yorker* (August 16, 1985). Rpt. in Andrew Porter, *Musical Events, A Chronicle, 1983–1986*. New York: Summit Books, 1989, pp. 345–49. ISBN 06–71635–37–9. ML60.P89552 1989.

A history and discussion of sopranos who have sung the role of Norma, beginning with the first Norma, Giuditta Pasta, and proceeding through Jenny Lind, Lilli Lehmann, Ester Mazzoleni, Giannina Russ, Celesta Boninsegna, Gina Cigna, and Rosa Ponselle (no mention is made of Zinka

Milanov), to more-recent sopranos such as Callas, Sutherland, Caballé, Sills, Deutekom, Verrett, Bumbry, Scotto, and Olivia Stapp, whose performance Porter reviews at New York's City Opera. He calls into question many of the production decisions made by Andrei Serban, such as presenting Norma as a bag lady who suddenly turns around and launches into "Sediziose voci" and having Adalgisa present in the final scene of the opera and joining Norma on the funeral pyre.

659. ——. "Footnotes on *Norma*." *About the House* 2/8 (Christmas 1967): 12–14+. ISSN 0001–3242. ML5.A22.

Porter begins by stating, "This is not an essay about the eloquence and beauty of Bellini's melody; nor a defence of his apt, skillful orchestration; nor a tribute to Felice Romani's masterly libretto. These things can be taken for granted now. If anything, Bellini is overpraised today, for his weaker operas are not sufficiently distinguished from the strong; and with the uneven pieces, pleasure in the general rediscovery of a style once despised can obscure perception of the specifically Bellinian achievements . . . Rather, this is a collection of 'footnotes' to that appreciation of *Norma* which no longer needs writing."

Gives genesis and sources for *Norma*. Points out that with the premiere of *Norma* Pasta was making her debut at La Scala. Background on the playwright Alexandre Soumet. "Romani, for his part, had had some previous experience with Norma-like characters": he cites the libretti for Mayr's *Medea in Corinto* (1813), one of Pasta's famous roles, and *La sacerdotessa d'Irminsul* for Pacini (1817). Notes differences between Soumet's play and Romani's libretto, the major one being the omission of Norma's fifth-act mad scene. Quotes from the letter written by Donzelli, the tenor who created Pollione, to Bellini. Cites six passages in *Norma* that are taken from earlier works; discusses editions: "None of the scores currently available faithfully represents Bellini's autograph; and that autograph (published in facsimile in 1835) presents problems in the form of cancellations, subsequently reinstated with the words 'si fa.' But we can distinguish between bars lightly crossed through, as if for a particular performance, and bars heavily excised in Bellini's emphatic way. On the whole the Boosey vocal score is the most accurate and the most complete. Without going into small matters, I list some larger points that markedly affect a performance." This he does on p. 14.

Following this article are 3 pp. of "Norma Archives," including information about Druids and their rituals, and copiously illustrated with pictures of Druidic ruins and famous Normas, with quotations about performances from Eduard Hanslick, Francis Robinson, and Henry Chorley.

660. Ricobi, Nicodemo [Domenico Biorci, pseud.]. *Norma: Opera nuovo del Maestro Bellini messa in scena il 26 p.p. dicembre nell'I. R. Teatro alla*

Scala—Alcuni cenni critico-drammtico-letterari di Nicodemo Ricobi. Milan: Giovanni Silvestri, 1832.

14 pp. Copy in Paris, Bibliothèque de l'Opéra [Liv. It. 3588]. Notes the merits of the work, discusses the singers, especially Pasta.

661. Schenkman, Walter. "Liszt's Reminiscences of Bellini's *Norma.*" *American Liszt Society Journal* 9/1 (June 1981): 55–64. ISSN 0147–4413. ML410.L7 A68.

A discussion of Liszt's *Réminiscences de Norma* as an operatic fantasy and in terms of pianistic style. Schenkman notes that Liszt's version of the "Piange" seems to have influenced Wagner's "Liebestod" from *Tristan und Isolde.*

662. Scherillo, Michele. "La *Norma* di Bellini e la *Velleda* di Chateaubriand." *Nuova antologia di scienze, lettere ed arti* (June 1892). AP37.N8.

Discusses one of the literary sources for *Norma*, Chateaubriand's *Les Martyrs.*

663. Stern, Kenneth A. "Norma's Gallic Roots." *Opera News* 43/17 (March 17, 1979): 12–15; 34. ISSN 0030–3607. ML1.O482.

Explores Soumet's play and French opera tradition upon which *Norma* is based.

Note: Additional sources include:

664. Angiolini, C. *La Norma resiada.* Milan, 1832. Rpt. in C. Angiolini, *La Norma resiada e altre sestine milanesi.* Ed. D. Isella and G. Folena. Milan: Allegretti, 1980.

665. *Atti del simposio belliniano celebrato in occasione del 150° anniversario della 1° esecuzione di* Norma. Catania, 1981.

666. Blaze de Bury, Henri, Baron. Article on *Norma. Revue des Deux Mondes* (January 1, 1836). AP20.R3.

667. Blier, Steven. "Reverse Angle." *Opera News* 61/9: 10–14. ISSN 0030–3607. ML1.O482.

668. Cametti, Alfredo. *La musica teatrale a Roma cento anni fa* (Norma *di Bellini*). Rome, 1932. See item 538.

669. Damerini, Adelmo. *Vincenzo Bellini*, Norma: *guida attraverso il dramma e la musica.* Milan: Bottega di Poesia, 1923. MT100.B5 N6.

670. D'Arcais, F. "La *Norma* di Bellini." *Nouva antologia di scienze, lettere ed arti* (December 1882): 802ff. AP37.N8.

671. Erasmi, Gabriele. "*Norma* ed *Aida*. Momenti estremi della concezione romantica." *Studi verdiana* 5. Parma: Istituto di Studi Verdiani, 1988–89, pp. 85–108.

672. Fano, Fabio. "*Norma* nella storia del melodramma italiano." *Rassegna Musicale* 8/5–6 (1935): 315–26. ML5.R18.

673. Gatti, Carlo. "Norma." *L'illustrazione italiana, Rivista settimanale* (December 27, 1931). AP37.I4.

674. Lippmann, Friedrich. "Lo stile belliniano in *Norma*." In *Opera & Libretto* 1. Ed. Gianfranco Folena, et al., pp. 211–34. Florence: L. Olschki, 1990. ML1700.O655 1990.

675. Pannain, Guido. "*Norma*: cento anni." In *Ottocento musicale italiano: saggi e note*. Milan: Edizioni Curci, 1952, pp. 49–51. ML290.4.P3.

676. Rosendorfer, Herbert. "Belcanto-Zeitalter und Risorgimento. Vincenzo Bellini und seine Oper *Norma*." In *Jahrbuch der Bayerischen Staatsoper 1985*. Ed. Hans-Peter Krellman, pp. 55ff. Munich: Die Gesellschaft zur Förderung der Münchner Opernfestspiele, 1985. ML5.J128.

***Beatrice di Tenda, tragedia lirica* in two acts**

Libretto by Felice Romani; premiere Venice, Teatro la Fenice, March 16, 1833

677. Boromé, Joseph A. "Bellini and 'Beatrice di Tenda'." *Music & Letters* 40 (1961): 319–35. ISSN 0027–4224. ML5.M64.

Genesis, sources, reception at premiere. Accusations of similarities to *Norma* and *Anna Bolena* discussed. Problems and break with Romani; accusations on both sides. Quotes from Bellini's letters. Also discusses the end of the affair with Giuditta Turina and Bellini leaving Italy for good. Performance history; assessment and possible future. This was written at a time when Joan Sutherland was performing the opera at Carnegie Hall. Analysis with plot synopsis and music examples. Gives sources of Bellini's self-borrowings in composing *Beatrice*.

678. Brauner, Charles S. "Textual Problems in Bellini's *Norma* and *Beatrice di Tenda*." *Journal of the American Musicological Society* 29/1 (1976): 99–118. See item 635. ISSN 0003–0139. ML27.U5 A83363.

679. Cametti, Alberto. *Bellini a Roma. Brevi appunti storici per cura di Alberto Cametti*. Rome: Tipografia della Pace di Filippo Cuggiani, 1900 (see item 636).

680. Gossett, Philip, ed. *Beatrice di Tenda*. Early Romantic Opera 5. New York: Garland, 1980. ISBN 08–24029–04–6. ML96.5.B47.

A facsimile edition of the nineteenth-century printed score, with an introduction by Gossett. This was the only Bellini opera to be published in full score during the nineteenth century and one of the few full opera scores published in Italy during this period. "Though further textual work is needed to evaluate fully the edition and its relation to the autograph and other sources, it seems to be an essentially accurate and clear presentation of the music." Two volumes. Sources, detailed genesis; notes which parts of the autograph are not in Bellini's own hand. Includes a synopsis of the opera.

681. Gui, Vittorio. "A proposito della mia revisione della *Beatrice di Tenda* di Bellini." *L'Approdo musicale* 19 (1965): 207–14. ML5.A617.

The conductor Vittorio Gui discusses his revision of this opera, a mangled performance version, in which, for example, the final cabaletta ("Ah, la morte a cui m'appresso"), is deleted and replaced with a choral repeat of the beautiful trio, "Angiol di pace." Cf. also by Gui: "*Beatrice di Tenda*." *Musica d'oggi*, New series 2 (1969): 194–97.

682. Lippmann, Friedrich. "Casta diva: la preghiera nell'opera italiana della prima metà dell'Ottocento." *Recercare* 2 (1990): 174ff. ML5.R184.

See item 650.

683. ——. "Pagine sconosciute de *I Capuleti e i Montecchi e Beatrice di Tenda* di Vincenzo Bellini." *Rivista italiana di musicologia* 2 (1967): 140–51. ISSN 0035–6867. ML5.R79.

Includes facsimiles. A study of the sources for these two operas. A number of newly discovered details in the sources for *Beatrice di Tenda* are presented. Examines sketches in Catania (reported on by Pastura in item 272); Ricordi's print (the manuscript this was based on is probably lost); manuscripts in Biblioteca del Conservatorio, Naples; and others. The problem of the final scene of *Beatrice* is explored. Lippmann ends the article with an exhortation for a Bellini Complete Works Edition, hoping that his work will help initiate the process.

684. Maguire, Simon, Elizabeth Forbes, and Julian Budden. "*Beatrice di Tenda*." In *The New Grove Dictionary of Opera*. 4 vols. Ed. Stanley Sadie. New York: Macmillan, 1992. Vol. 2: 361–63. ISBN 09–35859–92–6. ML102.O6 N5 1992.

Traces genesis, sources, problems and break with Romani; singers involved, reception and performance history. Plot summary. Musical and dramatic assessment of the opera, why it has ultimately failed to establish itself in the repertoire. Illustrated, with original set design from La Fenice of Act One scene in a grove in the gardens of the ducal palace.

685. Oehlmann, Werner. "*Beatrice di Tenda*." In *I teatri di Vincenzo Bellini*. Ed. Roberto Alajmo, pp. 129–35. Palermo: Edizioni Novecento, 1986. ISBN 88–37300–48–4. ML410.B44 T4 1986.

A volume about productions of Bellini's operas. Each work is given a separate chapter. There is an extensive prose introduction to each chapter, which then consists of numerous illustrations, many of them of set designs.

686. Porter, Andrew. "Unhappy Queen and Happy Prince." *The New Yorker* (December 23, 1985). Rpt. in Andrew Porter, *Musical Events, A Chronicle, 1983–1989*. New York: Summit Books, 1989, pp. 406–11. ISBN 06–71635–37–9. ML60.P89552 1989.

Porter suggests a profitable study could be made, comparing Donizetti's *Anna Bolena* and Bellini's *Beatrice di Tenda*, both with libretti by Romani and with the same basic plot, except that in *Beatrice* the mezzo soprano (Agnese) is in love with the tenor (Orombello). Bellini and Romani "were well aware of this, and they strove to avoid copycat charges. Such a study could open out to illumine the way that Bellini and Donizetti against the background of the Code Rossini . . . inspired one another, turn and turn about." Porter briefly recounts the crossing paths of Bellini and Donizetti and the feeling of rivalry on Bellini's part, noting that a musicological study could document these mutual influences.

687. Rishoi, Niel. Review of recording of *Beatrice di Tenda* with Lucia Aliberti, Fabio Luisi conducting. Berlin Classics. *Opera Quarterly* 11/4 (1995): 139–45. ISSN 0736–0053. ML1699.O65.

Good background and performance history of the opera. Makes a case for the strength of the opera, which has often been dismissed because of the circumstances of its premiere and its similarities in plot to Donizetti's *Anna Bolena*. Rishoi takes issue with, for example, Weinstock's assessment of the opera. See item 279. Anna and Beatrice, however, meet their fates in very different manners, one going mad and one dying with dignity. Rishoi deems Beatrice "the least conventional of Bellini's operas," with the heaviest orchestration and a great deal of atmosphere. Discusses Vittorio Gui's version, in which the final cabaletta ("Ah, la morte a cui m'appresso") is deleted and replaced with a choral repeat of the beautiful trio, "Angiol di pace." See item 681.

Quotations from conductor Nello Santi (*Opera News* interview, vol. 49/12, March 6, 1985—where it is stated that "Bellini wrote *Norma* in August 1833") about performance versions of this and primo ottocento opera in general. Rishoi discusses the proper casting of singers in the leading roles. He concludes that in this recording "there is almost nothing that deserves recommendation." The conductor, Fabio Luisi, "elects, perversely, to make this the only commercial recording not to include the verses from the autograph that smooth the way to the final cabaletta." Discusses the other commercial recordings of the opera in some detail, none of which is ideal. Gives best marks for overall vocalism to Bonynge on Decca, but Edita Gruberova on Nightingale Classics is the best Beatrice.

688. Salerno, Gildo. *Beatrice cerco marito: ritratto di una single belliniana*. Catania: Edizioni Greco, 1997.

Cited by Kimbell (see item 646) in terms of the shape of the overture, in four sections, all associated with the title character herself.

689. Seminara, Graziella. "La melodrammaturgia incompiuta di *Beatrice di Tenda*." In *Quaderni dell'Istituto musicale Vincenzo Bellini di Catania*, Vol. II. Ed. Roberto Carnevale, pp. 41–62. "Vincenzo Bellini 1801–2001, con una appendice su Francesco Pastura." Libreria Musicale Italiana. Lucca: LIM Editrice, 2001. See item 401. ISBN 88–7096–284–9. ML410.B44 V463x 2001.

    Deals with the choice of a "Romantic subject," Bellini's part in shaping the libretto, the language and formal structure of the libretto, musical setting, musical forms, problems with the work because of Romani's commitments elsewhere. Extensive source citations, music examples.

690. Tedeschi, Rubens. "*Beatrice di Tenda." Addio fiorito asil. Il melodramma italiano da Rossini al verismo*. Pordenone: Studio Tesi, 1992, pp. 174–84. ISBN 88–76923–42–X. ML1733.4.T4 1992.

    Contains a bibliography and an index. A survey of Italian opera from Rossini to the verismo composers. Within that context, a fairly extensive study of *Beatrice*.

Note: Additional sources include:

691. Pastura, Francesco. "*Beatrice di Tenda* fra cronica e storia." In *L'Opera italiana in musica (for Eugenio Gara)*. Ed. Franco Abbiati, pp. 45–58. Milan: Rizzoli, 1965. ML1733.O64.

692. ——. "Due frammenti della *Beatrice di Tenda* di Bellini." *Rassegna musicale* 8 (1935): 327ff. ML5.R18.

I puritani e i Cavalieri, melodramma serio in three acts

Libretto by Count Carlo Pepoli, based on the play by Jacques-Arsène Ancelot and Joseph-Xavier-Boniface Saintine, *Têtes Rondes et Cavaliers*, a drama with interpolated songs first given in Paris in September 1833.

Premiere January 24, 1835, Théâtre-Italien, Paris. Review of premiere: *Revue des deux mondes*, Series 4, I (January 1835), pp. 341–46.

Naples version for Malibran, Duprez, and Porto (no contemporary performances—premiere not until December 14, 1985, in London).

693. Alier, Roger. *I puritani de Vincenzo Bellini*. Barcelona: Ediciones Robinbook, 2000. ISBN 84–95601–04–4.

    A guide in Spanish to Bellini's final opera. Alier provides the original libretto, a Spanish translation of it with musical commentary interspersed throughout, and several essays about the genesis and sources of the work and historical aspects of the plot. No music examples; several small illustrations. Includes a very basic "Cronologia belliniana" and discography with essay, the latter by Marc Heilbron.

694. *L'Avant-Scène Opéra* 96 (March 1987). Issue devoted to *I puritani*. ML5. A86.

Copiously illustrated program book from the Paris Opéra. A plot synopsis by Jean Cabourg, the original Italian libretto with French translation by Michel Orcel, with extensive musical and literary commentary (with music examples) by the French Bellini expert, Pierre Brunel. Articles include:

- Jean-Louis Dutronc, "*Les Puritains*: une année de labeur": genesis of the work with respect to the quartet of singers who created the major roles;
- André Segond, "Vincenzo Bellini à Paris": portrait of the Paris in which Bellini created *I puritani* and met Chopin;
- Jean-Alexandre Ménétier, "Bellini et Chopin": the connection between Bellini and Chopin. Illustrated with music examples;
- Robert Pourvoyeur, "Rossini et les Puritains": Rossini as a sort of spiritual father of Italian opera in Paris at this time, and his role in the genesis of *I puritani*;
- Pierre Brunel, "Les différentes versions des Puritains": discusses the complex textual history of the opera;
- Catherine Clément, "Mademoiselle Le Bouc": female operatic mad scenes and their reflection of views of women;
- Gérard Corneloup, "Le Roman historique anglais face à l'opéra romantique": Walter Scott's influence on primo ottocento Italian opera;
- Alain Arnaud, "La Mélodie bellinienne ou la séduction de l'evanescence": various melodic types used by Bellini;
- Sylviane Falcinelli, "'L'Effet Rubini': prodige ou supercherie?": on one of the great bel canto virtuosi;
- Jean Cabourg, "Profil vocal des Puritains" by Jean Cabourg: the famous quartet that performed at the premiere;
- An extensive "Discography comparée" by André Tubeuf explores the studio and live recordings, with special attention to Callas (1953), Sutherland (1963), Sills (1973), Sutherland (1975), and Caballé (1979), the last conducted by Muti, who does not allow ornamentation even upon the repeat of cabalettas;
- "L'Oeuvre à l'affiche," researched by Michel Pazdro, with a bibliography by Elisabeth Giuliani, notes first performances, performance history at La Scala, the Metropolitan Opera, in Great Britain, at the Teatro Colón, in France, and other international venues.

695. Brunel, Pierre. "I puritani." In *I teatri di Vincenzo Bellini*. Ed. Roberto Alajmo, pp. 137–49. Palermo: Edizioni Novecento, 1986. ISBN 88–37300–48–4. ML410.B44 T4 1986.

A volume about productions of Bellini's operas. Each work is given a separate chapter. There is an extensive prose introduction to each chapter, which then consists of numerous illustrations, many of them of set designs.

696. Campana, Alessandra. " 'Ancor di nuovo questo suon molesto': Spazi e tempi della follia nei *Puritani*." *Vincenzo Bellini et la France (2007)*: 217–28. See item 404.

Quotes from Bellini's letter of April 11, 1834 to Filippo Santocanale, which includes the famous line "Il dramma per musica deve far piangere, inorridire, morire cantando." Examines madness in *Puritani* in the Paisiello tradition of "pazza per amore."

697. Cazaux, Chantal. "Giulia Grisi, Giovanni Battista Rubini, Antonio Tamburini, Luigi Lablache: Un quatuor vocal pour *I puritani* et *Marino Faliero*." *Vincenzo Bellini et la France* (2007): 307–25. See item 404.

The premieres of *Puritani* and *Marino Faliero* were less than two months apart, both given at the Théâtre-Italien with the same casts. Provides an examination of these singers' repertoires and a comparison of roles in these two operas. In Bellini's opera the soprano and the tenor dominate, whereas in *Marino Faliero* the character of Elena provides a chiaroscuro contrast to the three principal male voices, who represent a dominance of power and hierarchy.

698. Everist, Mark. " 'Tutti I francesi erano diventati matti': Bellini et le duo pour voix de deux basses." *Vincenzo Bellini et la France* (2007): 327–54. See item 404.

The famous bass duo from *I puritani*, which culminates in "Suoni la tromba," is examined as a great innovation in Italian opera. This duo is first compared with a buffo duet from Luigi Ricci's *Chiara di Rosemberg* and then the unison writing in Bellini's duo is examined in the light of Rossini's finales and a cabaletta written for Lablache by Pacini in *Amazilia* of 1825. Also treats the evolution of Tamburini's voice and how the change from bass to baritone provided a background for Verdi's development of the baritone voice. Music examples.

699. Everist, Mark, Sarah Hibberd, and Walter Zidaric. "Vincenzo Bellini, *I puritani*: Dossier de presse." *Vincenzo Bellini et la France* (2007): 405–81. See item 404.

An attempt to reprint the entire press coverage of the premiere of Bellini's final opera, although a few notices from after 1835 have been included.

700. Faria, Carlo. "A Cry of the Spirit: Bellini's Bel Canto in *I Puritani* Embodies Pure Romantic Emotion." *Opera News* 40/16 (February 28, 1976): 36–39. ISSN 0030–3607. ML1.O482.

An exploration of bel canto melodies in *I puritani* and the singers for whom Bellini created them. Questions addressed incude: How extensive was this vocabulary of bel canto? What do the terms mean? What was so peculiar to its mastery that for a while it became a dead art? Traces genesis of *I puritani* and then examines, providing music examples, certain parts of the score in terms of the vocal demands required.

701. Gherardi, Luciano. "Varianti ne *I puritani* e edizione a stampa." *Chigiana* 34/14 (1981): 217–32. ISSN 0069–3391. ML5.C38.

A comparison of two versions of *I puritani*, the second completed after the premiere in response to the singers' and public's reactions and intended to strengthen the drama. Studies by Francesco Pastura and Friedrick Lippmann are drawn upon.

702. Gossett, Philip. *I Puritani/Melodramma serio in three acts*. Early Romantic Opera. New York: Garland, 1983. ISBN 08–24029–05–4. ML96.5.B47.

A facsimile of Bellini's original autograph manuscript in the Biblioteca Comunale in Palermo together with the Naples revision, found in the Museo belliniano in Catania. In the introduction Gossett notes that *I puritani* "had a complex, even tormented history." There is extensive documentary evidence concerning its genesis: sketches, a copious interchange of letters between Bellini and his artistic colleagues both in Paris and in Italy, and musical manuscripts representing diverse layers in its history. The Naples composite manuscript, although a "revision" of *I puritani*, sometimes preserves music no longer present in the "original" Parisian source.

The editor takes into account: changes made during the composition of the Paris version before the Naples revision was prepared (shown in the Palermo manuscript); revisions made by Bellini for Naples (from the Catania manuscript); and changes made by Bellini for Paris after the Naples revision had been sent to Florimo (evidenced in the Palermo manuscript). This facsimile edition is meant to be a step in the direction of a critical edition of this opera.

703. Lippmann, Friedrich. "Quellenkundliche Anmerkungen zu einigen Opern Vincenzo Bellinis." *Analecta musicologica* 4 (1967): 131–53. ISSN 0585–6086. ML160.S893.

Details about variants and problems. States that a critical edition of *I puritani* should not, as with the other operas, merely include an appendix with text variants, but a complete extra volume producing the second, Naples, version of the opera. Only the first version has been printed (Paris, 1835). Describes the intended singers and changes for the Neapolitan version of 1835: Malibran, (Elvira); Duprez (Arturo); Pedrazzi (Riccardo); this originally was a baritone role but Pedrazzi was a tenor.

704. Maguire, Simon, Elizabeth Forbes, and Julian Budden. "*Puritani, I.*" *New Grove Dictionary of Opera*, 4 vols. Ed. Stanley Sadie. New York: Macmillan, 1992. Vol. 3: 1183–85. ISBN 09–35859–92–6. ML160.S893.

Genesis, sources, reception, singers involved. Discussion of Naples version for Malibran. Detailed plot summary. Musical assessment: *Puritani* has a "colorito" and in terms of harmony and orchestration is Bellini's most "sophisticated" opera. Contains "an unusual wealth of thematic recall" and is written, because of the Parisian audiences, on a spacious time-scale. Explores Elvira's mad scene, the storm scene, ensemble and vocal writing. Beethoven and Wagner are mentioned. This opera a portent to a non-existent future?

705. Mauceri, Marco. "Ancora su *I Puritani* per Napoli: un inedito." *Nuova rivista musicale italiana* 23 (1989): 410–17. ISSN 0029–6228. ML5.N93.

Brings to light a letter not included in Cambi, *Epistolario* (see item 288) from Bellini to Prince d'Ottaviano, written on October 14, 1834, about the "scrittura" offered by the Teatro San Carlo to adapt a version of *I puritani* for that theater. Presents a modern transcription of the entire document on pages 415–17. The negotiations were concluded on November 20, when Bellini received a contract from Naples. Mauceri mistakenly gives the date of the Paris premiere of *I puritani* as February 24, 1835, rather than January 24.

706. *Mémoire pour Le Sieur Dormoy, Directeur du Théâtre royal Italien, demandeur, contre Le Sieur Troupenas, Editeur de Musique, défendeur* [1841].

Legal issues about the rights to Bellini's last opera, *I puritani*, after his death. 24 pp. Followed by *Résumé pour M. Troupenas, éditeur de la musique, contre M. Dormoy, directeur du théâtre italien*. Two more pamphlets follow. Copy of these in Paris, Bibliothèque de l'Opéra, in a volume entitled Salle Ventadour, 1832–1865, call number [C. 7487 (1–19)].

707. Monterosso, Raffaello. "Le due redazioni dei Puritani." In *Letterature comparate, problemi e metodi: studi in onore di Ettore Paratore*. Bologna, 1981, pp. 589–609. PN863.L45.

A comparison of the Paris and Naples versions of *I puritani*.

708. Nicastro, Aldo. "Il caso Pepoli e il libretto de *I puritani.*" *Nuova rivista musicale italiana* 21 (1987): 214–27. ISSN 0029–6228. ML5.N93.

Biographical background on Carlo Pepoli. Quotes from his collected works, *Prose e poesie*.

709. Paduano, Guido. " 'Mesta e lieta': La coincidenza degli Opposti emotive nella situazione dei *Puritani*." *Vincenzo Bellini nel secondo centenario della nascita* (2004): 199–216. See item 406.

"Mesta e lieta" are the words spoken by Elvira's uncle, Giorgio, in the beginning of the second act, when the Chorus enquires about Elvira's mental state. Dichotomies between joy and sadness are examined. No source citations.

710. Pastura, Francesco. "L'edizione integrale de *I puritani* rappresentata al Teatro Massimo." Extract from *Rivista del Comune di Catania* 1 (January–March 1960). Published as a separate booklet.

Copy of this article in Museo belliniano with handwritten corrections to printed text, probably done by Pastura himself. On the evening of March 5, 1960, the public was able to hear, at the Teatro Massimo Bellini in Catania, the "complete" *I puritani*; this included three pieces and some recitative, none of which was published in the current edition. He traces the history of the published edition vis-à-vis the autograph manuscripts in the Museo belliniano (the version for Naples) and in the Biblioteca Comunale di Palermo (the original version for Paris). For various reasons the Naples version contains pieces not found in the Paris version, and the addition of these is what Pastura means by an "edizione integrale," even though that concept undoubtedly represents a version never actually written by Bellini.

711. ——. "Una lettera di Bellini a Maria Malibran e la storia della prima edizione de *I puritani*." Extract from *Rivista del Comune di Catania* (1954).

Separate bound copy in Museo belliniano. 6 pp. Pastura writes that in the library of the music conservatory in Brussels there is a letter from Bellini written from Paris on February 27, 1835, to Maria Malibran in Venice. The letter directly involves the complex textual history of *I puritani*, specifically the autograph score found in the Museo belliniano. Bellini expresses interest in getting to know Malibran better; it is not known if Malibran responded to this letter. Pastura provides not only the text but a facsimile of the letter.

712. Peschel, Richard E. and Enid Rhodes Peschel. "Music is Feeling, Then, Not Sound: Portrayals of Twentieth-Century Psychiatric Definitions in Three Nineteenth-Century Operas." In *Exploration: The Nineteenth Century*. Ed. Anne B. Dobbie, Jennifer Brantley, Katherine A. Holman, and Victoria H. Spaniol, pp. 66–99. Los Angeles: Levy, 1988. See item 615.

Discussion of Verdi's *Don Carlo* and Bellini's *La sonnambula* and *I puritani* from the viewpoint of psychiatry.

713. Petrobelli, Pierluigi. "Bellini e Paisiello: Altri documenti sulla nascita dei *Puritani*." In *Il melodramma italiano dell'ottocento: studi e ricerche per Massimo Mila*. Ed. G. Pestelli, pp. 351–63. Turin: G. Eunaudi, 1977. ML1733.4.M4; English trans. by Roger Parker as "Bellini and Paisiello:

Further Documents on the Birth of *I puritani*." In Pierluigi Petrobelli, *Music in the Theater: Essays on Verdi and Other Composers*. Princeton, N.J.: Princeton University Press, 1994, pp. 176–92. ISBN 06–91091–34–X. ML410.V4 P28 1994.

The author writes: "Bellini's correspondence with his librettist Pepoli and his Neapolitan friends Florimo, Barbo, etc., at the time he was working on *I puritani* in Paris (1835) clearly illustrates his method of composing as well as the principles that guided him in operatic compositions. His choice of librettist preceded the choice of plot, and the entire opera was fashioned as it would best suit the singers of the premiere. Individual numbers were composed as singers became available, and hence there was no overall conception of the score. Bellini regarded the clear representation of the passions as even more important a means of moving the audience than the dramatic incident, which could easily be moved from one point in the action to another. For example, a chorus in *I puritani* was moved several times during the period of composition. Eventually the piece was cut and its material was incorporated into the duet for two basses, 'Suoni la tromba.' The model for *I puritani* was clearly Paisiello's *Nina o la pazza per amore*; in fact the entire conception is typical of an eighteenth-century composer. Bellini's aim was to move his audience almost exclusively with the expressive strength of the vocal lines. However, the *I puritani* score also indicates that the composer was seeking new paths, e.g., the experiments with spatial effects at the opening of the first and third acts."

714. ——. "Nota sulla poetica di Bellini: a proposito de *I puritani*." *Muzikoloski Zbornik* 8 (1972): 70–85. English trans. by Roger Parker as "Notes on Bellini's Poetics: Apropos of *I puritani*." In Pierluigi Petrobelli, *Music in the Theater: Essays on Verdi and Other Composers*. Princeton, N.J.: Princeton University Press, 1994, pp. 162–75. ISBN 06–91091–34–X. ML410.V4 P28 1994.

Genesis of the opera, working relationship with Pepoli; the two versions of the work. Study of autograph documents.

715. Porter, Andrew. "Bellini's Last Opera." *Opera* 11/4 (May 1960): 315–22. ISSN 0030–3526. ML5.O66.

Informative article detailing the genesis of Bellini's last opera, using Cambi's *Epistolario* (see item 288) and Pastura's *Bellini secondo la storia* (see item 272) as main sources. Much on the "rivalry" between Donizetti and Bellini and Bellini "paying court" to Rossini to succeed in Paris. Lengthy quotation from a letter Bellini wrote to his uncle about these matters. Bellini notes that this is now the third time he and Donizetti have been thrown into direct confrontation and he considers that he has outdone his rival each time. Collaboration with Pepoli; the cast of the premiere; differences in the Naples version for Malibran. History of London performances. Ends not with Bellini's funeral, at which an arrangement of the tenor melody, "Creadeasi misera," from Act Three of *I puritani* was sung, but with Donizetti's response to *I puritani—Lucia di Lammermoor*. In this work "—which has so many parallels with *I puritani*—Donizetti was evidently determined to show what he could achieve on the same lines. It will be fascinating to compare the two." Illustrations: two from the *Illustrated London News* of scenes and rehearsals of *I puritani*; line engravings (after Challon) of the premiere cast; the room in Catania in which Bellini was born; a contemporary lithograph of the composer.

Note: On p. 322 are reproduced excerpts from three early English views of *I puritani*: from Chorley's *Thirty Years' Musical Recollections* (see item 38), from John E. Cox, *Musical Recollections of the Last Half-Century* (see item 40) and from *The Times* (London) on Jenny Lind's Elvira (July 31, 1848).

716. Pugliese, Giuseppe and Roman Vlad. *"I puritani" ritrovati: la versione inedita dedicata a Maria Malibran*. Manduria: P. Lacaita, 1986. ML410. B44 P84 1986.

A study of the Naples version of Bellini's final opera. Includes "La versione napoletana nell'Epistolario dell autore" by Pugliese, pp. 17–75.

717. Shawe-Taylor, Desmond. "A '*Puritani*' Discography." *Opera* 11 (June 1960): 387–95. ISSN 0030–3526. ML5.O66.

At the time of writing, there was only one "complete" *Puritani* in the catalogue, Callas conducted by Serafin, which was in fact somewhat heavily cut. Shawe-Taylor assesses many recordings from the past of individual numbers, by luminaries such as De Lucia, Battistini, De Luca, Bonci, Galli-Curci, up to Giuseppe Di Stefano and the very young Renata Scotto.

718. Smart, Mary Ann. "Bellini's Unseen Voices: Offstage Music and Quotation in *I puritani*." In *"Dalla tomba uscita": Representations of Madness in Early Nineteenth-Century Italian Opera*. Diss., Cornell University, 1994, pp. 87–154.

Elvira in *I puritani* in more than one instance is heard offstage. Other chapters treat *Lucia di Lammermoor* and the male mad scene in *Maria Padilla*. References to modern feminist writings.

719. Smith, Patrick J. "Heat of the Moment: Why Bellini's *I Puritani* is the Soul of Bel Canto." *Opera News* 55/14 (30 March 1991): 12–13. ISSN 0030–3607. ML1.O482.

Bel canto is "a vague term," but the operas of Bellini are the "*locus classicus* of the form [*sic*]" because of the nature of his melodies, which affected not only other opera composers but someone like Chopin. *Norma* is not the exemplar of bel canto because it "prefigures the later nineteenth century, as well as being a receptacle for the classic Gluckian opera of the eighteenth century." *Puritani*, instead, focuses on the voice and its expressive power and "gives more or less equal time to four voice types." The opera is also "unbelievable" dramatically, another component of bel canto, where the arias and scenes are "for the moment." Smith calls "Qui la voce" the "single finest example of the bel canto style" and discusses it in terms of the extraordinarily expansive scene in which it is heard. Concludes that "Had Bellini lived to write four or five more operas, I strongly believe he would have supplied a counterweight to Verdi's emerging, dramatically tinged type of vocabulary, and by keeping the drama within the vocal line would have continued and codified a tradition begun in the previous century. Perhaps then the subsequent history of Italian opera would have been something different."

720. Spina, Giuseppe. "Origine de *I puritani*." *Nuova rivista musicale italiana* 12 (January–March 1978): 29–33. ISSN 0029–6228. ML5.N93.

In 1835 Bellini's last opera was premiered in Paris as *I puritani di Scozia*, the title by which Scott's novel was known in France and Italy. Bellini wrote to Florimo that the title "I puritani" had been chosen because of the fame of Scott's novel. Thus began the idea that Bellini's opera was based on Scott's novel. The opera was instead based on the French play *Têtes rondes et cavaliers* by Jacques Ancelot and Xavier Saintine. This play in turn inspired Scott's novel *Woodstock*, but not, as has been asserted, his *Old Mortality*.

721. ——. "Scott–Ancelot–Pepoli–Bellini: genesi del libretto de *I Puritani*." *Nuova rivista musicale italiana* 23 (1989): 79–97. ISSN 0029–6228. ML5. N93.

Genesis and literary sources of Bellini's last opera. The fallacious connection with Walter Scott; Ancelot; the names of the characters; the historical epoch; the dramatic situations are points of discussion. Illustrated with reproductions of contemporary prints of singers, costumes, portraits of Pepoli and Bellini, facsimile of contemporary printed libretto.

722. Staffieri, Gloria. "*I puritani*: Una specie di *Grand Opéra*?" *Vincenzo Bellini nel secondo centenario della nascita* (2004): 229–49. See item 406.

In 1935 Alfred Einstein referred to Bellini's last opera as "a kind of grand opera." In 1969 Orrey (see item 270) returned to this idea, affirming that Bellini composd this opera for the French public with French opera tradition in mind. According to Orrey, Bellini had undoubtedly studied works such as Boïeldieu's *Dame blanche*, Auber's *Muette de Portici*, and Rossini's *Guillaume Tell*. There is even a definite correspondence between certain scenes in *Puritani* and those in *La Muette* and *Guillaume Tell*. In his letters, Bellini refers to operas by Auber, Meyerbeer, Halévy, Adam, Hérold, and Boïeldieu. Table One presents a formal and tonal outline of *I puritani* and use of recurring themes. Table Two concerns the Introductions to *La Muette* and *Guillaume Tell* and Table Three examines Rossini's *Donna del lago* and *Maometto Due* in light of Bellini's *Puritani*.

723. Tiby Ottavio, "*I puritani*." *A Vincenzo Bellini. Bollettino dei musicisti, Mensile del Sindicato Fascista Musicisti* 13/3 (December 1934): 63ff.

A Fascist publication, appearing approximately a century after Bellini's death, glorifying Italy through its artists.

724. Velly, Jean-Jacques. "*Les Puritains* face aux innovations orchestrales à Paris dans les années 1830." *Vincenzo Bellini et la France* (2007): 355–66. See item 404.

Paris was an important center for the development of the orchestra. Several orchestration treatises had appeared before that of Berlioz, beginning in the mid-1820s. A comparison of the many innovations in orchestration in works composed contemporaneously with *I puritani*, by composers such as Rossini, Halévy, Meyerbeer, and Berlioz.

725. Vlad, Roman. "Vicende di un capolavoro delle due versioni dei *Puritani*." Giuseppe Pugliese, Roman Vlad, with Franca Cella, et al. "*I puritani*" *ritrovati: la versione inedita dedicata a Maria Malibran*. Manduria: P. Lacaita, 1986, pp. 77ff. ML410.B44 P84 1986.

See item 716. A detailed comparison of the two versions of Bellini's final opera.

726. Zedda, Alberto and Federico Agostinelli. "I problemi musicologici della versione per Napoli de *I puritani*." In "*I puritani*" *ritrovati*. 1986, pp. 271ff.

See item 716. Editing considerations for the Naples version of *I puritani*.

727. Zidaric, Walter. "La Réception de *I puritani* dans la presse parisienne à partir de l'année de la creation (1835–1987)." *Vincenzo Bellini et la France* (2007): 367–403. See item 404.

To a great extent because of the great quartet of singers involved, the contemporary Parisian press unanimously declared *I puritani* a success. The bass duo was preferred over the soprano's aria. By 1987 the interest had shifted to Elvira's music, the need for a first-class quartet, and elements of *mise-en-scène.*

Note: Additional sources include:

728. Blaze de Bury, Henri, Baron. "*I puritani*." *Revue des Deux Mondes* (1835). AP20.R3.

729. Brofferio, A. "*I puritani e i cavalieri*. Opera seria del sig. C. Pepoli. Musica del Maestro Bellini." *Il messaggiere torinese* (Alexandria, 1839).

730. Petrobelli, Pierluigi. "Uno splendido affresco musicale." Program Booklet for *I puritani*, Teatro La Fenice, Venice (1968–69): 171–81.

731. Schenkman, Walter. "Two Contemporary Documents on Bellini's 'Suoni la tromba'." *Opera Journal* 9/4 (1976): 23–31. ISSN 0030–3585. ML1. O46.

BELLINI'S NON-OPERATIC WORKS

732. Arcidiacono, Angela, Giuseppe Cantone, Antonella Fiorino, and Letizia Spampinato. "Analisi melodica di alcune composizioni vocali da camera di Vincenzo Bellini." In *Quaderni dell'Istituto musicale Vincenzo Bellini di Catania*, Vol. II. Ed. Roberto Carnevale, pp. 75–112. "Vincenzo Bellini 1801–2001, con una appendice su Francesco Pastura." Libreria Musicale Italiana. Lucca: LIM Editrice, 2001. See item 401.

Analysis of melodic shapes and intervallic content (with graphs) in four of Bellini's songs: "Dolente immagine di Filla mia," "Vaga luna che inargenti," "Vanne, o rosa fortunata," and "Malinconia, ninfa gentile." Numerous music examples.

733. Bellini, Vincenzo. *Composizioni da camera per canto e pianoforte*. Milan: Ricordi, 1935.

734. ——. *Concerto for Oboe and Orchestra in E♭ Major (Concerto in Mib per oboe e archi)*. Milan: Ricordi, 1971. M1123.B43. Ebmaj. L5.

Various other editions also exist, also for piano accompaniment. See Library of Congress catalog.

Reviewed by Andrea Della Corte in *Musica d'oggi* 17/4 (April 1935): 160.

735. ——. *Messe di Gloria*: In G minor, from vocal and orchestral parts in Naples Conservatory Library. Recording: Bellini, Vincenzo. *Missa Seconda in sol minore*. Camerata Polifonica Siciliana. Cond. Douglas Bostock. Soloists: Katia Ricciarelli, soprano; Francesca Aparo, alto; Salvatore Fisichella, tenor; and Furio Zanasi, baritone. Class CD225.

World premiere recording of this work performed in Catania Cathedral. Bellini wrote more than thirty sacred works, among them four extant masses. This recording includes notes by Maria Rosaria Adamo.

736. ——. *Sei Ariette per camera del maestro Vincenzo Bellini*. Milan: Ricordi, 1829.

A publication of six of Bellini's songs during his lifetime.

737. ——. *Ventidue composizioni vocali da camera*, revisione di Francesco Cesari. Milan: Suvini Zerboni, 2000.

From the 1935 Ricordi edition, Cesari has excluded three compositions: "La farfalletta," "Quando incise su quel marmo," and "Torna, vezzosa Fillide" and has added "quattro titoli sconosciuti ai cataloghi belliniani,"

"Quattro composizioni presocchè dimenticate," and "due lavori pubblicati in questi ultimi anni."

738. Bongiovanni, Carmela. "Bellini e Paer a Parigi, Due musicisti e la loro produzione vocale cameristica a confronto." *Vincenzo Bellini et la France* (2007): 109–53. See item 404.

Paer was one of the most important Italian composers living in Paris. In 1835 he became director of chamber music and the musical chapel for King Louis-Philippe. Both Paer and Bellini wrote several chamber compositions to Italian poetry by Pepoli. Bellini in fact wrote nine compositions, rather than five as traditionally stated. Only one has survived, "La ricordanza." Music examples.

739. Cesari, Francesco. "Nuove acquisizioni al catalogo vocale da camera di Vincenzo Bellini." In *La romanza italiana da salotto*. Ed. F. Sanuitale. Turin: EDT, 2002.

New acquisitions to the catalog of Bellini's songs. See item 737.

740. Gallotta, Bruno. "La musica vocale da camera di Bellini e Donizetti." *Rassegna musicale Curci* 48/2 (May 1995): 5–11. ML5.R183.

An examination of the precursors of Bellini's and Donizetti's vocal chamber music, such as Rossini. Historical and cultural contexts are discussed in order to demonstrate the worth of this repertoire, which has often been overlooked or disdained.

741. Kim, Soo Yeon. *The Chamber Songs of Rossini, Bellini, and Donizetti*. DMA thesis, University of Illinois at Urbana-Champaign, 1992.

The author has included transcriptions of the songs and translations of the texts.

742. Mattina, Aldo. "Drammaturgia e lirismo delle Ariette con una breve indagine su una (im)probabile catalogazione." In *Quaderni dell'Istituto musicale Vincenzo Bellini di Catania*, Vol. II. Ed. Roberto Carnevale, pp. 63–74. "Vincenzo Bellini 1801–2001, con una appendice su Francesco Pastura." Libreria Musicale Italiana. Lucca: LIM Editrice, 2001. See item 401.

Considerations for cataloguing Bellini's songs and other non-operatic vocal works. Surveys current lists of these works from sources such as *Enciclopedia Storica—La Musica* (Guido M. Gatti, 1976, 36 listings); *Dizionario Enciclopedico Universale della Musica e dei Musicisti* (Alberto Basso, director, 35 listings); *15 Composizioni da camera per canto e pianoforte* (Ricordi, 1935); *Ventidue composizioni vocali da camera* (Francesco Cesari, 1999). Also looks at the composition of songs as leading to operatic versions, citing examples from *La straniera* and pointing out other occasions for this practice in *Sonnambula, Puritani, Adelson e Salvini* and *Beatrice di Tenda.*

743. Meloncelli, Raoul. "Le liriche da camera su versi di Felice Romani." In *Felice Romani, Melodrammi-poesie-documenti*. Ed. Andrea Sommariva. (*Historiae musicae cultures biblioteca* LXXVII), pp. 257–308. Florence: Olschki, 1966.

744. Morabito, Fulvia. *La romanza vocale da camera in Italia*. Turnhout: Brepols, 1997.

A great part of the first chapter is dedicated to the songs of Bellini and their stylistic relationships to similar works of other composers.

745. Pastura, Francesco. "Un' arietta inedita di Vincenzo Bellini." *Musica d'oggi; rassegna di vita e di coltura musicale* 18 (1936): 115–17. ML5. M721.

Reveals the unpublished arietta "Era felice un dì."

746. ——. "La 'Messa seconda' di Bellini." Estratto della *Rivista del Comune di Catania* 3–4 (July–December 1959).

Published as a separate booklet, 5 pp.; copy in Museo belliniano. Pastura makes the point that the main difficulty in definitively cataloging the non-operatic ("minori") compositions of Bellini is the problem of chronological order. Contains facsimiles.

747. Principe, Quirino. "L'Altro Bellini." In Giampiero Tintori, *Bellini*. Milan: Ruscon: Libri, 1983. p. 279 (see item 276).

On the songs, "arie di camera."

748. Stefani, Carlida. "La lirica da camera di Bellini: dal contesto funzionale alle questioni testuali." *Vincenzo Bellini nel secondo centenario della nascita* (2004): 521–34. See item 406.

Examines the twenty-two songs in Cesari's collection and updates information about them.

749. Touret, Corinne. "Une mélodie inquiète et subtile: 'L'Abbandono.'" *Vincenzo Bellini et la France* (2007): 197–214. See item 404.

After a brief review of the main features of Bellini's life in Paris, focuses on an analysis of "L'Abbandono," composed during the last months of Bellini's life. The work is placed in historical context and then compared with other Italian Romantic songs from composers such as Rossini, Donizetti, and Bellini himself. Music examples.

11

Bellini's Interpreters, Histories of Theaters, Bel Canto Style, Production Aspects

750. Alajmo, Roberto, ed. *I teatri di Vincenzo Bellini*. Palermo: Edizioni Novecento, 1986. ISBN 88–37300–48–4. ML410.B44 T4 1986.

Introduction by Ubaldo Mirabelli. A chapter for each of the operas, with an extensive prose introduction to each chapter, followed by a presentation of numerous illustrations, many of them of stage designs. Chapters are written by such Bellini authorities as Pierre Brunel, Maria Rosario Adamo, Giampiero Tintori, and others and are listed in this volume in the appropriate section in Studies of Individual Operas. In addition, the following topics are presented: Giampiero Tintori, *Bellini al museo Teatrale alla Scala; Iconografia belliniana*; Maria Rosario Adamo, *Regesto cronologico [Note biografiche; Avvenimenti culturale]; Esempi musicali, Schede e note.*

751. Ardoin, John. "A Footnote to Ponselle's Norma." *Opera* 27 (March 1976): 225–28. ISSN 0030–3526. ML5.O66.

Ponselle's preparation and performance of the role of Norma, using Marion Telva's (a notable Adalgisa) annotated score and various recordings as evidence. Transpositions, breath markings. Illustrated with facsimiles of Telva's score. Discussion of some of the same transpositions in the 1954 performances at the Metropolitan with Zinka Milanov as Norma.

752. —— and Gerald Fitzgerald. *Callas*. New York: Holt, Rinehart, and Winston, 1974. ISBN 00–30114–86–1. ML420.C18 C33.

Beautiful, lavishly produced iconography with essays. Numerous black and white photos. Ardoin wrote "The Art and the Life" and Fitzgerald "The Great Years." Ardoin writes in detail about the vocal style of the primo ottocento, emphasizing the roles that Giuditta Pasta created for Bellini and

Donizetti and how Maria Callas has served them in our own century. Includes a chronology of performances and recordings, beginning in 1938. 282 pp.

753. Barbiera, Raffaello. *Vite ardenti del teatro*. Milan: Fratelli Treves, 1931.

Dedicates a chapter to "Bellini. I suoi romanzi d'amore." But disregard it, for he talks of Bellini's *Poliuto*, written by Pepoli in Paris. "L'argomento del *Poliuto* era sublime: i martiri cristiani. Eppure col suo genio Vincenzo Bellini donò quel povero libretto e trionfò!" (p. 130).

754. Barthe, Vincent. "Diriger *Norma* aujourd'hui en France: Quels choix interprétaires." *Vincenzo Bellini et la France* (2007): 797–810. See item 404.

The lyric theater created by Bellini in Norma is a theater of the soul, according to Barthe. Norma is a masterpiece, an opera "of shadow and night," a catalogue of bel canto features full of long and gorgeous melodies. Believes that "Bellini's secret" was "a beautiful synthesis of recitative, arioso, and aria."

755. Biggi, Maria Ida. *Francesco Bagnara scenografio alla Fenice*. Venice: Marsilio, 1996. ISBN 88–31765–68- X. ND2888. B27 A4 1996.

Francesca Bagnara was a nineteenth-century Venetian set designer who designed sets for some Bellini operas.

756. —— and Maria Teresa Muraro. *Giuseppe e Pietro Bertoja scenografio alla Fenice 1840–1902*. Venice: Marsilio, 1998. See item 800. ISBN 88–31771–41–8. ND2888.B47 A4 1998.

The Bertojas were nineteenth-century Venetian set designers.

757. Blaze de Bury, Henri-Ange, Baron. *Musiciens contemporains*. Paris: Michel Lévy Frères, 1856. See item 36. ML385.B64.

In addition to discussing Bellini and other contemporary composers, Blaze de Bury explores the careers of famous Bellini interpreters such as Giuditta Pasta and Maria Malibran.

758. Bonardi, Alain. " 'Acclimater' *Norma*: Une proposition de scénographie interactive à l'Ile d'Yeu." *Vincenzo Bellini et la France* (2007): 811–19. See item 404.

Presents the principles of an interactive scenography for *Norma* performed in August 2001 at l'Ile d'Yeu, which "generated new relationships among sets, singers and music through interactive and generative computer techniques." Illustrations.

759. Bonynge, Richard. "Vincenzo Bellini: Vom Schöngesang der Klarinette—Maestro Richard Bonynge über Stil und Interpretation bei Bellini." *Opernwelt* 42 (2001): 76–77. ISSN 0030–3690.

The title translates as: Vincenzo Bellini: From the Beautiful Song of the Clarinet—Maestro Richard Bonynge on Bellinian Style and Interpretation. Bonynge maintains that Bellini was perhaps the composer who developed the strongest affinity to and understanding of the voice. He knew exactly how to pair instruments and voices; the clarinet is very close to the human voice and Bellini wrote for this instrument beautifully. Bellini is not often performed today because few performers understand true *bel canto* style and technique. Illustrated.

760. Brewer, Bruce. "Il cigno di Romano: Giovanni Battista Rubini: A Performance Study." *Donizetti Society Journal* 4 (1980): 117–65. ISSN 0307–1448. ML410.D7 A4.

A biography of the important Bellini tenor, including a chronological list of performances and a list of repertoire.

761. Brusotti, Roberto. "L'Arturo di Kraus, stilizzazione e Romanticismo." *Musica, rivista di informazione musicale e discografica* 131 (November 2001): 42–46.

An examination of the "aristocratic" tenor Alfredo Kraus as Arturo in *I puritani*. Discusses the vocal exigencies of the role and how Kraus fulfills them.

762. Bushnell, Howard. *Maria Malibran: A Biography of the Singer*. Foreword by Elaine Brody. University Park: Pennsylvania State University, 1979. ISBN 02–71002–22–0. ML420.M2 B87.

Because of her early death, Maria Malibran has always held a fascination for biographers and treatments of her have been fairly numerous. According to Stern, the strong point about Bushnell's work "is that now all the important Malibran history, anecdotes and legends are available in English and under one cover." Bushnell does little, however, with Malibran's embellishments and with her own compositions. Many of her letters are reproduced in English translation. A list of Malibran's complete opera roles, but without the number of performances, is included.

Reviews: Winton Dean in *Music & Letters* 62/2 (April 1981): 206–08; Charlotte Greenspan in *Nineteenth-Century Music* 4/3 (Spring 1981): 273–76; Dale Harris in *Notes* 37/3 (March 1981): 581–82; Kenneth Stern in *Opera News* 46/12 (February 13, 1982): 36.

763. Cella, Franca and Lorenzo Arruga. *Museo teatrale alla Scala: Bellini a Milano (November 30–December 28, 1935)*. Torino, 1935.

Contents of this eighty-page exhibition catalogue include "Il volto di Bellini"; "La voce negli autografi"; "Gli oggetti personali"; "I luoghi"; "Gli amici"; "Le opere milanesi" ("La fonte, il libretto," "gli interpreti"); "Gli interpreti belliniani: le altre opere"; and "Le scene, i costumi."

764. Celletti, Rodolfo. "Il vocalismo italiano da Rossini a Donizetti." Parte 1: Rossini; Parte 2: Bellini e Donizetti." *Analecta musicologica* 5 (1968): 267–94; 7 (1969): 214–47. ISSN 0585–6086. ML160.S893.

The author writes, "Between 1810 and 1840 the Italian vocal school underwent two fundamental upheavals. The first was determined by certain characteristics of Rossini's writing—in particular, the custom of writing out coloratura in full rather than letting the performers improvise it. . . . The second upheaval was tied to the advent of Romantic opera, which established a precise relation between the timbre of the voices and the basic nature of a character, in opposition to the abstract, asexual opera of the 17th and 18th centuries." The present essay describes the practical effects of these innovations on vocalism, 1810–40, and illustrates how Rossini, Bellini, Mercadante, and Donizetti treated the individual vocal ranges, both in terms of psychology and of tessitura, range, and ornamentation.

765. Chorley, Henry. *Thirty Years' Musical Recollections*. Ed. with an introduction by Ernest Newman. New York: Knopf, 1926. Originally published in 2 vols. London: Hurst and Blackett, 1862. ML423.C55 C5 1926. Rpt. in 2 vols. New York: Da Capo Press, 1984 (see item 38).

Mainly a chronicle of performances Chorley saw from 1830 to 1859 as a critic for the London *Atheneum*. In 1836, for example, he writes about (among other works) Bellini's *La straniera, Beatrice di Tenda, Norma*, and *I puritani*, and the singers Giulia Grisi, Rubini, Tamburini, Lablache, and others. Speaks rapturously of *I puritani* in London with Grisi, Rubini, and Lablache. Chorley was considered an excellent judge of singers and one who described them fairly, both their strengths and their faults.

766. Clayton, Ellen Creathorne. *Queens of Song: Being Memoirs of Some of the Most Celebrated Female Vocalists Who Have Performed on the Lyric Stage from the Earliest Days of Opera to the Present Time*. London, New York: Harper & Brothers, 1865. ML400.C51 1865.

Discusses many of the singers who participated in Bellini's operas. Includes portraits.

767. Cox, John E. "Gian Battista Rubini." *Donizetti Society Journal* 4 (1980): 172–79. ISSN 0307–1448. ML410.D7 A4.

Reprint of an article from Cox's *Musical Recollections of the Last Half Century*, originally published in 1872. See item 40. A short biography of Rubini and an assessment of his vocal qualities.

768. Cropsey, Eugene H. "American Premiers of Bellini's Lesser-Known Operas." *Opera Quarterly* 17/3 (Summer 2001): 435–50. ISSN 0736–0053. ML1699.O65.

The North American premieres of *Il pirata* and *La straniera* in New York and of *I Capuleti e i Montecchi* and *Beatrice di Tenda* in New Orleans. Chronicle of singers, productions, and reception. Illustrated.

769. Danzuso, D. and G. *Musica, musicisti e teatri a Catania (dal mito all cronica)*. Palermo, 1984; 2/1990.

770. De Angelis, Marcello. *Le carte dell'impresario. Melodramma e costume teatrale dell'800*. Florence: Sansoni, 1982. ML1733.4.D4 1982.

Activities of the impresario Alessandro Lanari, based on documents in the Fondo Lanari at the Biblioteca Nazionale Centrale in Florence. Published here are a new letter by Bellini (from 1830) and notes for the production of *Beatrice di Tenda* in 1837, among other items. Illustrations, portraits, and facsimiles are included.

771. De Biez, Jacques. *Tamburini et la musique italienne*. Paris, 1877.

Antonio Tamburini (1800–1876) was a leading bass-baritone who participated in four Bellini premieres: *Il pirata*, *Bianca e Fernando*, *La straniera*, and *I puritani*.

772. De Luca, Maria Rosa. "I bozzetti per opere belliniane del San Pietro a Majella." In *Vincenzo Bellini: Critica-Storia-Tradizione*. Ed. Salvatore Enrico Failla, pp. 76–81. Catania: Maimone, 1991. ISBN 88–77510–56–0. ML410.B44 V52 1991.

Contemporary costume designs for Bellini's operas. Several color illustrations.

773. Drake, James A. "A Perfect Voice: Ponselle in *Norma*." *Opera Quarterly* 14/1 (Autumn 1997): 67–77. ISSN 0736–0053. ML1699.O65.

Rosa Ponselle, one of the greatest sopranos of the twentieth century, was a famous Norma in the 1920s. Excerpt from Drake's biography, *Rosa Ponselle: A Centenary Biography*. Portland, Oregon: Amadeus Press, 1997.

774. Edwards, Henry Sutherland. *The Prima Donna: Her History and Surroundings from the Seventeenth to the Nineteenth Century*. 2 vols. London: Remington & Co., 1888; reprint New York: Da Capo Press, 1978. ISBN 03–06775–36–0. ML400.E28 1978.

Treats Pasta, Malibran, and other illustrious Bellini leading ladies.

775. Escudier, Léon, with Marie Escudier. *Etudes biographiques sur les chanteurs contemporains*. Paris, 1840.

Escudier was a noted French publisher who personally knew Bellini and many of the great singers of the day.

776. Farkas, Andrew. *Opera and Concert Singers: An Annotated International Bibliography of Books and Pamphlets*. New York: Garland, 1985. ISBN 08–24090–01–2. ML128.S295 F37 1985.

Extensive annotated bibliography, citing literature about nearly eight hundred singers. Periodical literature is not included.

777. Ferranti-Giulini, Maria. *Giuditta Pasta e i suoi tempi. Memorie e lettere raccolta a cura di Maria Ferranti nob. Giulini*. Milan: Cromotipia E. Sormani, 1935. ML420.P29 F4.

A 221-page biography of Pasta written in the late 1860s. A documentary study with illustrations, letters, facsimiles of letters, and a number of the many odes written in honor of Pasta.

778. Ferrarini, Mario, with a preface by Carlo Gatti. *Parma teatrale ottocentesca*. Parma: Casanova, 1946. ML1733.8.P28 F4.

Parma was the city where the fiasco of the premiere of Bellini's *Zaira* occurred.

779. Ferrero, M. V. *La scenografia dalle origini al 1936*. Turin: Cassa di Risparmio, 1980.

A study of stage production in Italian theaters to 1936. Numerous illustrations, portraits.

780. Fitzlyon, April. *Maria Malibran: Diva of the Romantic Age*. London: Souvenir Press, 1987. ISBN 02–85650–30–0. ML420.M2 F6 1987.

The author's aim was "to view La Malibran as a product and symbol of French Romanticism, an expression of Romantic attitudes," rather than to provide a fully documented account of her career, which Howard Bushnell (see item 762) has already done. Many references to Bellini. Contains bibliography and index.

781. Forbes, Elizabeth. *Mario and Grisi: A Biography*. London: Gollancz, 1985. ISBN 05–75036–06–0. ML420.M3296 F7 1985.

The soprano Giulia Grisi (1811–1869) created the roles of Adalgisa in *Norma* and Elvira in *I puritani*.

782. Gatti, Carlo. *Il teatro alla Scala nella storia e nell'arte (1778–1963)*. 2 vols. Milan: Ricordi, 1964. ML1733.8.M5 G3 1964a.

An important chronicle of the theater in Milan where several of Bellini's operas were premiered. Includes illustrations, facsimiles, and portraits. The second volume consists of a "Cronologia completa degli spettacoli e dei concerti," edited by Giampiero Tintori.

783. Giazotto, Remo. *Maria Malibran: una vita nei nomi di Rossini e Bellini*. Torino: ERI, 1986. ML420.M2 G5 1986.

A six-hundred-page study of one of the most important singers of the early-nineteenth century, one who interpreted a number of Bellini's heroines, and for whom he wrote a special version of *I puritani*.

784. Gutierrez, Beniamino. *Il Teatro Carcano (1803–1914); glorie artistiche e patrottiche, decadenza e resurrezione. Note e documenti inediti con*

illustrazioni dell'epoca. Milan: G. Abbiati, 1914. Rpt. Bologna: A. Forni, 1984. PN2686. M52 T454 1984.

The Milan theater where the premiere of *La sonnambula* was given. Illustrations, facsimiles, and portraits included.

785. Hanslick, Eduard. "Lili Lehmann," 1885. In *Musikalisches Skizzenbuch: Die moderne Oper*, 4. Berlin, 1888. Modern edition as *Musikalisches Skizzenbuch: neue Kritiken und Schilderungen*. Farnborough: Gregg, 1971. ML60.H24 1971.

Lehmann was one of the great Normas (and Isoldes and Brünnhildes) of the late nineteenth century. She is portrayed here by the famous Viennese critic.

786. Ivaldi, Armando Fabio. *Scene genovesi per opere di Bellini (1847–48)*. KC Edizione, 1998.

Michele Canzio was a noted set designer at Teatro Carlo Fenice, Genoa. Many illustrations of stage sets. Appendix I is the "Rappresentazione belliniane a Genova (1828–1900)" listed by opera. Appendix II is a Chronology of Opera by Bellini Given in Genoa from 1828 to 1900.

787. Jesurum, Olga. "Dal castello di Montolino al tempio d'Irminsul: Appunti per una visualità del teatro belliniano nelle scenografie italiane della prima metà dell'ottocento." *Vincenzo Bellini nel secondo centenario della nascita* (2004): 581–94. See item 406.

Treats the set designers Bertoja, Sanquirico, and Bagnara. Tables of productions and plates of stage sets.

788. Kaufman, Thomas G. "Giulia Grisi: A Re-Evaluation." *Donizetti Society Journal* 4 (1980): 181–225. ISSN 0307–1448. ML410.D7 A4.

A biography of the soprano Grisi, who created the roles of Adalgisa and Elvira, which includes a repertoire list and a chronology of performances.

789. Kesting, Jürgen. *Maria Callas*. Trans. from the German by John Hunt. Boston: Northeastern University Press, 1993. ISBN 15–55531–79–2. ML420.C18 K513 1993.

Intelligent discussions of bel canto style and Maria Callas's interpretations of Bellini heroines. Chapter 13, "Singing for the Imagination," is an extensive discussion of the Callas discography. Bibliography, discography, and index.

790. ——. "Vincenzo Bellini: Geschichte einer Verdrängung: Für welche Stimmen hat Bellini geschrieben? Und was macht seine Melodien aus? Anmerkungen zur Gesangspraxis gestern und heute." *Opern-Welt* 42 (2001): 72–73. ISSN 0030–3690.

The title translates as: Vincenzo Bellini: Story of a Repression: For which voices did Bellini write? And what determines his melodies? Notes on vocal practice yesterday and today. The author speculates why there is so little current interest in Bellini's music. Bellini's operas are "singer-operas" and the stage director and conductor are paramount today, perhaps explaining it. Examines the most famous singers who created the roles for Bellini: Grisi, Lablache, Pasta, and Rubini, citing contemporary accounts of their voices and artistry.

791. Locatelli, Agostino. *Cenni biografici sulla straordinaria carriera teatrale percorsa da Giovanni Battista Rubini da Romano, cantante di camera*. Milan: F. Colombo, 1844.

Rubini and Bellini met in connection with *Bianca e Gernando* in 1826 and the tenor then created roles in three subsequent operas by Bellini: *Il pirata* (Gualtiero), *La sonnambula* (Elvino), and *I puritani* (Arturo). The relationship was mutually beneficial; it was Bellini, who personally coached Rubini, who raised the tenor to international acclaim and in turn Rubini helped make Bellini's works renowned.

792. *Maria Callas alla Scala: Mostra documentaria a vent'anni dalla scomparsa: Teatro alla Scala, Ridotto dei Palchi, 16 settembre–16 novembre 1997*. Milan: Teatro alla Scala, 1997. ML141.M5 C356 1997.

An exhibition catalog with several essays on Maria Callas's art, including her roles at La Scala. These include roles in Bellini's operas *Norma*, *La sonnambula*, and *Il pirata* among others.

793. Merlin, Olivier. *Quand le bel canto régnait sur le Boulevard*. Paris: Fayard, 1978. ISBN 22–13006–66–0. ML1727.8 P2 M47.

A survey of Italian opera at the Théâtre-Italien in Paris in the first half of the nineteenth century. Bellini in the context of Rossini's dominance there and in terms of the Parisian milieu.

794. Migliavacca, Giorgio. "Bellinienne Extraordinaire: A Conversation with Mariella Devia." *Opera Quarterly* 17/3 (Summer 2001): 451–63. ISSN 0736–0053. ML1699.O65.

A biographical sketch and report of a conversation with the Italian soprano Mariella Devia, who has been singing bel canto roles for over thirty years. "If Rossini and Donizetti have been the bread-and-butter of Devia's career, it is Bellini that has earned her the tiara of prima donna assoluta." She has, for example, performed Elvira in *I puritani* over a hundred times. Discussion of her recordings and attitudes toward embellishment. Profusely illustrated with performance stills.

795. —— and Laura Scandariato. "Turin's Links with Bellini: A Northern Capital and a Successful Southerner." *Opera Quarterly* 17/3 (Summer 2001): 380–98. ISSN 0736–0053. ML1699.O65.

The importance of the Teatro Regio, Turin, which in the early-nineteenth century Stendhal placed fourth in importance after La Scala (Milan), San Carlo (Naples), and La Fenice (Venice). A chronicle of Bellini's personal connections with Turin; some of his works were also performed at the less important Teatro D'Angennes. Performance history, singers, drawing on nineteenth-century reviews and other documents. Illustrated with extensive source citations.

796. Monterosso, Raffaello. "Alcune osservazioni sulla prassi esecutiva delle opere di Bellini." *Nuovi annali della facoltà di Magisterio dell'Università di Messina* III (1985): 875–88.

Some observations on performing Bellini's operas.

797. Monteverdi, Mario, ed. and introduction. *La Scala: 400 Years of Stage Design from the Museo Teatrale alla Scala*. Alessandria, 1968. Washington, D.C.: International Exhibitions Foundation, 1971. PN2091. S8 M67.

Catalogue. The museum possesses an extensive collection devoted to the set designs of Alessandro Sanquirico—scenes from *Bianca e Fernando*, *Il pirata*, *La straniera*, *La sonnambula*, and *Norma*.

798. ——. *Scene di Alessandro Sanquirico nelle collezioni del Teatrale alla Scala*. Palazzo Cuttica di Cassine, April 20–May 31, 1968. Milan: Grafice Milli, 1968. PN2091.S8 S29.

An exhibition catalogue of Sanquirico's set designs, including those for Bellini's operas. See item 797 above.

799. Mount Edgcumbe, Richard. *Musical Reminiscences of the Earl of Mount Edgcumbe, Containing an Account of the Italian Opera in England from 1773 to 1834*. New York: Da Capo, 1973. Rpt. from the 4th ed., London, 1834. See item 66. ISBN 03–06700–08–5. ML1731.3.E23 1973.

Primo ottocento peformances of Bellini's operas in London from an eyewitness with over a half-century's experience of opera attendance.

800. Muraro, Maria Teresa. "Nuovi significati delle scene dei Bertoja alla Fenice di Venezia." In *La realizzazione scenica dello spettacolo verdiano. Atti del Congresso internazionale di Studi, Parma Teatro Regio—Conservatorio di Musica "Arrigo Boïto," le 28–30 novembre 1994*. Ed. Pierluigi Petrobelli and Fabrizio della Seta, pp. 83–108. Parma: Istituo di Studi verdiani, 1996. ISBN 88–85065–14–7. ML410.V4. R3 1996.

See item 756.

801. [Giuditta] Pasta Archive of the Lincoln Center Library for the Performing Arts, New York City.

Important collection of archival material about Giuditta Pasta, who created the roles of Amina, Norma, and Beatrice.

802. Pougin, Arthur. *Marie Malibran: histoire d'une cantatrice*. Paris: Plon, 1911. English trans. as *Marie Malibran, The Story of a Great Singer*. London: Eveleigh Nash, 1911. Rpt. of French version Geneva: Minkoff, 1973. ISBN 28–26600–36–2. ML420.M2 P69 1973.

Appendices include Mme Malibran's Dramatic Repertory, Mme Malibran's Compositions, Bibliography on Mme Malibran, One of Mme Malibran's Engagements, Mme Malibran's Tomb, and The Facts Attending Mme Malibran's Death and Burial.

803. Pullen, Robert and Stephen Taylor. *Montserrat Caballé: Casta Diva*. Boston: Northeastern University Press, 1994. ISBN 15–55532–28–4. ML420.C17 P85 1995.

An authorized biography, except for the Critical Discography. Caballé has an impressive list of Bellini recordings, both live and commercial, although not as extensive as that of either Callas or Sutherland. Listed with fairly extensive commentary are three versions of *Il pirata* (one commercial), four of *Norma* (one commercial and one of them the video of the famed Orange performance in 1974, truly remarkable), one studio recording of *I puritani*, and a live performance of *La straniera*. In addition, the text of the biography deals with the singer's experiences of performing and recording these Bellini operas, especially *Norma*, which she sang over a hundred times.

804. Radiciotti, Giuseppe. "Il Barbaia nella leggenda e quello della storia." *L'arte pianistica* 7/3 (1920): 5–6.

The impresario Domenico Barbaia, who was responsible for commissioning Bellini to write for San Carlo, Naples, and La Scala, Milan, at the beginning of his career.

805. Reparaz, Carmen de. *Maria Malibran 1808–36. Estudio biografico*. Madrid: Servicio de Publicaciones del Monisterio de Educaciòn y Ciencia, 1976. Trans. into French by F. Barberousse, 1979. ISBN 84–36900–33–0. ML420.M2 R5.

Includes bibliography and index. A Spanish study of the important Bellini soprano.

806. Ricci, Franco Carlo. *Momenti drammatici nel teatro belliniano*. Rome: Bulzoni, 1973. Biblioteca di cultura 34, 104 pp. ML410.B44 R54.

An investigation of musicodramatic aspects of Bellini's operas. One chapter is devoted to Bellini's recitative. Bibliography pertinent to the topic.

807. Scott, Michael. *Maria Meneghini Callas*. Boston: Northeastern University Press, 1991. ISBN 15–55531–46–6. ML420.C18 S35 1992.

A biography and highly perceptive assessment of the art of one of the most important Bellini interpreters of the twentieth century. Discussed at length are her vocal strengths and shortcomings and her recordings. Of Bellini's operas, these include two versions of *Norma*, a *Sonnambula*, a *Puritani*, and numerous "live" performances now available on CD, including the 1959 *Pirata* from Carnegie Hall. Scott even provides (courtesy Aspinall: Roberts) in notation the two embellished stanzas of "Sovra il sen" from *La sonnambula* that Callas sang at La Scala in 1955, a recording of which is available.

808. Sicari, Floriana. *Callas e Bellini: Analisi di una credità.* Preface by Gina Guandalini. Brugherio: Sinfonica jazz, 2002. ISBN 88–84000–37–8.

Study of Bellini interpretations by Maria Callas, with many comparisons with other sopranos such as Adelina Patti, Margherita Carosio, Rosa Ponselle, Zinka Milanov, Giannina Arangi-Lombardi, and Lily Pons. Source citations, illustrations, bibliography.

809. Soulies, Albert. *Le Théâtre-Italien de 1801 à 1913*. Paris: Librairie Fischbacher, 1913. ML1727.8.P2 S77.

Somewhat of a documentary study but with no source citations or bibliography. Letters, archival records about the management of the theater; much information about Edouard Robert and Carlo Severini, the director and administrator, respectively, of the theater during the time of Rossini, Donizetti, and Bellini. No index. Many engravings, including portraits of composers, singers (Giulia and Giuditta Grisi in *I Capuleti*, for example), facsimile of Bellini's handwriting in the finale of *Adelson e Salvini*, two measures of a score belonging to Tamburini, in which he has written in an embellishment of a cadence, one of many throughout the score.

810. Stern, Kenneth. "Pasta Diva: Bellini's First *Norma* at Home on Lake Como." *Opera News* 46/12 (February 13, 1982): 8–11. ISSN 0030–3607. ML1.O482.

Makes the point of how little we really know of the great singers who created Bellini's roles. About Pasta there has been much misinformation passed down over the generations. It is not true, for example, that Rossini disliked her. "The first full-length biography, incorporating the important points of over 3,000 letters written by, to, or about the diva, is nearing completion and will alter some prevailing misconceptions." Stern looks at Pasta's life at her villa on Lake Como, purchased in 1827. The Villa Pasta became "a place of pilgrimage for her admirers and a retreat for some of the great names in opera history." Pasta enjoyed her retirement there, gardening like a peasant woman. Discusses some of the roles she assumed, her correspondence, her furniture, the paintings she owned.

811. ——. "The Theater of Bel Canto: Pasta and a New School of Acting." *Opera News* 40/16 (February 28, 1976): 8–16. ISSN 0030–3607. ML1. O482.

Maintains that Giuditta Pasta, learning from masters of the English stage such as David Garrick and Sarah Siddons, "introduced a romantic new style of acting to early ninetenth-century opera." Pasta never thrived on acrobatic technical displays, which were now "an anachronism in the face of the burgeoning romantic revolution." Her coloratura "was channeled by her dramatic instincts." Allied with this is making recitative telling rather than perfunctory. This also is the key to the style of Bellini and Donizetti. Also important, because linked to the music, were Pasta's physical gestures. An extended comparison with Sarah Siddons is made. Includes an extended comparison between Pasta and Maria Malibran and Pasta and Henriette Sontag in terms of voice and acting technique. Notes the importance of the actor François-Joseph Talma to Romanticism. Discusses Pasta's creation of three operatic roles: Donizetti's Anna Bolena and Bellini's Amina and Norma. And finally compares Pasta with Maria Callas.

812. Sutherland, Joan. *The Autobiography of Joan Sutherland, A Prima Donna's Progress*. Washington, D.C.: Regnery Publishing, Inc., 1997. ISBN 08–95263–74–2. ML420.S96 A3 1997.

Contains numerous references to the works of Bellini. Dame Joan sang and recorded (twice each except for *Beatrice*) *La sonnambula*, *Beatrice di Tenda*, *Norma*, and *I puritani*. Much information is provided about recording sessions, rehearsals, productions, other artists, and vocal matters.

813. Tiby, Ottavio. *Il Real Teatro Carolina e l'Ottocento musicale palermitano*. Historiae Musicae Cultores Biblioteca 9. Florence: L. Olschki, 1957. ML 1733.P25 T5.

In 1860 the theater's name was changed to the Teatro Bellini. Tiby includes extensive material on Bellini. Uses unpublished archival material. Illustrations and portraits included.

814. Traini, Carlo. *Il cigno di Romani: Giovanni Battista Rubini, re dei tenori*. Bergamo: Tipografia Scuole Professional Orfanotrofio, 1954. ML420. R888 T7.

An important creator of Bellini's roles. Includes illustrations and portraits.

815. Vitali, Giovanni. "Kraus canta Sonnambula." *Musica, rivista di informazione musicale e discografica* 131 (November 2001): 47–48.

An assessment and chronicle of Alfredo Kraus's performances of Elvino in *La sonnambula* in various Italian and other cities in the early 1960s: Milan, Rome, Parma, Venice, Naples, Florence, and Geneva. The tenor's elegiac artistry, which made him an ideal Bellini interpreter, is emphasized, the author comparing him to Tito Schipa.

816. Williams, Jeannie. "La Rossiniana: A Conversation with Marilyn Horne." *The Opera Quarterly* IX (Summer 1993): 64–91. ISSN 0736–0053.

Marilyn Horne was one of the twentieth-century's greatest Rossini singers and a key figure in the revival of his serious operas. Here she discusses performance practice, the use of the mezzo soprano in "trousers roles" in nineteenth-century opera through Verdi and twentieth-century audience reaction to Rossini's unfamiliar operas. Music examples include Rossini's embellishments to Bellini's "La tremenda ultrice" from *I Capuleti e I Montecchi*.

817. Zucker, Stefan. "Last of a Breed." *Opera News* 46/12 (February 13, 1982): 24–27, 36. ISSN 0030–3607. ML1.O482.

Giovanni Battista Rubini was Bellini's favorite tenor. At the time of his death Bellini was planning to refashion the role of Pollione in *Norma* for Rubini to perform in the 1835–36 season at the Théâtre des Italiens. Zucker notes that Rubini "developed an even vibrato which became the model for many successors. Although his vocal means were limited, his technique allowed him to sing extremely demanding roles, including five created by Bellini." An overview of Rubini's life and career and the roles he created for Bellini, especially Elvino in *La sonnambula* and Arturo in *I puritani*. Of great importance are the questions of how high Rubini sang and in what keys he sang his arias, for they were published in transpositions in order to sell. As Zucker notes, "These transpositions have a drastic impact on the emotional character of the role." A comparison of the ranges of Rubini and the nineteenth-century tenor Giovanni David. Includes quotations from contemporary journals and illustrations.

Note: Additional sources include:

818. De Filippis, F. and R. Arnese. *Cronache del Teatro di San Carlo (1737–1960)*. 2 vols. Naples, 1959.

819. Della Corte, Andrea. "Noterelle sul canto." *A Vincenzo Bellini. Bollettino dei musicisti, Mensile del Sindicato Fascista Musicisti* 2/3 (December 1934): 67ff.

820. ——. "I problemi della scenografia e l'ottocento." In *Tempi e aspetti della scenografia*. Ed. A. Hyatt Major, Mercedes Viale, Andrea della Corte, and A. G. Bragaglia. Turin: Edizioni Radio Italiana, 1954.

821. Mariani, Valerio. *Storia della scenografia italiana*. Florence: Rinascimento del Libro, 1930. ML1733.M54 S8.

822. Monaldi, Gino. *Cantanti celebri (1829–1929)*. Rocca: Edizioni Tiber, 1929. ML400.M73.

823. ——. *Cantanti celebri del secolo XIX*. Rome: Nuova Antologia, 1906. ML400.M74.

824. ——. *Impresari celebri del secolo XIX*. Bologna: L. Cappelli, n.d.

825. ——. *Le prime rappresentazioni celebri: Bellini, Bizet, Boïto, et alia*. Milan: Fratelli Treves, 1910.

826. Nani-Mocenigo, Mario-Filippo. *Il Teatro La Fenice; note storiche e artistiche*. Venice: Industrie Poligrafiche Venete, 1926. ML1733.8.V4 N18.

827. Rinaldo, Mario. "Bellini interprete." *Rassegna dorica* 6 (1935): 70–82. ML5.R145.

828. Salvioli, Giovanni [anagram pseud. of Luigi Lianovosani and Livio Nino Galvani]. *La Fenice—Gran teatro di Venezia: Serie degli spettacoli dalla primavera 1792 a tutto il carnevale 1876*. Milan, ca. 1876.

829. Schlitzer, Franco. "Vincenzo Bellini." *Mondo teatrale dell'ottocento; episodi, testimonianze, musiche e lettere*. Naples: F. Fiorentino, 1954. ML1733.S85.

830. Silke, Leopold. "Bibliografie der italienischen Literatur zur Scenographie des Musiktheaters." *Analecta musicologica* 17 (1976): 296–309. ISSN 0585-6086. ML160.S893.

831. Terenzio, Vincenzo. "Bellini alla Fenice." *Teatri nel mondo. La Fenice*. Introduction by Floris L. Ammannatti. Milan: Nuove ed., 1972. ML1733.8. V42 F4.

832. Viola, Orazio. *I maggiori e più antichi interpreti delle opere belliniane*. Catania, n.d.

12

Discographies (Including Discography of Bellini's Operas, in Chronological Order), Videographies, and Reviews of Recordings

833. Albright, William. Review of recordings of *I puritani. Opera Quarterly* 17/3 (Summer 2001): 576–89. ISSN 0736–0053. ML1699.O65.

Extensive review of fifteen recordings, both live and studio, including multiple recordings by Maria Callas, Joan Sutherland, and Cristina Deutekom. History of performance and vocal demands. Recommends Sutherland's second Decca set as "indispensable" but notes that "Callas's historic but flawed EMI set has complementary virtues."

834. Ardoin, John. "Bellini behind the Iron Curtain." *Opera Quarterly* 6/4 (Summer 1989): 33–37. ISSN 0736–0053. ML1699.O65.

Review of two recordings of Bellini's operas from Eastern Europe: *Norma* from Moscow (1986) and *La sonnambula*, recorded in Bratislava (1987). Even though for most of the twentieth century, opera performance in these countries was of a national nature and not in the bel canto style, Ardoin sees these performances as evidencing the internationalization of performance style with the attendant blurring of individual and national styles.

835. ——. *The Callas Legacy; The Complete Guide to Her Recordings on Compact Discs*. 4th ed. Portland, Oregon: Amadeus, 1996. ISBN 09–31340–90–X. ML420.C18 A85 1995.

A detailed examination of the recordings of Maria Callas. Recordings of operas by Bellini include *Il pirata*, *I puritani*, multiple recordings, both live and studio, of *Norma* and *La sonnambula*. Also included are excerpts from recital albums. Organized chronologically. Includes a list of Recorded Interviews and Filmed Performances plus a fairly extensive bibliography, excluding items dealing with reviews of only one recording for the most part.

836. Baxter, Robert. Review of *Adelson e Salvini. Opera Quarterly* 12/4 (Spring–Summer 1996): 124–26. Rpt. in Bellini Commemorative Issue of *Opera Quarterly* 17/3 (Summer 2001): 477–79. ISSN 0736–0053. ML1699.O65.

This performance was recorded during a series of live performances at the Teatro Massimo "Bellini" in Catania during September 1992. Other than filling in a gap in the CD catalogue for Bellini, the performance is not noteworthy. The recording is marred by extraneous noises and, with the exception of Alicia Nafé (the Nelly), the singers fare poorly. The tenor role is especially difficult, requiring twenty-six high Cs, four Ds, and one high E. It was written for Rubini for the 1826–27 version of the opera, which was not performed until 1992 in Catania.

837. Bellingardi, Luigi. "Discografia." In *Vincenzo Bellini*. Ed. Maria Rosario Adamo and Friedrich Lippmann, pp. 557–62. Turin: Editione RAI Radiotelevisione, Italiana, 1981.

See item 262

838. Blyth, Alan. *Opera on CD: The Essential Guide to the Best CD Recordings of 100 Operas*. London: Kyle Cathie, Ltd., 1992. ISBN 18–56260–56–9. ML156.4.O46 B6 1992.

Blyth is a well-known, knowledgeable critic who has written for the English periodicals *Gramophone* and *Opera*. Bellini recordings are treated on pp. 38–40. For each opera treated, which includes *La sonnambula*, *Norma*, and *I puritani*, he gives one recommendation and then an alternate. Each receives extensive commentary, including information as to cuts and completeness.

839. Brunel, Pierre. "Eléments de discographie." In his monograph *Vincenzo Bellini*, 1981, pp. 392–97 (see item 263). ISBN 22–13002–63–5. ML410.B44 B7.

A short essay on the Bellini discography, listing, comparing, and rating available recordings, which were much fewer than currently.

840. Burroughs, Bruce. Review of recordings of *La sonnambula. Opera Quarterly* 17/3 (Summer 2001): 505–33. ISSN 0736–0053. ML1699.O65.

An exhaustive assessment of fifteen live and studio recordings, including three by Maria Callas and four by Joan Sutherland. Many valuable observations about bel canto style and vocal technique, with a special appreciation of Dame Joan and Richard Bonynge.

841. *Casta Diva—A Romanticized Biography of Bellini*. Italian/French film, dubbed in English. Bel Canto Society Videocassette item 410. Technicolor, 98 minutes, VHS, 1954.

Features Maurice Ronet as Bellini, Antonella Lualdi as Maddalena Fumaroli, Nadia Gray as Giuditta Pasta, Fausto Tozzi as Donizetti; directed by Carmino Gallone. Reviewed by William Ashbrook in *Opera Quarterly* 17/3 (Summer 2001): 598–99. Ashbrook calls it an "unhistorical gallimaufry." The film does feature the voice of Caterina Mancini in a staged performance of Imogene's final aria from *Il pirata* and a few other opera extracts, but these are a relatively small part of the overall film.

842. Fairman, Richard. "*La sonnambula*" and "*I puritani*." In *Opera on Record* 2. Ed. A. Blyth, pp. 115–28. Discographies compiled by Malcolm Walker. London: Hutchinson, 1983; New York: Beaufort Books, 1984. ISBN 08–25302–12–9. ML156.4.O46 O552 1984.

Survey and discussion of complete recordings and excerpted arias. List at end of chapter of "complete" recordings, of which several more have been added to the catalogue since this account was published. Discographies compiled by Malcolm Walker. Includes both studio and "live" recordings. In trying to determine the ideal singer for Amina in *La sonnambula*, Fairman quotes both Chorley and Romani, reminding us how seldom anyone on recording comes close to the ideal, who, in Romani's words, is "playful, ingenuous and innocent, and at the same time passionate, sensuous, and amorous; who has a cry for joy and also a cry for sorrow, an accent for reproach and another for entreaty." He deems the live 1955 La Scala recording sung by Maria Callas and directed by Leonard Bernstein one that captures the singer's "miraculously radiant and involving Amina." Problems with recordings of *I puritani*—as with live performances—include heavily cut scores and male singers without a proper sense of Bellinian style.

843. Gioviale, Fernando. "La evocativa. Appunti una interpretazione discografica del melodramma belliniano." In *Vincenzo Bellini: Critica-Storia-Tradizione*. Ed. Salvatore Enrico Failla, pp. 163–79. Catania: Maimone, 1991 (see item 439). ISBN 88–77510–56–0. ML410.B44 V52 1991.

Illustrated with reproductions of record covers, some of them rare, live recordings. Lists and assesses recordings, discussing conductors, singers, versions recorded.

844. Glasow, E. Thomas Review of recording of *I puritani* with Edita Gruberova on Nightingale Classics. *Opera Quarterly* 12/4 (1996): 126–29. ISSN 0736–0053. ML1699.O65.

Calls this "a welcome addition to the digital catalogue" even with weak male singers, the tenor being the worst. Gruberova as Elvira is very strong, at peak form, technically secure. "Although one may point affectionately to Maria Callas's emotional interpretation of this music, Gruberova's is equally affecting—and more beautifully vocalized." The text is virtually complete, including the final cabaletta (not heard in the Callas or Caballé recordings).

845. Graeme, Roland. Review of recordings of *I Capuleti e i Montecchi. Opera Quarterly* 17/3 (Summer 2001): 495–505. ISSN 0736–0053. ML1699. O65.

An extensive review of seven recordings of this opera, both live and studio. Genesis and sources, problems of conducting and casting this opera. Although he greatly admires performances by Baker and Katia Ricciarelli, Graeme concludes that the Teldec set with Hei-Kyung Hong and Jennifer Larmore "is definitely the *Capuleti* to start with."

846. Hamilton, David. "*I puritani*." *Opera News* 41 (January 25, 1997): 38–41. ISSN 0030–3607. ML1.O482.

Bibliography and discography for Bellini's final opera.

847. Harris, Kenn. *Opera Recordings: A Critical Guide*. New York: Drake, 1973. ISBN 08–77492–61–1. ML156.4 O46 H36.

As is always the case with discographical materials, many new recordings (both live and from the studio) have appeared since this book was published. Harris provides worthwhile discussions of the recordings then available: one of *Beatrice di Tenda*, six of *Norma*, one of *Il pirata*, two of I *puritani*, and two of *La sonnambula*. In several cases the choice is between Maria Callas and Joan Sutherland and heavily cut versus more-or-less complete.

848. Hastings, Stephen. "Norma, una rassegna discografica." *Musica, rivista di informazione musicale e discografica* 131 (November 2001): 49–57.

Extensive, informative essay about the merits of various recordings of *Norma*, both live and from the studio. The title heroines include Gina Cigna (two recordings), Zinka Milanov, Maria Callas (six recordings), Leyla Gencer, Joan Sutherland (two recordings), Montserrat Caballé (two recordings), Renata Scotto, Jane Eaglen, and M. Lagrange (with the orchestra and chorus of the Teatro Massimo "Bellini" with Alain Lombard conducting). The author was unable to hear recordings made by Anita Cerqueti, Elena Souliotis, and Beverly Sills. Includes illustrations of singers and conductors.

849. Jellinek, George. Review of recording of *Bianca e Fernando* (1828 Genoa version). Andrea Licata, cond., Teatro Massimo "Bellini," Catania: Nuova Era 7076/77. *Opera Quarterly* 11/3 (1995): 181–83. ISSN 0736–0053. ML1699.O65.

The recording includes extensive historical notes by Friedrich Lippmann, how Gernando became Fernando, improvements in both libretto and music. Jellinek assesses the style of numbers in the opera, noting, "The loveliest 'original' episode is unquestionably the soprano–mezzo duet, 'Sorgi, o padre,' with its delicate oboe accompaniment." (This duet has been recorded by Mirella Freni and Renata Scotto on London OS 26652.)

Jellinek finds this performance meretorious and concludes, "Nuova Era deserves praise for preserving this worthy performance."

850. ——. Review of recordings of *La straniera. Opera Quarterly* 17/3 (Summer 2001): 487–89. ISSN 0736–0053. ML1699.O65.

Review of two live recordings with Renata Scotto and Montserrat Caballé as Alaide. Genesis and sources of the work, premiere and reception are discussed. Jellinek finds both sopranos to be "expert Bellinians, but they stress different facets of the composer's art."

851. Law, Joe K. Review of recordings of *Il pirata. Opera Quarterly* 17/3 (Summer 2001): 479–85. ISSN 0736–0053. ML1699.O65.

A thorough assessment of the complete live and commercial recordings, including those with Maria Callas, two with Montserrat Caballé, and one with Lucia Aliberti. In addition, the author notes recordings of the final scene with Edita Gruberova and Jane Eaglen. Discusses the place of *Il pirata* in Bellini's oeuvre and the singers who first created the major roles.

852. McKee, David. Review of recordings of *Beatrice di Tenda. Opera Quarterly* 17/3 (Summer 2001): 555–76. ISSN 0736–0053. ML1699.O65.

Extensive assessment of nine recordings both live and studio. Genesis and sources, premiere, reception, performance history. Comparison with Donizetti's *Anna Bolena*. Vocal requirements, problems with the Ricordi piano-vocal score, lack of an authoritative edition. "For this writer's taste, the Beatrice of Edita Gruberova and Agnese of Elena Zilio are unequaled for both dramatic compulsion and musicological insight. Neither enjoys ideal freedom in the uppermost reaches of her writing, which gives Sutherland, and Horne or Veasey, an incontestable advantage."

853. Mordden, Ethan. *A Guide to Opera Recordings*. Oxford: Oxford University Press, 1987. ISBN 01–95044–25–8. ML156.4.O46 M7 1987.

A cogent single-volume guide to a wide variety of recordings from Nellie Melba to Stephen Sondheim, from cylinders and 78s to LPs and compact discs. The recordings of Bellini's music are discussed in Chapter 8, pp. 78–86. He speaks of the loss of the "bel canto" style by the late-nineteenth century and its *riesumazione* (exhumation) in the 1950s with Maria Callas. Mordden also deals with the importance of Tullio Serafin, Callas's greatest influence. He lists five sopranos who dominated the revival: Callas, Sutherland, Caballé, Sills, and Scotto; and one tenor, Luciano Pavarotti, "who has implanted himself through his collaboration with Sutherland and Bonynge." Discusses recordings beginning with *Il pirata*, the live performances versus the commercial ones, and the 78 rpm aria excerpts. Characterizes Bellini aptly as "a composer who, inheriting Rossinian *melodramma*, both expanded and tightened, partially dismantling the set aria form, for instance, to emphasize ensemble, and developing the characterological possibilities in recitative." In speaking of Wagnerian-type recordings (of *Norma*, for instance, with "earth-mother Adalgisas"), Mordden reminds us, "Bel canto . . . was a nostalgia, a lost ideal romantically moribund by 1850. It does not look ahead, but behind."

854. Osborne, Charles. *The Bel Canto Operas of Rossini, Donizetti, and Bellini*. Portland, Oregon: Amadeus, 1994. ISBN 09–31340–71–3. ML 390.O82 1994.

Selective discography for Bellini on pp. 364–65. Mostly one or two choices for each opera and indeed selective. For *Norma*, for example, Osborne chooses the flawed second recording by Sutherland-Bonynge, with Caballé as Adalgisa and Pavarotti as Pollione. He also lists the second Callas recording with Christa Ludwig and Franco Corelli.

855. Petkovic, Milan. Review of recordings of *Zaira*. *Opera Quarterly* 17/3 (Summer 2001): 489–95. ISSN 0736–0053. ML1699.O65.

An extensive assessment of two live recordings of the opera, with Renata Scotto and Katia Ricciarelli as the heroines. The recording with Scotto represents the first twentieth-century performance of *Zaira*, on March 30, 1976, at the Teatro Massimo "Bellini" in Catania. Also discussed are the failure and merits of the score, and the reworking of some dozen pieces for *I Capuleti e i Montecchi* and later *Beatrice di Tenda*. While Petkovic lauds Scotto's performance and striking projection of text, he concludes, "Neither of these CD versions of *Zaira* should be considered as a definitive recording of this lovely opera; each has more than one unsatisfactory aspect."

856. Porter, Andrew. "Baker and Sills as Romeo and Juliet (Angel Recording)." *High Fidelity/Musical America* 26 (April 1976): 89–90. ISSN 0018–1463. ML1.H45.

See item 883.

857. ——. "Opera on the Gramophone." *Opera* 9 (January 1958): 12–19. ISSN 0030–3526. ML5.O66.

A survey of *Norma* on record by one of the foremost critics and best writers on music. Written at a time when only one complete set of *Norma* (Callas, cond. Serafin) was available, traces the many aria recordings, beginning with Adelina Patti, who never sang the role onstage. Great names such as Marcella Sembrich, Lilli Lehmann, Celesta Boninsegna, Emma Calvé, and Rosa Ponselle are presented.

858. ——. "*Norma*." In *Opera on Record* 1. Ed. Alan Blyth, pp. 154–72. Discographies compiled by Malcolm Walker. London: Hutchinson, 1979. ISBN 00–91399–80–7. ML156.4.O46 O55.

Includes not only complete recordings but individual arias, including 78 rpm.

859. Rich, Alan. "Recordings [*I Capuleti e i Montecchi*, EMI Angel DSB-3969]." *Opera Quarterly* 4/2 (1986): 149–51. ISSN 0736–0053. ML1699.O65.

Denigrates the opera for not being faithful to Shakespeare, but "Both acts of *I Capuleti* work their way toward splendid finales." This recording includes a short cabaletta for Giulietta as she drinks Lorenzo's potion; this was discovered and appended to the score only in 1967 by Friedrich Lippmann. Lippmann's excellent historical note is included in the booklet that accompanies the recording.

860. Rishoi, Niel. Review of recording of *Beatrice di Tenda* with Lucia Aliberti, Fabio Luisi conducting. Berlin Classics. *Opera Quarterly* 11/4 (1995): 139–45. ISSN 0736–0053. ML1699.O65.

See item 941.

861. ——. Review of recordings of *Norma*. *Opera Quarterly* 17/3 (Summer 2001): 533–54. ISSN 0736–0053. ML1699.O65.

An extensive review of fifteen recordings, plus a listing of seven additional recordings not discussed. These include multiple recordings by Gina Cigna, Maria Callas, Montserrat Caballé, and Joan Sutherland, and performances by Elena Souliotis, Renata Scotto, Zinka Milanov, Beverly Sills, and others. Problems of casting, textual variations.

862. Schauer, J. "Recordings [London *Norma*]." *Opera Quarterly* 6/2 (1988–89): 141–43. ISSN 0736–0053. ML1699.O65.

A review of the second Sutherland–Bonynge recording, made in 1984 with Montserrat Caballé as Adalgisa and Luciano Pavarotti as Pollione. Bonynge includes some rarely-heard passages, for example Adalgisa's stanza of the trio in Act One and the coda to the "Guerra, guerra" chorus. Schauer concludes that "audiophiles seeking a state-of-the-digital-art *Norma* should be quite content with this [recording]."

863. Shawe-Taylor, Desmond. "A '*Puritani*' Discography." *Opera* 11 (June 1960): 387–95. ISSN 0030–3526. ML5.O66.

At this time only one complete *Puritani* in the catalogue, Callas conducted by Serafin. Shawe-Taylor assesses many recordings from the past of individual numbers, by luminaries such as De Lucia, Battistini, De Luca, Bonci, Galli-Curci, up to Giuseppe Di Stefano and the very young Renata Scotto.

864. Smith, Patrick J. "High Emotions, Radiant Melos—In a First *Beatrice di Tenda*." *High Fidelity/Musical America* 17 (December 1967): 76+. ISSN 0018–1463.

A review of first complete recording of the opera, made by London-Decca with Joan Sutherland, conducted by Richard Bonynge.

865. Thomas, C.J. "Two Valuable Callas Reissues." *Opera Quarterly* 4/4 (1986–87): 108–10. ISSN 0736–0053. ML1699.O65.

Norma and *I puritani* from the early 1950s.

866. Willier, Stephen. Review of Bellini, *La straniera* (Ricordi Fonicetra RFCG 2010, cond. Gianfranco Masini). *Opera Quarterly* 11/3 (1995): 172–75. ISSN 0736–0053. ML1699.O65.

Genesis and reception; modern performance history; vocal styles. Comparison with previous work, *Il pirata*. Finds Lucia Aliberti, who sings the title role, not in the same league with Caballé and other great Bellini sopranos of the recent past.

Note: An additional source:

867. Marinelli, C. "La sonnambula." In *Opere in disco*. Fiesole, 1982, pp. 136–47.

DISCOGRAPHY OF BELLINI'S OPERAS (IN CHRONOLOGICAL ORDER BY OPERA)

All items listed are compact discs unless otherwise noted.

Adelson e Salvini (revised version)

868. Andrea Licata, cond., Alicia Nafé (Nelly), Eleonora Jankovic (Madame Rivers), Lucia Ricci (Fanny), Bradley Williams (Salvini), Fabio Previati (Adelson), Aurio Tomicich (Bonifacio), Roberto Coviello (Struley). Nuova Era 7154–55.

Bianca e Fernando

869. Andrea Licata, cond., Orchestra and Chorus of the Teatro Massimo "Bellini," Catania; Young Ok Shim (Bianca), Gregory Kunde (Fernando), Haijing Fu (Filippo), Aurio Tomicich (Carlo). Nuova Era 7076–77.

Il pirata

870. Nicola Rescigno, cond., Orchestra and Chorus of the American Opera Society, New York; Maria Callas (Imogene), Pier Miranda Ferraro (Gualtiero), Constantino Ego (Ernesto); includes final scene sung by Maria Callas with the Concertgebouw Orchestra, Amsterdam, cond. Nicola Rescigno. EMI Classics D23261. Live performance, Carnegie Hall, 1959. Notes, libretto.

871. Franco Capuana, cond., Orchestra and Chorus of the Maggio Musicale Fiorentino; Montserrat Caballé (Imogene), Flaviano Labò (Gualtiero), Piero Cappucilli (Ernesto). Memories HR 4186/87; also Opera D'Oro OPD-1179. Live performance, 1967.

872. Gianandrea Gavazzeni, cond., Orchestra and Chorus of the Radio-televisione Italiana, Rome; Montserrat Caballé (Imogene), Bernabé Martì (Gualtiero), Piero Cappucilli (Ernesto). EMI CMS 7 64169 2. Recorded 1971. Notes (valuable essay by Andrew Porter), libretto.

873. Marcello Viotti, cond., Orchestra and Chorus of the Deutsche Oper, Berlin; Lucia Aliberti (Imogene), Stuart Neill (Gualtiero), Roberto Frontali (Ernesto). Berlin Classics 0011152BC © 1994.

La straniera

874. Nino Sanzogno, cond., Orchestra and Chorus of the Teatro Massimo, Palermo; Renata Scotto (Alaide), Renato Cioni (Arturo), Domenico Trimarchi (Valdeburgo), Elena Zilio (Isoletta). Melodram 37039. Live performance, 1968, Palermo.

875. Anton Guadagno, cond., unnamed orchestra and chorus, Carnegie Hall; Montserrat Caballé (Alaide), Amadeo Zambon (Arturo), Vincente Sardinero (Valdeburgo), Biancamaria Casoni (Isoletta). Legato Classics LCD-134–2. Live performance, 1969 (includes a live performance of Montserrat Caballé singing Richard Strauss's *Vier letzte Lieder*, 1979).

876. Ettore Gracis, cond., Orchestra and Chorus of the Teatro La Fenice, Venice; Renata Scotto (Alaide), Beniamino Prior (Arturo), Domenico Trimarchi (Valdeburgo), Elena Zilio (Isoletta). Opera D'Oro OPD-1261. Live performance, 1970, Venice.

877. Oliviero de Fabritis, cond., Orchestra and Chorus of the Teatro Massimo "Bellini," Catania; Elena Souliotis (Alaide), Veriano Luchetti (Arturo), Ugo Savarese (Valdeburgo), Elena Silio (Isoletta). GDS 21041. Live performance, 1971, Catania. Notes, Italian libretto.

     Bonus Tracks: Selections from *Norma*. Bruno Bartoletti, cond., Orchestra and Chorus of the Opera di Roma; Elena Souliotis (Norma), Gastone Limarilli (Pollione), Ivo Vinco (Oroveso). Live performance 1969, Rome.

878. Gianfranco Masini, cond., Orchestra and Chorus of the Teatro Comunale Giuseppe Verdi di Trieste; Lucia Aliberti (Alaide), Vincenzo Bello (Arturo), Roberto Frontali (Valdeburgo), Sara Mingardo (Isoletta). Ricordi Fonit Cetra RFCD 2010. Live performance, 1990, Trieste. Notes, libretto.

Zaira

879. Danilo Belardinelli, cond., Orchestra and Chorus of the Teatro Massimo "Bellini," Catania; Renata Scotto (Zaira), Maria Luisa Nave (Nerestano), Giorgio Casellato Lamberti (Corasmino), Luigi Roni (Orosmane). MYTO 3MCD 971.151. Live performance, 1976, Catania.

880. Paolo Olmi, cond., Orchestra and Chorus of the Teatro Massimo "Bellini," Catania; Katia Ricciarelli (Zaira), Alexandra Papadjakou (Nerestano),

Ramon Vargas (Corasmino), Simone Alaimo (Orosmane). Nuova Era 6982–3. Live performance, 1990, Catania.

I Capuleti e i Montecchi

881. Claudio Abbado, cond., Chorus of the Teatro Comunale di Bologna, Residentie Orkest Den Haag; Margherita Rinaldi (Giulietta), Giacomo Aragall (Romeo), Luciano Pavarotti (Tebaldo), Nicola Zaccaria (Capellio), Walter Monachesi (Lorenzo). Verona 28001/2; Opera D'Oro OPD-1171. Live performance, 1966, Amsterdam. Notes, libretto (Abbado's version with Romeo as a tenor and other changes).

882. Piero Belluggi, cond., Orchestra and Chorus of Teatro La Fenice; Katia Ricciarelli (Giulietta); Veriano Luchetti (Romeo), Giorgio Merighi (Tebaldo), Bruno Marangoni (Capellio), Walter Monachesi (Lorenzo). Mondo Musica MHOF 10604. Live performance, 1973, Venice.

883. Giuseppe Patanè, cond., New Philharmonic Orchestra, John Aldis Choir; Beverly Sills (Giulietta), Janet Baker (Romeo), Nicolai Gedda (Tebaldo), Robert Lloyd (Capellio), Raimund Herincx (Lorenzo). EMI Classics, recorded 1975.

884. Riccardo Muti, cond., Chorus and Orchestra of the Royal Opera House, Covent Garden; Edita Gruberova (Giulietta), Agnes Baltsa (Romeo), Dano Raffanti (Tebaldo), Gwynne Howell (Capellio), John Tomlinson (Lorenzo). EMI CMS 7 64846 2. Live performance, 1984, Covent Garden, London. Notes, libretto.

885. Bruno Campanella, cond.; Katia Ricciarelli (Giulietta), Diana Montague (Romeo), Dano Raffanti (Tebaldo), Marcello Lippi (Capellio), Antonio Salvadori (Lorenzo). Nuova Era 7020–21. Live performance, 1991, Venice.

886. Roberto Abbado, cond., Munich Radio Orchestra and Chorus of the Bavarian Radio; Eva Mei (Giulietta), Vesselina Kasarova (Romeo), Ramón Vargas (Tebaldo), Umberto Chiummo (Capellio), Simone Alberghini (Lorenzo). RCA Victor Red Seal 09026–68899–2. Recorded 1997. Notes, libretto.

887. Donald Runnicles, cond., Scottish Chamber Orchestra and Chorus; Hei-Kyung Hong (Giulietta), Jennifer Larmore (Romeo), Paul Groves (Tebaldo), Raymond Aceto (Capellio), Robert Lloyd (Lorenzo). Teldec 3984–21472–2 © 1999.

La sonnambula

Note: Since this list was compiled new commercial recordings with Natalie Dessay and Francesco Meli (Virgin, cond. Evelino Pidò) and Cecilia Bartoli and Juan Diego Flórez (Decca, cond. Alessandro De Marchi) have appeared.

888. Gianandrea Gavazzeni, cond., Orchestra and Chorus of the Teatro San Carlo, Naples; Margherita Carosio (Amina), Nicola Monti (Elvino), Marco

Stefanoni (Rodolfo), Anna Di Stasio (Lisa). Encore's Grand Tier ENGT-CD-2 item 3/92. Live performance, 1951, Naples.

889. Franco Capuana, cond., Turin RAI Symphony, Cetra Chorus; Lina Pagliughi (Amina), Ferrucio Tagliavini (Elvino), Cesare Siepi (Rodolfo), Wanda Ruggeri (Lisa). Fonit Cetra CDO 16. Recorded 1952.

890. Leonard Bernstein, cond., Orchestra and Chorus of the Teatro alla Scala, Milan; Maria Callas (Amina), Cesare Valletti (Elvino), Giuseppe Modesti (Rodolfo), Eugenia Ratti (Lisa). MYTO 89006; Opera D'Oro OPD-1139. Live performance, 1955, Milan.

891. Antonino Votto, cond., Orchestra and Chorus of the Teatro alla Scala, Milan; Maria Callas (Amina), Nicola Monti (Elvino), Nicola Zaccaria (Rodolfo). EMI CDS 7 47378–8. Recorded 1957. Notes, libretto.

892. Antonino Votto, cond., Orchestra and Chorus of the Teatro alla Scala, Milan; Maria Callas (Amina), Nicola Monti (Elvino), Nicola Zaccaria (Rodlfo), Mariella Angioletti (Lisa). Melodram CDM 26003. Live performance, 1957, Grosseshaus, Cologne.

893. Antonino Votto, cond., La Piccola Scala at the King's Theatre, Edinburgh; Maria Callas (Amina), Nicola Monti (Elvino), Nicola Zaccaria (Rodolfo), Edith Martelli (Lisa). Virtuoso 2697252. Live performance, 1957, Edinburgh.

894. Nicola Rescigno, cond., Chorus and Orchestra of the New York Opera Society; Joan Sutherland (Amina), Renato Cioni (Elvino), Ezio Flagello (Rodolfo), Eileen Di Tullio (Lisa) Gala GL 100.545. Live performance, 1961, New York.

Bonus Tracks: Excerpts from *La sonnambula*. Nello Santi, cond., Chorus and Orchestra of La Fenice, Venice; Renata Scotto (Amina), Alfredo Kraus (Elvino), Ivo Vinco (Rodolfo), Marisa Zotti (Lisa). Live performance, 1961, Venice.

895. Nello Santi, cond., Orchestra and Chorus of the Teatro La Fenice, Venice; Renata Scotto (Amina), Alfredo Kraus (Elvino), Ivo Vinco (Rodolfo), Marisa Zotti (Lisa). Bongiovanni GAO 111–112. Live performance, 1961, Venice.

896. Richard Bonynge, cond., Orchestra and Chorus of the Maggio Musicale Fiorentino; Joan Sutherland (Amina), Nicola Monti (Elvino), Fernando Corena (Rodolfo), Sylvia Stahlman (Lisa). Decca 448 966–2. Recorded 1962.

897. Richard Bonynge, cond., National Philharmonic Orchestra, London Opera Chorus; Joan Sutherland (Amina), Luciano Pavarotti (Elvino), Nicolai Ghiaurov (Rodolfo). Decca 417 424–2DH2. Recorded 1980.

898. Roberto Cecconi, cond., Orchestra and Chorus of the Teatro La Fenice, Venice; June Anderson (Amina), Aldo Bertolo (Elvino), Giorgio Surjan (Rodolfo), Patrizia Dordi (Lisa). Mondo Musica MFOH 10506. Live performance, 1984, Venice.

899. Marcella Viotti, cond., Piacenza Symphony Orchestra, Como City Chorus; Mariella Devia (Amina), Luca Canonici (Elvino), Alessandro Verducci (Rodolfo), Elisabetta Battaglia (Rodolfo). Nuova Era 6764/65. Live performance, 1988, Teatro Sociale in Como.

900. Gabriele Bellini, cond., Orchestra of Eastern Netherlands, National Reisopera Chorus; Eva Lind (Amina), William Matteuzzi (Elvino), Petteri Salomaa (Rodolfo), Stefania Donzelli (Lisa). Arts 47291–2. Recorded 1991.

901. Alberto Zedda, cond., The Netherlands Radio Chamber Orchestra and Radio Choir; Luba Orgonasova (Amina), Raúl Giménez (Elvino), Francesco Ellero d'Artegna (Rodolfo), Dilbèr (Lisa). Naxos 8.6600 42–43. Live performance, 1992, Amsterdam.

902. Giuliano Carelli, cond., Orchestra Internazionale d'Italia, Chamber Chorus Sluk of Bratislava; Patrizia Ciofi (Amina), Giuseppe Morino (Elvino), Giovanni Furlanetto (Rodolfo), Maria Costanza Nocentini (Lisa). Nuova Era 7215/16. Recorded 1994.

903. Marcello Viotti, cond., Chorus of the Bavarian Radio, Orchestra of the Munich Radio; Edita Gruberova (Amina), José Bros (Elvino), Roberto Scandiuzzi (Rodolfo), Dawn Kotoski (Lisa). Nightingale NC 0000 41–2. Recorded 1998.

Norma

904. Ettore Panizza, cond., Orchestra and Chorus of the Metropolitan Opera; Gina Cigna (Norma), Bruna Castagna (Adalgisa), Giovanni Martinelli (Pollione), Ezio Pinza (Oroveso). The Fourties FT 1517–18. Live performance, 1937, New York.

905. Vittorio Gui, cond., Orchestra and Chorus of the EIAR of Turin; Gina Cigna (Norma), Ebe Stignani (Adalgisa), Giovanni Breviario (Pollione), Tancredi Pasero (Oroveso). Nuova Era HMT 90014/15; Memories HR 4552–53. Recorded 1937. Notes, libretto.

906. Cesare Sodero, cond., Metropolitan Opera and Chorus, New York; Zinka Milanov (Norma), Jennie Tourel (Adalgisa), Frederick Jagel (Pollione), Norman Crordon (Oroveso). Encore Grand Tier ENGT-CD-2 item 1–92. Live performance, 1944, New York.

907. Guido Picco, cond., Palacio de las Bellas Artes, Mexico City; Maria Callas (Norma) Giulietta Simionato (Adalgisa), Kurt Baum (Pollione), Nicola Moscona (Oroveso). Melodram 26018. Live performance, 1950, Mexico City.

908. Vittorio Gui, cond., Covent Garden Orchestra and Chorus; Maria Callas (Norma), Ebe Stignani (Adalgisa), Mirto Picchi (Pollione), Giacomo Vaghi (Oroveso). Allegro Verona 27018/20; Legato 130. Live performance, 1952.

909. Antonino Votto, cond., Teatro Giuseppe Verdi, Trieste; Maria Callas (Norma), Elena Nicolai (Adalgisa), Franco Corelli (Pollione), Boris Christoff (Oroveso). Melodram 26031. Live performance, 1953.

910. Tullio Serafin, cond., Orchestra and Chorus of the Teatro alla Scala, Milan; Maria Callas (Norma), Ebe Stignani (Adalgisa), Mario Filipeschi (Pollione), Nicola Rossi-Lemeni (Oroveso). EMI Classics 7243 5 56271 2 4, Mono. Recorded 1954.

911. Fausto Cleva, cond., Metropolitan Opera and Chorus, New York; Zinka Milanov (Norma), Blanche Thebom (Adalgisa), Gino Penno (Pollione), Cesare Siepi (Oroveso). Melodram MRL 005 (LP, currently out of print). Live performance, 1954, New York.

912. Antonino Votto, cond., Orchestra and Chorus of the Teatro alla Scala, Milan; Maria Callas (Norma), Giulietta Simionato (Adalgisa), Mario Del Monaco (Pollione), Nicola Zaccaria (Oroveso). Gala GL 100.511. Live performance, 1955, Milan.

913. Gabriele Santini, cond., Rome Opera Orchestra and Chorus; Anita Cerqueti (Norma), Miriam Pirazzini (Adalgisa), Franco Corelli (Pollione), Giulio Neri (Oroveso). Great Opera Performances GOP 722–CD–2. Live performance, 1958, Rome.

914. Tullio Serafin, cond., Maria Callas (Norma), Christa Ludwig (Adalgisa), Franco Corelli (Pollione), Nicola Zaccaria (Oroveso). EMI CMS 7 63000–2. Recorded 1960. Notes, libretto.

915. Richard Bonynge, cond., London Symphony Orchestra and Chorus; Joan Sutherland (Norma), Marilyn Horne (Adalgisa), John Alexander (Pollione), Richard Cross (Oroveso). Decca 425 488–2. Recorded 1964. Notes, libretto.

916. Oliviero de Fabritis, cond.; Leyla Gencer (Norma), Fiorenza Cossotto (Adalgusa), G. Limarilli (Pollione), Ivo Vinco (Oroveso). MYTO 2 981177. Live performance, 1966, Lausanne.

917. Ettore Gracis, cond., Orchestra and Chorus of Teatro La Fenice, Venice; Elinor Ross (Norma), Fiorenza Cossotto (Adalgisa), Mario del Monaco (Pollione), Ivo Vinco (Oroveso). Mondo Musica MFOH 10281. Live performance, 1966, Venice.

918. Selections from *Norma*, Bruno Bartoletti, cond., Orchestra and Chorus of the Opera di Roma; Elena Souliotis (Norma), Gastone Limarilli (Pollione), Ivo Vinco (Oroveso). GDS 21041. Live performance, 1969, Rome. See item 877 above.

919. Carlo Felice Cillario, cond., Orchestra and Chorus of the Teatro del Liceo of Barcelona; Montserrat Caballé (Norma), Fiorenza Cossotto (Adalgisa), Bruno Prevedi (Pollione), Ivo Vinco (Oroveso). Melodram CDM 27089. Live performance, 1970 (Caballé's debut in the role). Italian libretto only.

920. Oliviero de Fabritis, cond. Chorus and Orchestra of the Teatro alla Scala di Milano; Elena Suliotis *[sic]* (Norma, Fiorenza Cossotto (Adalgisa), Gianfranco Cecchelle (Pollione), Ivo Vinco (Oroveso). Myto Devotion 2 MDCD 0007. Live performance, Milan, August 30, 1971.

921. Richard Bonynge. cond., Chorus and Orchestra of the San Francisco Opera; Joan Sutherland (Norma), Huguette Tourangeau (Adalgisa), John Alexander (Pollione), Clifford Grant (Oroveso). Gala GL 100.537, ADD. Live performance, San Francisco, 1972.

922. Gianandrea Gavazzeni, cond., Orchestra and Chorus of the Teatro alla Scala, Milan; Montserrat Caballé (Norma), Fiorenza Cossotto (Adalgisa), Gianni Raimondi (Pollione), Ivo Vinco (Oroveso). Great Opera Performances GOP 726. Live performance, 1972. Italian libretto only.

923. Carlo Felice Cillario, cond., London Philharmonic Orchestra and The Ambrosian Opera Chorus; Montserrat Caballé (Norma), Fiorenza Cossotto (Norma), Placido Domingo (Pollione), Ruggero Raimondi (Oroveso). RCA Victor Gold Seal LRC 0109 (3), ADD. Recorded 1972.

924. James Levine, cond., New Philharmonia Orchestra, John Aldis Chorus; Beverly Sills (Norma), Shirley Verrett (Adalgisa), Enrico Di Giuseppe (Pollione), Paul Plishka (Oroveso). Angel AVC 34030 (LP, currently out of print). Recorded 1974.

925. Giuseppe Patanè, cond., Orchestra and Chorus of the Teatro Regio of Turin; Montserrat Caballé (Norma), Josephine Veasey (Adalgisa), Jon Vickers (Pollione), Agostino Ferrin (Oroveso). Serenissima C 360. 140–42. Live performance, 1974.

926. Carlo Felice Cillario, cond., Chorus and Orchestra of the San Francisco Opera Association; Cristina Deutekom (Norma), Tatiana Troyanos (Adalgisa), Robleto Merolla (Pollione), Clifford Grant (Oroveso). Gala GL 100.548. Live performance, 1975, San Francisco.

927. Riccardo Muti, cond., Orchestra and Chorus of the Teatro Comunale, Florence; Renata Scotto (Norma), Margherita Rinaldi (Adalgisa), Ermanno Mauro (Pollione), Agostino Ferrin (Oroveso). Lyric LCD 203–2. Live performance, 1978, Florence.

928. James Levine, cond., The National Philharmonic Orchestra, The Ambrosian Opera Chorus; Renata Scotto (Norma), Tatiana Troyanos (Adalgisa), Giuseppe Giacomini (Pollione), Paul Plishka (Oroveso). Sony Classical Sync 35902. Recorded 1979.

929. Richard Bonynge, cond., Orchestra and Chorus of the Welsh National Opera; Joan Sutherland (Norma), Montserrat Caballé (Adalgisa), Luciano Pavarotti (Pollione), Samuel Ramey (Oroveso). Decca 414 476–2LH3. Recorded 1984. Notes, libretto.

930. Mark Ermler, cond., The USSR Ministry of Culture State Chamber Chorus and the Orchestra of the Bolshoi Theatre, Moscow; M. Bieshu (Norma), L. Nam (Adalgisa), G. Grigoryan (Pollione), G. Seleznev (Oroveso). Melodiya MCD 160 ABC; Olympia OCD 160 A, B, C AAD. Recorded 1986. Notes, libretto.

931. Riccardo Muti, cond., Orchestra and Chorus of the Maggio Musicale Fiorentino; Jane Eaglen (Norma), Eva Mei (Adalgisa), Vincenzo La Scola (Pollione), Dimitri Kavrakos (Oroveso). EMI 7243 5 55471 2 5; Opera D'Oro OPD-1183. Live performance, 1994. Ravenna, Notes, and libretto.

Beatrice di Tenda

932. Nicola Rescigno, cond., American Opera Society, Town Hall, New York; Joan Sutherland (Beatrice), Marilyn Horne (Agnese), Richard Cassilly (Orombello), Enzo Sordello (Filippo). Bella Voce BLV 107.226. Live performance, 1961, New York.

     Bonus Track: Antonino Votto, cond., Teatro alla Scala, Milan. Final Scene Joan Sutherland (Beatrice), Raina Kabaivanska (Agnese), Giuseppe Campra (Orombello). Live performance, 1961, Milan.

933. Antonio Votto, cond., Teatro alla Scala, Milan; Joan Sutherland (Beatrice), Raina Kabaivanska (Agnese), Giuseppe Campra (Orombello), Dino Dondi (Filippo). Opera D'Oro OPD-1259. Live performance, 1961, Milan.

934. Vittorio Gui, cond., Orchestra and Chorus of Teatro La Fenice, Venice; Leyla Gencer (Beatrice), Antigone Sgourda (Agnese), Juan Oncina (Orombello), Mario Zanasi (Filippo). Memories HR 4543/44. Live performance, 1964, Venice.

935. Alberto Zedda, cond., Prague Philharmonic Choir, Monte Carlo Orchestra; Marianna Nicolesco (Beatrice), Stefania Toczyska (Agnese), Vincenzo La Scola (Orombello), Piero Cappucilli (Filippo). Sony SM3K 64539 DDD. Recorded 1966, Monte Carlo.

936. Richard Bonynge, cond., London Symphony Orchestra and Ambrosian Opera Chorus; Joan Sutherland (Beatrice), Josephine Veasey (Agnese), Luciano Pavarotti (Orombello), Cornelius Opthof (Filippo). Decca 433 706–2. Recorded 1966.

937. Franco Mannino, cond., Orchestra and Chorus of RAI, Turin; Angela Gulin (Beatrice), Elena Zilio (Agnese), Jose Carreras (Orombello), Renato Bruson (Filippo). GAO GAO 158/59. Live performance, 1974.

938. Maurizio Arena, cond., Bologna; Mirella Freni (Beatrice), Irma Gonzales (Agnese), Renzo Casellato (Orombello), Claudio Desideri (Filippo). Legato Classics (out of print). Live performance, 1977, Bologna.

939. Gianfranco Masini, cond., Teatro La Fenice, Venice; June Anderson (Beatrice), Elena Zilio (Agnese), Don Bernardini (Orombello), Armando

Ariostini (Filippo). Opera D'Oro OPD-1174. Live performance, 198-, Venice.

940. Pinchas Steinberg, cond., ORF Symphony Orchestra, Wiener Jeunesse-Chor; Edita Gruberova (Beatrice), Vesselina Kasarova (Agnese), Don Bernardini (Orombello), Igor Morosov (Filippo). Nightingale Classics NC–070560–2. Live performances, 1992.

941. Fabio Luisi, cond., Orchestra and Chorus of Deutsche Oper, Berlin; Lucia Aliberti (Beatrice), Camille Capasso (Agnese), Martin Thompson (Orombello), Paolo Gavanelli (Filippo). Berlin Classics BC 1042. Recorded 1992.

I puritani

942. Guido Picco, cond., Orchestra and Chorus of the Teatro de Bellas Artes, Mexico City; Maria Callas (Elvira), Giuseppe Di Stefano (Arturo), Piero Campolonghi (Riccardo), Roberto Silva (Giorgio). Opera D'Oro OPD-1238. Live performance, 1952, Mexico City. Notes, no libretto.

943. Tullio Serafin, cond., Chorus and Orchestra of the Teatro alla Scala, Milan; Maria Callas (Elvira), Giuseppe Di Stefano (Arturo), Rolando Panerai (Riccardo), Nicola Rossi-Lemeni (Giorgio). EMI 47308. Recorded 1953. Notes, libretto.

944. Tullio Serafin, cond., Orchestra and Chorus of the Teatro Massimo, Palermo; Joan Sutherland (Elvira), Gianni Raimondi (Arturo), Mario Zanasi (Riccardo), Ferruccio Mazzoli (Giorgio). Bella Voce BLV 107.227. Live performance, 1961, Palermo.

945. Richard Bonynge, cond., Orchestra and Chorus of the Maggio Musicale Fiorentino; Joan Sutherland (Elvira), Pierre Duval (Arturo), Renato Cioni (Riccardo), Ezio Flagello (Giorgio). Decca 448 969–2. Recorded 1963. Notes, libretto.

946. Riccardo Muti, cond., Orchestra Sinfonica e Coro di Roma della RAI; Mirella Freni (Elvira), Luciano Pavarotti (Arturo), Sesto Bruscantini (Riccardo), Bonaldo Giaiotti (Giorgio). Opera D'Oro OPD-1141. Live performance, 1969, Rome.

947. Richard Bonynge, cond., London Symphony Orchestra, Chorus of the Royal Opera House, Covent Garden; Joan Sutherland (Elvira), Luciano Pavarotti (Arturo), Piero Cappucilli (Riccardo), Nicolai Ghiaurov (Giorgio). Decca 417 588–2LH3. Recorded 1973.

948. Julius Rudel, cond., Ambrosian Opera Chorus, London Philharmonic Orchestra; Beverly Sills (Elvira), Nicolai Gedda (Arturo), Louis Quilico (Riccardo), Paul Plishka (Giorgio). Universal MCD 80356 F BM720. Recorded 1973. Notes, no libretto.

949. Riccardo Muti, cond., Philharmonia Orchestra and Ambrosian Opera Chorus; Montserrat Caballé (Elvira), Alfredo Kraus (Arturo), Matteo

Manuguerra (Riccardo), Agostino Ferrin (Giorgio). EMI CMS 7 69663–2. Recorded 1979.

950. Richard Bonynge, cond., Orchestra and Chorus of the Teatro Massimo "Bellini," Catania; Mariella Devia (Elvira), William Matteuzzi (Arturo), Christopher Robinson (Riccardo), Paolo Washington (Giorgio). Nuova Era 6842/43. Live performance, 1989, Catania.

951. Fabio Luisi, cond., Munich Radio Orchestra and Bavarian Radio Chorus; Edita Gruberova (Elvira), Justin Lavender (Arturo), Ettore Kim (Riccardo), Francesco Ellero d'Artegna (Giorgio). Nightingale Classics NC 070562–2. Live performance, 1993, Munich. Notes, libretto.

13

Special Topics, Focuses, Contemporaries of Bellini and General Surveys that Include Bellini

SPECIAL TOPICS, FOCUSES

952. Besutti, Paola. "Bellini nella cultura italiana del primo novecento: Pizzetti e gli altri." *Vincenzo Bellini nel secondo centenario della nascita* (2004): 611–31. See item 406.

 Addresses Pizzetti's 1915 essay on Bellini (See item 466) and his subsequent writings representing Italian Fascist use of Bellini as a representative Italian composer, such as "La semplicità belliniana" in *Il musicista. Organo ufficiale del sindacato nazionale fascista musicisti* XVIII/2 (November 1939), pp. 25–29. Besutti presents many contemporary reviews of Pizzetti's writings on Bellini. Pizzetti's influence on Camille Bellaigue, who wrote an extensive, elegiac review about Bellini's music in *Revue des deux mondes* (see item 33) recognizing the "infinite beauty" of Bellini's melodies.

953. Black, John. "Donizetti and his Contemporaries in Naples, 1822–1848: A Study in Relative Popularity." *Donizetti Society Journal* 6 (1988): 11–27. ISSN 0307–1448. ML410.D7 A4.

 In order to gauge the popularity of various primo ottocento opera composers, the author examines five theaters in Naples in light of performances of works by eight composers: Donizetti, Rossini, Bellini, Mercadante, Pacini, Raimondi, Luigi Ricci, and Vincenzo Fioravanti. Donizetti's operas were the most performed; Bellini's were quite popular in the smaller theaters.

954. Blanco, Giuseppe. "Il 'capello' di Bellini." Extract from *Culture française* 26/5 (September–October 1979). Bari: Grafica Bigiemme. 6 pp. ISSN 0011–2925. DC339.C84.

Discusses Bellini's atrocious French accent and knowledge of the language, even though he lived there for nearly two years. Heine, in his famous posthumous portrait of the composer, speaks of this. Ferdinand Hiller, however, relates that the women were drawn to Bellini because of it: it added to "il suo grande fascino." Florimo tells of Bellini's gaff in trying to order a "chapeau de feutre," and asking for something entirely different (Florimo does not deign to say what); Rosselli (1996) repeats this story and makes it clear what was actually said, Bellini pronouncing "feutre" as "foutre."

955. Cafiero, R. and M. Marino, eds. *Francesco Florimo e l'Ottocento musicale.* 2 vols. Reggio Calabria: Jason, 1999. ISBN 88–81570–69–6. ML423.F63 F73 1999.

A publication devoted to Bellini's great friend, amanuensis, and biographer.

Articles include: Maria Girardi: "Florimo storiografo e biografo: concezione-scrittura. Raporti linguistici," pp. 11–49; Friedrich Lippmann: "Il ritratto di Bellini di Francesco Florimo," pp. 63–73; Jesse Rosenberg: "Il 'leista' Raimondi contro il 'durantista' Bellini," pp. 75–97; Pallogiovanni Maione: "Florimo committente musicale per un monumento a Bellini," pp. 99–119. See item 394.

956. Caldarella, Antonino. "Il primo incontro di Bellini con Rossini." *La rassegna musicale* 19 (1949): 45–47. ML5.R18.

The first encounter between Rossini and Bellini took place in July 1829 in Milan, when Rossini was on his way from Paris to Bologna, not in 1827 as reported in Luisa Cambi's *Bellini (la vita)* (see item 220) and elsewhere. The author uses as evidence and provides quotations from an unpublished autograph letter from Bellini to his uncle Vincenzo Ferlito, dated August 28, 1829, in which Bellini refers to this meeting. Facsimile reproduction of part of the letter is given. See items 99 and 312.

957. Cavazzuti, Pietro. *Bellini a Londra*. Florence: G. Barbèra, Editore Tipografia B. Coppini, 1945. 78 pp. ML410.B44 C17.

Copies in Museo belliniano and Paris, Bibliothèque de l'Opéra. 67 pp. Bellini in London: the state of opera during Bellini's visit, various artists. Quotes from Chorley. See item 38. Index of names. Many source citations and transcriptions of letters. Includes previously unpublished documents.

958. Clément, Catherine. *Opera: The Undoing of Women*. Trans. from the French by Betsy Wing. Minneapolis: University of Minnesota Press, 1998. Original French version, 1979. ISBN 08–16616–53–1 (hard-cover); 08–16616–55–8 (paperback). ML2100.C613 1988.

Foreword by Susan McClary. Feminist philosophical essays about the role of women in opera. Madness is discussed. Elvira, Amina, and Norma are treated. Bibliography, index.

959. Dellaborra, Mariateresa. " 'D'après une lecture de.' Sulla fortuna dei temi bellinianii en variation." *Vincenzo Bellini et la France* (2007): 755–96. See item 404.

Music examples. Lists of compositions. Explores the numerous French composers from 1834 to 1880 who used Bellini's themes as the basis for instrumental music such as Variations, Caprices, Quadrilles, Bluettes, Divertimenti, Fanasies.

960. Denaro, Alfio. *Bellini ed il suo canto supremo*. Radio-dramma in 3 parti. Milano: Gastaldi, 1954.

Copy in Museo belliniano. 39 pp. Radio play dealing with Bellini's last months in Paris, where he stayed with Samuel Levys (here Lewys) in Puteaux. The characters are Bellini, the "Lewys family," Giuditta Turina, and Dr. Montallegri, Bellini's last attending physician. Turina was of course never with Bellini in Paris; they did not see each other after Bellini left Italy in 1833 for London and Paris.

961. Denizeau, Gérard. "Paris, capitale artistique au temps de Bellini (1833–1835)." *Vincenzo Bellini et la France* (2007): 3–13. See item 404.

In the few years that Bellini lived in Paris, the city had a profusion of literary and cultural salons. Many architectural projects were completed and various ancient monuments (such as Notre-Dame, the Sainte-Chapelle, the Hall of Justice) were fully restored. Using a combination of Classicism and Romanticism, Parisian artists created new patterns that would have an influence on the lyric theater for the remainder of the century.

962. Döhring, Sieghart. "Die Wahnsinnszene." In *Die "Couleur Locale" in der Opera des neunzehnten Jahrhunderts*. Ed. Heinz Becker, pp. 279–310. Studien zur Musikgeschichte des neunzehnten Jahrhunderts 42. Regensburg: Bosse, 1976. ISBN 37–64921–01–3. ML1794.C68.

A survey of mad scenes in nineteenth-century opera. Bellini's Imogene (*Il pirata*) and Elvira (*I puritani*) are included.

963. Eigeldinger, Jean-Jacques. *L'Univers musical de Chopin*. Paris: Fayard, 2000. ISBN 221–13607–51–6. ML410.C54 E36 2000.

Contains a chapter, pp. 99–107, entitled "Chopin, Le Théâtre Italien et Bellini," discussing Chopin's attendance at Parisian performances of Bellini's operas and possible musical analogs. There is also a chapter on the "Hexameron," 229ff.

964. Gallo, Denise. "Giovanni Pacini and the Parisian Musical Scene." *Vincenzo Bellini et la France* (2007): 16–25. See item 404.

As with Bellini, Pacini was identified as a composer from Catania, where he was born in 1796 but only because his family, with their peripatetic existence, happened to find themselves there at the time. Pacini himself, however, often identified with Catania, referring to himself as "figlio della trinacria terra." In 1852 he dedicated his oratorio *Giuditta* to Catania; the text was written by the Catanese poet Giuseppe Raffaele Abate. Using Pacini's memoirs (see item 72), correspondence, and contemporary Parisian reviews, Gallo considers Pacini's relationshikp to the Parisian stage and suggests reasons for his poor reception in that city.

965. Gazzaniga, Arrigo. "Un intervallo nelle ultime scene di *Lucia*." *Nuova rivista musicale italiana* XIII/3 (July–September 1979): 620–33. ISSN 0029–6228. ML5.R8.

Examines the use of intervals wider than an octave to denote anxiety, tension, and madness in early nineteenth-century opera, especially in the "mad scene" of *Lucia di Lammermoor*. Such melodic writing, which culminates in twentieth-century Expressionism, was used by Bellini in his *Pirata* of 1827 and certain characters of Mozart also provide precedents, although some in a sly, comic manner (e.g., Fiordiligi in *Così fan tutte*).

966. Janis, Byron. "Chopin at the Opera." *Opera News* 46/12 (February 13, 1982): 12–14. ISSN 0030–3607. ML1.O482.

A distinguished Chopin pianist discusses Chopin's perennial fascination with the singing voice. "Was it pure chance that Chopin was laid to rest in a grave adjacent to that of Vincenzo Bellini at Père Lachaise cemetery in Paris?" Chopin always encouraged pianists to listen to the great singers and wrote much about his experiences at the opera and at vocal recitals. He met Bellini in 1833. Janis states, rather than Bellini's music influencing Chopin, who had not heard a note of it before he came to Paris in 1830, it was "merely a case of kindred spirits meeting and reveling in certain creative similarities and shared musical tastes, even in their fastidious elegance." Chopin collaborated with Liszt, Thalberg, Pixis, Herz, and Czerny to produce "Hexameron," a set of variations on "Suoni la tromba" from Bellini's *Puritani*. Discusses some singers Chopin knew well, such as the tenor Adolphe Nourrit, Pauline Viardot, and Jenny Lind. Notes the "operatic mood" of some of Chopin's piano compositions, such as the Etude op. 25, no. 7, and the Nocturne op. 27, no. 1.

967. Kolodin, Irving. "Mad Scene." Chapter 6 in *The Opera Omnibus: Four Centuries of Operatic Give and Take*. New York: E.P. Dutton, 1976. ISBN 08–41504–38–5. ML1700.K65.

Discusses roots of the operatic mad scene but focuses on works of Donizetti and Bellini. Singers, interpreters of the roles are emphasized. "What Bellini and Donizetti had in common, beyond a profound knowledge of the voice and its capabilities, was a strong sense of the drama inherent in dementia, hallucination, mental derangement, or whatever English equivalent one prefers for *la pazzia*. Out of their mutual involvement came some of the greatest vocal music ever written."

968. La Magna, Franco. *Vi rivviso, o lunghi ameni: Vincenzo Bellini nel cinema e nella televisione*. Reggio Calabria: Città del sole, 2007. ISBN 97–88873–51–120–5.

The subject of Bellini on film and on television. 206 pp. Bibliography, pp. 283–86.

969. Levi L'Italico, Primo. *Paesaggi e figure musicali*. Milan: Fratelli Treves, 1913. ML60.L38.

Includes an essay on Bellini.

970. Lippmann, Friedrich. "Casta diva: la preghiera nell'opera italiana della prima metà dell'Ottocento." Trans, from German into Italian by Renato Bossa, *Recercare* 2 (1990): 173–209. ML5.R184.

Lippmann examines various types of prayer scenes in nineteenth-century Italian opera, ranging from the intimate, static prayer with limited melodic range, the antiphonal solo-choral prayer, the dramatic prayer with heightened orchestral accompaniment, to the prayer that is a combination of the previous three, providing stasis yet furthering action at the same time. He provides specific examples of all of the above types. Notes the frequency of the *preghiera* but maintains that this is not due to religious feelings on the part of the public, but that the prayer scene was instead a vehicle for strong theatrical emotion.

971. ——. "Verdi e Bellini." In *Atti del primo congresso internazionale di studi verdiani: Venice 1966*. Parma, 1969, pp. 184–96. German trans. in *Beiträge zur Geschichte der Oper*. Ed. H. Becker, pp. 77–88. Regensburg, 1969. ML1700.B395.

Bellini's style influenced Verdi in a number of ways discussed by Lippmann: the emotional expression contained within formal structure; the avoidance of banalities; careful, expressive text treatment; limited use of fioriture; lengthening of the vocal melody. Notes Verdi's many fragmentary quotations (probably unconscious) of Bellini's melodies.

972. McClary, Susan. "Excess and Frame: The Musical Representation of Madwomen." In *Feminine Endings: Music, Gender, and Sexuality*, pp. 80–111. Minneapolis: University of Minnesota Press, 1991. ISBN 08–16618–99–2. M182.M38 1991.

An examination of several operatic madwomen from musical and sociological viewpoints. Claims that musicologists have not deigned to deal with this subject, which is not quite true. Uses theoretical writings of Michel Foucault and Klaus Doerner.

973. Miozzi, Dario. "Francesco Florimo 'stratega' del mito belliniano." In *Francesco Florimo a Vincenzo Bellini*. Ed. D. Miozzi, pp. 245–64. Catania: Giuseppe Maimone, 2001.

Florimo's considerable role in creating the Bellini legend.

974. Poniatowski, Irena, ed. *W kregu przyjaciol Chopina [Bellini and His Acquaintances]*. 5 vols. Warsaw, 1995–2000.

The Chopin–Bellini connection. Poniatowski is a noted Polish Chopin scholar.

975. Sala, Emilio. "Women Crazed by Love: An Aspect of Romantic Opera." Trans. William Ashbrook. *Opera Quarterly* 10/3 (Spring 1994): 19–41. ISSN 0736–0053. ML1699.O65.

A survey of madness among mainly nineteenth-century heroines. Bellini's Amina *(La sonnambula)*, Imogene *(Il pirata)*, and Elvira (*I puritani*) are included. Other works examined include Dalayrac's *Nina*, Donizetti's *Anna Bolena* and *Lucia di Lammermoor*, and Catalani's *Edmea*. The idea that the bond between the original literary sources and such opera libretti is often engineered by contemporary French boulevard plays is also discussed.

976. Sawall, Michael. "Der gesungene Krieg kostet euch kein Blut: Verdi, Bellini und Patriotismus in der Oper in der Epoche des Risorgimento aus Sicht der Ausburger *Allgemeine Zeitung*." *Zeitschrift des historischen Vereins für Schwaben* XCIII (2000): 145–65.

Bellini's and Verdi's music as an expression of the Risorgimento as viewed by a nineteenth-century German music journal.

977. ——. "*Guerra, Guerra*: La recezione politica di Bellini durante il Risorgimento." *Vinceno Bellini nel secondo centenario della nascita* (2004): 595–604. See item 406.

Even though Bellini was seemingly non-political, the Italians of the Risorgimento identified him as such, to the point that on July 2, 1871 *Norma* was given at the Teatro Apollo in Rome for a gala evening for Vittorio Emanuele II on the occasion of the official proclamation of Rome as the capital of the Kingdom of Italy.

978. Scaglione, Nitto. *Vincenzo Bellini a Messina*. Messina: Editrice "La Sicilia," 1934. ML410.B44 S3.

Copy in Museo belliniano. 64 pp. Various aspects of Bellini's connections with Messina, including the possibility of the young composer obtaining a post as *maestro di cappella* in that city. Details the performances of Bellini's works at two theaters in Messina. Explores Messina's mourning Bellini's death; inclusions of homages and elegies.

979. Suttoni, C. "Liszt's Letter: Reminiscences of *Norma*." *Journal of the American Liszt Society* 7/1 (June 1980): 77–79. ISSN 0147–4413.

Liszt's fantasy on themes from *Norma*.

980. Tarallo, Alfredo. *La biblioteca del Conservatorio di San Pietro a Majella a duecento anna dalla fondazione*. Naples: Istituto italiano per gli studi filosofici, 1991.

The library at the Naples Conservatory, which contains many holdings on Bellini.

981. Toye, Francis. "The New Interest in Italian Nineteenth-Century Opera." In *Fanfare for Ernest Newman*. Ed. Herbert von Thal, pp. 157–72. London: Barker, 1955. ML55.V3.

Reception of primo ottocento opera from the author of the first study in English of the operas of Rossini and Verdi. At the beginning of the twentieth century Bellini "lived more or less in a bracket with Donizetti—a curious bracket because no two men could well have been more different in every way. Perhaps the bracket may be defined as one of common contempt and neglect." "I do not remember a single performance of any of his operas—and, oh! how the pundits hated him! Fuller Maitland's edition of Grove (1904) could scarcely be more contemptuous, whereas Colles's edition (1927), though still patronizing, is definitely kinder." Dates the change in Bellini's reputation as beginning when Rosa Ponselle sang *Norma* in Europe in the late 1920s. Cities Maria Callas in recent years (this is 1955) as having "done a lot to further the good work." When Bellini's operas "have been sung as they should be sung under a conductor with a proper sense of style they are seen to retain much of their old magic." Notes the importance Ildebrando Pizzetti has played when he decided to "break a lance on Bellini's behalf." Pizzetti's "championship sufficed to reawaken much interest in Italy itself" and he then "began to affect the opinion abroad." The composer and theorist "set out to prove, and did prove, that the traditional view of Bellini as a slapdash, careless composer, incapable alike of counterpoint and orchestration, was completely erroneous." Bellini concentrated on melody, "gradually eschewing complication more and more. So far from being careless he took enormous trouble." Toye exhorts us, "Remember how Wagner at Riga raved over the elegiac beauty of *Norma*. Remember how Chopin on his deathbed asked to have a Bellini aria sung to him."

Summarizes the importance of the Italian school: "It is axiomatic everywhere, to the best of my belief, that in the domain of Music there are two nations of outstanding importance: the German and the Italian. As a rule, precedence is allotted to the German; rightly, I suppose, except in the matter of Opera. This, however, by no means implies justification of the dismissal of the Italian contribution as negligible. It is the reverse of negligible; it is of fundamental importance if only because it is so usefully complementary to the Teutonic contribution. In science, in complexity, probably in profundity, the Germans excel; the Italians excel in simplicity, directness and all that is implied in the French word *verve*."

Note: Additional sources include:

982. Jaloux, Edmond. "Bellini et le romantisme." *Le Temps*. July 12, 1935.

983. Levi L'Italico, Primo. "Vincenzo Bellini a Santa Cecilia." *Rivista politica e letterraria* 4/13 (1900).

984. Magali del Giudice, G. *Francesco Florimo l'amico di Vincenzo Bellini*. Naples: G. Acampora, 1901.

985. Monti, Antonio. *Milano romantico, 1814–1848*. Milan: Editoriale Domus, 1946.

986. Pastura, Francesco. "Bellini a Palermo." In *Conservatorio di Musica "Vincenzo Bellini" Annuario* 1960/61, pp. 35–39.

987. Petrocchi, G. "Natura ideale di Bellini." *Rassegna musicale* (July–August, 1942). ML5.R18.

988. Poggi, Cencio. *Vincenzo Bellini a Moltrasio*. Como, 1891.

989. Policastro, Guglielmo. *Catania nel settecento; costumi, architettura, scultura, pittura, musica*. Turin: Società Editrice Internazionale, 1950. DG975.C28 P64.

990. Scholes, Robert. "The Blood of an Innocent Woman: Bel Canto and the Gothic." *Yearbook of Interdisciplinarian Studies in the Fine Arts* 1 (1989): 225–37.

CONTEMPORARIES OF BELLINI AND GENERAL SURVEYS THAT INCLUDE A DISCUSSION OF BELLINI

991. Ashbrook, William. *Donizetti and His Operas*. Cambridge: Cambridge University Press, 1982. ISBN 95–21235–26–X. ML410.D7.

An expanded version of the original 1965 edition. Life and works of Donizetti, his use of operatic conventions, his relationship to other composers before and after, especially Vincenzo Bellini, Gioachino Rossini, and Giuseppe Verdi.

992. Brombert, Beth Archer. *Cristina: Portrait of a Princess*. New York: Knopf, 1977. ISBN 03–94408–07–1. DG551.8.B3 B76 1977.

A biography of the Princess Belgioioso, who held important salons in Milan and Paris where Bellini met many other famous artists, literary figures, and musicians. Bellini appears on pp. 248–50. Brombert quotes from Cristina's letter (Athens, 1849) to Madame Jaubert about the meeting at her country house, La Jonchère, between Heine and Bellini that provided the impetus for Heine's famous posthumous essay on Bellini found in *Florentinische Nächte*.

This account is often drawn from Jaubert's *Memoirs* but her information came from Belgioioso. Heine talked to Bellini about the death of young geniuses, saying maybe Bellini had nothing to worry about, unless he were a genius. Bellini was notoriously superstitious and considered Heine to have the "evil eye" because he wore glasses and had reddish tints in his blond hair, the latter an attribute of the devil. See items 31, 51, and 1001.

993. Budden, Julian. *The Operas of Verdi*. 3 vols. *From Oberto to Rigoletto*, vol. 1. London: Cassell, 1973. ISBN 01–95200–30–6. ML410.V4 B88.

Excellent introduction and background to the period in the opening chapter, "Verdi and the World of the Primo Ottocento," pp. 1–24. Written in 1973, Budden's essay begins with the observation that Italian opera from the first half of the nineteenth century "has up to now received scant attention from scholars; nor does it form any part of the ordinary music student's education. Most professors, with the authority of Berlioz, Schumann, Mendelssohn and Wagner to support them, have been content to dismiss it as a provincial backwater, the era of decadence in taste and craftsmanship." Budden discusses the conditions under which opera was produced in Italy during this period and explores the relationship between the singer and composer, citing examples from the careers of Bellini, Donizetti, Pacini, Rossini, and Verdi. He makes a point of the continuity between eighteenth-century Metastasian opera seria and Italian opera of the primo ottocento, a continuity that rendered early-nineteenth-century opera part of a conservative tradition. Counts Rossini as a key transition figure between the eighteenth century and the nineteenth: "a composer who sums up all the paradoxes and ambiguities of the ottocento." It was Rossini, for instance, who most extensively developed the two-part aria into the "scena." Discusses Bellini as the composer who evidences the widest variety of andante structures. Discusses aria and duet structures and verse-forms, how they differ from Germanic practice. The Italian libretto and how it, as with musical features, is "relatively fixed." Categories of singers and censorship are also explored.

994. Dahlhaus, Carl. *Nineteenth-Century Music*. Trans. from the German by J. Bradford Robinson. Berkeley: University of California Press, 1989. ISBN 05–20052–91–9. ML196.D2513 1989.

On pp. 117–20 Dahlhaus discusses "*Melodie lunghe*: Bellini and Donizetti." He declares, "The melodic style of Bellini's arias, above all his slow cantabiles, was the quintessence of what the nineteenth century, with astounding unanimity, understood by melody in the strong sense of the term." He notes the influence of Bellini's melodies on Chopin and Wagner. Specifically Dahlhaus analyses—"Ah! non credea mirarti"—from *La sonnambula* as "one of those paradigms of Bellini's melodic style." He notes that it may be hopeless "for even a painstakingly detailed analysis to capture in words the full individuality and the aesthetic essence of a melody," yet "our enthusiasm will ultimately devolve into sloganizing unless we take up the technical aspects of a composition." After this detailed analysis he continues by discussing the double aria structure of the period and its relation to the drama.

995. Dean, Winton. "Donizetti's Serious Operas." *Proceedings of the Royal Music Association* 100 (1973–74): 123–41.

The decisive influence on Donizetti's tragic romantic operas, "after he had digested those of Mayr and Rossini, may have been his contact with Bellini. From 1828 Donizetti composed nearly 30 serious operas which reflect growing care for dramatic detail and a conscious desire to expand available forms of expression, and which exerted an important influence on Verdi as late as *La forza del destino*."

996. ——. "Italian Opera." In *New Oxford History of Music.* Vol 8: *The Age of Beethoven*, 1790–1830. Ed. Gerald Abraham, pp. 376–451. London: Oxford University Press, 1982. ISBN 01–931–6308–X. ML160.N44.

Composers treated include Paisiello, Cimarosa, Paêr, Mayr, Rossini, Meyerbeer, Donizetti, and Mercadante (together, and very briefly). Genres include opera buffa, opera seria, and opera semiseria. Bellini is discussed at relative length, 431–51, and introduced as "The one composer to introduce something new before 1830," and his close connection to the eighteenth-century Neapolitan style is recognized. His libretti, melodies, and specific operas are discussed.

997. Dent, Edward J. "Donizetti: An Italian Romantic." In *Fanfare for Ernest Newman*. Ed. Herbert von Thal, pp. 86–107. London: Barkey, 1955. ML55.V3.

Dent writes at a time when only a handful of the operas of Rossini, Bellini, and Donizetti were given. Some of his views are thus no longer valid but many of them are still valuable in providing insight into primo ottocento opera scholarship and reception. He presents Italian opera of the primo ottocento as seen in Paris and London as "the most degraded age through which opera has ever passed," noting, "What we can actually see on the stage to-day is the merest handful out of a gigantic output of long-forgotten rubbish." Discusses the fallacy that we do not have the singers to do justice to these operas. Treats the sociological, artistic, and political nature of opera of this period, what Italian "romanticism" means: French and German composers were ready to try experiments with new techniques; "the Italians clung to standard patterns which even Verdi for a long time hardly dared ignore." Dates the "degradation of Italian opera . . . back to the death of Metastasio in 1782." Considers the librettista as a hack: "Among the innumerable *librettisti* of the romantic period there is only one who can justly claim the title of *poeta*—Felice Romani."

Comments on Bellini: "Rossini and Bellini have always attracted biographers who are more interested in personal lives than in musical analysis." Notes the "decidedly beneficial effect on the style of . . . [Donizetti]" of the rivalry between him and Bellini. This influence is "clearly apparent" in *Lucia di Lammermoor*. He discusses this influence in the broadest terms, not mentioning *Il pirata*. Bellini, "despite his often amateurish and feeble technique, created something new in opera by approaching it more from the angle of opera semi-seria . . . [I]t was only rarely that he achieved the heroic, and his real genius was for the expression of tenderness and delicacy."

998. ——. *The Rise of Romantic Opera*. Ed. Winton Dean. Cambridge: University Press, 1976. ISBN 05–21213–37–1. ML1704.D46.

A series of lectures delivered at Cornell University in the winter of 1937–38. As Winton Dean notes in the preface, Dent's lectures do "in fact convey a great deal of information, much of it recondite; but his principal aim was to serve as a kind of *agent provocateur* to goad his listeners into thinking for themselves." To this end he makes a number of generalized statements and exaggerations to stimulate thinking and perhaps revise viewpoints. These lectures provide an excellent background to Romantic opera. Dent rightly contends that the most important source of Romantic opera was French opera, that Romantic opera derived its most salient characteristics not from serious but from comic opera, and, as Dean states, "it was the principal source of the nineteenth-century German symphonic and instrumental style."

Bellini is treated in Chapter 11, pp. 162–75. Bellini's indebtedness to Pergolesi, Cimarosa, and Paisiello is emphasized. Discusses the important Romantic features of most of Bellini's oeuvre and provides earlier examples of these found in works by other composers. Calls Bellini "the great exponent of the barcarolle style, which became the rage of all the drawing-rooms of Europe in the early part of the nineteenth century," and may or may not be genuine folk music. Discusses such topics as the requirements for singing Bellini's music effectively, how much German music Bellini knew, formal structures, collaboration with Felice Romani, and Bellini's text setting.

999. Einstein, Alfred. *Music in the Romantic Era*. New York: Norton, 1947. ML196.E35.

In this survey of nineteenth-century music, Einstein discusses Bellini on pp. 264–68; he considers *Norma* "an exceptional work," while calling its composer a "master of the routine of operatic composition: ten or eleven operas packed into a bare ten years." This is a somewhat baffling viewpoint, in light of what Rossini and Donizetti's careers represented; Bellini worked much more slowly and usually more carefully than they.

1000. Lippmann, Friedrich. "Verdi und Donizetti." In *Anna Amalie Abert zum 65. Geburstag: Opernstudien*. Ed. Klaus Hortschansky, pp. 153–73. Tutzing: Schneider, 1975. ML55.A15 1975.

Explores aspects of Donizetti's stylistic connections with the works of Verdi, such as the structure of ensembles, rhythm and meter, and melodic types. The styles of Rossini and Bellini are also extensively explored.

1001. Malvezzi de Medici, Aldobrandino (Marchese). *Cristina di Belgiojoso*. 3 vols. Milan: Fratelli Treves, 1936–1937.

Belgioioso was a patroness of the arts whose salons Bellini frequented in Milan and Paris. Volume 1 covers "Le prime anni" (1808–1832); Volume 2 "La seduttrice" (1833–1842); and Volume 3 "Pensiero ed azione" (1843–1871). See items 31, 51, and 992.

1002. Mastrigli, Leopoldo. *La Sicilia musicale*. Bologna: C. Schmidl, 1891.

A publication for a national exposition held in Palermo in 1891–92. Part 1 deals with "La musica nei costumi del popolo siciliano" and includes an essay on forty popular Sicilian melodies. Part 2 treats Sicilian musicians of the seventeenth, eighteenth, and nineteenth centuries.

1003. Miragoli, Livia. *Il melodramma italiano nell'ottocento*. Rome: Maglione e Strini, 1924.

Discusses libretti, dramatists, musical style, and historical background of nineteenth-century Italian opera.

1004. Pistone, Danièle. *Nineteenth-Century Italian Opera from Rossini to Puccini*. Trans. from the French by E. Thomas Glasow. Portland, Oregon: Amadeus, 1995. ISBN 09–31340–82–9. ML1733.P5813 1995.

An overview of Italian opera of the period. Includes a pertinent bibliography.

1005. Pizzetti, Ildebrando. *La musica italiana dell'Ottocento*. Turin: Palatine, 1947. ML290.4.P6.

An overview of nineteenth-century Italian opera by the crucial figure in the twentieth-century revival of Bellini's music. Includes a chapter "La musica di Vincenzo Bellini." Other composers covered include Spontini and Donizetti.

1006. Rosselli, John. *The Opera Industry in Italy from Cimarosa to Verdi*. Cambridge: Cambridge University Press, 1984. ISBN 05–21257–32–8. ML1733.R78 1984.

The conditions under which opera was produced, from the standpoint of the impresario. Chapters include "A Season in the Life of the Impresario"; "The Impresario as Businessman"; "Agents and Journalists"; "The

Impresario and the Public"; and "The End of the Impresari." In the appendix Rosselli discusses "problems of evidence for the economic history of Italian opera," evidence for which includes correspondence, contracts, information from lawsuits, and "rather few complete accounts of receipts and expenditures for a whole opera season." Rosselli cautions against accepting figures on contracts as necessarily correct.

1007. ——. "Verdi e la storia della retribuzione del compositore italiano." In *Studi verdiani* 2 (1983): 11ff. ISSN 0393–2532. ML410.V4 S85.

The business side of Verdi's operatic life, contracts and efforts to establish copyright. Also takes the economic situations of Donizetti and Bellini into consideration. Explores materials on singers and also documents of individual impresarios.

1008. Steiner-Isenmann, Robert. *Gaetano Donizetti, Sein Leben und seine Opern*. Bern: Hallwag, 1982. ISBN 34–44102–72–0. ML410.D7 S8 1982.

Uses all previously published Donizetti correspondence. Written from the view-point of the composer, presenting Donizetti as a tragic Romantic figure. The author claims, however, that it uses "linguistic means which provide objectivity." Discussed are the "repertory of forms in Donizetti's operas, their development from copies of Rossini to models for Verdi, and the strong mutual influences between Donizetti and Bellini."

1009. Walker, Frank. *The Man Verdi*. New York: Knopf, 1962. Rpt. Chicago: University of Chicago Press, 1982. ISBN 02–26871–32–0. ML410.V4 W3.

Invaluable study of Verdi with many letters in English translation. Many passing references to Bellini and his works with reference to Verdi, the opera repertory of the time, and Giuseppina Strepponi the singer.

1010. Weaver, William. *The Golden Century of Italian Opera from Rossini to Puccini*. New York: Thames and Hudson, 1980. ISBN 05–0012–40–7. ML1733.W4.

A survey of Italian opera from the premiere of *Il barbiere di Siviglia* in 1816 to *Turandot* in 1926. The connections among Rossini, Bellini, Donizetti are explored. Copious contemporary illustrations; social and musical history of nineteenth-century opera.

1011. Weinstock, Herbert. *Donizetti and the World of Opera in Italy, Paris, and Vienna in the First Half of the Nineteenth Century*. New York: Pantheon Books, 1963; New York: Octagon Books, 1979. ISBN 03–74983–37–2. ML410.D7 W4.

The numerous connections between Bellini and Donizetti are explored. Includes twenty plates, illustrations, portraits, facsimiles, music examples.

1012. Zavadini, Guido. *Donizetti: Vita–Musiche–Epistolario*. Bergamo: Istituto Italiano d'Arti Grafiche, 1948.

In addition to letters written by Donizetti, also includes letters written by others that mention Donizetti. Indexes point to a number of references to Bellini.

Note: Additional sources include:

1013. Colombani, Alfredo. *L'Opera italiana nel secolo XIX, Corriere della sera*. Special Issue, Milan: Tipografia del Corriere della Sera, 1900.

1014. Curzon, Henri de. *Meyerbeer*. Paris, n.d.

1015. D'Arienzo, N. *La musica in Napoli*. Naples, 1900.

1016. Hucke, Helmut. "Die neapolitanische Tradition der Oper." In *Atti del convegno musicologico, New York, 1961*. Kassel: Bärenreiter, 1962, pp. 253–77.

1017. Medicus, Lotte. *Die Koloratur in der italienischen Opera des 19. Jahrhunderts*. Zurich: Aktienbuchdruckerei Wetzikon und Rüti, 1939. ML1733.M6 K6.

1018. Raffaelli, Pietro. *Il Melodramma in Italia dal 1600 fino ai nostri giorni*. Florence, 1881.

1019. Verga, E. *Storia della vita milanese*. Milan, 1931.

14

Glossary of People Associated with Bellini

This glossary, while it does include some of the more familiar figures in Bellini's life, is principally intended to provide information about some of the lesser-known figures whose names might be encountered in Bellini research.

Acquino, Baron Aimé d' Friend of Bellini in Paris and Florimo in Naples, attaché in the Paris embassy of the Kingdom of the Two Sicilies, nephew of the composer Michele Carafa. He kept a diary in French in which he recorded his visits to Bellini in the weeks before his death, where he was several times denied entrance; arrived on the morning of September 23, to be told that Bellini had died that morning at 5 a.m. Quotations from his diaries were first published by Florimo in *Memorie e lettere* (see item 297) and subsequently often reprinted.

Alincourt, V.C. Prevôt D' French writer whose theatrical work, *L'Etrangère*, which enjoyed a success in Paris, was the basis for *La straniera*.

Appiani, Contessa Giuseppina Bellini stayed in her palazzo from November 1830 through 1831, where he composed both *La sonnambula* and *Norma*. Née Strigelli ca. 1797, daughter of a prominent politician, conte Antonio Strigelli. Later became friendly with both Donizetti and Verdi. A noted salon hostess. *Cf.* Frank Walker, item 278, in which he discusses her "real and supposed relations with Donizetti and Verdi."

Barbaja, Domenico (ca. 1778–1841) The most important opera impresario of his time, responsible for establishing Bellini at San Carlo, Naples, and at La Scala, Milan. Operated at various times at La Scala; Kärtnerthortheater, Vienna; and San Carlo, and Teatro Fondo, and others in Naples; member of a management group called Giuseppe Cruvelli e Compagni that ran two Milanese theaters, La Scala and the Teatro Canobbiana.

Barbò di Castelmorano, Count Giacomo (1786–1849) One of the most loyal of Bellini's friends in Milan and author of *Cenni illustrativi alla nuova opera* La straniera (Milan, 1829). There is extant correspondence from Bellini to him.

Belgioioso, Cristina di Trivulzio (1808–1871) Held salons in Milan and Paris frequented by Bellini. In Paris she met Heinrich Heine and also undoubtedly such luminaries as Victor Hugo, Alfred de Musset, George Sand, Franz Liszt, and many others at her home, in addition to Italian exiles such as Vincenzo Gioberti, Alessandro Poerio, Pellegrino Rossi, Nicolò Tommaseo, and the librettist for his final opera, Count Carlo Pepoli.

Bonfigli, Lorenzo (1800–1878) Tenor, the first Tebaldo in *I Capuleti e i Montecchi*. Also appeared as Pollione in *Norma*, Elvino in *La sonnambula*, and Gualtiero in the Venetian premiere of *Il pirata*, adapted and rehearsed by Bellini.

Branca, Emilia Married Felice Romani in 1844; she was the daughter of Paolo Branca who, with his wife and daughters, presided over a notable Milanese salon. In 1882 she published "a blindly partisan biography of him [Romani], which ever since has been supplying misinformation and tendentious opinion about Romani himself, Rossini, Donizetti, Bellini, and the other composers with whom Romani collaborated." See item 335. The book is "prevailingly undependable." (Weinstock, item 279, p. 37).

Cantù, Gaetano Brother of Bellini's mistress, Giuditta Cantù Turina.

Carafa, Michele (1787–1872) Italian composer who after training in Naples studied in Paris with Cherubini and Kalkbrenner. Had a lifelong friendship with Rossini. Wrote for Italy but did well in Paris. Set a number of operas to works of Walter Scott, including *Le nozze di Lammermoor*.

Carradori-Allan, Rosalbina (1800–1865) Italian soprano who created the role of Giulietta in *I Capuleti e i Montecchi*.

Ciccimara, Giuseppe (1790–1836) Tenor from Puglia, active as a singer from 1816 to 1826. Became master of singing at the Kärntnerthor Theater in Vienna.

Conti, Carlo (1796–1868) Studied at San Sebastiano in Naples, where he was Bellini's "maestrino." Followed Saverio Mercadante as vice-director of the Real Collegio in 1862.

Cortesi, Antonio (1796–1879) Dancer, choreographer; composer of ballets for Italian theaters.

Cottrau, Guglielmo Luigi (1797–1847) Franco-Neapolitan composer and publisher and friend of Bellini. Like Bellini, he had studied the art of singing with Crescentini. He was the head of the publishing firm of Girard as well as the author of romances. He subsequently established himself in Naples.

Crescentini, Girolamo (1762–1846) Famous castrato singer and composer who returned to Italy from London, Lisbon, Vienna, and Paris in 1812 and became a voice teacher at the Naples Conservatory in 1825. Among his famous pupils was Isabella Colbrán, the first wife of Rossini and creator of a number of Rossini roles.

Crivelli, Giuseppe Head of "Società Crivelli e Compagni," an impresario of La Scala and the Teatro La Fenice, for which Bellini wrote *I Capuleti e i Montecchi*. Domenico Barbaja (q.v.) was a member of Crivelli e Compagni. Antonio Villa (q.v.) was his partner at La Scala.

Curioni, Alberico (1785–1885) Created the role of Orombello in Beatrice di Tenda. Sustained a long career, singing in operas by Manfroce, Rossini, Mercadante, et alia.

Delmas (Doctor) Performed the autopsy on Bellini on September 25, 1835; he said that Bellini had "succombé à une inflammation aiguë du gros intestin, compliquée d'abcès au foie" (died of acute inflammation of the large intestine, complicated by an abscess of the liver).

Donzelli, Domenico (1790–1873) Fine Italian tenor who created the role of Pollione in *Norma*. Rossini, Donizetti, and Mercadante also created roles for him. He was a close friend of Rossini and also his landlord.

Ferlito, Vincenzo Bellini's maternal uncle; Bellini often corresponded with him because he was more literate than Bellini's own parents.

Festa, Giuseppe Leader of the San Carlos opera orchestra and friend of Bellini in Naples.

Fioravanti, Valentino (1764–1837) Italian opera composer. Maestro di cappella of the Julian Chapel, Rome (1816).

Florimo, Francesco (1802–1888) Fellow student and lifelong friend and supporter of Bellini. Appointed archivist-librarian at the Naples Conservatory in May 1826, he built it into a formidable collection. His most significant historical work is *Scuola musicale di Napoli*. See item 131.

Fumaroli, Maddalena (ca. 1802–1834) Daughter of the Neapolitan magistrate Francesco Saverio Fumaroli; early love interest of Bellini. Much of what we know about her and Bellini comes from Florimo, which information was then romanticized by later writers. Her father forbade their marriage and Bellini lost interest in her after he left Naples in April 1827. She died before Bellini, who wrote of his reaction to her death to Florimo, who then "amplified" this letter to show the composer in a more favorable light.

Furno, Giovanni (1748–1837) Bellini's teacher at the Naples Conservatory when he first arrived in 1819. An inconsequential composer of sacred vocal and instrumental works and comic operas. He also taught Mercadante, the Ricci brothers, and Lauro Rossi. Author of *Regole per accompagnare i partimenti*. Milan, n.d

Gabussi, Vincenzo (1800–1846) Italian composer who moved to London in 1825. Bellini met him in London and in Paris. Successful voice teacher in London.

Galeota, Cavaliere As director of the Royal Theaters of Naples, he invited Bellini in late 1833 to compose an opera for the Teatro San Carlo for Carnival 1834–35.

Gallo, Agostino Bellini's spurious (?) "Letter to Agostino Gallo." May have been first published in Florence in 1843 in a pamphlet by Gallo entitled *Sull'Estetica di Vincenzo Bellini, notizie comunicate da lui stesso al Gallo.*

Gilardoni, Domenico (1798–1831) Librettist for *Bianca e Gernando.* He was based in Naples; wrote twenty libretti in five years for various theaters and eleven for Donizetti. He died at an early age.

Greville, Henry William (1801–1872) An exact contemporary of Bellini who was friendly with him in London and Paris, where Greville was posted to the British Embassy. His diary provides information about Bellini's final years. Diplomat, who was the younger brother of Charles Cavendish Fulke Greville.

Grisi, Carlotta (1819–1899) Famous ballerina who created the role of Giselle in Adolphe Adam's ballet in 1841.

Grisi, Giuditta (1805–1840) Carlotta Grisi's cousin; mezzo-soprano who created the role of Romeo in Bellini's *I Capuleti e i Montecchi.* Left the stage when she married in 1834.

Grisi, Giulia (1811–1869) Giuditta Grisi's sister; studied with Giuditta Pasta and others. Created the roles of Adalgisa in *Norma* and Elvira in *I puritani.* Her second marriage was to the tenor Mario.

Guerrera, Filippo Bellini's uncle in Messina, the husband of Bellini's paternal aunt Anna; Bellini corresponded with him.

Heine, Heinrich (1797–1856) German lyric poet and journalist who lived in Paris for many years. He wrote the famous posthumous "Portrait" of Bellini. See item 51.

Hiller, Ferdinand (1811–1885) German pianist and composer. Conducted the Leipzig Gewandhaus concerts for a certain period. Close friend of Mendelssohn; knew most of the famous musicians of the day, including Bellini.

Hunloke [Hundlocke?], Lady Charlotte Bellini knew her in his last weeks in Paris; she wrote to Giuditta Pasta, describing Bellini's final illness, a letter preserved in the Pasta Collection at the Lincoln Center Library for the Performing Arts in New York City.

Lablache, Luigi (1794–1858) One of the greatest bass voices of his time. As a boy contralto he sang in Mozart's *Requiem* at Haydn's funeral in 1809. He sang in the premieres of *Bianca e Gernando*, *Zaira*, and was part of the famous *Puritani* quartet; also known for the role of Oroveso in *Norma.*

Lamperi, Alessandro Friend of Bellini and in 1829 under secretary of state in the Ministry of Foreign Affairs of the Kingdom of Sardinia and Piedmont; he and Bellini met either in Genoa in 1828 or during a brief visit by Bellini to Turin in

October 1829. The earliest extant letter from Bellini to him is dated November 3, 1829. Sixteen autograph letters from Bellini to Lamperi are in the Houghton Library at Harvard University.

Lanari, Alessandro (1790–1862) Opera impresario connected with theaters in Florence (long associated with the Pergola there), Rome, Naples, Venice, and Bologna; often worked with Crevelli (q.v). He commissioned *Norma*, *I Capuleti*, *Beatrice di Tenda*, and also operas by Donizetti and Verdi. At the Pergola, Florence, he gave the first Italian performances of Meyerbeer's *Robert le diable* (1840) and Weber's *Der Freischütz* (1843).

Laporte, Pierre François (1790–1841) Actor and theater manager who introduced Bellini's operas to the English public. He was a key figure in bringing Bellini to England.

Levys, Samuel An English banker. Bellini died in his house in Puteaux, a suburb of Paris on the Left Bank of the Seine; Levys lived there with a woman named Olivier and had been entrusted with investing some of Bellini's money. In various sources he appears as "Lewis".

Litta, Duchess Camilla (Lomellini) Milanese aristrocrat to whom Bellini dedicated *Il pirata*.

Manzi, Antonio Fellow student and companion of Bellini at the Naples Conservatory. He sang the baritone role of Lord Adelson in *Adelson e Salvini* for the college production.

Marras, Giacinto Fellow student of Bellini. A singing teacher in Naples and Paris. Sang the soprano role of Nelly in *Adelson e Salvini* at the college on December 1, 1825.

Martini, Countess Virginia (1778–1836) A daughter of Count Lodovico della Torre Rezzonico and Giuditta Turina's closest female friend. She wrote to Florimo about Giuditta Turina and was helpful to her when Ferdinando Turina threatened actions against his wife. The letter from Bellini to Countess Martini of April 7, 1835, is not in Cambi's *Epistolario*. See item 288. Printed, however, in Barbiera's *Grandi e piccole memorie*. Florence, 1910, pp. 484–87; this letter refers to Giuditta Turina and her possible involvement with Count Neipperg.

Mercadante, Francesco Saverio (1795–1870) Italian opera composer who was a friend of Bellini. Studied at Real Collegio, Naples, where he succeeded Zingarelli as director. His operatic career lasted from Rossini's day almost to Verdi's *Aida*. *Il giuramento* is considered his best opera.

Merelli, Bartolomeo (1794–1879) Italian librettist and impresario at Genoa who commissioned the 1828 version of *Bianca e Fernando* for a new theater in that city. From 1829 to 1850 he managed La Scala, where he was responsible for the staging of *Norma* in 1831. He gave the libretto of *Nabucco* to Verdi.

Méric-Lalande, Henriette (1798–1867) French soprano who created the role of Alaide in *La straniera*.

Montallegri, Luigi Bellini's last attending physician, sent to Puteaux by Princess Belgioioso.

Moriani, Napoleone (1808–1878) Tuscan tenor. Sang in operas by Donizetti and Bellini, including roles in *Pirata*, *Norma*, and *Puritani*. After many successes had to leave the stage because of a malady of the throat.

Musumeci, Mario On the occasion of Bellini's visit to Catania in the spring of 1832, Musumeci gave what Weinstock (see item 279) deems a "flatulent" speech, lauding Bellini's art (see item 68). Musumeci also announced that Bellini had given the autograph score of *I Capuleti e i Montecchi* to the city of Catania (now in the Museo belliniano), and that a medal was to be struck in his honor. The latter did not occur, to the composer's intense displeasure. Vincenzo Percolla describes Musumeci's speech (see item 204), which was reprinted in *Omaggio a Bellini nel primo centenario della sua nascita*, 1901. See item 238.

Noja, Duca di One of the triumvirate governing the Naples Conservatory and superintendent of the royal theaters. Bellini came under the patronage of the Duke and Duchess of Noja in Naples.

Pacini, Giovanni (1796–1867) Opera composer and native of Catania; considered himself helpful in Bellini's career, whereas Bellini considered him a dangerous rival. Pacini was the lover of Paolina Borghese, sister of Napoleon, and then of the Russian countess Giulia Samoyloff. His most famous opera was *Saffo* (1840); others included *Margherita, regina d'Inghilterra* (1827) and *Ultimi giorni di Pompei* (1825). He published his memoirs, *Le mie memorie artistiche*, in 1865 (see item 72).

Paer, Ferdinando (1771–1839) Italian composer who was important for the development of opera semiseria at the beginning of the nineteenth century and who was a link between late eighteenth-century composers such as Cimarosa and Paisiello, and Rossini and his successors. He spent from 1807 until his death in Paris as Napoleon's maître de chapelle, director of the Opéra-Comique, music director of the Théâtre-Italien, maître de chapelle to Louis-Philippe, and finally teacher of composition at the Conservatoire.

Pagliari, Rocco A successor of Florimo at the library of the Naples Conservatory; published *Intermezzi musicali*. Naples, 1889.

Pasta, Giuditta, née Negri (1798–1865) Great singing-actress, she and Maria Callas are often compared to each other; creator of Amina, Norma, and Beatrice and a number of roles by other composers, including Donizetti's Anna Bolena.

Pepoli, Carlo (1796–1881) Poet-librettist and exiled patriot from Italy after the unsuccessful revolution in 1831. While living in Paris he wrote the libretto for *I puritani* in 1835. He was finally able to return permanently to his native country in 1859, where he served as a member of parliament for the united Italy.

Perucchini, Giovanni Battista Born in Bergamo, 1784. Venetian musical amateur, an accomplished pianist and composer of "romanze di camera" who made friends with Bellini, Rossini, and other composers who visited Venice.

Perugini, Leonardo Fellow student of Bellini at the Naples Conservatory; sang the tenor role of Salvini in *Adelson e Salvini* at the college.

Pollini, Francesco (1763–1847) Pianist, composer, and pedagogue who had studied briefly with Mozart in Vienna and with Zingarelli in Milan. First professor of piano at the Milan Conservatory. Bellini dedicated *La sonnambula* to him. He and his wife, Marianna, both musicians in their sixties without children, practically adopted Bellini in Milan; after Bellini's death Pollini acted as his agent in Milan and had difficulties with Giuditta Turina.

Ponzani, Pietro A lawyer who met Bellini in 1828, exchanged letters with him while Bellini was living in France, informing him in detail of the news in Milan.

Porto, Carlo Ottolini (ca. 1800–1836 or later) Italian bass who was to sing in the Naples version of *I puritani* along with Malibran and Duprez. He created roles in four operas by Donizetti and sang several Bellini roles: Capellio in *I Capuleti e i Montecchi*, Rodolfo in *La sonnambula*, Oroveso in *Norma*, and Giorgio in *I puritani* in Bologna (1836).

Pugni, Cesare (1802–1870) The author of several melodramme and balletti. Bellini met him in Paris in 1834 and engaged him to copy parts for *I puritani*, which Pugni furtively sold to various Italian impresarios.

Reina, Domenica (1797–1843) Tenor who created the role of Arturo in *La straniera*, for which Bellini had wanted but was unable to obtain Rubini (q. v.).

Ricci brothers, Luigi (1805–1859) and **Federico** (1802–1877) Fellow students and companions of Bellini at the Naples Conservatory. Together the Riccis wrote the famous opera *Crispino e la comare* (1850) to a libretto by Francesco Maria Piave.

Ricordi, Giovanni (1785–1853) A violinist, founded the famous publishing firm in Milan in 1808 after having studied the workings of Breitkopf und Härtel in Leipzig. He later was given the rights to publish the music performed at La Scala. At the time of his death he had 25,000 publications to his credit. The Ricordi archives now possesses some 4,000 music manuscripts, chiefly autographes.

Robert, Edouard Friend of Rossini and director of the Théâtre-Italien during Bellini's time in Paris. He and Carlo Severini (q.v.), the administrator of the theater, reserved an orchestra seat for Bellini at the Salle Favart and produced several of his operas.

Romani, Felice (1788–1865) Bellini's chief librettist, for whom he fashioned seven libretti. Studied law at Pisa University; wrote some 125 libretti—was the best and most in demand of the period—wrote for some forty composers, including Donizetti, Mercadante, Meyerbeer, Pacini, Rossini, and Vaccai. Was also a close friend of Bellini until they had a falling-out in 1833.

Rubini, Giovanni Battista (1795–1854) Great bel canto tenor with little acting ability; created tenor roles in *Bianco e Fernando*, *Il pirata*, *La sonnambula*, and *I Puritani*; Bellini revised the role Arturo in *La straniera* for him.

Ruggiero, Giuseppe Bass of modest talent, friend of Bellini, who used him in certain productions.

Samoyloff, Countess Giulia von Pahlen Pacini's mistress; Bellini felt the two plotted against him, specifically against Pasta in *Norma*. Although Bellini called her "that madwoman," he dedicated the Ricordi edition of *Bianca e Fernando* to her.

Sanquirico, Alessandro (1777–1849) La Scala's great scene designer; created several Bellini productions.

Santocanale, Filippo (1798–1884) A lawyer from Palermo; a friend of Rossini and Bellini's close friend and frequent correspondent; met during Bellini's last trip to Sicily in 1832. In 1876 Santocanale traveled to Catania to participate in the ceremonies involving the transferral of Bellini's remains from Paris to Catania Cathedral. On January 26, 1835 Rossini wrote to him of the great success of Bellini's *I puritani.*

Severini, Carlo (1800–1838) Friend from Bologna of Rossini and administrator of the Théâtre-Italien during Bellini's time in Paris. He and Edouard Robert (q.v.), the director of the theater, reserved an orchestra seat for Bellini at the Salle Favart and produced several of his operas. Severini died in the tragic fire that destroyed the Parisian theater in 1838.

Soumet, Alexandre (1788–1845) French playwright and author of *Norma; ou, L'Infanticide* (Paris, 1831), on which *Norma* was based.

Statella, La Duchessa Eleonora (1791–1836) Wife of Stefano Notarbartolo, Duke of Sammartino. She was one of Bellini's benefactors, helping him to realize his desire to study music in Naples.

Tadolini, Eugenia (1809–after 1851) Soprano who appeared in many Donizetti and Verdi roles, and as Amina, Norma, and Elvira in works by Bellini. Verdi considered her voice too beautiful for Lady Macbeth.

Tamburini, Antonio (1800–1876) Leading bass-baritone. Participated in four Bellini premieres: *Il pirata*, *Bianca e Fernando*, *La straniera*, and *I puritani*.

Tosi, Adelaide (ca. 1800–1859) Soprano who studied with Crescentini (q.v.). She sang the leading role in the second version (Genoa, 1828) of *Bianca e Fernando* and created three roles in operas by Donizetti at the San Carlo, Naples.

Tottola, Andrea Leone (ca. 1770–1831) Court poet at Naples; librettist for *Adelson e Salvini* and many libretti for Rossini, Donizetti, and others.

Tritto, Giacomo (1733–1824) One of Bellini's teachers at the Real Collegio. Composer of operas and church music.

Turina, Giuditta, née Cantù Daughter of a silk merchant and wife of Fernando Turina; love interest of Bellini's in Milan. Their relationship began at the time of the Genoese performance of *Bianca e Fernando* and lasted for around five years, until Bellini left Italy for London in late April 1833.

Unger, Caroline (1803–1877) Hungarian soprano engaged by Barbaja for La Scala. Created the role of Isoletta in *La straniera*.

Vaccai, Nicola (1790–1848) Italian opera composer. He wrote *Romeo e Giulietta* in 1825, the libretto of which was adapted by Romani for Bellini's *I Capuleti*.

Villa, Antonio Crivelli's partner who served as artistic director of La Scala.

Zingarelli, Nicola Antonio (1752–1837) Composer of operas and church music. Educated in Naples where he returned in 1813 as director of the Real Collegio; one of Bellini's teachers. Composed a *Romeo e Giulietta* in 1796.

Index of Authors, Editors, Translators, and Reviewers

The numbers in the following lists represent item numbers, not page numbers.

Index of Names and Subjects

D